Betty Crocker's
Best of Baking

More Than 350 of America's Favorite Recipes

Betty Crocker's
Best of Baking

More Than 350 of America's Favorite Recipes

Macmillan • USA

MACMILLAN
A Simon & Schuster Macmillan Company
1633 Broadway
New York, NY 10019-6785

Library of Congress Cataloging-in-Publication data

Crocker, Betty.
    Betty Crocker's best of baking: more than 350 of America's
favorite recipes.—1st ed.
        p.   cm.
    Includes index.
    1. Baking.   2. Cookery, American.   I. Title.
TX763.C754   1998
641.7′1—dc21   97-22856
                                                            CIP

ISBN: 0-02-862066-6
        0-02-862219-7 (Bulk Quantity Edition)
        0-02-862319-3 (Special Sales Edition)

GENERAL MILLS, INC.
Betty Crocker Kitchens Director: Marcia Copeland
Managing Editor: Lois Tlusty
Recipe Development: Betty Crocker Kitchens Home Economists
Food Styling: Betty Crocker Kitchens Food Stylists
Photography: Photographic Services Department

For consistent baking results, the Betty Crocker Kitchens recommends Gold Medal Flour.

Manufactured in the United States of America

10 9 8 7 6 5 4 3 2 1

First Edition

Cover design by Iris Jeromnimon
Cover photograph by David Bishop
Book design by designLab, Seattle

Cover Food: French Bread (page 34); Linzer Torte Bars (page 152);
Best Chocolate Cake with Fudge Frosting (page 238); Deep-Dish Cherry-Berry Pie
(page 260); Easy Sugar Cookies (page 291); Banana-Blueberry Muffins (page 52);
Turtle Brownies (page 161); The Ultimate Chocolate Chip Cookie (page 118)

Introduction

Is there anything more delightful than the smell of baking bread or muffins wafting from the kitchen? Remember the pleasure of freshly baked pies and cakes, the fun of making cookies? Then you'll love *Betty Crocker's Best of Baking*. We have gathered more than 350 favorite recipes for baking, from classic favorites such as Brownies to exciting new ideas such as Garlic Bread made in a bread machine.

First, savor breads of all kinds, from classic White Bread to Chocolate Swirl Coffee Cake. Then turn to an entire chapter on cookies, delicious morsels that are right for just about every occasion. Want some new dinner ideas? Then try our chapter on main dishes and sides that are warm from the oven. Serve hearty Au Gratin Potatoes to make simple grilled chicken special or try Wild Mushroom Pie for a delicious new dinner.

Looking for great cakes, pies and other goodies? Then head for the Desserts chapter. Enjoy Best Chocolate Cake with Fudge Frosting, Blueberry Pie, Cream Puffs or Gingerbread. And what's more fun than kids cooking in the kitchen? An entire chapter written just for kids! You and your kids can bake up a storm—try Rocky Road Cookies, Candy Bar Cupcakes, Strawberry Shortcakes or Top-It-Your-Way Pizza.

And when it comes to the holidays, baking just seems to be the thing to do. Use the holiday chapter to make home-made treats, even plan menus. Whether you want Classic Pumpkin Pie, a Fruited Christmas Wreath, a Gingerbread House or main dish ideas for a festive dinner—it's all here.

Complete with useful tips and helpful hints, *The Best of Baking* provides everything you need to feel comfortable with baking, from making a pie crust to shaping bread. With Betty Crocker, baking is easy—and delicious!

Betty Crocker

Contents

All About Baking

Measuring Ingredients

Graduated Nested Measuring Cups

Cups range in size from 1/4 cup to 1 cup; some sets have 1/8 cup (2 tablespoons), 2/3 cup and 3/4 cup measures as well. Use to measure dry ingredients and solid fats, such as shortening.

For flour, baking mix and sugar, spoon ingredient lightly into cup, then level with a straight edged spatula or knife. Sift powdered sugar only if lumpy.

For cereal and dry bread crumbs, pour into cup. Level with a straight-edged spatula or knife.

For shredded cheese, chopped nuts, coconut and soft bread crumbs, spoon into cup and pack down lightly.

For solid fats and brown sugar, spoon into cup and pack down firmly with spatula or spoon.

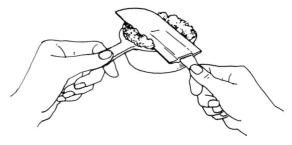

Graduated Measuring Spoons

Spoons range from 1/4 teaspoon to 1 table-spoon; some sets contain a 1/8 teaspoon and a 3/4 teaspoon. Use spoons to measure liquids and dry ingredients. *For thin liquids,* pour into spoon until full. *For thick liquids and dry ingredients,* pour or scoop into spoon until full, then level with a straight-edged spatula or knife.

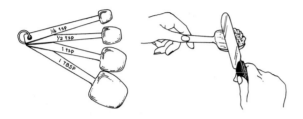

Glass Measuring Cups

Glass cups can be purchased in 1-, 2-, 4- and 8-cup sizes. Use to measure liquids. For an accurate amount, always read the measurement at eye level while the cup is on a flat surface. To measure sticky liquids, such as honey, molasses and corn syrup, first coat the cup lightly with oil so the liquid will be easier to remove.

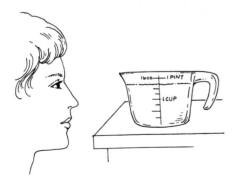

Mixing Ingredients

There's more than one way to combine ingredients and more than one tool to make it easy. If you've ever found the following terms confusing or aren't sure which tools to use, refer to this guide for help. The tools you choose for combining ingredients are determined by the job.

Mixing Terms

Beat: Combine ingredients vigorously with a spoon, fork, wire whisk, hand beater or electric mixer until smooth and uniform.

Blend: Combine ingredients with a spoon, wire whisk or rubber scraper until very smooth and uniform. A blender, hand blender or food processor may also be used.

Cut in: Distribute solid fat in dry ingredients until particles are desired size by crisscrossing two knives, using the side of a table fork, a wire whisk or by cutting with a pastry blender using a rolling motion.

Fold: Combine ingredients lightly while preventing loss of air by using two motions: Use a rubber spatula and first cut down vertically through mixture. Next, slide the spatula across the bottom of bowl and up the side, turning the mixture over. Continue the down-across-up-over motion while rotating bowl one-fourth turn with each series of strokes. For example, to fold dry ingredients into beaten egg whites for angel food cake or to fold liqueur into whipped cream.

Mix: Combine ingredients in any way that distributes them evenly.

Process: Use either a food processor or a mini chopper to liquefy, blend, chop, grind or knead food.

Stir: Combine ingredients with circular or figure 8 motion until of uniform consistency. Stir once in a while for "stirring occasionally," stir often for "stirring frequently" and stir continuously for "stirring constantly."

Whip: Beat ingredients to add air and increase volume until the ingredients are light and fluffy. Cream and egg whites are whipped.

Mixing Tools

Fork or Hand Beater: For lightly beating eggs, sauces and salad dressings and for small amount of mixing of moist and dry ingredients for quick breads.

Hands: For doughs, streusel toppings and very thick mixtures, such as meat loaf. Wash hands thoroughly before handling food. Wear plastic or rubber gloves, if desired.

Pastry Blender: For cutting solid fat into flour to make desired particle size for pie crust and biscuit doughs. Lift up and down with rolling motion.

Rubber Spatula: For folding, mixing and stirring batters or sauces (use heatproof rubber spatula for mixing hot foods in saucepans and skillets).

Spoon: For general all-purpose mixing and stirring, sturdy wooden or plastic cooking spoons are most commonly used.

Wire Whisk: For beating eggs, egg whites and thin batters; for stirring puddings, sauces and gravies to remove lumps.

Electric Mixing Appliances

Hand-Held Mixer: For all but the thickest batters as well as for eggs. Use for recipes in this book that specify "electric mixer," as a hand-held mixer was used for testing.

Stand Mixer: More powerful motor than a hand-held mixer. Allows more freedom of hands. May have added attachments, including a dough hook.

Blender: For liquefying or blending mixtures or chopping small amounts of nuts, herbs or bread crumbs. Not for most batters or doughs.

Hand-Held Blender: For liquefying or blending mixtures. May not perform as well as a regular blender for some mixtures.

Food Processor: For blending, pureeing, chopping, slicing, dicing, grinding, pulverizing and shredding many foods. Some will knead dough.

Mini Chopper: For mixing small amounts of sauces and dips or chopping small amounts of vegetables, nuts and herbs.

Helpful How-To's

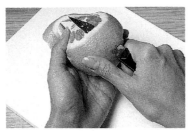

Peel: Cut off outer covering with a knife or vegetable peeler, or strip off outer covering with fingers.

Julienne: Stack thin slices; cut into matchlike sticks.

Cube: Cut into 1/2-inch or wider strips; cut across into cubes.

Dice: Cut into 1/2-inch or narrower strips; cut across into cubes.

Chop: Cut food into pieces of irregular sizes.

Cut up: Cut into small irregular pieces with kitchen scissors or knife.

Shred: Cut into long thin pieces by rubbing food across the large holes of a shredder or by using a knife to slice very thinly.

Grate: Cut into tiny particles by rubbing food across the small rough holes of a grater.

Technique How-To's

Toasting Coconut or Nuts: Sprinkle 1/2 cup coconut or nuts in ungreased heavy skillet. Cook over medium-low heat 6 to 14 minutes for coconut or 5 to 7 minutes for nuts, stirring frequently, until browning begins, then stirring constantly. (Watch carefully; time varies greatly between gas and electric ranges.)

Cutting up Pineapple: Twist top from pineapple. Cut pineapple into fourths. Holding pineapple securely, cut fruit from rind. Cut off pineapple core and remove "eyes." Cut crosswise or lengthwise into chunks or spears.

Hulling Strawberries (removing the caps): Use the tip of a table knife or an inexpensive strawberry huller (a very short, fat tweezers), or push one end of a plastic drinking straw into the point of the berry and push it through to pop off the cap.

Separating Eggs: Eggs are easiest to separate when cold. Purchase an inexpensive egg separator and place over a small bowl. Crack egg; open shell, allowing yolk to fall into center of separator. The white will slip through the slots of the separator and into the bowl. Do not pass the yolk back and forth from shell half to shell half. Bacteria may be present in the pores of the shell, which could contaminate the yolk or white.

Cooking Terms Glossary

Cooking has its own vocabulary just as any other activity does. Although not all-inclusive, this glossary is a handy reference for both beginning and experienced cooks. We've included examples of foods, in most cases, to help you quickly familiarize yourself with the terms. For other food or cooking definitions, see "Ingredients Glossary" (page 17).

Bake: Cook in oven surrounded by dry heat. Bake uncovered for dry, crisp surfaces (breads, cakes, cookies, chicken) or covered for moistness (vegetables, casseroles, stews).

Baste: Spoon liquid over food (pan juices over turkey) during cooking to keep it moist.

Batter: An uncooked mixture of flour, eggs and liquid with other ingredients; thin enough to be spooned or poured (muffins, pancakes).

Blanch: Plunge food into boiling water for a brief time to preserve color, texture and nutritional value or to remove skin (vegetables, fruits, nuts).

Boil: Heat liquid until bubbles rise continuously and break on the surface and steam is given off. For rolling boil, the bubbles form rapidly.

Broil: Cook directly under or above a red-hot heating unit.

Caramelize: Melt sugar slowly over low heat until it becomes a golden brown, caramel-flavored syrup. Or sprinkle granulated, powdered or brown sugar on top of a food, then place under a broiler until the sugar is melted and caramelized.

Chop: Cut into coarse or fine irregular pieces, using knife, food chopper, blender or food processor.

Coat: Cover food evenly with crumbs or sauce.

Cool: Allow hot food to stand at room temperature for a specified amount of time. Placing hot food on a wire rack will help it cool more quickly. Stirring mixtures occasionally also will help them cool more quickly and evenly.

Core: Remove the center of a fruit (apple, pear, pineapple). Cores contain small seeds (apple, pear) or are woody in texture (pineapple).

Crisp-tender: Doneness description of vegetables cooked until they retain some of the crisp texture of the raw food.

Crush: Press into very fine particles (crushing a clove of garlic, using a chef's knife or garlic press).

Cube: Cut food into squares 1/2 inch or larger, using a knife.

Cut up: Cut into small, irregular pieces with kitchen scissors or a knife. Or cut into smaller pieces (broiler-fryer chicken).

Dash: Less than 1/8 teaspoon of an ingredient.

Deep-fry or French-fry: Cook in hot fat that's deep enough to float the food.

Dice: Cut food into squares smaller than 1/2 inch, using a knife.

Dissolve: Stir a dry ingredient (flavored gelatin) into a liquid ingredient (boiling water) until the dry ingredient disappears.

Dot: Drop small pieces of an ingredient (margarine or butter) randomly over food (sliced apples in an apple pie).

Dough: Mixture of flour and liquid with other ingredients (often including a leavening); it is stiff but pliable. Dough can be dropped from a spoon (cookies), rolled (pie crust) or kneaded (bread).

Drain: Pour off liquid by putting the food into a strainer or colander that has been set in the sink. If draining fat from meat, place strainer in disposable container. If liquid is to be saved, place the strainer in a bowl or other container.

Drizzle: Pour topping in thin lines from a spoon or liquid measuring cup in an uneven pattern over food (glaze on a cake, cookies).

Dust: Sprinkle lightly with flour, cornmeal, powdered sugar or cocoa; for example, dust coffee cake with powdered sugar.

Flake: Break lightly into small pieces, using a fork (flaking cooked fish).

Flute: Squeeze a pastry edge with the fingers to make a finished, ornamental edge.

Fry: Cook in hot fat over moderate or high heat. Also see *Panfry* and *Sauté*.

Glaze: Brush, spread or drizzle an ingredient or mixture of ingredients (jam, melted chocolate) on hot or cold foods to give a glossy appearance or hard finish.

Grate: Rub a hard-textured food against the small, rough, sharp-edged holes of a grater, reducing them to tiny particles (citrus peel, chocolate, Parmesan cheese). For citrus peel, grate only the skin, not the bitter white membrane.

Grease: Rub the inside surface of a pan with shortening, using pastry brush, waxed paper or paper towel, to prevent food from sticking during baking (muffins, some casseroles). Nonstick cooking spray may also be used. Margarine and butter usually contain salt that may cause hot foods to stick.

Grease and Flour: Rub the inside surface of a pan with shortening before dusting it with flour, to prevent food from sticking during baking (cakes). After flouring the pan, turn the pan upside down, and tap the bottom to remove excess flour.

Heat Oven: Turn the oven controls to the desired temperature, allowing the oven to heat thoroughly before adding food. Heating takes about 10 minutes for most ovens. Also called preheating.

Julienne: Cut into thin, matchlike strips, using knife or food processor (fruits, vegetables, meats).

Knead: Work dough on a floured surface into a smooth, elastic mass, using hands or an electric mixer with dough hook. Kneading develops the gluten in flour and results in an even texture and a smooth, rounded top. It can take up to about 15 minutes by hand.

Marinate: Let food stand in a savory, usually acidic liquid in a glass or plastic container for several hours to add flavor or to tenderize. Marinade is the savory liquid in which the food is marinated.

Mince: Cut food into very fine pieces, smaller than chopped food.

Panfry: Fry meat or other food, starting with a cold skillet, using little or no fat and usually pouring off fat from meat as it accumulates during cooking.

Peel: Cut off outer covering, using knife or vegetable peeler (apples, potatoes). Also, to strip off outer covering, using fingers (bananas, oranges).

Poach: Cook in simmering liquid just below the boiling point (eggs, fish).

Reduce: Boil liquid uncovered to evaporate liquid and intensify flavor.

Roast: Cook meat uncovered on rack in shallow pan in oven without adding liquid.

Sauté: Cook over medium-high heat in hot fat with frequent tossing or turning motion.

Scald: Heat liquid to just below the boiling point. Tiny bubbles will form at the edge. A thin skin will form on the top of milk.

Score: Cut surface of food about 1/4 inch deep, using knife, to facilitate cooking, flavoring, tenderizing or for appearance (meat, yeast bread).

Shred: Cut into long, thin pieces, using round, smooth holes of shredder, a knife or food processor (cabbage, carrots, cheese).

Simmer: Cook in liquid on range top, just below the boiling point. Usually done after reducing heat from a boil. Bubbles will rise slowly and break just below the surface.

Slice: Cut into uniform-size flat pieces (bread, meat).

Soft Peaks: Egg whites beaten until peaks are rounded or curl when beaters are lifted from bowl, while still moist and glossy. Also see *Stiff Peaks.*

Soften: Let cold food stand at room temperature, or microwave at low power setting, until no longer hard (margarine, butter, cream cheese).

Steam: Cook food by placing on a rack or special steamer basket over a small amount of boiling or simmering water in a covered pan. Steaming helps retain flavor, shape, color, texture and nutritional value.

Stew: Cook slowly in a small amount of liquid for a long time (stewed fruit, beef stew).

Stiff Peaks: Egg whites beaten until peaks stand up straight when beaters are lifted from bowl, while still moist and glossy. Also see *Soft Peaks.*

Strain: Pour mixture or liquid through a fine sieve or strainer to remove larger particles.

Tear: Break into pieces, using fingers (lettuce for salads; bread slices for soft bread crumbs).

Toss: Tumble ingredients lightly with a lifting motion (salad with greens).

Ingredients Glossary

Baking Powder: Leavening mixture made from baking soda, an acid and a moisture absorber. Double-acting baking powder forms carbon dioxide twice: once when mixed with moist ingredients and once during baking. Do not substitute for baking soda because acid proportions may be unbalanced in recipe.

Baking Soda: Leavening known as bicarbonate of soda. Must be mixed with an acid ingredient (lemon juice, buttermilk or molasses) to release carbon dioxide gas bubbles.

Chocolate: Made from ground, liquefied roasted shelled cocoa beans, processed in various ways:

- **Baking cocoa:** Dried chocolate liquor (cocoa butter removed) is ground into unsweetened cocoa. Does not substitute directly for cocoa drink mixes that contain added milk powder and sugar.

- **Semisweet, bittersweet, sweet and milk chocolates:** Contain from 10 to 35 percent chocolate liquor; varying amounts of cocoa butter; sugar and, for some, milk and flavorings. Available in bars and chips, use for baking or eating. Quality varies, so follow package directions for melting.

- **White chocolate:** Not a true chocolate. Contains some cocoa butter but no cocoa or chocolate liquor. Often called vanilla milk chips or vanilla baking bar.

Corn Syrup: Clear, thick liquid (dark and light are interchangeable in recipes) made from corn sugar mixed with acid. It's one sweetener that doesn't crystallize and is especially good for pecan pie, frostings, fruit sauces and jams.

Cornstarch: A thickener for soups, sauces and desserts that comes from a portion of the corn kernel. This finely ground flour keeps sauces clear, not opaque as sauces thickened with wheat flour are. To substitute for all-purpose flour, use half as much cornstarch.

Cream: Smooth, rich product made from separating butterfat from the liquid in whole milk. Pasteurized and processed into several forms:

- **Half-and-half:** Milk and cream are mixed, containing 10 to 12 percent butterfat. It won't whip, but it can be used in place of whipping (heavy) cream in many recipes.

- **Sour cream:** Commercially cultured with lactic acid to give a tangy flavor. Regular sour cream is 18 to 20 percent butterfat. Reduced-fat sour cream is made from half-and-half and can be substituted for regular sour cream in most recipes. Nonfat sour cream has all fat removed and may not be successful in all recipes that call for regular sour cream.

- **Whipping (heavy) cream:** The richest cream available in the United States, it has 36 to 40 percent butterfat. It doubles in volume when whipped.

Fats and Oils: In cooking, they add richness and flavor to food, aid browning, help bind ingredients together, tenderize baked goods and are used for frying. But all fats are not created equal in texture and flavor. In our recipes, ingredient listings for fats vary because of their cooking and baking characteristics. See specific examples that follow.

- **Butter:** A saturated fat made from cream that must be at least 80 percent butterfat by U.S. Department of Agriculture (USDA) standards. It is high in flavor and has a melt-in-your-mouth texture. Butter is sold in sticks, whipped in tubs and as butter-flavored granules. Use only sticks for baking; whipped butter will give a different texture because of the air beaten into it.

- **Butter-margarine blends:** Available in sticks and tubs, blends usually are a combination of 60 percent margarine and 40 percent butter and are interchangeable with butter or margarine. Use only sticks for baking.

- **Lard:** A saturated fat made from rendered and refined pork fat, lard is not used as much now as in the past. Lard is softer and richer than butter and margarine and makes very tender, flaky biscuits and pastry.

- **Margarine:** An unsaturated butter substitute made with no less than 80 percent fat (most use vegetable oils made from soybeans, cottonseed and corn) by weight and flavoring from dairy products. Textures and flavors vary. Use as a table spread and for cooking and baking. Sold in sticks and as soft spreads in tubs. Use only sticks for baking.

- **Reduced-calorie or low-fat butter or margarine:** These products have water and air added and contain at least 20 percent less fat than regular butter or margarine. Do not use for baking.

- **Vegetable spreads:** Margarine products with less than 80 percent fat (vegetable oil) by weight usually are labeled as vegetable oil spreads. These products, like margarine, can be used for a variety of purposes, from spreading to cooking to baking.

    Because the percentage of fat is lower than for margarine, the amount of water is increased, which can affect the texture and quality of baked items, some

candies and other foods that need to be crisp. We do not recommend vegetable oil spreads with less than 65 percent fat be used for baking. And in some instances, we do not recommend spreads be used for baking at all.

Products with less than 60 percent fat are made to be used as table spreads, although they can be used for some cooking.

Some spreads may have unusual odors when heated and can spatter at high temperatures.

Vegetable oil spreads are sold in sticks (for all-purpose use), in tubs (to use as a table spread—do not use for baking) and as liquid squeeze spreads (to use for topping vegetables and popcorn or for basting—do not use for baking).

Manufacturers of vegetable oil spreads may recommend their product for baking and provide recipes. Keep in mind those recipes are developed specifically for a particular vegetable oil spread.

- **Oils for cooking:** Low in saturated fats and containing no cholesterol, these liquid fats are delicate to bland in flavor and are treated to withstand high-temperature cooking and long storage. In our recipes, they are listed as follows:

    Nonstick cooking spray: Used to spray cookware and bakeware before using, to prevent food from sticking during cooking and baking. Sometimes used directly on foods in low-fat cooking.

    Olive oil: Pressed from fully pitted ripe (black) olives. Olive oil is graded based on its acidity. The lower the acidity, the stronger the "olive" flavor. Cold-pressed (processed without heat) oil is called extra virgin. For the second olive pressing, solvents are used, and this yields virgin olive oil. Successive pressings yield less delicate oil. Use olive oil in marinades, salad dressings and cooking.

Vegetable oil: An economical blend of oils from various vegetables, such as corn, cottonseed, peanut, safflower and soybean. Use in all cooking and baking.

Shortening: Vegetable oils are hydrogenated to change them from liquid to solid at room temperature. Shortening is used especially for flaky, tender pastry and greasing baking pans. Butter-flavored shortening and regular shortening can be used interchangeably. Sold in cans and in stick form.

Flour: The primary ingredient in breads, cakes, cookies and quick breads.

- **All-purpose flour:** Selected wheats blended to be used for all kinds of baking. Available both bleached and unbleached.

- **Bread flour:** Wheats higher in gluten-forming protein than all-purpose flour, which gives more structure to bread. Bread flour absorbs more liquid and produces a more elastic dough, resulting in greater volume. Best choice for bread machine breads and yeast breads. For other bakings, bread flour can make some recipes too tough.

- **Cake flour:** Milled from soft wheats. It's lower in protein than all-purpose flour and not recommended to substitute for either all-purpose flour or bread flour. Cake flour results in tender, fine-textured cakes.

- **Quick-mixing flour:** Enriched, all-purpose flour that's granular and processed to blend easily with liquid to make gravies or sauces or to thicken main dishes.

- **Rye flour:** Milled from rye grain and low in gluten-forming protein, it is usually combined with wheat flour to increase the dough's gluten-forming capabilities.

- **Self-rising flour:** A convenience flour made from a blend of hard and soft wheats that includes leavening and salt. It's a favorite for light and fluffy biscuits and tender cakes. For best results, don't substitute self-rising flour for other kinds of flour unless directed in the recipe, as leavening and salt proportions won't be accurate.

- **Whole wheat flour:** Ground from the complete wheat kernel, whole wheat flour gives a nutty flavor and dense texture to breads and other baked goods. Stone-ground whole wheat flour is coarser than roller-milled whole wheat flour. Baked goods made with whole wheat flour rise less than those made with all-purpose flour.

Gingerroot: Plump tubers with knobby branches. Side branches have a milder tangy ginger flavor than the main root. Grate unpeeled gingerroot, or peel and chop or slice, to add flavor to foods such as stir-fries, sauces and baked goods. Look for gingerroot in the produce section of your supermarket.

Leavening: Ingredients that cause baked goods to rise and develop lighter textures (Also see *Baking Powder, Baking Soda, Yeast*).

Milk: Refers to cow's milk throughout this cookbook.

- **Buttermilk:** Thick, smooth liquid that results when skim or part-skim milk is cultured with lactic acid bacteria. Used in baking for tangy flavor.

- **Evaporated milk:** Whole milk with more than half of the water removed before the mixture is homogenized. Mixture is slightly thicker than whole milk. Use in recipes calling for evaporated milk, or mix with equal volume of water to substitute for whole milk.

- **Low-fat milk:** Contains 0.5 to 2 percent butterfat.

- **Skim milk:** Contains less than 0.5 percent butterfat.

- **Sweetened condensed milk:** Made when about half of the water is removed from whole milk and sweetener is added. Use for desserts.

- **Whole milk:** Contains at least 3.25 percent butterfat.

Phyllo (Filo): These paper-thin pastry sheets, whose name comes from the Greek word for "leaf," are the basis of many Greek and Middle Eastern main dishes and sweets. Available frozen or refrigerated. Sheets dry out quickly; cover unused sheets with waxed paper and a damp kitchen towel while working with phyllo.

Puff Pastry: Dozens of layers of chilled butter rolled between sheets of pastry dough. The basis of croissants, puff pastry shells for creamed poultry or seafood and such desserts as Napoleons and fruit pastries.

Sugar: Sweetener that may come from sugar beets or cane sugar. Available in several forms:

- **Granulated:** Standard white sugar available from 1-pound boxes to 100-pound bags as well as in cubes and 1-teaspoon packets.

- **Brown:** Either produced after refined white sugar is removed from beets or cane or is the result of mixing refined molasses syrup with white sugar crystals. Dark brown sugar has a more intense flavor. If brown sugar hardens, store in closed container with a slice of apple or a moist slice of bread. When measuring, firmly pack it into the measuring cup.

- **Powdered:** Crushed granulated sugar used for frostings and for dusting pastries and cakes.

Yeast: Leavening whose fermentation is the essence of yeast bread. The combination of warmth, food (sugar) and liquid causes yeast to release carbon dioxide bubbles that cause dough to rise. Always use yeast before its expiration date.

- **Bread machine yeast:** Special strain of fine-grained, dehydrated yeast, designed to be thoroughly dissolved during mixing and kneading in bread machines.

- **Compressed cake yeast:** Moist yeast whose individual 0.6-ounce square can be substituted directly for each package of active dry yeast. Store in refrigerator up to two weeks, or freeze up to two months and use immediately after defrosting.

- **Quick-acting active dry yeast:** Special strain of dehydrated yeast that allows bread to rise in less time than does regular yeast. It is often mixed with part of the flour to withstand higher water temperatures (120° to 130°).

- **Regular active dry yeast:** Dehydrated yeast that can be substituted directly for quick-acting active dry yeast.

Equipment Used in Recipe Testing

We use equipment for testing that the majority of consumers use in their homes. If a specific piece of equipment (such as a wire whisk) is necessary for recipe success, it will be listed in the recipe.

- Cookware and bakeware without non-stick coating were used, unless indicated.

- No dark colored, black or insulated bakeware was used.

- When a baking pan is specified in a recipe, a metal pan was used; a baking dish or pie plate means oven-proof glass was used.

- An electric hand mixer was used for mixing only when mixer speeds are specified in the recipe directions. When a mixer speed is not given, a spoon or fork was used.

Equivalent Measures

3 teaspoons = 1 tablespoon
4 tablespoons = 1/4 cup
5 tablespoons + 1 teaspoon = 1/3 cup
8 tablespoons = 1/2 cup
12 tablespoons = 3/4 cup
16 tablespoons = 1 cup (8 ounces)
2 cups = 1 pint (16 ounces)
4 cups (2 pints) = 1 quart (32 ounces)
8 cups (4 pints) = 1/2 gallon (64 ounces)
4 quarts = 1 gallon (128 ounces)

Special Directions for Refrigerated or Frozen Baked Foods

Baked Products: Cool completely before wrapping in airtight packaging for freezing. Allow frosting to set or freeze uncovered before packaging.

- **Breads:** Refrigerate only during hot, humid weather. Loosen wrap on frozen bread and thaw at room temperature two to three hours.

- **Cakes:** Refrigerate cakes with custard or whipped cream filling or frosting; do not freeze, as these toppings can separate. Loosen wrap on frozen unfrosted cakes and thaw at room temperature two to three hours. Loosen wrap on frozen frosted cakes and thaw overnight in refrigerator.

- **Cheesecakes:** Thaw wrapped in refrigerator four to six hours.

- **Cookies:** Freeze delicate or frosted and decorated cookies in single layers separated by waxed paper. Thaw covered in container at room temperature one to two hours. Crisp-textured cookies should be removed from container to thaw.

- **Pies:** For frozen unbaked fruit pies: Unwrap and carefully cut slits in top crust. Bake at 425° for 15 minutes. Reduce oven temperature to 375° and bake 30 to 45 minutes longer or until crust is golden brown and juice begins to bubble through slits.

  For baked fruit, pecan and pumpkin pies: Unwrap and thaw at room temperature until completely thawed. Or unwrap and thaw at room temperature 1 hour, then heat in 375° oven for 35 to 40 minutes or until warm. Unwrap and thaw baked pumpkin pies in refrigerator.

Dairy Products: Check packages for the freshness date, and refrigerate in original containers. Refrigeration time is for opened products.

- **Cream cheese and hard cheese:** If hard cheese is moldy, trim 1/2 inch from affected area and replace wrap each time. Thaw frozen cheese in refrigerator, use only in baked goods because of to texture changes.

- **Ice cream, sorbet, frozen yogurt:** Freeze in original container. Cover surface directly with aluminum foil or plastic wrap, to reduce ice crystals. For best quality, do not thaw and refreeze.

- **Whipped cream:** Freeze in small mounds on waxed paper until firm, then place in airtight container. Let stand about 15 minutes at room temperature to thaw.

Eggs: To refrigerate yolks only, cover with cold water and refrigerate tightly covered. To freeze yolks and whites, add 1/8 teaspoon salt or 1/2 teaspoon sugar for every four yolks or yolks and whites of two whole eggs and freeze tightly covered.

Meat Products: Check packages for the freshness date. Refrigerate or freeze meat in original packages, because repeated handling can introduce bacteria to meat and poultry. To freeze, overwrap with heavy-duty aluminum foil or freezer wrap or place in freezer bags.

Cold Food Storage Chart

Foods	Refrigerator (34° to 40°)	Freezer (0° or below)
Breads—coffee cakes, muffins, quick breads and yeast breads	5 to 7 days	2 to 3 months
Cakes—unfrosted and frosted	3 to 5 days	Unfrosted—3 to 4 months Frosted—2 to 3 months
Cheesecakes—baked	3 to 5 days	4 to 5 months
Cookies—baked	Only if stated in recipe	Unfrosted—no longer than 12 months Frosted—no longer than 3 months
Pies—unbaked or baked fruit pies, baked pecan and baked pumpkin pies	Baked pumpkin pies, 3 to 5 days. Store fresh fruit or baked fruit pies and baked pecan pies loosely covered at room temperature no longer than 3 days.	Unbaked fruit pies— 2 to 3 months Baked fruit pies— 3 to 4 months
Pie shells—unbaked or baked	Store in freezer.	Unbaked shells—no longer than 2 months Baked shells—no longer than 4 months

Cooking at Higher Altitudes

People who live at elevations of 3,500 feet or higher face some unique cooking challenges. Air pressure is lower than it is at sea level, so water has a lower boiling point and liquid evaporates faster. Because certain foods and methods of preparation are affected by the pressure at high elevations, recipes for both conventional and microwave cooking must be adjusted for optimum performance. Unfortunately, trial and error often is the only way to make improvements, as no set of rules applies to all recipes. Try the following guidelines.

- Most baked goods (leavened with baking powder or baking soda, not yeast) will be improved by one or more of the following adjustments: increased temperature (25°), increased liquid, decreased leavening, decreased sugar and/or a larger pan size. For very rich recipes, such as pound cakes, decreasing the fat will improve results. Quick breads and cookies usually require the fewest adjustments.

- Yeast bread dough rises more rapidly at high altitudes and can over-rise easily. Allow dough to rise for a shorter time. Flour dries out more quickly too, so use the minimum amount called for or use 1/4 to 1/2 cup less than the total amount.

- Boiled candy and cooked frostings (sugar mixtures) become concentrated more rapidly because of the faster evaporation of water. Watch cooking closely to prevent scorching. Reduce recipe temperature by 2° for every 1,000 feet of elevation.

If you are new to high-altitude cooking, call your USDA Extension Service office, listed in the phone book under county government, for help with any questions you may have. Recipes are also available from Colorado State University, Fort Collins, Colorado 80521. Local libraries and bookstores carry high-altitude cookbooks.

Breads

Blueberry Buckle Coffee Cake (page 61)

Continued on next page

About Yeast Breads

Almost nothing smells as wonderful or is more tempting than bread fresh and warm from the oven! Yeast breads require some rising time, but the final results are definitely worth the wait. Sample delicious kneaded breads, biscuits, coffee cakes, sweet rolls and more—these breads rise to any occasion!

Pans and Pan Preparation

- Use loaf pans of anodized aluminum, darkened metal or glass for bread with well-browned crusts. If using pans with dark nonstick coating, watch carefully so bread doesn't overbrown. Follow manufacturer's directions, because reducing the oven temperature by 25° is often recommended.

- Use shiny cookie sheets and muffin cups, which reflect heat, for tender, golden brown crusts on rolls and sweet rolls.

Ingredients

When mixed together, kneaded and baked, these basic ingredients provide a variety of breads.

Flour: All-purpose flour is the most widely used flour. The amount of protein in flour varies with the wheat crop, as does the moisture within the flour itself. This is why most kneaded dough recipes give a range of amount of flour.

Yeast: Yeast is a live plant that gives off a gas that makes dough rise. It is very sensitive—too much heat will kill it, but cold will stunt its growth. Always check the expiration date on the yeast before using.

Many recipes follow the "quick-mix" method of mixing the yeast with part of the flour, then beating in very warm liquid (120° to 130°). Some recipes, however, yield better results by the traditional method of dissolving the yeast in warm water (105° to 115°). The water temperature is higher for the quick-mix method as the flour and other ingredients dilute the yeast.

If using quick active dry yeast, you can omit the first rising, if desired. After kneading, cover the dough and let it rest 10 minutes before continuing with the next step.

Be sure you correctly follow the temperatures for liquids stated in each recipe, because using the wrong temperature for either method will give poor results.

Liquids: Water and milk are the most commonly used liquids. Water gives bread a crispier crust; milk, a velvety texture and added nutrients.

Sweeteners: Sugar, honey and molasses provide "food" for the yeast to help it grow, enhance flavor and help brown the crust. Do not use artifical sweeteners because they do not properly "feed" the yeast.

Salt: Salt is a flavoring needed to control yeast growth and prevent over-rising, which can cause bread to collapse. If salt is reduced, decrease both rising times.

Fat: Margarine, butter, shortening or vegetable oil is added to contribute tenderness and flavor.

Eggs: Eggs are sometimes added for flavor, richness and color.

Baking Yeast Breads

- Stagger loaf pans on a lower oven rack so they do not touch the sides of the oven or each other. The top of each pan should be level with, or slightly above, the middle of the oven.

- If baking round loaves on a cookie sheet, place the sheet on a rack in the center of the oven.

- Determine the doneness by tapping the crust. The loaf will have a hollow sound when done.

- Remove loaves from pans immediately so the sides remain crusty, and place on wire racks away from drafts to cool.

- For a shiny, soft crust, brush just-baked bread with margarine, butter or shortening.

Cutting Bread

- Cut into slices with a serrated bread knife or an electric knife on a cutting board or other surface designed for cutting.

- If bread is very fresh or warm, turn the loaf on its side to avoid squashing the top.

- Bread can be cut into fun shapes such as wedges (round loaves) or from slices, cut into fingers. Use cookie cutters for special shapes—leftover pieces can be used for croutons.

Storing Bread

- Breads and rolls can be stored in airtight containers in a cool, dry place up to five days. Refrigerate only in hot, humid weather.

- Breads can be stored tightly wrapped in moistureproof or vaporproof material,

labeled and dated, in the freezer for up to three months. To thaw, let stand wrapped at room temperature for two to three hours.

Types of Yeast Doughs

There are two kinds of yeast doughs: batter and kneaded. Batter breads are shortcut, no-knead yeast breads. Kneaded breads require more time to prepare as well as energy for kneading the dough. Both kinds need to rise before shaping and baking to allow the yeast to activate. To let dough rise, cover and keep in a warm, draft-free place. If necessary, place the covered bowl of dough on a wire rack over a bowl of warm water.

Batter dough: Because less flour is used than for kneaded dough, batter dough is stickier and instead of being kneaded, is beaten with an electric mixer with the first addition of flour. The batter is generally not shaped but is spread in the pan. There is usually only one rising time. Batter bread has a coarser texture than kneaded bread and has a pebbled surface.

Kneaded dough: Kneading develops the gluten and results in even texture and a smooth, rounded top. If dough is not sufficiently kneaded, the bread will be coarse, heavy, crumbly and dry. A standard countertop electric mixer with a dough-hook attachment mixes dough enough for satisfactory loaves of bread, although the loaves may have slightly less volume than those kneaded by hand. A heavy-duty mixer yields loaves of higher volumes. Be sure to follow manufacturer's directions for the size of recipe the mixer can handle as well as mixing time.

How to Shape Yeast Bread Loaves

1. Flatten dough with hands or rolling pin into rectangle, 18×9 inches.

2. Roll dough up tightly toward you, beginning at one of the open ends.

3. Press with thumbs to seal after each turn; pinch edge of dough into roll to seal.

4. Press each end with side of hand to seal; fold ends under loaf.

How to Cut Special Doughs

French Bread: Make 1/4-inch deep slashes across loaf at 2-inch intervals.

Caramel-Pecan Sticky Rolls: To cut even slices, place a piece of dental floss or heavy thread under roll. Bring ends of floss up and crisscross at top of roll. Pull strings in opposite directions.

Traditional White Bread

2 loaves, 16 slices each

Do you need to use less salt in your diet? If so, decrease sugar to 2 tablespoons and salt to 1 teaspoon. Substitute vegetable oil for the shortening. Each rising time will be 10 to 15 minutes shorter.

6 to 7 cups all-purpose* or bread flour
3 tablespoons sugar
1 tablespoon salt
2 tablespoons shortening
2 packages regular or quick active dry yeast
2 1/4 cups very warm water (120° to 130°)
Margarine or butter, melted

Mix 3 1/2 cups of the flour, the sugar, salt, shortening and yeast in large bowl. Add warm water. Beat with electric mixer on low speed 1 minute, scraping bowl frequently. Stir in enough remaining flour, 1 cup at a time, to make dough easy to handle.

Turn dough onto lightly floured surface. Knead about 10 minutes or until smooth and elastic. Place in greased bowl and turn greased side up. Cover and let rise in warm place 40 to 60 minutes or until double. Dough is ready if indentation remains when touched.

Grease bottoms and sides of 2 loaf pans, 8 1/2 × 4 1/2 × 2 1/2 or 9 × 5 × 3 inches, with shortening.

Punch down dough and divide in half. Flatten each half with hands or rolling pin into rectangle, 18×9 inches, on lightly floured surface. Roll dough up tightly, beginning at 9-inch side, to form a loaf. Press with thumbs to seal after each turn. Pinch edge of dough into roll to seal. Press each end with side of hand to seal. Fold ends under loaf. Place seam side down in pan. Brush loaves lightly with margarine. Cover and let rise in warm place 35 to 50 minutes or until double.

Move oven rack to low position so that tops of pans will be in center of oven. Heat oven to 425°.

Bake 25 to 30 minutes or until loaves are deep golden brown and sound hollow when tapped. Remove from pans to wire rack. Brush loaves with margarine; cool.

*If using self-rising flour, omit salt.

Cinnamon-Raisin Bread: *Stir in 1 cup raisins with the second addition of flour. Mix 1/4 cup sugar and 2 teaspoons ground cinnamon. After rolling dough into rectangles, sprinkle each with 1 tablespoon water and half of the sugar mixture.*

Fresh Herb Bread: *Stir in 2 tablespoons chopped fresh chives, 2 tablespoons chopped fresh sage leaves and 2 tablespoons chopped fresh thyme leaves just before the second addition of flour.*

Cinnamon-Raisin Bread

Honey–Whole Wheat Bread

2 loaves

2 packages active dry yeast
1/2 cup warm water (105° to 115°)
1/3 cup honey
1/4 cup shortening
1 tablespoon salt
1 3/4 cups warm water
3 cups whole wheat flour
3 to 4 cups all-purpose flour*
Margarine or butter, softened

Dissolve yeast in 1/2 cup warm water in large mixing bowl. Stir in honey, shortening, salt, 1 3/4 cups warm water and the whole wheat flour. Beat until smooth. Mix in enough all-purpose flour to make dough easy to handle.

Turn dough onto lightly floured surface; knead until smooth and elastic, about 10 minutes. Place in greased bowl; turn greased side up. Cover; let rise in warm place until double, about 1 hour. (Dough is ready if indentation remains when touched.)

Punch down dough; divide into halves. Flatten each half with hands or rolling pin into rectangle, 18×9 inches. Fold crosswise into thirds, overlapping the 2 sides. Roll up tightly, beginning at one of the open ends. Press with thumbs to seal after each turn. Pinch edge firmly to seal. Press each end with side of hand to seal; fold ends under loaf. Place loaves, seam sides down, in 2 greased baking pans, 9 × 5 × 3 inches or 8 1/2 × 4 1/2 × 2 1/2 inches. Brush with margarine; sprinkle with whole wheat flour or crushed oats, if desired. Let rise until double, about 1 hour.

Heat oven to 375°. Bake until loaves are deep golden brown and sound hollow when tapped, 40 to 45 minutes. Remove from pans; cool on wire rack.

*If using self-rising flour, decrease salt to 1 teaspoon.

Country Crust Bread

2 loaves

2 packages active dry yeast
2 cups warm water (105° to 115°)
1/2 cup sugar
1 tablespoon salt
2 eggs
1/4 cup vegetable oil
6 to 6 1/2 cups all-purpose flour*
Vegetable oil
Margarine or butter, softened

Dissolve yeast in warm water in large mixing bowl. Stir in sugar, salt, eggs, 1/4 cup oil and 3 cups of the flour. Beat until smooth. Mix in enough remaining flour to make dough easy to handle.

Turn dough onto lightly floured surface; knead until smooth and elastic, 8 to 10 minutes. Place in greased bowl; turn greased side up. (At this point, dough can be refrigerated 3 to 4 days.) Cover; let rise in warm place until double, about 1 hour. (Dough is ready if indentation remains when touched.)

Punch down dough; divide into halves. Roll each half into rectangle, 18×9 inches. Roll up tightly, beginning at 9-inch side. Press with thumbs to seal after each turn. Pinch edge firmly to seal. Press each end with side of hand to seal; fold ends under loaf. Place loaf, seam side down, in greased baking pan, 9×5×3 inches. Brush with oil. Let rise until double, about 1 hour.

Heat oven to 375°. Bake until loaves are deep golden brown and sound hollow when tapped, 30 to 35 minutes. Remove from pans. Brush with margarine; cool on wire rack.

*If using self-rising flour, omit salt.

Country Cinnamon-Raisin Bread: *Divide dough into halves. Knead 1/2 cup raisins into each half. Roll each half into rectangle, 18×9 inches. Brush with oil. Mix 1/2 cup sugar and 1 tablespoon ground cinnamon; sprinkle over rectangles. Continue as directed.*

Sally Lunn

16 servings

2 packages active dry yeast
1/2 cup warm water (105° to 115°)
5 1/2 cups all-purpose flour*
1/4 cup shortening
1 1/2 cups lukewarm milk (scalded then cooled)
2 tablespoons sugar
1 1/2 teaspoons salt
2 eggs

Dissolve yeast in warm water in large mixing bowl. Stir in remaining ingredients. Beat until smooth. Cover; let rise in warm place until double, about 1 hour.

Stir down batter by beating about 25 strokes. Spread in greased tube pan, 10×4 inches. Let rise to within 1 inch of top of pan, about 45 minutes.

Heat oven to 350°. Bake until loaf is golden brown and crusty, 45 to 50 minutes. Remove from pan; serve warm.

*If using self-rising flour, omit salt.

TIP

To get a head start, measure the dry ingredients into a plastic bag or a bowl, then seal or cover, so they're ready when needed.

Sally Lunn

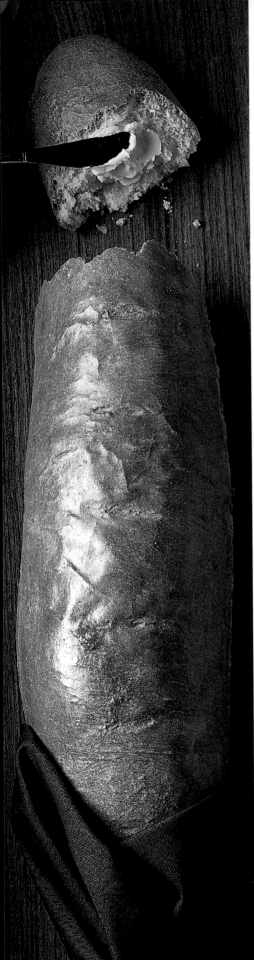

French Bread

1 loaf

1 package active dry yeast
1 1/4 cups warm water (105° to 115°)
1 1/2 teaspoons salt
1 tablespoon shortening
3 1/2 to 4 cups all-purpose flour
1 tablespoon cornmeal
Cold water
1 egg white
2 tablespoons cold water

Dissolve yeast in warm water in large mixing bowl. Stir in salt, shortening and 1 1/2 cups of the flour. Beat with spoon until smooth. Mix in enough remaining flour (first with spoon, then by hand) to make dough easy to handle.

Turn dough onto lightly floured surface; knead until smooth and elastic, about 5 minutes. Place in greased bowl; turn greased side up. Cover; let rise in warm place until double, 1 1/2 to 2 hours. (Dough is ready if indentation remains when touched.)

Punch down dough; round up and let rise until almost double, about 45 minutes. Punch down; cover and let rest 15 minutes. Sprinkle with cornmeal. Roll dough into rectangle, 15×10 inches. Roll up tightly, beginning at 15-inch side. Pinch edge firmly to seal. Roll gently back and forth to taper ends. Place loaf on lightly greased cookie sheet. If desired, make 1/4-inch slashes across loaf at 2-inch intervals. Brush with cold water. Let rise about 1 1/2 hours. Brush with cold water.

Heat oven to 375°. Bake 20 minutes. Beat egg white and 2 tablespoons cold water slightly; brush over loaf. Bake 25 minutes longer. Remove from cookie sheet; cool on wire rack.

TIP

Place warm water (heat only to 110° to 115°) and yeast in food processor. Cover and process, using quick on and off motions, until yeast is dissolved. Add flour, sugar and salt. Cover and process about 30 seconds or until dough forms a ball. (If dough is too sticky, add flour, 1 tablespoon at a time.) Do not knead dough. Place in greased bowl, and continue as directed.

French Bread

Italian Foccacia

2 flatbreads (12 slices each)

**2 1/2 to 3 cups all-purpose or unbleached
    flour**
2 teaspoons sugar
1/4 teaspoon salt
**1 package regular or quick-acting active
    dry yeast**
1/4 cup olive or vegetable oil
1 cup very warm water (120° to 130°)
Olive or vegetable oil
**2 tablespoons chopped fresh herbs (such as
    basil, oregano or rosemary)**
2 tablespoons grated Parmesan cheese

Mix 1 cup of the flour, the sugar, salt and yeast in large bowl. Add 1/4 cup oil and the warm water. Beat on medium speed 3 minutes, scraping bowl occasionally. Stir in enough remaining flour until dough is soft and leaves side of bowl.

Turn dough onto lightly floured surface; gently roll in flour to coat. Knead 5 to 10 minutes or until dough is smooth and elastic. Place in greased bowl; turn greased side up. Cover and let rise in warm place 1 to 1 1/2 hours or until double. (Dough is ready if indentation remains when touched.)

Heat oven to 425°. Grease 2 cookie sheets. Punch down dough, and divide in half. Shape each half into flattened 12-inch round on cookie sheet. Cover and let rise in warm place 20 minutes. Prick centers and 1 inch in from edge thoroughly with fork. Brush with oil. Sprinkle each with 1 tablespoon herbs and cheese. Bake 12 to 15 minutes or until golden brown. Serve warm.

Red Pepper Foccacia: *For each flatbread, cook 1 medium red bell pepper, cut into 1/4-inch rings, and 1 small onion, sliced, in 1 tablespoon olive or vegetable oil in 10-inch skillet over medium heat, stirring frequently, until softened. Arrange on each oil-brushed flatbread and sprinkle with herbs and cheese before baking.*

Italian Breadsticks

3 dozen breadsticks

1 package active dry yeast
2/3 cup warm water (105° to 115°)
1 tablespoon sugar
1 teaspoon salt
1/4 cup vegetable or olive oil
2 to 2 1/4 cups all-purpose flour
Vegetable or olive oil
1 egg white
1 tablespoon water
Coarse salt or toasted sesame seed

Dissolve yeast in warm water in large mixing bowl. Stir in sugar, 1 teaspoon salt, 1/4 cup oil and 1 cup of the flour. Beat until smooth. Mix in enough remaining flour to make dough easy to handle.

Turn dough only lightly floured surface; knead until smooth and elastic, about 5 minutes. Shape dough into roll, 10 inches long. Cut into 36 equal parts. Roll each part into rope, 8 inches long for thick breadsticks, 10 inches long for thin breadsticks. Place about 1 inch apart on greased cookie sheet. Brush with oil. Cover; let rise in warm place about 20 minutes.

Heat oven to 350°. Beat egg white and 1 tablespoon water slightly; brush over breadsticks and sprinkle with coarse salt. Bake until golden brown, 20 to 25 minutes.

Chile Pepper–Cheese Bread

1 loaf

1 package active dry yeast
1/2 cup warm water (105° to 115°)
1/2 cup lukewarm milk (scalded then
    cooled)
2/3 cup margarine or butter, softened
2 eggs
1 teaspoon salt
2 1/2 cups all-purpose flour*
1/2 cup cornmeal
1 cup shredded hot pepper cheese (about
    4 ounces)
2 to 4 tablespoons chopped green chiles,
    drained on paper towels
Cornmeal

Dissolve yeast in warm water in large mixing bowl. Stir in milk, margarine, eggs, salt and 1 cup of the flour. Beat on low speed, scraping bowl constantly, 30 seconds. Beat on medium speed, scraping bowl occasionally, 2 minutes. Stir in remaining flour, 1/2 cup cornmeal, the cheese and chiles. Scrape batter from side of bowl. Cover; let rise in warm place until double, about 30 minutes.

Stir down batter by beating about 25 strokes. Spread in greased 2-quart round casserole. Cover; let rise until double, about 40 minutes.

Heat oven to 375°. Sprinkle loaf with cornmeal. Bake until loaf is brown and sounds hollow when tapped, 40 to 45 minutes. Remove from casserole; cool on wire rack. To serve, cut into wedges with serrated knife.

*If using self-rising flour, omit salt.

Onion-Dill Bread: *Omit cornmeal, cheese and chiles. Increase flour to 3 cups. Stir in 1/4 cup chopped onion and 1 tablespoon dried dill weed with the second addition of flour. Brush top of loaf with margarine or butter, softened, and sprinkle with sesame seed or poppy seed before baking.*

Chile-Pepper Cheese Bread

Granola-Yogurt Bread

2 loaves

2 packages active dry yeast
1/2 cup warm water (105° to 115°)
2 teaspoons sugar
1 cup warm water
1 carton (8 ounces) plain yogurt
1 tablespoon salt
5 to 5 1/2 cups all-purpose flour
2 cups granola (any flavor)
Margarine or butter, softened

Dissolve yeast in 1/2 cup warm water. Stir in sugar. Let stand until bubbly and double in volume, about 10 minutes. Mix 1 cup warm water, the yogurt and salt in large mixer bowl. Stir in yeast mixture. Beat in 3 cups of the flour on medium speed, scraping bowl occasionally, 2 minutes. Mix in granola and enough remaining flour to make dough easy to handle.

Turn dough onto lightly floured surface; knead until smooth and elastic, about 10 minutes. Place in greased bowl; turn greased side up. Cover; let rise in warm place until double, about 1 hour. (Dough is ready if indentation remains when touched.)

Punch down dough; divide into halves. Shape each half into oval; place on lightly greased cookie sheet. Brush with margarine. Let rise until double, about 40 minutes.

Heat oven to 375°. Bake until loaves are golden brown and sound hollow when tapped, 30 to 35 minutes. Remove from cookie sheet. Brush with margarine; cool on wire rack.

Potato Refrigerator Dough

This versatile dough makes so many delicious rolls! Use it to make any of the rolls on the next page, from Braided Dinner Rolls to Hamburger Buns.

1 package active dry yeast
1 1/2 cups warm water (105° to 115°)
2/3 cup sugar
1 1/2 teaspoons salt
2/3 cup shortening
2 eggs
1 cup lukewarm mashed potatoes*
6 1/2 to 7 cups all-purpose flour**

Dissolve yeast in warm water in large mixing bowl. Stir in sugar, salt, shortening, eggs, potatoes and 4 cups of the flour. Beat until smooth. Mix in enough remaining flour to make dough easy to handle.

Turn dough onto lightly floured surface; knead until smooth and elastic, about 5 minutes. Place in greased bowl; turn greased side up. Cover bowl tightly; refrigerate at least 8 hours but no longer than 5 days. Punch down dough. Shape, let rise and bake as directed.

*Instant mashed potatoes can be substituted for the mashed potatoes; prepare as directed on package for 2 servings
**If using self-rising flour, omit salt.

Left to right: *Hamburger Buns, Crescent Rolls, Parker House Rolls, Braided Dinner Rolls*

Braided Dinner Rolls

6 rolls

1/3 Potato Refrigerator Dough (page 37)
1 egg
1 tablespoon water
3/4 teaspoon poppy seed
3/4 teaspoon sesame seed

Divide dough into 18 equal parts. Roll each part into rope, 7 inches long, on lightly floured surface. Place groups of 3 ropes each close together on lightly greased cookie sheet. Braid ropes gently and loosely. Do not stretch. Pinch ends to fasten; tuck under securely. Let rise until double, 45 to 60 minutes.

Heat oven to 375°. Beat egg and water slightly; brush over braids. Sprinkle each of 3 braids with 1/4 teaspoon poppy seed and each of remaining 3 braids with 1/4 teaspoon sesame seed. Bake until golden brown, about 15 minutes.

Parker House Rolls: *Prepare Potato Refrigerator Dough (page 37). Divide into halves (refrigerate 1 half for future use or use for Crescent Rolls, page 00). Divide remaining half of dough into halves. Roll 1 half into rectangle, 13×9 inches. Cut into 3-inch circles; brush with margarine or butter, softened. Fold each so top half overlaps slightly. Press edges together. Place close together in greased round baking pan, 9×1 1/2 inches. Brush with margarine or butter, softened. Repeat with remaining dough. Let rise until double, 45 to 60 minutes. Heat oven to 400°. Bake until light brown, 13 to 15 minutes. 20 rolls*

Crescent Rolls: *Prepare Potato Refrigerator Dough (page 37). Divide into halves (refrigerate 1 half for future use or use for Parker House Rolls). Divide* remaining half of dough into halves. Roll 1 half into 12-inch circle. Spread with margarine or butter, softened. Cut circle into 16 wedges. Roll up, beginning at rounded edges. Place rolls, with points underneath, on greased cookie sheet; curve ends slightly. Brush with margarine or butter, softened. Repeat with remaining dough. Let rise until double, 45 to 60 minutes. Heat oven to 400°. Bake until light brown, 13 to 15 minutes. 32 rolls

Hamburger Buns: *Divide one-third of Potato Refrigerator Dough (page 37) into 12 equal parts. Shape each part into smooth ball on lightly floured surface with lightly greased fingers; flatten. Place about 1 inch apart on greased cookie sheet. Let rise until double, 45 to 60 minutes. Heat oven to 400°. Brush buns with margarine or butter, softened; sprinkle with sesame seed or poppy seed. Bake until golden brown, 13 to 15 minutes. 1 dozen rolls*

Herb Buns

1 dozen rolls

1 package active dry yeast
1 cup warm water (105° to 115°)
1 teaspoon caraway seed
1/2 teaspoon dried sage leaves
1/4 teaspoon ground nutmeg
2 tablespoons sugar
1 teaspoon salt
1 egg
2 tablespoons shortening
2 1/4 cups all-purpose flour*

Dissolve yeast in warm water in large mixing bowl. Add caraway seed, sage and nutmeg. Stir in sugar, salt, egg, shortening and 1 cup of the flour. Beat until smooth. Stir in remaining flour until smooth. Scrape batter from side of bowl. Cover; let rise in warm place until double, about 30 minutes.

Stir down batter by beating about 25 strokes. Spoon into 12 greased muffin cups, 2 1/2 × 1 1/4 inches, filling each about half full. Let rise until batter reaches tops of cups, 20 to 30 minutes.

Heat oven to 400°. Bake 15 minutes.

*If using self-rising flour, omit salt.

Sour Cream–Chive Buns: *Decrease warm water to 1/4 cup. Omit caraway seed, sage and nutmeg. Mix 3/4 cup dairy sour cream, the sugar, salt and shortening. Heat just to boiling; cool to lukewarm. Stir sour cream mixture and half of the flour into yeast. Beat until smooth. Mix in remaining flour, the egg and 1 tablespoon plus 1 1/2 teaspoons snipped chives.*

Herb Buns

Chocolate-Caramel Sticky Buns

15 buns

3 1/2 cups all-purpose flour
1/2 cup cocoa
1/3 cup granulated sugar
1/2 teaspoon salt
2 packages quick-acting or regular active
   dry yeast
1 cup very warm milk (120° to 130°)
1/3 cup margarine or butter, softened
1 egg
1 cup packed brown sugar
1/2 cup (1 stick) margarine or butter
1/4 cup dark corn syrup
3/4 cup pecan halves
2 tablespoons margarine or butter, softened
1/2 cup miniature chocolate chips
2 tablespoons packed brown sugar
1 teaspoon ground cinnamon

Mix 2 cups of the flour, cocoa, granulated sugar, salt, and yeast in large bowl. Add warm milk, 1/3 cup margarine, and egg. Beat on low speed 1 minute, scraping bowl frequently. Beat on medium speed 1 minute, scraping bowl frequently. Stir in remaining flour (dough will be stiff).

Turn dough onto lightly floured surface. Knead about 5 minutes or until smooth and elastic. Place in greased bowl and turn greased side up. Cover and let rise in warm place about 1 1/2 hours or until double. (Dough is ready if indentation remains when touched.)

Heat 1 cup brown sugar and 1/2 cup margarine to boiling, stirring constantly; remove from heat. Stir in corn syrup. Pour in ungreased rectangular pan, 13×9×2 inches. Sprinkle with pecan halves.

Punch dough down. Flatten with hands or rolling pin into rectangle, 15×10 inches, on lightly floured surface. Spread with 2 tablespoons margarine. Mix chocolate chips, 2 tablespoons brown sugar and the cinnamon. Sprinkle evenly over margarine. Roll up tightly, beginning at 15-inch side. Pinch edge of dough into roll to seal. Stretch and shape until even. Cut roll into fifteen 1-inch slices. Place slightly apart in pan. Let rise in warm place about 30 minutes or until double.

Heat oven to 350°. Bake 30 to 35 minutes or until dark brown. Immediately invert on heat-proof tray or serving plate. Let stand 1 minute so caramel will drizzle down; remove pan.

Chocolate-Caramel Sticky Buns

Caramel-Pecan Sticky Rolls

15 rolls

3 1/2 to 4 cups all-purpose* or bread flour
1/3 cup granulated sugar
1 teaspoon salt
2 packages regular or quick active dry yeast
1 cup very warm milk (120° to 130°)
1/3 cup *stick* margarine or butter, softened**
1 large egg
1 cup packed brown sugar
1/2 cup *stick* margarine or butter, softened
1/4 cup dark corn syrup
1 cup pecan halves (4 ounces)
2 tablespoons *stick* margarine or butter, softened**
1/2 cup chopped pecans or raisins, if desired
1/4 cup granulated or packed brown sugar
1 teaspoon ground cinnamon

Mix 2 cups of the flour, 1/3 cup granulated sugar, the salt and yeast in large bowl. Add warm milk, 1/3 cup margarine and the egg. Beat with electric mixer on low speed 1 minute, scraping bowl frequently. Beat on medium speed 1 minute, scraping bowl frequently. Stir in enough remaining flour to make dough easy to handle.

Turn dough onto lightly floured surface. Knead about 5 minutes or until smooth and elastic. Place in greased bowl and turn greased side up. Cover and let rise in warm place about 1 hour 30 minutes or until double. Dough is ready if indentation remains when touched.

Heat 1 cup brown sugar and 1/2 cup margarine to boiling in 2-quart saucepan, stirring constantly; remove from heat. Stir in corn syrup. Pour into ungreased rectangular pan, 13×9×2 inches. Sprinkle with pecan halves.

Punch down dough. Flatten with hands or rolling pin into rectangle, 15×10 inches, on lightly floured surface. Spread with 2 tablespoons margarine. Mix chopped pecans, 1/4 cup granulated sugar and the cinnamon; sprinkle evenly over margarine. Roll rectangle up tightly, beginning at 15-inch side. Pinch edge of dough into roll to seal. Stretch and shape until even. Cut roll into fifteen 1-inch slices. Place slightly apart in pan. Cover and let rise in warm place about 30 minutes or until double.

Heat oven to 350°.

Bake 30 to 35 minutes or until golden brown. *Immediately* turn upside down onto heatproof tray or serving plate. Let stand 1 minute so caramel will drizzle over rolls; remove pan. Serve warm.

* If using self-rising flour, omit salt.
** Spreads with at least 65% vegetable oil can be substituted.

Lighter Caramel-Pecan Sticky Rolls: *For less fat and fewer calories per serving, omit 1 cup brown sugar, 1/2 cup margarine, the corn syrup, pecan halves and omit heating brown sugar, margarine, corn syrup and pecans.*

Line pan with aluminum foil; spray with non-stick cooking spray. Drizzle 3/4 cup light caramel ice-cream topping over foil. Sprinkle with 2/3 cup chopped pecans. Continue as directed in steps 4, 5 and 6—except omit the chopped pecans from the filling.

Overnight Danish Twists

27 twists

2 packages regular or quick active dry yeast
1/2 cup warm water (105° to 115°)
4 cups all-purpose flour*
1/3 cup sugar
2 teaspoons salt
1 cup cold *stick* butter, cut into small
    pieces**
4 large eggs
1 cup milk
Jam or preserves
Powdered Sugar Glaze (right)

Dissolve yeast in warm water in large bowl. Mix in flour, sugar and salt. Cut in butter, using pastry blender or crisscrossing 2 knives, until mixture looks like fine crumbs.

Separate egg yolks from egg whites; refrigerate egg whites for use in steps 5 and 7. Stir egg yolks and milk into flour mixture until soft dough forms. Cover bowl with plastic wrap and refrigerate at least 8 hours but no longer than 24 hours. Lightly grease 2 large cookie sheets with shortening.

Punch down dough. Divide dough into 3 equal parts. Roll 1 part dough at a time into rectangle, 9 × 7 inches, on lightly floured surface. (If dough becomes too sticky while shaping, refrigerate 5 to 10 minutes.) Cut rectangle crosswise into nine 1-inch strips.

For each twist, pinch ends of each strip together to form ring, stretching strip slightly, then twist to form figure 8. Place at least 2 inches apart on cookie sheet. Brush with egg white. Let rise uncovered at room temperature about 25 minutes or until dough is puffy and loops fill in.

Heat oven to 350°.

Make an indentation in center of each loop. Fill with 1/2 to 1 teasoon jam. Brush dough with egg white. Bake about 15 minutes or until light golden brown. Immediately remove to wire rack; cool slightly. Drizzle Powdered Sugar Glaze over warm twists.

POWDERED SUGAR GLAZE

1 1/2 cups powdered sugar
3/4 teaspoon vanilla
2 to 3 tablespoons water or milk

Mix all ingredients until smooth. If necessary, stir in additional water, 1/2 teaspoon at a time, until drizzling consistency.

* Do not use self-rising flour in this recipe.
** We do not recommend using margarine or vegetable oil spreads.

Honey Almond-Apple Puffs

9 puffs

1/2 package (17 1/4-ounce size) frozen puff
    pastry, thawed
1 large pared cooking apple, cut into
    6 wedges
Ground nutmeg
1/4 cup honey
1/4 cup sliced almonds

Heat oven to 425°. Unfold pastry and cut into 9 squares. Cut apple wedges crosswise in half (only 9 apple pieces are needed). Place 1 apple piece on each pastry square and sprinkle with nutmeg. Moisten corners of pastry with water. Gather corners over apple and pinch to seal well. Place on ungreased cookie sheet. Bake 15 to 20 minutes or until deep golden brown and puffed. Heat honey until thin. Brush honey over warm puffs. Sprinkle with almonds.

Tips for Biscuits

- When making biscuits, cut in shortening or other fat by using a pastry blender, crisscrossing 2 table knives, using the side of a fork or cutting with a wire whisk. "Cutting in" results in cutting the shortening into tiny lumps that will produce a flaky texture throughout the biscuits as the shortening melts during baking.

- Roll or pat biscuit dough to an even thickness for attractive biscuits and even baking. A clever way to roll dough evenly is between two wooden sticks that are 1/2 inch high and 14 inches long. Anyone who works with wood can make a pair. See photo 3, "How to Make Biscuits" (right).

- Cut the dough with a biscuit cutter dipped into flour. Cut the biscuits out of the dough as close together as possible. Push the cutter straight down into the dough—twisting as you cut will result in uneven biscuits.

- If a biscuit cutter is not available, cut biscuits with an opened 6-ounce juice can or other narrow can or glass dipped into flour. Or use cookie cutters to make fun shapes.

- After cutting as many biscuits as possible, press the scraps of dough together lightly, but do not knead. Roll or pat the remaining dough to 1/2-inch thickness and cut. These biscuits will have a slightly uneven appearance.

How to Make Biscuits

1. Cut shortening into flour mixture until the mixture resembles fine crumbs.

2. Stir in enough milk until dough leaves side of bowl (dough will be soft).

3. Roll or pat the dough 1/2-inch thick. Cut with floured 2 1/2-inch round cutter.

Baking Powder Biscuits

Baking Powder Biscuits

About 1 dozen biscuits

1/3 cup shortening
1 3/4 cups all-purpose flour*
2 1/2 teaspoons baking powder
3/4 teaspoon salt
3/4 cup milk

Heat oven to 450°. Cut shortening into flour, baking powder and salt with pastry blender until mixture resembles fine crumbs. Stir in just enough milk so dough leaves side of bowl and rounds up into a ball. (Too much milk makes dough sticky; not enough milk makes biscuits dry.)

Turn dough onto lightly floured surface. Knead lightly 10 times. Roll or pat to 1/2 inch thick. Cut with floured 2-inch biscuit cutter. Place on ungreased cookie sheet about 1 inch apart for crusty sides, touching for soft sides.

Bake until golden brown, 10 to 12 minutes. Immediately remove from cookie sheet.

*If using self-rising flour, omit baking powder and salt.

Biscuit Sticks: *Heat 1/3 cup margarine or butter in baking pan, 9×9×2 inches, in oven until melted; remove from oven. Roll dough into 8-inch square. Cut dough into halves; cut each half into eight 1-inch strips. Dip strips into margarine, coating all sides. Arrange strips in 2 rows in pan. Bake until golden brown, about 15 minutes. 16 sticks.*

Baking with Confidence

PERFECT BAKING POWDER BISCUITS ARE:

Light golden brown outside
High with fairly smooth, level tops
Tender and light
Flaky and slightly moist inside

Problem	Possible Cause
Not high	• too little baking powder • too much mixing • too hot oven
Dark bottom crust	• baking sheet was dull or dark, not shiny • oven rack placed too low in oven
Tough	• too little baking powder • too much mixing • too hot oven
Not flaky	• too little shortening • too much mixing • too little kneading

Buttermilk Biscuits

About 10 biscuits

1/2 cup shortening
2 cups all-purpose flour
1 tablespoon sugar
2 teaspoons baking powder
1 teaspoon salt
1/4 teaspoon baking soda
About 3/4 cup buttermilk

Heat oven to 450°. Cut shortening into flour, sugar, baking powder, salt and baking soda with pastry blender in large bowl until mixture resembles fine crumbs. Stir in just enough buttermilk so dough leaves side of bowl and forms a ball.

Turn dough onto lightly floured surface; gently roll in flour to coat. Knead lightly 10 times. Roll or pat 1/2 inch thick. Cut with floured 2 1/2-inch biscuit cutter. Place about 1 inch apart on ungreased cookie sheet.

Bake 10 to 12 minutes or until golden brown. Immediately remove from cookie sheet. Serve hot.

Pesto Biscuits

About 10 biscuits

1/3 cup shortening
1/4 cup pesto
2 cups all-purpose flour
3 teaspoons baking powder
1/2 teaspoon salt
About 1/2 cup milk
Grated Parmesan cheese

Heat oven to 450°. Cut shortening and pesto into flour, baking powder and salt with pastry blender in large bowl until mixture resembles fine crumbs. Stir in just enough milk so dough leaves side of bowl and forms a ball.

Turn dough onto lightly floured surface; gently roll in flour to coat. Knead lightly 10 times. Roll or pat 1/2 inch thick. Cut with floured 2 1/2-inch biscuit cutter. Place about 1 inch apart on ungreased cookie sheet. Sprinkle with cheese.

Bake 10 to 12 minutes or until golden brown. Immediately remove from cookie sheet. Serve hot.

Breakfast Puffs

15 puffs

1/3 cup shortening
1/2 cup sugar
1 egg
1 1/2 cups all-purpose flour*
1 1/2 teaspoons baking powder
1/2 teaspoon salt
1/4 teaspoon ground nutmeg
1/2 cup milk
1/2 cup sugar
1 teaspoon ground cinnamon
1/2 cup margarine or butter, melted

Heat oven to 350°. Grease 15 muffin cups, 2 1/2 × 1 1/4 inches. Mix shortening, 1/2 cup sugar and the egg. Stir in flour, baking powder, salt and nutmeg alternately with milk. Fill muffin cups about two-thirds full.

Breakfast Puffs

Bake until golden brown, 20 to 25 minutes. Mix 1/2 cup sugar and the cinnamon. Immediately after baking, roll puffs in melted margarine, then in sugar-cinnamon mixture.

*If using self-rising flour, omit baking powder and salt.

Sausage Biscuits

About 10 biscuits

Making a delicious breakfast sandwich is a snap with these biscuits. Use a 3-inch biscuit cutter and bake the biscuits just a few minutes longer. Split the warm biscuits and fill with eggs and cheese. (photograph on page 49)

1/2 pound bulk pork sausage
1/3 cup shortening
2 cups all-purpose flour
3 teaspoons baking powder
1/4 teaspoon salt
About 3/4 cup milk

Heat oven to 450°. Cook sausage in 10-inch skillet over medium heat, stirring frequently, until brown. Drain if necessary. Cool sausage slightly; crumble.

Cut shortening into flour, baking powder and salt with pastry blender in large bowl until mixture resembles fine crumbs. Stir in sausage. Stir in just enough milk so dough leaves side of bowl and forms a ball.

Turn dough onto lightly floured surface; gently roll in flour to coat. Knead lightly 10 times. Roll or pat 1/2 inch thick. Cut with floured 2 1/2-inch biscuit cutter. Place about 1 inch apart on ungreased cookie sheet.

Bake 10 to 12 minutes or until golden brown. Immediately remove from cookie sheet. Serve hot. Refrigerate any remaining biscuits.

Basil-Pepper Biscuits

About 10 biscuits

(photograph on page 58)

1/4 cup shortening
2 cups all-purpose or whole wheat flour
2 tablespoons chopped fresh or 2 teaspoons dried basil leaves
1 tablespoon sugar, if desired
3 teaspoons baking powder
1 teaspoon salt
1 teaspoon cracked black pepper
About 3/4 cup milk

Heat oven to 450°. Cut shortening into remaining ingredients except milk with pastry blender in medium bowl until mixture resembles fine crumbs. Stir in just enough milk so dough leaves side of bowl and rounds up into a ball. (Too much milk makes dough sticky, not enough makes biscuits dry.)

Turn dough onto lightly floured surface; gently roll in flour to coat. Knead lightly 20 to 25 times. Roll or pat 1/2 inch thick. Cut with floured 2 1/2-inch biscuit cutter. Place on ungreased cookie sheet about 1 inch apart for crusty sides, touching for soft sides. Bake 10 to 12 minutes or until golden brown. Immediately remove from cookie sheet. Serve warm.

Cornmeal–Basil-Pepper Biscuits: *Substitute 1/2 cup yellow, white or blue cornmeal for 1/2 cup of the flour. Sprinkle cornmeal over biscuits before baking, if desired.*

Cinnamon Biscuit Fans

8 biscuits

1/3 cup firm margarine or butter
2 cups all-purpose flour
2 tablespoons sugar
3 teaspoons baking powder
1/2 teaspoon salt
About 3/4 cup milk
3 tablespoons margarine or butter, softened
3 tablespoons sugar
1 teaspoon ground cinnamon
Glaze (below)

Heat oven to 425°. Grease 8 medium muffin cups, 2 1/2 × 1 1/4 inches. Cut 1/3 cup margarine into flour, 2 tablespoons sugar, the baking powder and salt with pastry blender in large bowl until mixture resembles fine crumbs. Stir in just enough milk so dough leaves side of bowl and forms a ball.

Turn dough onto lightly floured surface; gently roll in flour to coat. Knead lightly 10 times. Roll into rectangle, 12×10 inches. Spread 3 tablespoons margarine over rectangle. Mix 3 tablespoons sugar and the cinnamon; sprinkle over rectangle. Cut rectangle crosswise into 6 strips, 10×2 inches. Stack strips; cut crosswise into 8 pieces. Place cut sides up in muffin cups.

Bake 16 to 18 minutes or until golden brown. Immediately remove from pan. Drizzle Glaze over warm biscuits.

GLAZE

1/2 cup powdered sugar
2 to 2 1/2 teaspoons milk

Mix ingredients until smooth and of drizzling consistency.

Cinnamon Biscuit Fans, Sausage Biscuits (page 47)

About Quick Breads

Quick breads are fast and easy to make. They range from light and fluffy pancakes to tender, flaky biscuits and moist, rich nut breads. Some quick breads are made from batters while other are made from doughs. The proportions of liquid to flour, fat and eggs create the different quick bread categories, such as muffins, biscuits or pancakes.

Double-acting baking powder, rather than slower-acting yeast, is most often the leavening used in quick breads. It consists of an acid, such as cream of tartar, and an alkali, such as baking soda, which react with one another when liquid is added, giving off a harmless gas (carbon dioxide). In batter or dough, this gas forms tiny bubbles that expand quickly, creating the structure of the quick bread. This happens twice, once when mixed with wet ingredients and again during baking. To be sure baking powder is always fresh, purchase only a small quantity at a time, and stir it before using.

Pans and Pan Preparation

- Use shiny pans and cookie sheets, which reflect heat, for golden, delicate and tender crusts on muffins, coffee cakes and nut breads.

- Dark pans or pans with dark nonstick coating absorb heat more readily than shiny pans, so watch carefully to be sure foods don't overbrown. Follow manufacturer's directions for both baking and greasing. Many suggest reducing the oven temperature by 25°, and some do not recommend greasing or using nonstick cooking spray at all.

- If using insulated pans, you may need to increase baking times slightly.

- Only the bottoms of pans are usually greased with shortening for muffins and nut breads. This prevents a lip from forming around the edge of the bread.

Mixing Quick Breads

- Follow individual recipes for mixing instructions. Some batters are mixed until smooth, others only until moistened. Overmixing can result in less tender breads.

- We recommend that stick margarine or butter be used for quick breads when margarine or butter is specified. Vegetable oil spreads (also in stick form) with at least 65 percent fat can be substituted; the baked result will be satisfactory, although the batter or dough may have a slightly softer consistency.

- We do not recommend using vegetable oil spreads with less than 65 percent fat, tub margarines or whipped products whether butter, margarine or spreads. Because these products contain more water and less fat, using them can result in poor quality overall (thinner or softer consistency when mixing; less tender or wet and gummy after baking).

Baking Quick Breads

- For the best circulation of heat, place the oven rack in the center of the oven, unless otherwise directed.

- Ovens vary, so check for doneness at the minimum baking time, and add one- or two-minute intervals before checking again.

- Quick breads are usually removed from their pans to a wire rack to cool immediately or shortly after baking. This gives the bread a drier, crisper surface; if left in the pan, the bread would be steamed and soft.

Making the Perfect Muffin
Greasing

- Grease the bottoms only of muffin cups with shortening. Ungreased, the sides give the batter a surface to cling to as it bakes, resulting in muffins with nicely rounded tops. You can eliminate the greasing and make cleanup easier by using paper baking cups.

- Use shiny muffin pans for best browning. Even if you use dark nonstick muffin pans, grease the bottoms as directed. Dark pans absorb heat more readily than do shiny pans, so with dark pans, better results are often achieved by reducing the oven temperature by 25°.

Mixing

- Mix the egg and other liquid ingredients with a fork until well blended. Occasionally, dry ingredients such as brown sugar or orange peel will be added at this point to ensure their even distribution throughout the batter.

- Stir in the dry ingredients just until the flour is moistened. The batter should be lumpy. Overmixed batter will result in tough muffins with peaked tops and an uneven texture.

Folding

- If the recipe calls for folding in chopped nuts, pieces of fruit or other stir-ins, first sprinkle them over the batter. To fold, cut down through the center of the batter with a rubber spatula. Draw the spatula across the bottom and up the side of the bowl, folding the batter over the stir-ins on the top of the batter. Give the bowl a quarter turn and do it again.

Repeat just until the stir-ins are distributed through the batter.

Baking

- Place the oven rack in the center of the oven for the best circulation of heat.

- Divide batter evenly among muffin cups, using a large spoon or ice-cream scoop. Wipe off any batter that spills onto the edge of the pan to avoid burning. Fill empty cups in the muffin pan half full of water to ensure even baking.

- Bake muffins for the minimum time specified in the recipe, then check for doneness. If necessary, bake a minute or two longer; then check them again.

- When muffins are done, immediately remove them from the muffin pan. Muffins left to cool in the pan will become soggy from trapped steam. If paper baking cups are used, muffins should lift out easily. Otherwise, loosen the muffins with a knife or metal spatula, then lift them out. Occasionally, a recipe will specify that muffins be left in the pan for a few minutes before removing; this allows fragile muffins to set up.

Reheating

- Muffins are best served warm. If they become too cool, heat uncovered in the microwave on medium (50%) just until warm—one muffin for 15 to 30 seconds, two muffins for 25 to 40 seconds, three muffins for 35 to 60 seconds and four muffins for 45 seconds to 1 minute 15 seconds.

- Or to reheat in a conventional oven, wrap muffins in aluminum foil and heat in a 400° oven about 5 minutes or until warm.

Banana-Blueberry Muffins

1 dozen muffins

If you can't use up all of your ripe bananas, freeze them in their peels. When you're ready to bake with them, just thaw them and they'll be ready to use.

2/3 cup milk
1/4 cup vegetable oil
1/2 cup mashed ripe banana (about 1 medium)
1 egg
2 cups all-purpose flour
2/3 cup sugar
2 1/2 teaspoons baking powder
1/2 teaspoon salt
1/4 teaspoon ground nutmeg
1 cup fresh or frozen (thawed and well-drained) blueberries

Heat oven to 400°. Grease bottoms only of 12 medium muffin cups, 2 1/2 × 1 1/4 inches, or line with paper baking cups. Beat milk, oil, banana and egg in large bowl. Stir in remaining ingredients except blueberries just until flour is moistened. Fold in blueberries. Divide batter evenly among muffin cups (cups will be almost full). Sprinkle with sugar if desired.

Bake 18 to 20 minutes or until golden brown. Immediately remove from pan.

Bran-Date Muffins

1 dozen muffins

1/2 cup hot water
1/4 cup chopped dates
1 1/2 cups wheat bran
1 cup whole wheat flour
1 teaspoon baking powder
1/2 teaspoon baking soda
1/2 teaspoon salt
1/3 cup vegetable oil
1 egg
1 cup buttermilk
1/2 cup chopped dates

Pour water over 1/4 cup dates; set aside.

Heat oven to 400°. Grease bottoms only of 12 medium muffin cups, 2 1/2 × 1 1/4 inches, with shortening, or line with paper baking cups.

Mix wheat bran, flour, baking powder, baking soda and salt in large bowl.

Place date-water mixture, the oil and egg in blender or food processor. Cover and blend on medium speed about 1 minute or until smooth. Stir date mixture and buttermilk into flour mixture just until flour is moistened (batter will be lumpy). Gently stir in 1/2 cup dates. Divide batter evenly among muffin cups.

Bake 20 to 22 minutes or until toothpick inserted in center comes out clean. Cool muffins in pan 5 minutes; remove from pan to wire rack. Serve warm, if desired.

Lighter Bran-Date Muffins: *For less fat and fewer calories per serving, substitute fat-free buttermilk for the milk, 1/4 cup fat-free cholesterol-free egg product for the egg and 1/4 cup prune baby food for 1/4 cup of the oil.*

Apricot-Ginger Muffins

1 dozen muffins

Crystallized ginger is made by cooking pieces of gingerroot in a sugar syrup and then coating them with coarse sugar. Look for crystallized ginger in the spice section of your supermarket.

1 cup plain yogurt
1/3 cup vegetable oil
2 tablespoons finely chopped crystallized
  ginger
1 egg
2 cups all-purpose flour
1/2 cup sugar
2 teaspoons baking powder
1 teaspoon baking soda
1/2 cup chopped dried apricots

Heat oven to 400°. Grease bottoms only of 12 medium muffin cups, 2 1/2 × 1 1/4 inches, or line with paper baking cups. Beat yogurt, oil, ginger and egg in large bowl. Stir in remaining ingredients except apricots just until flour is moistened. Fold in apricots. Divide batter evenly among muffin cups (cups will be very full). Sprinkle with sugar if desired.

   Bake 16 to 18 minutes or until golden brown. Immediately remove from pan.

Strawberry-Macadamia Nut Muffins

1 dozen muffins

Macadamia nuts have a rich, buttery, slightly sweet flavor. To keep them fresh, store opened containers of macadamia nuts in the refrigerator or freezer. If you'd like, you can substitute chopped pecans or almonds for the macadamia nuts in this recipe.

3/4 cup milk
1/3 cup margarine or butter, melted
1 egg
2 cups all-purpose flour
2/3 cup sugar
2 teaspoons baking powder
1/2 teaspoon salt
1 cup chopped fresh strawberries
1/2 cup chopped macadamia nuts

Heat oven to 400°. Grease bottoms only of 12 medium muffin cups, 2 1/2 × 1 1/4 inches, or line with paper baking cups. Beat milk, margarine and egg in large bowl. Stir in flour, sugar, baking powder and salt just until flour is moistened. Fold in strawberries and macadamia nuts. Divide batter evenly among muffin cups (cups will be almost full). Sprinkle with sugar if desired.

   Bake 20 to 22 minutes or until golden brown. Immediately remove from pan.

Spiced Honey-Lemon Muffins

8 muffins

Some of the warm glaze will drip off the warm muffins, so place muffins on a serving plate, cookie sheet or waxed paper for easier cleanup.

3/4 cup milk
1/3 cup vegetable oil
1/4 cup honey
2 teaspoons grated lemon peel
1 egg
2 cups all-purpose flour
2 1/2 teaspoons baking powder
1/2 teaspoon salt
1/2 teaspoon ground cinnamon
1/4 teaspoon ground allspice
Honey-Lemon Glaze (below)

Heat oven to 400°. Grease bottoms only of 8 medium muffin cups, 2 1/2 × 1 1/4 inches, or line with paper baking cups. Beat milk, oil, honey, lemon peel and egg in large bowl. Stir in remaining ingredients except Honey-Lemon Glaze just until flour is moistened. Divide batter evenly among muffin cups (cups will be about 3/4 full).

Bake 20 to 22 minutes or until golden brown. Immediately remove from pan. Brush Honey-Lemon Glaze over warm muffins.

HONEY-LEMON GLAZE

2 tablespoons honey
1/4 teaspoon grated lemon peel
2 teaspoons lemon juice

Mix all ingredients until well blended.

Lemon Yogurt-Poppy Seed Muffins

1 dozen muffins

1/3 cup milk
1/4 cup vegetable oil
1 container (6 ounces) lemon yogurt (2/3 cup)
1 egg
1 3/4 cups all-purpose flour
1/4 cup sugar
2 tablespoons poppy seed
1 tablespoon grated lemon peel
2 1/2 teaspoons baking powder
1/2 teaspoon baking soda
1/2 teaspoon salt
Lemon Glaze (below)

Heat oven to 400°. Grease bottoms only of 12 medium muffin cups, 2 1/2 × 1 1/4 inches, or line with paper baking cups. Beat milk, oil, yogurt and egg in large bowl. Stir in remaining ingredients except Lemon Glaze just until flour is moistened. Divide batter evenly among muffin cups (cups will be about 3/4 full).

Bake 16 to 18 minutes or until golden brown. Immediately remove from pan. Drizzle Lemon Glaze over warm muffins.

LEMON GLAZE

1/2 cup powdered sugar
2 to 3 teaspoons lemon juice

Mix ingredients until smooth and of drizzling consistency.

Molasses Bran Muffins

1 dozen muffins

3/4 cup milk
1 1/2 cups shreds of wheat bran cereal
1 egg
1/2 cup vegetable oil
1/3 cup molasses
1 1/4 cups all-purpose* or whole wheat flour
3 teaspoons baking powder
1 teaspoon salt

Heat oven to 400°. Grease bottoms only of 12 medium muffin cups, 2 1/2 × 1 1/4 inches, or line with paper baking cups. Pour milk on cereal in medium bowl and let stand 1 minute. Beat in egg, oil and molasses. Mix remaining ingredients. Stir into cereal mixture all at once just until flour is moistened (batter will be lumpy). Divide batter evenly among muffin cups. Bake about 20 minutes or until golden brown. Immediately remove from pan.

If using self-rising flour, omit baking powder and salt.

Fresh Herb-Yogurt Muffins

1 dozen muffins

1 cup plain yogurt
1/3 cup olive or vegetable oil
2 tablespoons chopped fresh or 2 teaspoons
    dried basil, oregano or rosemary leaves
1 egg
2 cups all-purpose flour
2 teaspoons baking powder
1/2 teaspoon baking soda
1/2 teaspoon salt

Heat oven to 400°. Grease bottoms only of 12 medium muffin cups, 2 1/2 × 1 1/4 inches, or line with paper baking cups. Beat yogurt, oil, basil and egg in large bowl. Stir in remaining ingredients just until flour is moistened. Divide batter evenly among muffin cups (cups will be about 3/4 full).

Bake 18 to 20 minutes or until golden brown. Immediately remove from pan.

Baking with Confidence

PERFECT MUFFINS ARE:

Golden brown
Slightly rounded with bumpy tops
Tender and light
Even-textured with medium, round holes
Moist inside
Easy to remove from the pan

Problem	Possible Cause
Pale muffins	• oven too cool
Peaked and smooth tops	• too much mixing
Tough and heavy	• too much flour
	• too much mixing
Uneven texture with long holes and tunnels	• too much mixing
Dry	• too much flour
	• oven too hot
	• baked too long
Sticks to pan or paper liners	• not enough fat
Dark crust but center not done	• muffin pan was dull or dark
	• oven too hot

Cheese and Spinach Muffins

1 dozen muffins

1 1/4 cups milk
1/3 cup margarine or butter, melted
1 egg
2 cups all-purpose flour
1/4 cup grated Parmesan cheese
2 tablespoons chopped green onions
3 teaspoons baking powder
1/4 teaspoon salt
1/2 cup coarsely chopped fresh or 1/4 cup very well drained, frozen (thawed) chopped spinach
1/2 cup shredded Swiss cheese
Grated Parmesan cheese

Heat oven to 400°. Grease bottoms only of 12 medium muffin cups, 2 1/2 × 1 1/4 inches, or line with paper baking cups. Beat milk, margarine and egg in large bowl. Stir in flour, 1/4 cup Parmesan cheese, the green onions, baking powder and salt just until flour is moistened. Fold in spinach and Swiss cheese. Divide batter evenly among muffin cups (cups will be almost full). Sprinkle with Parmesan cheese.

Bake 18 to 20 minutes or until golden brown. Immediately remove from pan.

Parmesan-Tomato Muffins

1 dozen muffins

1 cup milk
1/4 cup vegetable oil
1 egg
2 cups all-purpose flour
1/4 cup grated Parmesan cheese
1 tablespoon chopped fresh or 1 teaspoon dried basil leaves
2 1/2 teaspoons baking powder
1/4 teaspoon salt
1/2 cup chopped sun-dried tomatoes in olive oil, drained
1/4 cup chopped pimiento-stuffed olives
Grated Parmesan cheese

Heat oven to 400°. Grease bottoms only of 12 medium muffin cups, 2 1/2 × 1 1/4 inches, or line with paper baking cups. Beat milk, oil and egg in large bowl. Stir in flour, 1/4 cup Parmesan cheese, the basil, baking powder and salt just until flour is moistened. Fold in tomatoes and olives. Divide batter evenly among muffin cups (cups will be almost full). Sprinkle with Parmesan cheese.

Bake 18 to 20 minutes or until golden brown. Immediately remove from pan.

Specialty Muffins

Convert your favorite 12-muffin regular muffin recipe to mini, bakery-style (very large regular muffins), or jumbo muffins or to regular or jumbo muffin tops, using the guidelines below. When you determine the bake times for your favorite muffin recipes, be sure to write them down for future use.

- There is a wide range in bake times, so check for doneness at the minimum time, then every minute or two until done.

- When making bakery-style muffins with softer, more fluid batters, make ten muffins. Stiffer, thicker batters can be used to make eight bakery-style muffins.

- Muffin batters with large pieces of nuts, fruit or chocolate work better as bakery-style or jumbo muffins because the stir-ins are too large for mini muffins.

- Muffin batters that are very rich work better as mini muffins because a larger muffin may be too much for one serving.

- Muffin top pans often have a dark nonstick surface. Be sure to check the manufacturer's directions to see if reducing the oven temperature by 25° is recommended.

SPECIALTY MUFFIN BAKING CHART

Muffin Size	Muffin Cup Size	Oven Temperature	Bake Time	Yield
MUFFINS				
Mini	1 3/4 × 1 inch (small)	400°	10 to 17 minutes	24
Bakery-style	2 1/2 × 1 1/4 inches (medium)	400°	20 to 26 minutes	8 to 10
Jumbo	3 1/2 × 1 3/4 inches (large)	375°	25 to 35 minutes	4
MUFFIN TOPS				
Regular	2 3/4 × 3/8 inch	400°	8 to 10 minutes	18
Jumbo	4 × 1/2 inch	400°	15 to 20 minutes	6

Lemon-Oat Scones, Basil-Pepper Biscuits (page 48)

Lemon-Oat Scones

About 15 scones

1/3 cup margarine or butter
1 1/4 cups all-purpose flour
1/2 cup quick-cooking oats
3 tablespoons sugar
2 1/2 teaspoons baking powder
2 teaspoons grated lemon peel
1/2 teaspoon salt
1 egg, beaten
1/2 cup chopped almonds, toasted
4 to 6 tablespoons half-and-half
1 egg, beaten

Heat oven to 400°. Cut margarine into flour, oats, sugar, baking powder, lemon peel and salt with pastry blender in medium bowl until mixture resembles fine crumbs. Stir in 1 egg, the almonds and just enough half-and-half so dough leaves side of bowl.

Turn dough onto lightly floured surface; gently roll in flour to coat. Knead lightly 10 times. Roll or pat 1/2 inch thick. Cut with floured 2-inch round cutter or cut into diamond shapes with sharp knife. Place on ungreased cookie sheet. Brush 1 egg over dough.

Bake 10 to 12 minutes or until golden brown. Immediately remove from cookie sheet. Cool on wire rack. Split scones; spread with margarine and serve with strawberry preserves if desired.

Spicy Fruit Scones: *Omit lemon peel. Add 3/4 teaspoon ground cinnamon and 1/8 teaspoon ground cloves with the salt. Substitute 1/2 cup diced fruits, chopped figs, currants or dates for the nuts.*

Orange-Currant Scones

About 20 scones

Scones come from Scotland and are often cooked on a griddle. Here they are baked for ease—but not lack of flavor!

1/2 cup currants
1/3 cup margarine or butter
1 3/4 cups all-purpose flour
3 tablespoons sugar
2 1/2 teaspoons baking powder
1/4 teaspoon salt
1 tablespoon grated orange peel
1 egg, beaten
4 to 6 tablespoons half-and-half
1 egg white, beaten

Heat oven to 400°. Soak currants in warm water for 10 minutes to soften; drain. Cut margarine into flour, sugar, baking powder and salt with pastry blender until mixture resembles fine crumbs. Stir in orange peel, egg, currants and just enough half-and-half until dough leaves side of bowl.

Turn dough onto lightly floured surface. Knead lightly 10 times. Divide dough into 2 parts. Roll or pat into two 6-inch circles about 1/2 inch thick. Place on ungreased cookie sheet; brush with beaten egg white.

Bake 10 to 12 minutes or until golden brown. Immediately remove from cookie sheet. Cut into wedges to serve.

Easy Pull-Apart Coffee Cake

16 servings

1 cup pecan halves
3/4 cup packed brown sugar
1/4 cup (1/2 stick) plus 2 tablespoons margarine or butter
2 tablespoons milk
1 package (6-serving size) vanilla regular pudding and pie filling
4 cups Bisquick® Original baking mix
2/3 cup milk
2 tablespoons granulated sugar
1 teaspoon vanilla
1 egg

Heat oven to 350°. Grease 12-cup bundt cake pan. Sprinkle pecan halves in pan. Heat brown sugar, margarine, 2 tablespoons milk and the pudding and pie filling (dry) in 1-quart saucepan over medium heat, stirring constantly, until mixture begins to boil around edge; remove from heat and reserve.

Mix remaining ingredients until stiff dough forms; beat 30 seconds. (If dough is too sticky, stir in additional baking mix.) Turn dough onto surface dusted with baking mix; roll in baking mix to coat. Knead lightly 10 times. Cut dough into 32 pieces. Stack pieces of dough in pan. Pour brown sugar mixture evenly over dough.

Bake 25 to 30 minutes or until golden brown. Immediately invert onto heatproof serving plate; let pan remain over coffee cake 1 minute. Serve warm.

Raspberry–Cream Cheese Coffee Cake

12 servings

Even though this elegant coffee cake is made with yeast, it's quick because there's no kneading or long rising time.

1 1/2 to 2 cups all-purpose flour
2 tablespoons sugar
2 tablespoons margarine or butter, softened
1/2 teaspoon salt
1 package regular or quick-acting active
   dry yeast
2/3 cup very warm water (120° to 130°)
Cream Cheese Filling (right)
Streusel Topping (right)
1 jar (10 ounces) raspberry or strawberry
   preserves

Grease rectangular pan, 13 × 9 × 2 inches. Mix 3/4 cup of the flour, the sugar, margarine, salt and yeast in large bowl. Stir in warm water. Beat on medium speed 2 minutes, scraping bowl occasionally. Stir in enough remaining flour until dough pulls away from side of bowl (dough will be sticky). Pat dough evenly in bottom and 1/2 inch up side of pan, using floured fingers. Cover and let rest 15 minutes.

Heat oven to 375°. Prepare Cream Cheese Filling and Streusel Topping; reserve.

Bake crust 10 to 15 minutes or just until edges begin to brown. Spread Cream Cheese Filling over crust, almost to edges. Stir raspberry preserves; spoon evenly over filling. Sprinkle with Streusel Topping. Bake 20 to 25 minutes or just until almonds in topping begin to brown. Serve warm or let stand until cool. Refrigerate any remaining coffee cake.

CREAM CHEESE FILLING

1 package (8 ounces) cream cheese,
   softened
1/4 cup sugar
1/2 teaspoon almond extract

Beat all ingredients on low speed about 1 minute or until smooth.

STREUSEL TOPPING

1 tablespoon firm margarine or butter
3 tablespoons all-purpose flour
3 tablespoons sugar
1/4 cup sliced almonds

Cut margarine into flour and sugar with pastry blender until crumbly. Stir in almonds.

Blueberry Buckle Coffee Cake

9 servings

(photograph on page 24)

2 cups all-purpose flour
3/4 cup sugar
2 1/2 teaspoons baking powder
3/4 teaspoon salt
1/4 cup shortening
3/4 cup milk
1 egg
2 cups fresh or frozen (thawed and drained) blueberries
Crumb Topping (below)
Glaze (below)

Heat oven to 375°. Grease square pan, 9 × 9 × 2 inches, or round pan, 9 × 1 1/2 inches. Blend flour, sugar, baking powder, salt, shortening, milk and egg; beat 30 seconds. Carefully stir in blueberries. Spread batter in pan; sprinkle with Crumb Topping.

Bake 45 to 50 minutes or until toothpick inserted in center comes out clean. Drizzle with Glaze. Serve warm.

CRUMB TOPPING

1/2 cup sugar
1/3 cup all-purpose flour
1/4 cup butter or margarine, softened
1/2 teaspoon ground cinnamon

Mix all ingredients until crumbly.

GLAZE

1/2 cup powdered sugar
1/4 teaspoon vanilla
1 1/2 to 2 teaspoons hot water

Mix all ingredients until of drizzling consistency.

Chocolate Swirl Coffee Cake

9 servings

Topping (below)
2 cups Bisquick Original baking mix
1/4 cup sugar
2/3 cup water or milk
2 tablespoons margarine or butter, melted
1 egg
1/3 cup semisweet chocolate chips, melted

Heat oven to 400°. Grease square pan, 8 × 8 × 2 inches. Prepare Topping; reserve.

Mix baking mix, sugar, water, margarine and egg; beat vigorously 30 seconds. Spread in pan. Spoon chocolate over batter; cut through batter and chocolate with knife several times to marble. Sprinkle with Topping.

Bake 20 to 25 minutes or until brown and cake feels firm when touched in center. Serve warm or let stand until cool.

TOPPING

1/3 cup flaked coconut
1/4 cup sugar
1/4 cup chopped walnuts or pecans
1 tablespoon margarine or butter, melted

Mix all ingredients.

Tips for Nut Breads

- Grease only the bottoms of loaf pans for fruit or nut breads. The ungreased sides allow the batter to cling while rising during baking which helps form a gently rounded top. If sides of pan are greased, edges of the loaf may have ridges.

- Chop or shred fruits, vegetables or nuts before you start making the batter. If you prepare the batter and then stop to chop or shred ingredients, the batter may become too stiff.

- To avoid overmixing, mix by hand instead of using an electric mixer.

- A large, lengthwise crack in the thin, tender top crust is typical.

- Cool nut breads completely before slicing to prevent crumbling (preferably, store tightly covered twenty-four hours after cooling). Cut with a sharp, thin-bladed knife, using a light sawing motion.

- After cooling, loaves can be wrapped tightly and refrigerated for one week.

Zucchini Bread

2 loaves (24 slices)

Cut sliced Zucchini Bread into interesting shapes with cookie cutters. Spread the cutouts with cream cheese for pretty (and delicious) treats.

3 cups shredded zucchini (about 3 medium)
1 2/3 cups sugar
2/3 cup vegetable oil
2 teaspoons vanilla
4 eggs
3 cups all-purpose flour
1/2 cup coarsely chopped walnuts or pecans
1/2 cup raisins, if desired
4 teaspoons baking powder
1 teaspoon salt
1 teaspoon ground cinnamon
1/2 teaspoon ground cloves

Heat oven to 350°. Grease bottoms only of 2 loaf pans, 8 1/2 × 4 1/2 × 2 1/2 inches or 9 × 5 × 3 inches. Mix zucchini, sugar, oil, vanilla and eggs in large bowl. Stir in remaining ingredients. Pour into pans.

Bake 50 to 60 minutes or until toothpick inserted in center comes out clean. Cool 10 minutes. Loosen sides of loaves from pans; remove from pans. Cool completely on wire rack before slicing. Store tightly wrapped in refrigerator up to 1 week.

*Zucchini Bread, Banana-Nut Bread (page 64),
Pumpkin Bread (page 406)*

Baking with Confidence

PERFECT NUT BREAD IS:

Golden brown, rounded top
Lengthwise crack (or split) along the top
Thin, tender crust
Moist texture with small even holes
Fruits and/or nuts are evenly distributed

Problem	Possible Cause
Didn't rise	• too much mixing
	• check expiration date on leavening
Tough	• too much mixing
	• not enough fat
Tunnels	• too much mixing
Rims around the edges	• sides of pan were greased
Compact texture	• too much flour
	• too little leavening
Crumbly	• not cooled completely, cut too soon after baking

Heat oven to 350°. Grease bottom only of loaf pan, 8 1/2×4 1/2×2 1/2 inches or 9×5×3 inches. Mix carrots, sugar, oil and eggs in large bowl. Stir in remaining ingredients. Pour into pan. Bake 50 to 60 minutes or toothpick inserted in center comes out clean. Cool 10 minutes. Loosen sides of loaf from pan; remove from pan. Cool completely on wire rack before slicing. Store tightly wrapped in refrigerator up to 1 week.

Banana-Nut Bread

2 loaves (12 slices each) or 1 loaf (24 slices)

(photograph on page 63)

1 1/4 cups sugar
1/2 cup (1 stick) margarine or butter, softened
2 eggs
1 1/2 cups mashed ripe bananas
1/2 cup buttermilk
1 teaspoon vanilla
2 1/2 cups all-purpose flour
2 teaspoons baking powder
1/2 teaspoon salt
1/4 teaspoon baking soda
1 cup chopped walnuts or pecans

Heat oven to 350°. Grease bottoms only of 2 loaf pans, 8 1/2×4 1/2×2 1/2 inches, or 1 loaf pan, 9×5×3 inches. Mix sugar and margarine in large bowl. Stir in eggs. Add bananas, buttermilk and vanilla until smooth; beat until smooth. Stir in flour, baking powder, salt and baking soda just until flour is moistened. Stir in walnuts. Pour into pans.

Bake 8-inch loaves about 1 hour, 9-inch loaf about 1 hour 15 minutes or until toothpick inserted in center comes out clean. Cool 5 minutes. Loosen sides of loaves from pans; remove from pans. Cool completely on wire rack before slicing. Store tightly wrapped in refrigerator up to 1 week.

Carrot-Nut Bread

1 loaf (24 slices)

1 1/2 cups shredded carrots (about 3 medium)
3/4 cup sugar
1/3 cup vegetable oil
2 eggs
3/4 cup all-purpose flour
3/4 cup whole wheat flour
1/4 cup coarsely chopped walnuts or pecans
2 teaspoons baking powder
1/2 teaspoon salt
1/2 teaspoon ground cinnamon
1/2 teaspoon ground cloves

Glazed Cinnamon-Raisin Batter Bread

1 loaf (16 slices)

Cinnamon-raisin bread is an all-time favorite. You'll love this recipe because it's easier and faster to make than ever!

3 1/2 to 3 3/4 cups all-purpose flour
2 tablespoons sugar
1 teaspoon ground cinnamon
1/2 teaspoon salt
**1 package regular or quick-acting active
    dry yeast**
1 1/2 cups very warm water (120° to 130°)
2 tablespoons margarine or butter, softened
3/4 cup raisins
Glaze (right)

Generously grease loaf pan, 8 1/2 × 4 1/2 × 2 1/2 inches or 9 × 5 × 3 inches. Mix 2 cups of the flour, the sugar, cinnamon, salt and yeast in large bowl. Add warm water and margarine. Beat on low speed until moistened. Beat on medium speed 3 minutes, scraping bowl occasionally. Stir in raisins and enough remaining flour to make a stiff batter. Smooth and pat batter in pan with floured hands. Cover and let rise in warm place about 30 minutes or until batter is about 1/2 inch above top of 8-inch pan or about 1/2 inch below top of 9-inch pan.

Place oven rack in lowest position. Heat oven to 375°. Bake 45 to 50 minutes or until loaf is golden brown and sounds hollow when tapped; remove from pan. Cool completely on wire rack before slicing. Drizzle with Glaze.

GLAZE

1/2 cup powdered sugar
1/4 teaspoon vanilla
2 to 2 1/2 teaspoons milk

Mix all ingredients until smooth and of drizzling consistency.

Irish Soda Bread

8 slices

3 tablespoons margarine or butter, softened
2 1/2 cups all-purpose flour
2 tablespoons sugar
1 teaspoon baking soda
1 teaspoon baking powder
1/2 teaspoon salt
1/3 cup raisins
About 3/4 cup buttermilk

Heat oven to 375°. Grease cookie sheet. Cut margarine into flour, sugar, baking soda, baking powder and salt in large bowl with pastry blender until mixture resembles fine crumbs. Stir in raisins. Stir in just enough buttermilk so dough leaves side of bowl.

Turn dough onto lightly floured surface; gently roll in flour to coat. Knead 1 to 2 minutes or until smooth. Shape into round loaf, about 6 1/2 inches in diameter. Place on cookie sheet. Cut an X shape about 1/4 through loaf with floured knife.

Bake 35 to 45 minutes or until golden brown. Remove from cookie sheet. Brush with softened margarine or butter if desired. Cool on wire rack.

Chile-Cheese Batter Bread

8 pieces

You can substitute 1 cup of milk and 1 tablespoon vinegar for the buttermilk if need be.

2 cups all-purpose flour
2 teaspoons baking powder
3/4 teaspoon salt
1/2 teaspoon baking soda
1 cup shredded Cheddar cheese (4 ounces)
1 can (4 ounces) chopped green chiles, well drained
1 cup buttermilk
1 tablespoon vegetable oil
1 egg

Heat oven to 350°. Grease pie plate, 9 × 1 1/4 inches. Mix flour, baking powder, salt and baking soda in large bowl. Add cheese and chiles; toss. Stir in remaining ingredients just until flour is moistened (batter will be lumpy). Pour into pie plate.

Bake 40 to 45 minutes or until golden brown and toothpick inserted in center comes out clean; remove from pie plate. Cool on wire rack.

Fresh Herb Batter Bread

1 loaf

3 cups all-purpose flour
1 tablespoon sugar
1 teaspoon salt
1 package regular or quick-acting active dry yeast
1 1/4 cups very warm water (120° to 130°)
2 tablespoons chopped fresh parsley
2 tablespoons shortening
1 1/2 teaspoons chopped fresh or 1/2 teaspoon dried rosemary leaves
1/2 teaspoon chopped fresh or 1/4 teaspoon dried thyme leaves
Margarine or butter, softened

Grease loaf pan, 9 × 5 × 3 inches. Mix 2 cups of the flour, the sugar, salt and yeast in large bowl. Add warm water, parsley, shortening, rosemary and thyme. Beat on low speed 1 minute, scraping bowl frequently. Beat on medium speed 1 minute, scraping bowl frequently. Stir in remaining flour until smooth. Smooth and pat batter in pan with floured hands. Cover and let rise in warm place about 40 minutes or until double.

Heat oven to 375°. Bake 40 to 45 minutes or until loaf sounds hollow when tapped; remove from pan. Brush with margarine. Cool on wire rack.

Potato-Tarragon Casserole Bread

12 slices

Casserole breads are no-knead yeast breads that are baked in casserole dishes. If you don't have any leftover mashed potatoes, prepare instant mashed potatoes as a quick alternative.

3 1/2 cups all-purpose flour
1 tablespoon chopped fresh or 1 teaspoon
**   dried tarragon leaves**
1 teaspoon salt
1 package regular or quick-acting active
**   dry yeast**
3/4 cup very warm milk (120° to 130°)
1/2 cup very warm water (120° to 130°)
1/3 cup margarine or butter, softened
1 egg
3/4 cup lukewarm mashed potatoes

Grease 2-quart casserole. Mix 1 1/2 cups of the flour, the tarragon, salt and yeast in large bowl. Add warm milk, warm water, margarine and egg. Beat on low speed 30 seconds, scraping bowl constantly. Beat on medium speed 2 minutes, scraping bowl occasionally. Stir in remaining flour and the potatoes. Spread evenly in casserole. Cover and let rise in warm place about 45 minutes or until double. (Batter is ready if indentation remains when touched with floured finger.)

Place oven rack in lowest position. Heat oven to 375°. Bake 45 to 50 minutes or until loaf is golden brown and sounds hollow when tapped; remove from casserole. Cool on wire rack.

Baking with Confidence

PERFECT YEAST BREADS AND ROLLS ARE:

High and evenly shaped
Uniformly golden brown with a tender crust
Even in texture with no large air holes
Moist and silky with an elastic quality

Problem	Possible Cause
Not high	• water too hot for yeast
	• too little flour
	• too little kneading
	• too short rising period
	• pan too large
Coarse texture	• rising time too long
	• too little flour
	• too little kneading
	• oven too cool
Harsh, dry and not silky	• too much flour
	• not kneaded enough
Yeasty taste	• rising time too long
	• temperature too high during rising time

Cheesy Breadsticks

24 breadsticks

1/4 cup grated Parmesan cheese
1/2 teaspoon paprika
2 cups all-purpose flour
1/2 cup shredded Cheddar cheese
3/4 cup milk
2 tablespoons margarine or butter, melted
2 teaspoons baking powder
1 teaspoon sugar
1 teaspoon salt
1 egg, beaten

Mix Parmesan cheese and paprika; reserve. Mix remaining ingredients except egg until dough leaves side of bowl. Turn dough onto lightly floured surface; gently roll in flour to coat. Knead lightly 20 to 25 times. Cover and let stand 15 minutes.

Heat oven to 400°. Grease 2 cookie sheets. Divide dough in half. Cover and reserve one-half of dough. Roll other half of dough into rectangle, 10×8 inches. Brush with half of the egg; sprinkle with half of the cheese mixture. Press cheese mixture lightly into dough. Cut rectangle lengthwise into 12 strips. Gently twist each strip several times; place on one of the cookie sheets.

Bake 12 to 15 minutes or until golden brown. Immediately remove from cookie sheet. Cool on wire rack. Repeat with remaining dough, egg and cheese mixture.

Cheesy Pretzels: *Roll each half of the dough into rectangle, 12×8 inches. Cut each rectangle lengthwise into 8 strips. Fold each strip lengthwise in half; pinch edges to seal. Twist folded strips into pretzel shapes; place seam sides down on greased cookies sheet. Brush pretzels with egg; sprinkle with the cheese mixture. Bake as directed.*

Bread Bowls

6 bread bowls

Yeast gives a terrific, slightly chewy texture to these fun bread bowls. Bowls filled with salad, chowder, chile or a thick stew are sure to be real crowd pleasers!

1 package regular or quick-acting active dry yeast
1/4 cup warm water (105° to 115°)
2 tablespoons sugar
1/4 cup shortening
3 cups all-purpose flour
3 teaspoons baking powder
3/4 teaspoon salt
About 1 cup buttermilk

Dissolve yeast in warm water. Stir in sugar; reserve. Cut shortening into flour, baking powder and salt with pastry blender in large bowl until mixture resembles fine crumbs. Stir in yeast mixture and just enough buttermilk so dough leaves side of bowl and forms ball.

Turn dough onto lightly floured surface; gently roll in flour to coat. Knead about 1 minute or until smooth. Cover and let rise 10 minutes.

Heat oven to 375°. Grease outsides of six 10-ounce custard cups. Place cups upside down on ungreased jelly roll pan, 15 1/2×10 1/2×1 inch. Divide dough into 6 equal parts. Pat or roll each part into 7-inch circle. Shape dough circles over outsides of custard cups. (Do not allow dough to curl under edges of cups.)

Bake 18 to 22 minutes or until golden brown. Carefully lift bread bowls from custard cups—custard cups and bread will be hot. Cool bread bowls upright on wire rack.

Cheesy Bread Sticks, Bread Bowls

Onion-Anchovy Tart

About 35 appetizers

3 tablespoons olive or vegetable oil
3 large onions, thinly sliced
1 tablespoon chopped fresh basil or thyme
    leaves
1/8 teaspoon white pepper
1 loaf (1 pound) frozen white or whole
    wheat bread dough, thawed
2 cans (2 ounces *each*) anchovy fillets,
    drained
10 oil-cured Greek olives, cut in half and
    pitted

Heat oil in 10-inch skillet until hot. Stir in onions; reduce heat. Cover and cook about 25 minutes, stirring occasionally, until onions are very tender. Stir in basil and pepper.

Lightly grease cookie sheet. Shape bread dough into flattened rectangle on lightly floured surface. Roll dough with floured rolling pin into rectangle, 14×11 inches. Place on cookie sheet. Let stand 15 minutes.

Spoon onion mixture evenly over dough to within 1 inch of edge. Arrange anchovies in lattice pattern on onion mixture. Top with olives. Let stand 15 minutes.

Heat oven to 425°. Bake 15 to 20 minutes or until crust is brown. Cut into 2-inch squares.

Sweet Bread Wreath

1 wreath

Pizza dough takes on a new life in this pretty—and delicious—wreath.

Basic Pizza Dough for Three Crusts
    (page 167)
2 eggs, beaten
1/4 cup sugar
1/2 teaspoon ground cinnamon
1/2 teaspoon ground anise
1/4 teaspoon freshly grated nutmeg

Prepare Basic Pizza Dough. Heat oven to 350°. Grease cookie sheet. Divide dough into thirds. Roll each third dough into rope, 26 inches long. Braid ropes gently and loosely; pinch ends together. Shape braid into wreath on cookie sheet; pinch ends together. Let rise in warm place about 1 hour or until double.

Brush wreath with eggs. Mix remaining ingredients; sprinkle on wreath.

Bake 25 to 30 minutes or until golden brown.

Sweet Bread Wreath

Cornbread

12 servings

This cornbread is sweeter and lighter in texture than the Southern Buttermilk Cornbread recipe (right). Choose the one that best suits your taste.

1 cup milk
1/4 cup stick margarine or butter, melted*
1 large egg
1 1/4 cups yellow, white or blue cornmeal
1 cup all-purpose flour**
1/2 cup sugar
1 tablespoon baking powder
1/2 teaspoon salt

Heat oven to 400°. Grease bottom and side of round pan, 9 × 1 1/2 inches, or square pan, 8 × 8 × 2 inches, with shortening.

Beat milk, margarine and egg in large bowl. Stir in remaining ingredients all at once just until flour is moistened (batter will be lumpy). Pour batter into pan.

Bake 20 to 25 minutes or until golden brown and toothpick inserted in center comes out clean.

*Spreads with at least 65% vegetable oil can be substituted.
**If using self-rising flour, omit baking powder and salt.

Corn Muffins: *Grease bottoms only of 12 medium muffin cups, 2 1/2 × 1 1/4 inches, with shortening, or line with paper baking cups. Fill about 3/4 full.*

Southern Buttermilk Cornbread

1 loaf

1 1/2 cups yellow, white or blue cornmeal
1/2 cup all-purpose flour*
1 1/2 cups buttermilk
1/4 cup vegetable oil or shortening
2 teaspoons baking powder
1 teaspoon sugar
1 teaspoon salt
1/2 teaspoon baking soda
2 large eggs

Heat oven to 450°. Grease bottom and side of round pan, 9 × 1 1/2 inches, square pan, 8 × 8 × 2 inches, or 10-inch ovenproof skillet with shortening.

Mix all ingredients. Beat vigorously 30 seconds. Pour batter into pan.

Bake round or square pan 25 to 30 minutes, skillet about 20 minutes or until golden brown. Serve warm.

* If using self-rising flour, decrease baking powder to 1 teaspoon and omit salt.

Lighter Southern Buttermilk Cornbread: *For 3 grams of fat and 120 calories per serving, use fat-free buttermilk, decrease oil to 2 tablespoons and substitute 1/2 cup fat-free cholesterol-free egg product for the eggs.*

Cheesy Mexican Cornbread: *Decrease buttermilk to 1 cup. Stir in 1 can (about 8 ounces) cream-style corn, 1 can (4 ounces) chopped green chiles, well drained, 1/2 cup shredded Monterey Jack or Cheddar cheese (2 ounces) and 1 teaspoon chile powder.*

Corn Sticks: *Grease 18 corn stick pans with shortening. Fill about 7/8 full. Bake 12 to 15 minutes. Makes 18 corn sticks.*

Antipasto Pull-Apart

2 loaves (about 16 slices each)

4 to 5 cups all-purpose flour
1 tablespoon sugar
2 teaspoons salt
1/4 cup olive oil or 1/4 cup (1/2 stick)
    margarine or butter, melted
2 packages regular or quick-acting active
    dry yeast
2 1/4 cups very warm water (120° to 130°)
3/4 cup finely chopped salami (about
    4 ounces)
2 cloves garlic, finely chopped
1 3/4 cups whole wheat flour
1/4 cup grated Romano or Parmesan cheese
2 tablespoons chopped fresh or 2 teaspoons
    dried basil leaves
1 egg white
1 tablespoon cold water

Mix 3 cups of the all-purpose flour, the sugar, salt, oil and yeast in large bowl. Add warm water. Beat on low speed 1 minute, scraping bowl frequently. Beat on medium speed 1 minute, scraping bowl frequently. Divide dough between 2 medium or large bowls.

Stir salami, garlic and whole wheat flour into dough in 1 bowl. If necessary, stir in enough all-purpose flour to make dough easy to handle. Turn dough onto lightly floured surface; gently roll in flour to coat. Knead about 10 minutes or until smooth and elastic. Place in greased bowl; turn greased side up. Cover and let rise in warm place 40 to 60 minutes or until double. (Dough is ready if indentation remains when touched.)

Stir cheese and basil into dough in other bowl. Stir in enough remaining all-purpose flour to make dough easy to handle. Turn dough onto lightly floured surface; gently roll in flour to coat. Knead about 10 minutes or until smooth and elastic. Place in greased bowl; turn greased side up. Cover and let rise in warm place 30 to 50 minutes or until double.

Grease large cookie sheet. Punch down whole wheat dough and let rest 5 minutes. Punch down white dough and let rest 5 minutes. Gently pat each dough into 7 1/2-inch square. Cut each square into twenty-five 1 1/2-inch squares. Randomly arrange white and whole wheat squares on cookie sheet in 2 round mounds, about 6 inches across. Cover and let rise in warm place 35 to 50 minutes or until double. Beat egg white and cold water; brush over loaves.

Heat oven to 375°. Bake 35 to 40 minutes or until loaves are golden brown and sound hollow when tapped. Remove from cookie sheet. Cool on wire rack. Pull apart to serve.

Bread Machine Recipes

Five Steps to Perfect Bread

1. Read All Instructions Carefully
Read your bread machine manual carefully, especially the tips and hints. They can provide a good troubleshooting guide should your bread not come out perfectly. Understand how your machine's cycles work, and use them properly. Do not reset the machine in the middle of a cycle. Although you can check the dough while it's mixing, never open your machine during the rising or baking stages to check the progress, because the rising loaf could collapse.

2. Assemble Your Machine Correctly
Make sure the pan, blade and other parts are correctly assembled for proper mixing and kneading. If the bread machine parts are used incorrectly, the dough may not mix, knead, rise and bake properly.

3. Read Your Recipe
Understand the recipe you are making before you begin to use your machine. Be sure to use only the ingredients called for, and measure them carefully because overmeasuring or undermeasuring can affect the results.

- Use standard household measuring cups and spoons for all ingredients.

- To measure bread flour, spoon into standard dry-ingredient measuring cup and level with a knife or spatula.

- To measure liquid, pour into see-through liquid measuring cup, place cup on flat surface and read measurement at eye level.

4. Prepare Ingredients before Baking
Assemble ingredients, measuring carefully, before putting any of them in the machine. For best results, ingredients should be at room temperature except for those ingredients normally stored in the refrigerator, such as fresh milk and eggs. Check the recipe carefully to be sure that all of the ingredients have been added in the proper order.

5. Adjust Recipes One Change at a Time
As you become familiar with your bread machine and find a favorite recipe, you may get the urge to experiment by changing the ingredients. If you do experiment with reliable bread machine recipes, make just one change at a time so you know what does or does not work.

Classic White Bread

This traditional bread is great for sandwiches, or to serve with soup.

1-Pound Recipe (8 slices)		1 1/2-Pound Recipe (12 slices)
3/4 cup plus 1 tablespoon	**Water**	1 cup plus 2 tablespoons
1 tablespoon	**Margarine or butter, softened**	2 tablespoons
2 cups	**Bread flour**	3 cups
2 tablespoons	**Dry milk**	3 tablespoons
1 tablespoon	**Sugar**	2 tablespoons
1 teaspoon	**Salt**	1 1/2 teaspoons
1 1/4 teaspoons	**Bread machine yeast**	2 teaspoons

Make 1 1/2-pound recipe for bread machines that use 3 cups flour, or make 1-pound recipe for bread machines that use 2 cups flour.

Measure all ingredients carefully and place in bread machine pan in the order recommended by the manufacturer.

Select Basic/White cycle. Use Medium or Light crust color. Remove baked bread from pan and cool on wire rack.

Harvest Loaf

Dehydrated soup greens can be found in jars in the spice section of your supermarket.

1-Pound Recipe (8 slices)		1 1/2-Pound Recipe (12 slices)
3/4 cup	**Water**	1 cup plus 2 tablespoons
2 teaspoons	**Margarine or butter, softened**	1 tablespoon
2 cups	**Bread flour**	3 cups
2 tablespoons	**Dehydrated soup greens**	1/4 cup
1 tablespoon	**Dry milk**	2 tablespoons
1 tablespoon	**Sugar**	2 tablespoons
1 teaspoon	**Salt**	1 1/2 teaspoons
1/8	**Garlic powder**	1/4 teaspoon
1 1/2 teaspoons	**Bread machine yeast**	2 teaspoons

Make 1 1/2-pound recipe for bread machines that use 3 cups flour, or make 1-pound recipe for bread machines that use 2 cups flour.

Measure carefully, placing all ingredients in bread machine pan in the order recommended by the manufacturer.

Select Basic/White cycle. Use Medium or Light crust color. Remove baked bread from pan and cool on wire rack.

Harvest Loaf, Sticky Orange-Almond Rolls (page 108)

Dijon-Thyme Bread

1-Pound Recipe (8 slices)		**1 1/2-Pound Recipe** (12 slices)
2/3 cup	**Water**	1 cup
2 tablespoons	**Dijon mustard**	3 tablespoons
2 teaspoons	**Vegetable oil**	1 tablespoon
2 cups	**Bread flour**	3 cups
1 tablespoon	**Sugar**	2 tablespoons
1/2 teaspoon	**Salt**	3/4 teaspoon
1/2 teaspoon	**Dried thyme leaves**	1 teaspoon
1 1/4 teaspoons	**Bread machine yeast**	2 teaspoons

Make 1 1/2-pound recipe for bread machines that use 3 cups flour, or make 1-pound recipe for bread machines that use 2 cups flour.

Measure carefully, placing all ingredients in bread machine pan in the order recommended by the manufacturer.

Select Basic/White cycle. Use Medium or Light crust color. Remove baked bread from pan and cool on wire rack.

Cutting and Storing Loaves

Because loaves baked in a bread machine are shaped differently than traditional bread loaves, there are several ways to cut them:

- Use an electric knife for best results when cutting warm bread loaves. Otherwise, a sharp serrated or sawtooth bread knife works well.

- For square slices, place the loaf on its side and slice across the loaf. We find this the easiest way to cut loaves.

- For rectangular slices, place the loaf upright and cut from the top down. Slices may be cut in half, lengthwise or crosswise.

- For wedges, place the loaf upright and cut through to the center from the top down into wedges. Or cut loaf in half from the top down, then place *each half* cut side down and cut lengthwise into four, six or eight wedges.

- For other interesting shapes, use your imagination! Bread slices can be cut into triangles, fingerlike strips, chunks or other interesting shapes using cookie cutters.

STORING BREAD MACHINE LOAVES

If you have leftover bread machine bread, store it as follows:

- Store bread tightly covered at room temperature up to three days. If weather is hot and humid, store in the freezer.

- Store bread tightly covered in the freezer up to two months. Slice the loaves before freezing, so using one slice at a time will be easy.

- Do not store bread machine bread in the refrigerator because it tends to dry out and become stale more quickly than commercially made bread.

- Leftover bread can be used in your favorite bread pudding, crouton and stuffing recipes. Keep a tightly closed container in the freezer to add to as needed.

Pepperoni Pizza Bread

1-Pound Recipe (8 slices)		1 1/2-Pound Recipe (12 slices)
3/4 cup	**Water**	1 cup plus 2 tablespoons
2 cups	**Bread flour**	3 cups
1/4 cup	**Shredded mozzarella cheese**	1/3 cup
1 tablespoon	**Sugar**	2 tablespoons
1 teaspoon	**Garlic salt**	1 1/2 teaspoons
1 teaspoon	**Dried oregano leaves**	1 1/2 teaspoons
1 teaspoon	**Bread machine yeast**	1 3/4 teaspoons
1/2 cup	**Sliced pepperoni**	2/3 cup

Make 1 1/2-pound recipe for bread machines that use 3 cups flour, or make 1-pound recipe for bread machines that use 2 cups flour.

Measure carefully, placing all ingredients in bread machine pan in the order recommended by the manufacturer. Add pepperoni at the Raisin/Nut signal or 5 to 10 minutes before last kneading cycle ends.

Select Basic/White cycle. Use Medium or Light crust color. Do not use delay cycles. Remove baked bread from pan and cool on wire rack.

Note: *We do not recommend this recipe for 1 1/2-pound bread machines with cast-aluminum pans in horizontal-loaf shape.*

Pepperoni Pizza Bread

Potato-Chive Bread

This bread, flavored with chives, is very nice toasted and served with salmon or salmon cream cheese.

1-Pound Recipe (8 slices)		1 1/2-Pound Recipe (12 slices)
3/4 cup	**Water**	1 cup plus 2 tablespoons
1 tablespoon	**Margarine or butter, softened**	2 tablespoons
2 cups	**Bread flour**	3 cups
1/3 cup	**Mashed potato mix (dry)**	1/2 cup
2 tablespoons	**Chopped fresh chives** **OR**	1/4 cup
1 tablespoon	**Freeze-dried chives**	2 tablespoons
2 teaspoons	**Sugar**	1 tablespoon
1 teaspoon	**Salt**	1 1/2 teaspoons
1 3/4 teaspoons	**Bread machine yeast**	2 3/4 teaspoons

Make 1 1/2-pound recipe for bread machines that use 3 cups flour, or make 1-pound recipe for bread machines that use 2 cups flour.

Measure carefully, placing all ingredients in bread machine pan in the order recommended by the manufacturer.

Select Basic/White cycle. Use Medium or Light crust color. Do not use delay cycles. Remove baked bread from pan and cool on wire rack.

Salsa Bread

1-Pound Recipe (8 slices)		1 1/2-Pound Recipe (12 slices)
1/2 cup	**Prepared salsa**	3/4 cup
1/4 cup	**Water**	1/3 cup plus 1 tablespoon
1 tablespoon	**Margarine or butter, softened**	2 tablespoons
2 cups	**Bread flour**	3 cups
1 tablespoon	**Chopped fresh cilantro**	2 tablespoons
1 tablespoon	**Sugar**	2 tablespoons
1 teaspoon	**Salt**	1 1/2 teaspoons
1 1/4 teaspoons	**Bread machine yeast**	2 teaspoons

Make 1 1/2-pound recipe for bread machines that use 3 cups flour; make 1-pound recipe for bread machines that use 2 cups flour.

Measure carefully, placing all ingredients in bread machine pan in the order recommended by the manufacturer.

Select Basic/White cycle. Use Medium or Light crust color. Remove baked bread from pan and cool on wire rack.

Cajun Bread

1-Pound Recipe **(8 slices)**		**1 1/2-Pound Recipe** **(12 slices)**
1/2 cup	**Water**	3/4 cup
1/4 cup	**Chopped onion**	1/3 cup
1/4 cup	**Chopped green bell pepper**	1/3 cup
1 clove	**Garlic, finely chopped**	1 clove
2 teaspoons	**Margarine or butter, softened**	1 tablespoon
2 cups	**Bread flour**	3 cups
1 tablespoon	**Sugar**	2 tablespoons
1 teaspoon	**Cajun or Creole seasoning**	2 teaspoons
3/4 teaspoon	**Salt**	1 1/4 teaspoons
1 teaspoon	**Bread machine yeast**	1 3/4 teaspoons

Make 1 1/2-pound recipe for bread machines that use 3 cups flour, or make 1-pound recipe for bread machines that use 2 cups flour.

Measure carefully, placing all ingredients in bread machine pan in the order recommended by the manufacturer.

Select Basic/White cycle. Use Medium or Light crust color. Do not use delay cycles. Remove baked bread from pan and cool on wire rack.

Savory Roasted Pepper Bread

1-Pound Recipe (8 slices)		1 1/2-Pound Recipe (12 slices)
1/2 cup	**Water**	3/4 cup
3 tablespoons	**Chopped roasted red bell peppers (from a jar)**	1/4 cup
2 teaspoons	**Margarine or butter, softened**	1 tablespoon
1 clove	**Garlic, crushed**	2 cloves
2 cups	**Bread flour**	3 cups
2 tablespoons	**Grated Parmesan cheese**	3 tablespoons
1 tablespoon	**Sugar**	2 tablespoons
1 teaspoon	**Salt**	1 1/2 teaspoons
1 teaspoon	**Dried basil leaves**	1 1/2 teaspoons
1 1/4 teaspoons	**Bread machine yeast**	2 teaspoons

Make 1 1/2-pound recipe for bread machines that use 3 cups flour, or make 1-pound recipe for bread machines that use 2 cups flour.

Measure carefully, placing all ingredients in bread machine pan in the order recommended by the manufacturer.

Select Basic/White cycle. Use Medium or Light crust color. Do not use delay cycles. Remove baked bread from pan and cool on wire rack.

Guide to Great Bread

Your bread machine occasionally may produce a loaf that might not meet your expectations. Since each bread machine works a little differently, you may wish to try slight ingredient adjustments to improve results. Remember that it is very important to measure all ingredients carefully. Short, heavier loaves are to be expected when whole grains, whole-grain flours or all-purpose flour is substituted, because they have less protein.

We have listed unsatisfactory characteristics, possible causes and solutions. To pinpoint a problem, choose only one change at a time, rather than trying several different changes at once. Increase or decrease an ingredient by the amount listed and note the result.

LOAF DIDN'T RISE

Cause	Solution
Too much salt, which can inhibit yeast action	Decrease salt by 1/4 teaspoon
Too little sugar, which can inhibit rising	Increase sugar by 1 teaspoon
Too little fat, which can inhibit rising	Increase fat by 1 teaspoon
Old or improperly stored yeast	Check date of yeast
Delay cycle used	Do not use delay cycle

Cause	Solution
Ingredients placed in pan incorrectly	Place ingredients in pan as directed

MUSHROOM-SHAPED TOP

Cause	Solution
Too much yeast causing too much rising	Decrease yeast by 1/4 teaspoon
Too much sugar causing too much rising	Decrease sugar by 1 teaspoon
Too little salt causing too much rising	Increase salt by 1/4 teaspoon
Too much liquid	Decrease liquid by 1 tablespoon
Too much sugary ingredients (applesauce, raisins, candied fruit, etc.)	Decrease by 1 tablespoon

LOAF IS TOO BROWN

Cause	Solution
Too much sugar, causing excess browning	Decrease sugar by 1 teaspoon
Too much fat, causing excess browning	Decrease fat by 1 teaspoon
Dark setting, causing excess browning	Try using a light-crust setting

LOAF COLLAPSED

Cause	Solution
Too much yeast, causing too much rising	Decrease yeast by 1/4 teaspoon
Too much sugar, causing too much rising	Decrease sugar by 1 teaspoon
Too little salt, causing too much rising	Increase salt by 1/4 teaspoon
Too much liquid	Decrease liquid by 1 tablespoon
Too many ingredients	Use correct size recipe for correct size of pan
Opening machine during rising and baking	Do not open machine
Hot and humid weather	Bake during coolest part of the day and use refrigerated liquid; do not use delay cycles
Leaving baked loaf in machine	Remove loaf from machine and pan immediately after baking cycle is complete

LOAF IS DIFFICULT TO SLICE

Cause	Solution
Too much liquid, causing it to be crumbly	Decrease liquid by 1 tablespoon

LOAF IS HEAVY AND DRY

Cause	Solution
Too much flour	Decrease flour by 1 tablespoon
Too little liquid	Increase liquid by 1 tablespoon
Too little yeast	Increase yeast by 1/4 teaspoon

LOAF IS UNDERBAKED OR GUMMY IN THE CENTER

Cause	Solution
Too much flour, causing an underbaked loaf	Decrease flour by 1 tablespoon
Too much liquid or moist ingredients (bananas, applesauce, yogurt, etc.)	Decrease liquid by 1 tablespoon

LOAF HAS A YEASTY AROMA OR COARSE TEXTURE OR IS OVER-RISEN

Cause	Solution
Too much yeast	Decrease yeast by 1/4 teaspoon
Salt was omitted	Measure and add ingredients carefully

Pesto-Tomato Bread

The pesto adds a wonderful flavor to this bread. You can use any pesto you want, whether it is conveniently bought from the grocery store or you make it yourself with your favorite recipe. Either way, it's delicious!

1-Pound Recipe (8 slices)		1 1/2-Pound Recipe (12 slices)
1/4 cup	**Coarsely chopped, softened* sun-dried tomatoes (not oil-packed)**	1/3 cup
3/4 cup	**Water**	1 cup plus 2 tablespoons
1/4 cup	**Pesto**	1/3 cup
2 cups	**Bread flour**	3 cups
1 tablespoon	**Sugar**	2 tablespoons
1 teaspoon	**Salt**	1 1/2 teaspoons
3/4 teaspoon	**Bread machine yeast**	1 1/4 teaspoons

Make 1 1/2-pound recipe for bread machines that use 3 cups flour, or make 1-pound recipe for bread machines that use 2 cups flour.

Measure carefully, placing all ingredients in bread machine pan in the order recommended by the manufacturer.

Select Basic/White cycle. Use Medium or Light crust color. Do not use delay cycles. Remove baked bread from pan and cool on wire rack.

*Soak tomatoes in 1 cup very hot water about 10 minutes or until softened; drain.

Pesto-Tomato Bread

Garlic-Basil Bread

1-Pound Recipe **(8 slices)**		**1 1/2-Pound Recipe** **(12 slices)**
3/4 cup	**Water**	1 cup plus 1 tablespoon
2 teaspoons	**Margarine or butter, softened**	1 tablespoon
1 clove	**Garlic, finely chopped**	2 cloves
2 cups	**Bread flour**	3 cups
1 tablespoon	**Dry milk**	2 tablespoons
1 tablespoon	**Sugar**	2 tablespoons
1 teaspoon	**Salt**	1 1/2 teaspoons
1 teaspoon	**Dried basil leaves**	1 1/2 teaspoons
1 1/2 teaspoons	**Bread machine yeast**	2 1/4 teaspoons

Make 1 1/2-pound recipe for bread machines that use 3 cups flour, or make 1-pound recipe for bread machines that use 2 cups flour.

Measure carefully, placing all ingredients in bread machine pan in the order recommended by the manufacturer.

Select Basic/White cycle. Use Medium or Light crust color. Remove baked bread from pan and cool on wire rack.

Fresh Herb Bread

1-Pound Recipe (8 slices)		1 1/2-Pound Recipe* (12 slices)
3/4 cup plus 1 tablespoon	**Water**	1 cup plus 2 tablespoons
1 tablespoon	**Margarine or butter, softened**	2 tablespoons
2 cups	**Bread flour**	3 cups
1 teaspoon	**Chopped fresh sage leaves**	2 teaspoons
2 teaspoons	**Chopped fresh basil leaves**	1 tablespoon
2 teaspoons	**Chopped fresh oregano leaves**	1 tablespoon
1 teaspoon	**Chopped fresh thyme leaves**	2 teaspoons
2 tablespoons	**Chopped fresh parsley**	1/4 cup
2 tablespoons	**Dry milk**	3 tablespoons
1 tablespoon	**Sugar**	2 tablespoons
3/4 teaspoon	**Salt**	1 teaspoon
1 teaspoon	**Bread machine yeast**	1 1/2 teaspoons

Make 1 1/2-pound recipe for bread machines that use 3 cups flour, or make 1-pound recipe for bread machines that use 2 cups flour.

Measure carefully, placing all ingredients in bread machine pan in the order recommended by the manufacturer.

Select Basic/White cycle. Use Medium or Light crust color. Remove baked bread from pan and cool on wire rack.

We recommend using bread machines with 9-cup or larger bread pan for the 1 1/2-pound recipe.

Almond Honey-Whole Wheat Bread

1-Pound Recipe **(8 slices)**		**1 1/2-Pound Recipe** **(12 slices)**
2/3 cup	**Water**	1 cup plus 2 tablespoons
2 tablespoons	**Honey**	3 tablespoons
1 tablespoon	**Margarine or butter, softened**	2 tablespoons
1 cup	**Bread flour**	1 1/2 cups
1 cup	**Whole wheat flour**	1 1/2 cups
2 tablespoons	**Toasted slivered almonds**	1/4 cup
3/4 teaspoon	**Salt**	1 teaspoon
1 teaspoon	**Bread machine yeast**	1 1/2 teaspoons

Make 1 1/2-pound recipe for bread machines that use 3 cups flour, or make 1-pound recipe for bread machines that use 2 cups flour.

Measure carefully, placing all ingredients in bread machine pan in the order recommended by the manufacturer.

Select Basic/White cycle. Use Medium or Light crust color. Remove baked bread from pan and cool on wire rack.

Whole Wheat–Cranberry Bread

Try this for the Thanksgiving holidays!

1-Pound Recipe (8 slices)		1 1/2-Pound Recipe (12 slices)
3/4 cup	**Water**	1 cup plus 2 tablespoons
2 tablespoons	**Honey**	1/4 cup
1 tablespoon	**Margarine or butter, softened**	2 tablespoons
1 1/4 cups	**Bread flour**	2 cups
3/4 cup	**Whole wheat flour**	1 1/4 cups
1 teaspoon	**Salt**	1 1/2 teaspoons
1/4 teaspoon	**Ground mace**	3/4 teaspoon
1 1/4 teaspoons	**Bread machine yeast**	2 teaspoons
1/3 cup	**Dried cranberries or golden raisins**	1/2 cup

Make 1 1/2-pound recipe for bread machines that use 3 cups flour, or make 1-pound recipe for bread machines that use 2 cups flour.

Measure carefully, placing all ingredients except cranberries in bread machine pan in the order recommended by the manufacturer. Add cranberries at the Raisin/Nut signal or 5 to 10 minutes before last kneading cycle ends.

Select Basic/White cycle. Use Medium or Light crust color. Remove baked bread from pan and cool on wire rack.

Jalapeño Cornbread

1-Pound Recipe (8 slices)		1 1/2-Pound Recipe (12 slices)
1/2 cup	**Water**	3/4 cup plus 2 tablespoons
1/2 cup	**Frozen whole kernel corn, thawed**	2/3 cup
1 tablespoon	**Margarine or butter, softened**	2 tablespoons
2 teaspoons	**Chopped jalapeño chile**	1 tablespoon
2 cups	**Bread flour**	3 1/4 cups
1/4 cup	**Cornmeal**	1/3 cup
1 tablespoon	**Sugar**	2 tablespoons
1 teaspoon	**Salt**	1 1/2 teaspoons
1 1/2 teaspoons	**Bread machine yeast**	2 1/2 teaspoons

Make 1 1/2-pound recipe for bread machines that use 3 cups flour, or make 1-pound recipe for bread machines that use 2 cups flour.

Measure carefully, placing all ingredients in bread machine pan in the order recommended by the manufacturer.

Select Basic/White cycle. Use Medium or Light crust color. Do not use delay cycles. Remove baked bread from pan and cool on wire rack.

Note: *We do not recommend this recipe for bread machines with glass-domed lids.*

Jalapeño Cornbread

Roasted Garlic Bread

It's easy to roast your own garlic for this bread. The garlic adds such a wonderful flavor, you'll want to make it again and again.

1-Pound Recipe (8 slices)		1 1/2-Pound Recipe (12 slices)
1 bulb	**Roasted Garlic (below)**	2 bulbs
2/3 cup	**Water**	1 cup plus 2 tablespoons
1 teaspoon	**Olive or vegetable oil**	1 tablespoon
2 cups	**Bread flour**	3 cups
1 tablespoon	**Sugar**	2 tablespoons
1/2 teaspoon	**Salt**	1 teaspoon
1 teaspoon	**Bread machine yeast**	1 1/4 teaspoons

Make 1 1/2-pound recipe for bread machines that use 3 cups flour, or make 1-pound recipe for bread machines that use 2 cups flour.

Prepare Roasted Garlic. After squeezing garlic out of cloves, mash garlic slightly to measure 2 tablespoons for 1-pound recipe, or 3 tablespoons for 1 1/2-pound recipe.

Measure carefully, placing all ingredients except Roasted Garlic in bread machine pan in the order recommended by the manufacturer. Add mashed garlic at the Raisin/Nut signal or 5 to 10 minutes before last kneading cycle ends.

Select Basic/White cycle. Use Medium or Light crust color. Do not use delay cycles. Remove baked bread from pan and cool on wire rack.

ROASTED GARLIC

Heat oven to 350°. Carefully peel away paper-like skin from around 1 or 2 garlic bulbs, leaving just enough to hold bulbs intact. Trim top of garlic bulb about 1/2 inch to expose cloves. Place stem end down on 12-inch square of aluminum foil. Drizzle each bulb with 2 teaspoons olive or vegetable oil. Wrap securely in foil; place in pie plate or shallow baking pan. Bake 45 to 50 minutes or until garlic is tender when pierced with toothpick or fork. Cool slightly. Gently squeeze garlic out of cloves.

Note: *A 1-ounce bulb of garlic, roasted, equals about 1 tablespoon mashed garlic; a 2-ounce bulb equals about 2 tablespoons mashed garlic.*

Double Apricot-Almond Bread

1-Pound Recipe (8 slices)		1 1/2-Pound Recipe (12 slices)
1/3 cup	Lukewarm water	1/2 cup
1 jar (4 ounces)	Apricot baby food (reserve 1 teaspoon)	1 jar (6 ounces)
1 tablespoon	Margarine or butter, softened	2 tablespoons
2 cups	Bread flour	3 cups
1 tablespoon	Dry milk	2 tablespoons
1 tablespoon	Sugar	2 tablespoons
1 teaspoon	Salt	1 1/2 teaspoons
1/8 to 1/4 teaspoon	Ground nutmeg	1/4 to 1/2 teaspoon
1 teaspoon	Bread machine yeast	2 teaspoons
1/3 cup	Quartered dried apricots	1/2 cup
1/3 cup	Coarsely chopped toasted almonds	1/2 cup
	Apricot Glaze (below)	

Make 1 1/2-pound recipe for bread machines that use 3 cups flour, or make 1-pound recipe for bread machines that use 2 cups flour.

Measure carefully, placing all ingredients except the 1 teaspoon reserved baby food, apricots, almonds and Apricot Glaze in bread machine pan in the order recommended by the manufacturer. Add apricots and almonds at the Raisin/Nut signal or 5 to 10 minutes before last kneading cycle ends.

Select Sweet or Basic/White cycle. Use Medium or Light crust color. Do not use delay cycles. Remove baked bread from pan and cool on wire rack. Prepare Apricot Glaze; drizzle onto cooled loaf.

APRICOT GLAZE

1/2 cup powdered sugar
1 teaspoon reserved apricot baby food
1 teaspoon milk
Dash of nutmeg

Mix all ingredients until smooth and thin enough to drizzle.

Multigrain Loaf

Look for 7-grain cereal in the health food or hot cereal section of your supermarket.

1-Pound Recipe (8 slices)		1 1/2-Pound Recipe (12 slices)
3/4 cup plus 2 tablespoons	**Water**	1 1/4 cups
1 tablespoon	**Margarine or butter, softened**	2 tablespoons
1 cup	**Bread flour**	1 1/3 cups
3/4 cup	**Whole wheat flour**	1 1/3 cups
2/3 cup	**7-grain cereal**	1 cup
2 tablespoons	**Packed brown sugar**	3 tablespoons
1 teaspoon	**Salt**	1 1/4 teaspoons
2 teaspoons	**Bread machine yeast**	2 1/2 teaspoons

Make 1 1/2-pound recipe for bread machines that use 3 cups flour, or make 1-pound recipe for bread machines that use 2 cups flour.

Measure carefully, placing all ingredients in bread machine pan in the order recommended by the manufacturer.

Select Whole Wheat or Basic/White cycle. Use Medium or Light crust color. Remove baked bread from pan and cool on wire rack.

Spicy Apple Bread

Apple Pie Spice can be made by mixing 2 parts cinnamon with 1 part nutmeg to equal the amount called for.

1-Pound Recipe (8 slices)		1 1/2-Pound Recipe (12 slices)
2/3 cup	**Water**	1 cup plus 1 tablespoon
1 tablespoon	**Margarine or butter, softened**	2 tablespoons
2 cups	**Bread flour**	3 cups
1/4 cup	**Cut-up dried apples**	1/3 cup
1 tablespoon	**Dry milk**	2 tablespoons
1 tablespoon	**Sugar**	2 tablespoons
1 teaspoon	**Salt**	1 1/2 teaspoons
1 1/2 teaspoons	**Apple pie spice**	2 1/2 teaspoons
1 1/2 teaspoons	**Bread machine yeast**	2 teaspoons

Make 1 1/2-pound recipe for bread machines that use 3 cups flour, or make 1-pound recipe for bread machines that use 2 cups flour.

Measure carefully, placing all ingredients in bread machine pan in the order recommended by the manufacturer.

Select Sweet or Basic/White cycle. Use Medium or Light crust color. Remove baked bread from pan and cool on wire rack.

Blueberry-Lemon Loaf

For a special treat, spread with softened cream cheese.

1-Pound Recipe (8 slices)		1 1/2-Pound Recipe (12 slices)
3/4 cup	**Water**	1 cup plus 1 tablespoon
1 teaspoon	**Grated lemon peel**	1 1/2 teaspoons
1 tablespoon	**Margarine or butter, softened**	2 tablespoons
2 cups	**Bread flour**	3 cups
1 tablespoon	**Dry milk**	2 tablespoons
2 tablespoons	**Sugar**	3 tablespoons
1 teaspoon	**Salt**	1 1/2 teaspoons
1 1/4 teaspoons	**Bread machine yeast**	2 teaspoons
1/4 cup	**Dried blueberries or currants**	1/3 cup

Make 1 1/2-pound recipe for bread machines that use 3 cups flour, or make 1-pound recipe for bread machines that use 2 cups flour.

Measure carefully, placing all ingredients except blueberries in bread machine pan in the order recommended by the manufacturer. Add blueberries at the Raisin/Nut signal or 5 to 10 minutes before last kneading cycle ends.

Select Sweet or Basic/White cycle. Use Medium or Light crust color. Remove baked bread from pan and cool on wire rack.

Cherry-Almond Loaf

1-Pound Recipe (8 slices)		1 1/2-Pound Recipe (12 slices)
2/3 cup	**Water**	3/4 cup plus 2 tablespoons
1/3 cup	**Whole maraschino cherries, well-drained**	1/2 cup
1 tablespoon	**Margarine or butter, softened**	2 tablespoons
2 cups	**Bread flour**	3 cups
1 tablespoon	**Sugar**	2 tablespoons
2 teaspoons	**Dry milk**	1 tablespoon
1 teaspoon	**Salt**	1 1/2 teaspoons
1 1/4 teaspoons	**Bread machine yeast**	2 teaspoons
1/4 cup	**Slivered almonds**	1/2 cup

Make 1 1/2-pound recipe for bread machines that use 3 cups flour, or make 1-pound recipe for bread machines that use 2 cups flour.

Measure carefully, placing all ingredients except almonds in bread machine pan in the order recommended by the manufacturer.

Add almonds at the Raisin/Nut signal or 5 to 10 minutes before last kneading cycle ends.

Select Sweet or Basic/White cycle. Use Medium or Light crust color. Do not use delay cycles. Remove baked bread from pan and cool on wire rack.

Coffee-Amaretto Bread

1-Pound Recipe (8 slices)		1 1/2-Pound Recipe (12 slices)
2 teaspoons	**Instant coffee granules**	1 tablespoon
3 tablespoons	**Amaretto or other almond-flavored liqueur***	1/4 cup
1/2 cup plus 2 tablespoons	**Water**	3/4 cup plus 2 tablespoons
1 tablespoon	**Margarine or butter, softened**	2 tablespoons
2 cups	**Bread flour**	3 cups
3 tablespoons	**Sugar**	1/4 cup
1 tablespoon	**Dry milk**	2 tablespoons
3/4 teaspoon	**Salt**	1 1/4 teaspoons
1 1/2 teaspoons	**Bread machine yeast**	2 1/2 teaspoons

Make 1 1/2-pound recipe for bread machines that use 3 cups flour, or make 1-pound recipe for bread machines that use 2 cups flour.

Dissolve coffee granules in amaretto. Measure carefully, placing coffee-amaretto mixture and remaining ingredients in bread machine pan in the order recommended by the manufacturer.

Select Sweet or Basic/White cycle. Use Medium or Light crust color. Remove baked bread from pan and cool on wire rack.

*Substitute 1 teaspoon almond extract plus enough water to equal 3 tablespoons for the 3 tablespoons amaretto or 2 teaspoons almond extract plus enough water to equal 1/4 cup for the 1/4 cup amaretto.

Almond–Chocolate Chip Bread

1-Pound Recipe (8 slices)		**1 1/2-Pound Recipe (12 slices)**
3/4 cup plus 1 tablespoon	**Water**	1 cup plus 2 tablespoons
1 tablespoon	**Margarine or butter, softened**	2 tablespoons
1/4 teaspoon	**Vanilla**	1/2 teaspoon
2 cups	**Bread flour**	3 cups
1/2 cup	**Semisweet chocolate chips**	3/4 cup
2 tablespoons	**Sugar**	3 tablespoons
2 teaspoons	**Dry milk**	1 tablespoon
1/2 teaspoon	**Salt**	3/4 teaspoon
1 teaspoon	**Bread machine yeast**	1 1/2 teaspoons
1/4 cup	**Sliced almonds**	1/3 cup

Make 1 1/2-pound recipe for bread machines that use 3 cups flour, or make 1-pound recipe for bread machines that use 2 cups flour.

Measure carefully, placing all ingredients except almonds in bread machine pan in the order recommended by the manufacturer.

Add almonds at the Raisin/Nut signal or 5 to 10 minutes before last kneading cycle ends.

Select Sweet or Basic/White cycle. Use Medium or Light crust color. Do not use delay cycles. Remove baked bread from pan and cool on wire rack.

Almond–Chocolate Chip Bread

Glazed Cinnamon Rolls

9 rolls

These cinnamon rolls are easy to whip together, perfect for any breakfast or brunch.

2 1/2 cups bread flour
1/4 cup sugar
3/4 cup plus 2 tablespoons water
2 tablespoons margarine or butter, softened
1 teaspoon salt
1 teaspoon bread machine yeast
Cinnamon Filling (right)
2 tablespoons margarine or butter, softened
Vanilla Glaze (right)

Measure carefully, placing all ingredients except Cinnamon Filling, 2 tablespoons margarine and Vanilla Glaze in bread machine pan in the order recommended by the manufacturer. Select Dough/Manual cycle.

Grease square pan, 9×9×2 inches. Prepare Cinnamon Filling. Flatten dough with hands or rolling pin into 9-inch square on lightly floured surface. Spread with 2 tablespoons margarine; sprinkle with Cinnamon Filling. Roll dough up tightly; pinch edge of dough into roll to seal. Cut roll into 1-inch slices. Place in pan. Cover and let rise in warm place 1 to 1 1/4 hours or until double.

Heat oven to 375°. Bake 25 to 30 minutes or until golden brown. Remove from pan to wire rack. Drizzle Vanilla Glaze over warm rolls. Serve warm.

CINNAMON FILLING

1/3 cup sugar
2 teaspoons ground cinnamon

Mix ingredients.

VANILLA GLAZE

1 cup powdered sugar
1/2 teaspoon vanilla
1 to 2 tablespoons milk

Mix all ingredients until smooth and thin enough to drizzle.

Note: *If you prefer evenly shaped rolls, roll dough pieces into balls before dipping into orange mixture.*

Glazed Cinnamon Rolls

Sticky Orange Rolls

1 dozen rolls

(photograph on page 77)

1 cup water
1/4 cup (1/2 stick) margarine or butter,
    softened
3 1/2 cups bread flour
1/3 cup packed brown sugar
1 teaspoon salt
1 1/2 teaspoons bread machine yeast
1/2 cup (1 stick) margarine or butter,
    melted
2 tablespoons grated orange peel
1/2 cup granulated sugar

Measure carefully, placing all ingredients except 1/2 cup melted margarine, the orange peel and granulated sugar in bread machine pan in the order recommended by the manufacturer. Select Dough/Manual cycle.

Grease rectangular pan, 13×9×2 inches. Divide dough in half. Roll each half into 12-inch rope on lightly floured surface. Cut each rope into 6 pieces.

Mix 1/2 cup melted margarine, the orange peel and granulated sugar in medium bowl. Dip dough pieces into orange mixture, covering dough completely. Place slightly apart in pan. Cover and let rise in warm place about 30 minutes or until double.

Heat oven to 350°. Bake 20 to 30 minutes or until golden brown.

Sticky Orange-Almond Rolls: *Place 1 cup sliced unblanched almonds in small bowl. Roll dough pieces in almonds after dipping into orange mixture.*

Note: *If you prefer evenly shaped rolls, roll dough pieces into balls before dipping into orange mixture.*

Caramelized Onion Focaccia

8 pieces

2 cups bread flour
3/4 cup water
2 tablespoons olive or vegetable oil
1 tablespoon sugar
1 teaspoon salt
1 1/2 teaspoons bread machine yeast
Onion Topping (below)
3/4 cup shredded mozzarella cheese
    (3 ounces)
2 tablespoons grated Parmesan cheese

Measure carefully, placing all ingredients except Onion Topping and cheeses in bread machine pan in the order recommended by the manufacturer. Select Dough/Manual cycle.

Grease cookie sheet. Pat dough into 12-inch circle on cookie sheet. Cover and let rise in warm place about 30 minutes or until almost double. Prepare Onion Topping.

Heat oven to 400°. Make deep depressions in dough at 1-inch intervals with finger or handle of wooden spoon. Spread topping over dough. Sprinkle with cheeses. Bake 15 to 18 minutes or until edge is golden brown. Remove from cookie sheet to wire rack. Cut into wedges; serve warm.

ONION TOPPING

3 tablespoons margarine or butter
2 medium onions, sliced
2 cloves garlic, finely chopped

Melt margarine in 10-inch skillet over medium-low heat. Cook onions and garlic in margarine 15 to 20 minutes, stirring occasionally, until onions are brown and caramelized.

Caramelized Onion Focaccia

Savory Calzones

6 calzones

2 1/2 cups bread flour
1 cup water
1 tablespoon olive or vegetable oil
2 1/4 teaspoons bread machine yeast
1 teaspoon sugar
1 teaspoon salt
Savory Filling (below)
1 egg, slightly beaten

Measure carefully, placing all ingredients except Savory Filling and egg in bread machine pan in the order recommended by the manufacturer. Select Dough/Manual cycle.

Heat oven to 375°. Grease cookie sheet. Divide dough into 6 equal pieces. Roll each piece into 7-inch circle on lightly floured surface with floured rolling pin. Add Savory Filling. Fold dough over filling; fold edge up and pinch securely to seal. Place on cookie sheet. Brush with egg. Bake 25 to 30 minutes or until golden brown.

SAVORY FILLING

6 sun-dried tomato halves (not oil-packed)
1/3 cup pesto
1 1/2 cups shredded mozzarella or
    provolone cheese (6 ounces)
4 ounces Canadian-style bacon or ham,
    cut into thin strips (about 1 cup)
1 cup sliced mushrooms (3 ounces)
Freshly ground pepper

Soak tomatoes in 1 cup very hot water about 10 minutes or until softened; drain and finely chop. Spread 1 tablespoon pesto on each circle to within 1 inch of edge. Layer cheese, bacon, mushrooms and tomatoes on half of each circle to within 1 inch of edge. Sprinkle with pepper.

Favorite Cheese Pizza

2 pizzas, 6 pieces each

3 cups bread flour
1 cup plus 2 tablespoons water
2 tablespoons olive or vegetable oil
2 tablespoons grated Parmesan cheese,
    if desired
2 1/2 teaspoons bread machine yeast
1 1/2 teaspoons Italian seasoning, if desired
1 teaspoon sugar
1 teaspoon salt
Pizza Topping (below)

Measure carefully, placing all ingredients except Pizza Topping in bread machine pan in the order recommended by the manufacturer. Select Dough/Manual cycle.

Move oven rack to lowest position. Heat oven to 400°. Grease 2 cookie sheets. Divide dough in half. Pat each half into 12-inch circle on cookie sheet with floured fingers. Add Pizza Topping.

Bake 18 to 20 minutes or until crust is light brown.

PIZZA TOPPING

1 can (8 ounces) tomato sauce
1 teaspoon Italian seasoning
1 clove garlic, finely chopped
1 small onion, thinly sliced and separated
    into rings
3 cups shredded mozzarella cheese (12 ounces)
1/4 cup grated Parmesan cheese

Mix tomato sauce, Italian seasoning and garlic. Spread half the sauce over each crust. Arrange onion on sauce. Sprinkle with cheeses.

Favorite Cheese Pizza

Savory Breadsticks

30 breadsticks

3 cups bread flour
1 cup plus 2 tablespoons water
3 tablespoons margarine or butter, softened
2 tablespoons sugar
2 1/4 teaspoons bread machine yeast
2 teaspoons dried rosemary leaves, crushed
1 1/2 teaspoons salt
1 teaspoon dried oregano leaves, crushed
1 tablespoon water
1 egg white

Measure carefully, placing all ingredients except 1 tablespoon water and the egg white in bread machine pan in the order recommended by the manufacturer. Select Dough/Manual cycle.

Grease cookie sheet. Divide dough into 30 equal pieces. Roll each piece into 8-inch rope. Place 1 inch apart on cookie sheet. Cover and let rise in warm place 20 to 25 minutes or until puffy.

Heat oven to 350°. Beat 1 tablespoon water and the egg white; brush over dough. Bake 15 to 20 minutes or until golden brown.

Garlic Twists

18 twists

2 cups bread flour
3/4 cup water
1 tablespoon sugar
1 teaspoon salt
1 1/2 teaspoons bread machine yeast
1/3 cup margarine or butter, melted
2 tablespoons grated Parmesan cheese
2 cloves garlic, finely chopped

Measure carefully, placing all ingredients except margarine, cheese and garlic in bread machine pan in the order recommended by the manufacturer. Select Dough/Manual cycle.

Grease 2 cookie sheets. Divide dough into 18 equal pieces. Roll each piece into 14- to 16-inch rope on lightly floured surface. Bring ends together; twist 3 or 4 times. Place on cookie sheets.

Mix margarine, garlic and cheese. Brush twists generously with cheese mixture. Cover and let rise in warm place 20 to 30 minutes or until double.

Heat oven to 400°. Bake 12 to 15 minutes or until golden brown.

Cheesy Garlic Monkey Bread

10 slices

3 1/2 cups bread flour
1/4 cup shortening
1/3 cup sugar
3/4 cup water
1 teaspoon salt
1 1/2 teaspoons bread machine yeast
1 egg
1/3 cup grated Parmesan cheese
4 cloves garlic, finely chopped
1/2 cup (1 stick) margarine or butter, melted

Measure carefully, placing all ingredients except Parmesan cheese, garlic and margarine in bread machine pan in the order recommended by the manufacturer. Select Dough/Manual cycle.

Grease tube pan, 10×4 inches, or 12-cup bundt cake pan. Divide dough into 20 equal pieces. Mix cheese and garlic. Dip dough pieces into melted margarine, then roll in cheese mixture. Arrange in layers in pan. Cover and let rise in warm place about 45 minutes or until double.

Heat oven to 350°. Bake 35 to 45 minutes or until golden brown. Remove from pan. Serve warm.

Whole Wheat Dinner Rolls

12 rolls

Bring back memories of grandmother's kitchen and treat your family to the heavenly aroma of home-made rolls baking in the oven.

1 1/4 cups bread flour
1 cup whole wheat flour
1 tablespoon shortening
3/4 cup water
2 tablespoons packed brown sugar
1 tablespoon dry milk
1 1/4 teaspoons bread machine yeast
1/2 teaspoon salt

Measure carefully, placing all ingredients in bread machine pan in the order recommended by the manufacturer. Select Dough/Manual cycle.

Grease large cookie sheet. Punch down dough; place on lightly floured surface. Divide dough into 12 equal pieces. Shape each piece into a ball. Place slightly apart on cookie sheet. Cover and let rise in warm place about 30 minutes or until double.

Heat oven to 375°. Bake 15 to 20 minutes or until golden brown.

Wild Rice Breadsticks

10 breadsticks

The wild rice in these breadsticks gives them a great, nutty flavor.

1 2/3 cups bread flour
1/2 cup whole wheat flour
1/2 cup cooked wild rice or brown rice
3/4 cup water
1 tablespoon molasses
1 tablespoon vegetable oil
1 teaspoon fennel seed, if desired
1 teaspoon salt
1 teaspoon bread machine yeast

Measure carefully, placing all ingredients in bread machine pan in the order recommended by the manufacturer. Select Dough/Manual cycle.

Grease large cookie sheet. Divide dough into 10 equal pieces. Roll each piece into 9-inch rope. Place on cookie sheet. Brush with vegetable oil. Cover and let rise in warm place 5 to 15 minutes or until slightly risen.

Heat oven to 375°. To make breadsticks resemble sheaves of grain, make short angled cuts with scissors at one end of each breadstick. For a shiny finish, brush breadsticks with slightly beaten egg, if desired.

Bake 15 to 20 minutes or until golden brown. Remove from cookie sheet to wire rack. Serve warm or cool.

Cookies

The Ultimate Chocolate Chip Cookie (page 118)

Continued on next page

About Cookies

There's probably no dessert so well loved as cookies! Whether warm from the oven, packed in school lunches or enjoyed with cold milk or a good cup of coffee, the cookie recipes that follow will please anyone. To make the best cookies, read the helpful tips that follow and the ones throughout the chapter.

Pans and Pan Preparation

- Use a shiny cookie sheet at least two inches narrower and shorter than the oven. The sheet may be open on one to three sides. If the cookie sheet has four sides, cookies may not brown as evenly.

- If cookie sheets are thin, consider using two cookies sheets (one on top of the other) for insulation.

- Insulated cookie sheets help prevent cookies from becoming too dark on the bottom. Cookies baked on insulated cookie sheets may take longer to bake.

- Grease the cookie sheet only if directed in the recipe, using solid shortening (not margarine or butter) or nonstick cooking spray.

Mixing Cookies

- Sugars, fats and liquids are usually mixed together first, either by electric mixer or by hand, until ingredients are well combined. Then the dry ingredients are stirred in by hand just until moistened.

- Use an electric mixer only when specified in the recipe.

- Cookies mixed by hand will be more compact and dense than cookies mixed with an electric mixer because less air is beaten into the fat.

- Do not overmix dough or the cookies will be tough.

Baking Cookies

- Bake a "test" cookie. If it spreads more than desired, add 1 to 2 tablespoons flour or refrigerate the dough. If it is too dry, stir in 1 to 2 tablespoons milk.

- Check cookies at the minimum baking time—just one minute can make a difference, especially for cookies high in sugar and fat.

- Unless the recipe states otherwise, remove baked cookies immediately from the cookie sheet with a wide spatula, and place on a wire rack to cool. Cool completely.

Cookie Storage

- Store crisp, thin cookies in a container with a loose-fitting cover, which allows the flow of air to keep them crisp. If they soften, recrisp them by placing in a 300° oven for 3 to 5 minutes.

- Store unfrosted soft cookies in an airtight container to preserve their moistness. A piece of bread or apple (replaced frequently) in the container will help keep them soft.

- Store frosted soft cookies in a single layer in an airtight container so the frosting will maintain its shape and the cookies will retain their moistness.

- Do not mix crisp and soft cookies in the same container, or the crisp cookies will become soft.

- Store bar cookies in a tightly covered container, or leave them in the pan and cover tightly with aluminum foil.

The Ultimate Chocolate Chip Cookie

About 4 dozen cookies

(photograph on page 114)

3/4 cup granulated sugar
3/4 cup packed brown sugar
1 cup margarine or butter, softened
1 egg
2 1/4 cups all-purpose or whole wheat flour
1 teaspoon baking soda
1/2 teaspoon salt
1 cup coarsely chopped nuts
1 package (12 ounces) semisweet chocolate chips (2 cups)

Heat oven to 375°. Mix sugars, margarine and egg in large bowl. Stir in flour, baking soda and salt. (Dough will be stiff.) Stir in nuts and chocolate chips.

Drop dough by rounded tablespoonfuls about 2 inches apart onto ungreased cookie sheet.

Bake 8 to 10 minutes or until light brown. Cool slightly; remove from cookie sheet.

Chocolate Chip Shortbread Cookies

About 3 dozen cookies

1 cup margarine or butter, softened
3/4 cup packed brown sugar
2 cups all-purpose flour
1 cup miniature semisweet chocolate chips

Heat oven to 350°. Mix margarine and brown sugar in large bowl until well blended. Stir in flour. Stir in chocolate chips.

Roll dough into 1 1/4-inch balls. Place about 3 inches apart on ungreased cookie sheet. Flatten to about 1/2-inch thickness with greased bottom of glass dipped in sugar.

Bake 12 to 14 minutes or until set. Cool slightly; remove from cookie sheet.

TIP

Make all cookies on each cookie sheet the same size to ensure uniform baking. Mixing cookie sizes will cause some to be overbaked or underbaked.

Chocolate-Orange–Chocolate Chip Cookies

About 2 1/2 dozen cookies

1 cup sugar
2/3 cup margarine or butter, softened
1 tablespoon grated orange peel
1 egg
1 1/2 cups all-purpose flour
1/3 cup cocoa
1/4 teaspoon salt
1/4 teaspoon baking powder
1/4 teaspoon baking soda
1 cup chopped pecans
1 package (6 ounces) semisweet chocolate chips (1 cup)
1/3 cup sugar
1 teaspoon grated orange peel

Heat oven to 350°. Mix 1 cup sugar, the margarine, 1 tablespoon grated orange peel and the egg in large bowl. Stir in flour, cocoa, salt, baking powder and baking soda. Stir in pecans and chocolate chips.

Roll dough into 1 1/2-inch balls. Mix 1/3 cup sugar and 1 teaspoon grated orange peel. Roll balls of dough in sugar mixture. Place about 3 inches apart on ungreased cookie sheet. Flatten to about 1/2 inch thickness with bottom of glass. Bake 9 to 11 minutes or until set. Cool slightly; remove from cookie sheet.

Fresh Mint-Chocolate Chip Cookies

About 3 1/2 dozen cookies

Fresh mint is a delicious surprise in these unusually delicate cookies—perfect with a cup of tea.

1 1/3 cups sugar
3/4 cup margarine or butter, softened
1 tablespoon finely chopped mint leaves*
1 egg
2 cups all-purpose flour
1 teaspoon baking soda
1/2 teaspoon salt
1 package (10 ounces) mint chocolate chips

Heat oven to 350°. Mix sugar, margarine, mint leaves and egg in large bowl. Stir in flour, baking soda and salt. Stir in chocolate chips.

Drop dough by rounded tablespoonfuls about 2 inches apart onto ungreased cookie sheet. Bake 11 to 13 minutes or until golden brown. Cool slightly; remove from cookie sheet.

* 1/4 teaspoon mint extract can be substituted for the chopped mint leaves.

Mini Fresh Mint-Chocolate Chip Cookies: *Drop dough by level teaspoonfuls onto ungreased cookie sheet. Bake 6 to 8 minutes or until golden brown. About 10 1/2 dozen cookies*

Giant Toffee–Chocolate Chip Cookies

About 1 1/2 dozen cookies

Mini chips make these big toffee-flavored cookies look positively monstrous. Don't try to fit more than six cookies to a cookie sheet because they spread.

1 cup packed brown sugar
1/2 cup margarine or butter, softened
1/2 cup shortening
1/4 cup honey
1 egg
2 cups all-purpose flour
1 teaspoon baking soda
1/2 teaspoon baking powder
1/4 teaspoon salt
1 package (12 ounces) miniature semisweet chocolate chips
1 package (6 ounces) almond brickle chips

Heat oven to 350°. Mix brown sugar, margarine, shortening, honey and egg in large bowl. Stir in flour, baking soda, baking powder and salt. Stir in chocolate chips and brickle chips.

Drop dough by level 1/4 cupfuls about 2 inches apart onto ungreased cookie sheet.

Bake 12 to 14 minutes or until edges are golden brown. (Centers will be soft.) Cool 3 to 4 minutes; remove from cookie sheet.

Regular Toffee-Chocolate Chip Cookies: *Drop dough by rounded tablespoonfuls 2 inches apart onto ungreased cookie sheet. Bake 10 to 12 minutes or until golden brown. About 4 dozen cookies.*

TIP

Some people like chocolate chip cookies crisp and golden brown, others like them chewy and just kissed with color. For chewy cookies, reduce minimum bake time by one to two minutes, adjusting for your personal preference.

Giant Toffee–Chocolate Chip Cookies

Candy Cookies

About 3 dozen cookies

A pleasing variation on the classic chocolate chip cookie—have fun selecting the type of candy you use.

1/2 cup granulated sugar
1/2 cup packed brown sugar
1/3 cup margarine or butter, softened
1/3 cup shortening
1 teaspoon vanilla
1 egg
1 1/2 cups all-purpose flour
1/2 teaspoon baking soda
1/2 teaspoon salt
1 package (8 ounces) chocolate-coated
    candies

Heat oven to 375°. Mix sugars, margarine, shortening, vanilla and egg. Stir in remaining ingredients.

Drop dough by heaping teaspoonfuls about 2 inches apart onto ungreased cookie sheet.

Bake until light brown, 8 to 10 minutes. (Centers will be soft.) Cool slightly; remove from cookie sheet.

TIP

When a recipe says "drop dough by rounded teaspoonfuls (or tablespoonfuls)," use regular teaspoons and tablespoons from your every-day flatware.

Inside-Out Chocolate Chip Cookies

About 4 1/2 dozen cookies

Creamy white chips in dark, chocolaty cookies— these chocolate chip cookies have been turned inside-out!

1 cup granulated sugar
3/4 cup packed brown sugar
3/4 cup margarine or butter, softened
1/2 cup shortening
2 eggs
1 teaspoon vanilla
2 1/2 cups all-purpose flour
1/2 cup cocoa
1 teaspoon baking soda
1/4 teaspoon salt
1 1/2 cups vanilla milk chips
1 cup chopped nuts

Heat oven to 350°. Mix sugars, margarine, shortening, eggs and vanilla in large bowl. Stir in flour, cocoa, baking soda and salt. Stir in vanilla milk chips and nuts.

Drop dough by rounded tablespoonfuls about 2 inches apart onto ungreased cookie sheet.

Bake 10 to 12 minutes or until set. Cool slightly; remove from cookie sheet.

Inside-Out Chocolate Chip Cookies

Triple-Chocolate Chunk Cookies

About 3 dozen cookies

A sweet trio of chocolate makes these cookies three times as delightful—creamy milk chocolate, more assertive bittersweet chocolate and soft white chocolate.

1 1/2 cups packed brown sugar
1 cup (2 sticks) margarine or butter, softened
1 egg
2 1/4 cups all-purpose flour
2 teaspoons ground cinnamon
1 teaspoon baking soda
1/2 teaspoon salt
1 cup chopped nuts
4 ounces bittersweet chocolate, chopped
4 ounces sweet cooking chocolate, chopped
4 ounces white chocolate (white baking bar), chopped
Three-Chocolate Glaze (right)

Heat oven to 375°. Mix brown sugar, margarine and egg in large bowl. Stir in flour, cinnamon, baking soda and salt (dough will be soft). Stir in nuts, chocolates and white chocolate.

Drop dough by rounded tablespoonfuls about 2 inches apart onto ungreased cookie sheet.

Bake 8 to 10 minutes or until light golden brown. Cool slightly; remove from cookie sheet. Dip cookies in Three-Chocolate Glaze.

THREE-CHOCOLATE GLAZE

3 teaspoons shortening
3 ounces bittersweet chocolate
3 ounces sweet cooking chocolate
3 ounces white chocolate (white baking bar)

Heat 1 teaspoon of the shortening with bittersweet chocolate over low heat, stirring constantly, until chocolate is melted and smooth. Remove from heat. Dip each cookie 1/2 inch deep into chocolate along one edge. Repeat with remaining shortening and chocolates. Rotate dipped edge of cookie for each type of chocolate if desired.

Triple-Chocolate Chunk Cookies,
Ultimate Chocolate Chip Cookies (page 118)

Left to right: *Favorite Chocolate Chip Cookies, Honey-Oatmeal Cookies, Chocolate Drop Cookies*

Favorite Chocolate Chip Cookies

About 3 1/2 dozen cookies

1/2 cup granulated sugar
1/2 cup packed brown sugar
1/3 cup margarine or butter, softened
1/3 cup shortening
1 egg
1 teaspoon vanilla
1 1/2 cups all-purpose flour*
1/2 teaspoon baking soda
1/2 teaspoon salt
1/2 cup chopped nuts
1 package (6 ounces) semi-sweet chocolate
   chips

Heat oven to 375°. Mix sugars, margarine, shortening, egg and vanilla. Stir in remaining ingredients. Drop dough by rounded teaspoonfuls about 2 inches apart onto ungreased cookie sheet. Bake until light brown, 8 to 10 minutes. Cool slightly before removing from cookie sheet.

* If using self-rising flour, omit baking soda and salt.

Honey-Oatmeal Cookies

About 5 dozen cookies

1 1/4 cups sugar
1/2 cup shortening
2 eggs
1/3 cup honey
2 cups quick-cooking or regular oats
1 3/4 cups all-purpose flour*
1 cup raisins
1/2 cup chopped nuts
1 teaspoon baking soda
1 teaspoon salt

Heat oven to 375°. Mix sugar, shortening, eggs and honey. Stir in remaining ingredients.

Drop dough by rounded teaspoonfuls about 2 inches apart onto ungreased cookie sheet.

Bake until light brown, 8 to 10 minutes. Immediately remove from cookie sheet.

*If using self-rising flour, omit baking soda and salt.

Chocolate Drop Cookies

About 4 1/2 dozen cookies

1 cup sugar
1/2 cup margarine or butter, softened
1 egg
2 ounces melted unsweetened chocolate
1/3 cup buttermilk or water
1 teaspoon vanilla
1 3/4 cups all-purpose flour*
1/2 teaspoon baking soda
1/2 teaspoon salt
1 cup chopped nuts, if desired
Chocolate Frosting (right)

Heat oven to 400°. Mix sugar, margarine, egg, chocolate, buttermilk and vanilla in large bowl. Stir in flour, baking soda, salt and nuts.

Drop dough by rounded teaspoonfuls about 2 inches apart onto ungreased cookie sheet.

Bake until almost no indentation remains when touched, 8 to 10 minutes. Immediately remove from cookie sheet. Cool; frost with Chocolate Frosting.

If using self-rising flour, omit baking soda and salt.

CHOCOLATE FROSTING

2 squares (1 ounce each) unsweetened chocolate
2 tablespoons margarine or butter
3 tablespoons water
About 2 cups powdered sugar

Heat unsweetened chocolate squares and margarine over low heat until melted; remove from heat. Beat in water and powdered sugar until smooth and of spreading consistency.

Cranberry Chip Cookies

About 5 1/2 dozen cookies

A lovely, soft cookie bursting with cranberries and nuts. Try pistachio nuts for a unique flavor and even more color! You can use frozen cranberries, but be sure to pat them dry after chopping and don't overmix, or they may smear.

1 cup granulated sugar
3/4 cup packed brown sugar
1/2 cup (1 stick) margarine or butter, softened
1/4 cup milk
2 tablespoons orange juice
1 egg
3 cups all-purpose flour
1 teaspoon baking powder
1/2 teaspoon salt
1/4 teaspoon baking soda
2 1/2 cups coarsely chopped cranberries
1 cup chopped nuts
1/2 cup vanilla milk or semisweet chocolate chips
Chocolate Glaze (right), if desired

Heat oven to 375°. Grease cookie sheet. Mix sugars and margarine in large bowl. Stir in milk, orange juice and egg. Stir in flour, baking powder, salt and baking soda. Carefully stir in cranberries, nuts and vanilla milk chips.

Drop dough by rounded teaspoonfuls about 2 inches apart on cookie sheet.

Bake 10 to 15 minutes or until light brown. Remove from cookie sheet. Cool on wire rack. Spread with Chocolate Glaze.

CHOCOLATE GLAZE

1/2 cup semisweet chocolate chips
2 tablespoons margarine or butter
2 tablespoons corn syrup
1 to 2 teaspoons hot water

Heat chocolate chips, margarine and corn syrup over low heat, stirring constantly, until chocolate chips are melted; cool slightly. Stir in water, 1 teaspoon at a time, until consistency of thick syrup.

TIP

Use shortening when greasing cookie sheets, and only grease if specified in the recipe. Margarine or butter can cause the cookies to stick and overbrown. Regrease sheets as needed during baking.

Soft Pumpkin Drops

About 4 dozen cookies

1 cup sugar
1 cup canned pumpkin
1/2 cup shortening
1 tablespoon grated orange peel
2 cups all-purpose or whole wheat flour
1 teaspoon baking powder
1 teaspoon baking soda
1 teaspoon ground cinnamon
1/4 teaspoon salt
1/2 cup raisins
1/2 cup chopped nuts
Creamy Vanilla Frosting (right)

Heat oven to 375°. Mix sugar, pumpkin, shortening and orange peel. Stir in flour, baking powder, baking soda, cinnamon and salt. Mix in raisins and nuts.

Drop by rounded teaspoonfuls about 2 inches apart onto ungreased cookie sheet.

Bake until light brown, 8 to 10 minutes; cool. Frost with Creamy Vanilla Frosting.

CREAMY VANILLA FROSTING

3 cups powdered sugar
1/3 cup margarine or butter, softened
1 1/2 teaspoons vanilla
About 2 tablespoons milk

Mix powdered sugar and margarine. Stir in vanilla and milk; beat until smooth and of spreading consistency.

Mocha Macaroons

About 3 1/2 dozen cookies

3 egg whites
1 teaspoon freeze-dried instant coffee (dry)
1/4 teaspoon cream of tartar
1/8 teaspoon salt
1/2 cup sugar
2 tablespoons cocoa
2 cups flaked coconut

Heat oven to 300°. Grease cookie sheet lightly. Beat egg whites, coffee, cream of tartar and salt in medium bowl on high speed until foamy. Beat in sugar, 1 tablespoon at a time, on high speed. Continue beating until stiff. Do not underbeat. Fold in cocoa. Fold in coconut.

Drop mixture by rounded teaspoonfuls 1 inch apart onto cookie sheet.

Bake 20 to 25 minutes or until set. Cool 10 minutes; remove from cookie sheet. Cool on wire rack. Sprinkle with additional cocoa or drizzle with melted chocolate, if desired.

Tips for Drop Cookies

• Spoon dough with a tableware spoon (not a measuring spoon, unless a level teaspoon or tablespoon is specified). Push dough onto cookie sheet with another spoon or rubber spatula.

• Use a spring-handle ice-cream scoop for making uniformly shaped cookies. These are sold in various sizes and are referred to by number. (The number corresponds to the number of level scoops per quart of ice cream.) For example, if your recipe says to drop dough by rounded teaspoonfuls, use a number 70 scoop.

• Drop dough about two inches apart (or as directed in the recipe) onto cookie sheet to prevent cookies from baking together, as the dough spreads during baking.

• If edges are dark and crusty, cookies were overbaked, the cookie sheet was too large for oven or a dark cookie sheet was used. If center of cookies is doughy, they were underbaked.

• Excess spreading may be caused by dough being too warm, the cookie sheet being too hot or incorrect oven temperature. Chill soft doughs before dropping onto cookie sheet. Also, let cookie sheet cool between bakings.

Traditional Almond Cookies

About 4 dozen cookies

3 cups slivered almonds, toasted
3 egg whites
1 1/2 cups granulated sugar
1 teaspoon powdered sugar
1 teaspoon amaretto or 1/4 teaspoon
    almond extract
Granulated sugar

Heat oven to 300°. Line cookie sheet with cooking parchment paper, or grease and flour cookie sheet. Place almonds in food processor or blender. Cover and process, or blend, until finely ground but not pastelike.

Beat egg whites in medium bowl on high speed until stiff. Stir in almonds, 1 1/2 cups granulated sugar and the powdered sugar. Stir in amaretto.

Drop mixture by rounded teaspoonfuls about 2 inches apart onto cookie sheet. Sprinkle with granulated sugar. Bake 20 to 25 minutes or until brown. Remove from cookie sheet. Cool on wire rack. Drizzle with melted bittersweet chocolate, if desired.

Salted Peanut Crisps

About 6 dozen cookies

1 1/2 cups packed brown sugar
1/2 cup margarine or butter, softened
1/2 cup shortening
2 eggs
2 teaspoons vanilla
3 cups all-purpose flour*
2 cups salted peanuts
1/2 teaspoon salt
1/2 teaspoon baking soda

Heat oven to 375°. Mix brown sugar, margarine, shortening, eggs and vanilla. Stir in remaining ingredients.

Drop dough by rounded teaspoonfuls about 2 inches apart onto lightly greased cookie sheet. Flatten with greased bottom of glass dipped in sugar.

Bake until golden brown, 8 to 10 minutes. Immediately remove from cookie sheet.

*If using self-rising flour, omit baking soda and salt.

Chocolate Crinkles

About 6 dozen cookies

2 cups granulated sugar
1/2 cup vegetable oil
4 ounces melted unsweetened chocolate
  (cool)
2 teaspoons vanilla
4 eggs
2 cups all-purpose flour*
2 teaspoons baking powder
1/2 teaspoon salt
1/2 cup powdered sugar

Mix granulated sugar, oil, chocolate and vanilla in large bowl. Mix in eggs, one at a time. Stir in flour, baking powder and salt. Cover and refrigerate at least 3 hours.

Heat oven to 350°. Shape dough by rounded teaspoonfuls into balls. Roll in powdered sugar. Place about 2 inches apart on greased cookie sheet.

Bake 10 to 12 minutes or until almost no indentation remains when touched.

*If using self-rising flour, omit baking soda and salt.

Snickerdoodles

About 6 dozen cookies

1 1/2 cups sugar
1/2 cup margarine or butter, softened
1/2 cup shortening
2 eggs
2 3/4 cups all-purpose flour*
2 teaspoons cream of tartar
1 teaspoon baking soda
1/4 teaspoon salt
2 tablespoons sugar
2 teaspoons ground cinnamon

Heat oven to 400°. Mix 1 1/2 cups sugar, the margarine, shortening and eggs. Stir in flour, cream of tartar, baking soda and salt.

Shape dough by rounded teaspoonfuls into balls. Mix 2 tablespoons sugar and the cinnamon; roll balls in mixture to coat. Place about 2 inches apart on ungreased cookie sheet.

Bake until set, 8 to 10 minutes. Immediately remove from cookie sheet.

If using self-rising flour, omit baking soda and salt.

TIP

Cool the cookie sheets between batches; otherwise cookie dough placed on warm cookie sheets will spread.

Top to bottom: *Salted Peanut Crisps, Chocolate Crinkles, Snickerdoodles*

Applesauce-Granola Cookies

About 3 1/2 dozen cookies

1 cup packed brown sugar
1/2 cup shortening
1 teaspoon vanilla
1 egg
1/2 cup applesauce
2 cups all-purpose flour
2 cups granola
1/2 teaspoon baking soda
1/2 teaspoon salt

Heat oven to 375°. Mix brown sugar, shortening, vanilla and egg in large bowl. Stir in applesauce. Stir in remaining ingredients.

Drop dough by rounded tablespoonfuls about 2 inches apart onto ungreased cookie sheet.

Bake 11 to 13 minutes or until almost no indentation remains when touched in center. Cool slightly; remove from cookie sheet.

TIP

If using a cookie sheet with a nonstick coating, watch carefully, as cookies may brown quickly. Follow manufacturers' directions as many may suggest reducing the oven temperature by 25°.

Chocolate Oatmeal Chewies

About 3 1/2 dozen cookies

1 1/2 cups sugar
1 cup margarine or butter, softened
1/4 cup milk
1 egg
2 2/3 cups quick-cooking or old-fashioned oats
1 cup all-purpose flour
1/2 cup cocoa
1/2 teaspoon salt
1/2 teaspoon baking soda

Heat oven to 350°. Mix sugar, margarine, milk and egg in large bowl. Stir in remaining ingredients.

Drop dough by rounded tablespoonfuls about 2 inches apart onto ungreased cookie sheet.

Bake 10 to 12 minutes or until almost no indentation remains when touched in center. Cool slightly; remove from cookie sheet.

Pineapple Puffs

About 6 1/2 dozen cookies

1 1/2 cups sugar
1/2 cup margarine or butter, softened
1/2 cup sour cream or plain yogurt
1 egg
1 can (8 1/4 ounces) crushed pineapple, undrained
3 1/2 cups all-purpose flour
1/2 cup chopped almonds
1 teaspoon baking soda
1 teaspoon vanilla
1/2 teaspoon salt
Vanilla Frosting (below)

Heat oven to 375°. Mix sugar, margarine, sour cream, egg and pineapple in large bowl. Stir in remaining ingredients except Vanilla Frosting.

Drop dough by teaspoonfuls about 2 inches apart onto ungreased cookie sheet.

Bake 8 to 10 minutes or until almost no indentation remains when touched in center. Immediately remove from cookie sheet. Cool completely. Prepare Vanilla Frosting and spread on cookies.

VANILLA FROSTING

2 cups powdered sugar
2 to 3 tablespoons milk
1 teaspoon vanilla

Mix ingredients until smooth and of spreading consistency.

Moravian Ginger Cookies

About 1 dozen 1/8-inch thick cookies or about 1 1/2 dozen paper-thin cookies

1/3 cup molasses
1/4 cup shortening
2 tablespoons packed brown sugar
1 1/4 cups all-purpose or whole wheat flour
1/4 teaspoon salt
1/4 teaspoon baking soda
1/4 teaspoon baking powder
1/4 teaspoon ground cinnamon
1/4 teaspoon ground ginger
1/4 teaspoon ground cloves
Dash of ground nutmeg
Dash of ground allspice
Easy Creamy Frosting (below)

Mix molasses, shortening and brown sugar in large bowl. Stir in remaining ingredients except Easy Creamy Frosting. Cover and refrigerate about 4 hours or until firm.

Heat oven to 375°. Roll half of dough at a time 1/8 inch thick or paper-thin on floured cloth-covered surface. Cut into 3-inch rounds with floured cutter. Place about 1/2 inch apart on ungreased cookie sheet.

Bake 1/8-inch-thick cookies about 8 minutes, paper-thin cookies about 5 minutes or until light brown. Immediately remove from cookie sheet. Cool completely. Prepare Easy Creamy Frosting and spread on cookies.

EASY CREAMY FROSTING

1 cup powdered sugar
1 to 2 tablespoons half-and-half
1/2 teaspoon vanilla

Mix ingredients until of spreading consistency.

Almond-Filled Crescents

4 dozen crescents

1 cup powdered sugar
1 cup whipping (heavy) cream
2 eggs
3 3/4 cups all-purpose flour
1 teaspoon baking powder
1/2 teaspoon salt
1 can (8 ounces) almond paste
3/4 cup margarine or butter, softened
Glaze (below)

Mix powdered sugar, whipping cream and eggs in large bowl. Stir in flour, baking powder and Salt. (Dough will be stiff.) Cover and refrigerate about 1 hour or until firm.

Heat oven to 375°. Break almond paste into small pieces in medium bowl; add margarine. Beat on low speed until blended. Beat on high speed until fluffy (tiny bits of almond paste will remain).

Roll one-fourth of dough at a time into 10-inch circle on lightly floured surface. Spread one-fourth of almond paste mixture (about 1/2 cup) over circle. Cut into 12 wedges. Roll up, beginning at rounded edge. Place on ungreased cookie sheet with points underneath. Curve cookies to form crescents. Repeat with remaining dough and almond paste mixture.

Bake 14 to 16 minutes or until golden brown. Remove from cookie sheet. Cool completely. Prepare Glaze and drizzle on crescents.

GLAZE

1 cup powdered sugar
6 to 7 teaspoons milk

Mix until smooth and of drizzling consistency.

Hungarian Poppy Seed Cookies

About 3 dozen cookies

Lemon peel, clove and poppy seed often flavor Eastern European cookies. Look for commercially prepared poppy seed filling next to canned pie fillings at the supermarket.

1/2 cup margarine or butter
1/4 cup granulated sugar
1 teaspoon grated lemon peel
1 egg
1 1/4 cups all-purpose flour
1/2 teaspoon baking soda
1/4 teaspoon ground cloves
3/4 cup poppy seed filling
Powdered sugar

Beat margarine and granulated sugar in large bowl until light and fluffy. Beat in lemon peel and egg. Stir in flour, baking soda and cloves. Roll dough between pieces of waxed paper into 1/4-inch-thick rectangle, 12×10 inches. Refrigerate 30 minutes or until firm.

Heat oven to 350°. Grease cookie sheet. Remove waxed paper from one side of dough. Spread poppy seed filling to within 1/4 inch of edges. Roll up tightly, beginning at 12-inch side, peeling off waxed paper as dough is rolled. Pinch edge of dough to seal well. Cut dough into 1/2-inch slices. Place on cookie sheet about 1 inch apart.

Bake 10 to 12 minutes or until edges are light brown. Cool slightly; remove from cookie sheet. Sprinkle with powdered sugar.

Hungarian Poppy Seed Cookies,
Mint Ravioli Cookies (page 144)

Ladyfingers

About 3 1/2 dozen cookies

Homemade ladyfingers are a treat, delicate and fresh. They are essential to Charlotte Russe and trifle.

3 eggs, separated
1/4 teaspoon cream of tartar
1/4 cup sugar
1/3 cup sugar
3/4 cup all-purpose flour
3 tablespoons water
1/2 teaspoon vanilla
1/4 teaspoon baking powder
1/4 teaspoon lemon extract, if desired
1/8 teaspoon salt

Heat oven to 350°. Grease and flour cookie sheet. Beat egg whites and cream of tartar in large bowl until foamy. Gradually beat in 1/4 cup sugar until stiff peaks form. Beat egg yolks and 1/3 cup sugar in medium bowl about 3 minutes or until thick and lemon colored. Stir in remaining ingredients. Fold egg yolk mixture into egg white mixture.

Place batter in decorating bag with #9 tip or cookie press with #32 tip. Form 3-inch fingers about 2 inches apart on cookie sheet. Bake 10 to 12 minutes or until set and light brown. Immediately remove from cookie sheet. Dust tops with powdered sugar.

Almond Macaroons

About 3 dozen cookies

1 can (8 ounces) almond paste
1/4 cup all-purpose flour
1 1/4 cups powdered sugar
1/4 teaspoon almond extract
2 egg whites
3 dozen blanched whole almonds

Grease cookie sheet. Mix almond paste, flour, powdered sugar, almond extract and egg whites in large bowl. Beat on medium speed 2 minutes, scraping bowl occasionally, until smooth.

Place dough in decorating bag fitted with #9 rosette tip. Pipe 1 1/2-inch cookies about 2 inches apart on cookie sheet. Top each with whole almond. Refrigerate 30 minutes. Heat oven to 325°. Bake about 12 minutes or until edges are light brown. Immediately remove from cookie sheet. Cool completely. Store in airtight container.

Ladyfingers, Almond Macaroons

Lime Meltaways

About 3 dozen cookies

These cookies are a refreshing dessert on summer days. They really do melt in your mouth.

1 cup margarine or butter
1/2 cup powdered sugar
1 3/4 cups all-purpose flour
1/4 cup cornstarch
1 tablespoon grated lime peel
1/2 teaspoon vanilla
Lime Glaze (below)

Heat oven to 350°. Beat margarine and powdered sugar in large bowl until light and fluffly. Stir in remaining ingredients except Lime Glaze until well blended. Place dough in cookie press with ribbon tip. Form long ribbons of dough on ungreased cookie sheet. Cut into 3-inch lengths. Bake 9 to 11 minutes or until edges are golden brown. Remove from cookie sheet. Cool completely. Prepare Lime Glaze and brush on cookies.

LIME GLAZE

1/2 cup powdered sugar
4 teaspoons lime juice
2 teaspoons grated lime peel

Mix all ingredients.

Swedish Half-Moon Cookies

About 3 dozen cookies

This tender cookie is made with potato flour (sometimes called "potato starch"). It is often found in stores near the cornstarch, in a section with gluten-free products and in health-food stores.

1 3/4 cups all-purpose flour
1/2 cup potato flour
1/2 cup powdered sugar
1 cup margarine or butter, well chilled and cut into cubes
1/8 teaspoon almond extract
1 egg
1/2 cup cherry preserves
1 egg white, beaten
1/4 cup sanding sugar
1/4 cup finely chopped blanched almonds

Mix flours and powdered sugar in large bowl. Cut margarine into dry mixture using pastry blender until mixture resembles fine crumbs. Stir in almond extract and egg until dough leaves side of bowl. Cover and refrigerate 1 hour.

Heat oven to 350°. Line cookie sheet with cooking parchment paper. Roll one-fourth of dough at a time 1/8 inch thick between 2 sheets of waxed paper. (Keep remaining dough refrigerated until ready to roll.) Cut with fluted 3-inch round biscuit cutter. Spoon 1/2 teaspoon cherry preserves onto half of each cookie. Fold dough over preserves to form half-moon shape. Pinch edges to seal. Place on cookie sheet. Brush with egg white; sprinkle with sanding sugar and almonds. Bake 10 to 12 minutes or until edges are light brown. Remove from cookie sheet.

Orange Madeleines

About 2 dozen cookies

Sponge cakes in miniature, French madeleines are baked in shell-shaped molds. If you must bake the recipe in two batches, don't let the batter sit any longer than it has to or the second batch will not be as tender as the first.

1 egg, separated
1/2 cup sugar
1 cup all-purpose flour
1/2 cup milk
2 tablespoons vegetable oil
1 tablespoon orange-flavored liqueur or milk
1 1/2 teaspoons baking powder
1 1/2 teaspoons grated orange peel
1/4 teaspoon salt
Powdered sugar

Heat oven to 375°. Grease and flour twenty-four 3-inch* madeleine molds. Beat egg white in small bowl until foamy. Beat in 1/4 cup of the sugar, 1 tablespoon at a time. Continue beating until very stiff and glossy. Set meringue aside. Beat remaining 1/4 cup sugar with remaining ingredients except powdered sugar in medium bowl on high 2 minutes, scraping bowl occasionally. Fold in meringue.

Fill molds two-thirds full. Tap pan firmly on counter to remove air bubbles. Bake 10 to 12 minutes or until edges are light brown. Cool slightly; remove from pan. Sprinkle with powdered sugar just before serving.

One 12-mold pan can be used. Bake half of batter; wash, grease and flour pan. Bake remaining batter.

Chocolate-Cherry Sand Tarts

About 4 1/2 dozen cookies

3/4 cup sugar
3/4 cup margarine or butter, softened
1 egg white
1 3/4 cups all-purpose flour
1/4 cup cocoa
About 1 3/4 cups cherry preserves
Chocolate Glaze (below)

Mix sugar, margarine and egg white in large bowl. Stir in flour and cocoa. Cover and refrigerate about 2 hours or until firm.

Heat oven to 350°. Press 1-inch ball of dough in bottom and up side of each ungreased sandbakelse mold, about 1 3/4 × 1/2 inch. Spoon about 1 1/2 teaspoons cherry preserves into each mold. Place on cookie sheet. Bake 12 to 15 minutes or until crust is set. Cool about 10 minutes. Carefully remove cookies from molds. Cool completely. Prepare Chocolate Glaze and drizzle on cookies.

CHOCOLATE GLAZE

2/3 cup semisweet chocolate chips
1 tablespoon shortening

Heat and stir ingredients until melted and smooth.

Chocolate Shortbread

About 4 dozen cookies

As an alternative to the frosted spiderweb design described below, drizzle straight lines of chocolate across the white frosting; draw a toothpick across the lines, alternating directions.

2 cups powdered sugar
1 1/2 cups margarine or butter
3 cups all-purpose flour
3/4 cup cocoa
2 teaspoons vanilla
4 ounces semisweet chocolate, melted
    and cooled
1/2 teaspoon shortening
Creamy Frosting (right)

Heat oven to 325°. Beat powdered sugar and margarine in large bowl until light and fluffy. Stir in flour, cocoa and vanilla.

Roll half of dough at a time 1/2 inch thick on lightly floured surface. Cut into 3-inch rounds. Place 2 inches apart on ungreased cookie sheet.

Bake 9 to 11 minutes or until firm. (Do not let cookies get dark brown.) Remove from cookies sheet. Cool completely.

Mix chocolate and shortening until smooth. Prepare Creamy Frosting and spread each cookie with about 1 teaspoon. Immediately drizzle chocolate mixture on frosting making 3 concentric circles. Starting at center, draw a toothpick 5 to 6 times through chocolate circles to make spiderweb design. Let stand until chocolate is firm.

CREAMY FROSTING

3 cups powdered sugar
1/3 cup margarine or butter, softened
1 1/2 teaspoons vanilla
About 2 tablespoons milk

Mix powdered sugar and margarine. Stir in vanilla and milk. Beat until smooth and of spreading consistency.

Butterscotch Shortbread

About 4 dozen cookies

If you prefer shortbread cutouts, use a 2-inch cookie cutter.

1/2 cup margarine or butter, softened
1/2 cup shortening
1/2 cup packed brown sugar
1/4 cup granulated sugar
2 1/4 cups all-purpose flour
1 teaspoon salt

Heat oven to 300°. Mix margarine, shortening and sugars in large bowl. Stir in flour and salt. (Dough will be dry and crumbly. Use hands to mix completely.)

Roll dough into rectangle, 15×7 1/2 inches, on lightly floured surface. Cut into 1 1/2-inch squares. Place about 1 inch apart on ungreased cookie sheet.

Bake about 25 minutes or until set. (These cookies brown very little and the shape does not change.) Remove from cookie sheet.

Tips for Shaped Cookies

- Rich, soft dough must be chilled before shaping. Work with small amounts, keeping remaining dough refrigerated.

- If dough is too soft after chilling, mix in 1 to 2 tablespoons flour. If dough is too dry and crumbly, work in 1 to 2 tablespoons milk, water or softened stick margarine or butter.

- Take the time to mold fancy shapes (such as crescents, candy canes, wreaths, bells) so that cookies are uniform in shape and size. This helps them bake evenly.

- Shape refrigerator cookie dough firmly into a smooth roll of the length or diameter specified in the recipe. Wrap rolled dough in waxed paper, plastic wrap or aluminum foil, twisting ends.

- Refrigerate rolled dough until firm enough to slice easily. Use a thin, sharp knife to slice dough.

- Rolls of dough can be refrigerated up to twenty-four hours or wrapped airtight and frozen up to twelve months.

Peachy Pinwheels

About 5 dozen cookies

For the freshest nutmeg flavor, grate your own nutmeg.

1 cup finely chopped dried peaches
3/4 cup water
1/2 cup sugar
1/2 teaspoon freshly ground nutmeg
1/2 cup margarine or butter, softened
1/4 cup shortening
1 cup sugar
2 eggs
1 teaspoon vanilla
2 1/2 cups all-purpose flour
1 teaspoon baking powder
1/4 teaspoon salt

Mix peaches, water, 1/2 cup sugar and the nutmeg in 1-quart saucepan. Heat to boiling; reduce heat. Cover and simmer about 35 minutes or until peaches are tender and water is almost absorbed; cool slightly. Mash with fork.

Mix margarine, shortening, 1 cup sugar, the eggs and vanilla. Stir in remaining ingredients. Cover and refrigerate at least 1 hour.

Divide dough in half. Roll each half into rectangle, 11×7 inches, on floured surface. Spread half of the peach mixture to within 1/2 inch of edges of each rectangle. Roll up tightly, beginning at long side. Pinch to seal. Wrap and refrigerate at least 4 hours or until firm.

Heat oven to 375°. Cut roll into 1/4-inch slices. Place on ungreased cookie sheet.

Bake about 10 minutes or until light brown; cool.

Tips for Rolled Cookies

- Roll only part of the chilled dough at a time, and keep the remainder refrigerated.

- To prevent dough from sticking, sprinkle rolling surface with flour and rub flour onto rolling pin. Use only enough flour to prevent dough from sticking during rolling. Too much flour and rerolling the dough results in dry, tough cookies.

- To ensure even baking, roll dough evenly to maintain uniform thickness. Rolling dough between two 15- or 18-inch rulers or wooden dowels or sticks of the correct height helps keep dough even.

- Dip cookie cutter into flour or powdered sugar and shake off excess before each cut.

- Cut cookies close together to avoid rerolling leftover dough (rerolled dough will be a little tougher).

- Use a wide metal spatula to lift cut dough to the cookie sheet to avoid stretching the dough.

Sugar Cookie Tarts

About 2 1/2 dozen cookies

2 cups sugar
1 cup shortening
3/4 cup margarine or butter, softened
2 teaspoons vanilla
1 egg
3 1/2 cups all-purpose flour
1 teaspoon baking powder
1/4 teaspoon salt
Cream Cheese Spread (below)
Toppings (sliced fresh fruit, miniature chocolate chips, chopped pecans or jam and toasted sliced almonds)

Heat oven to 375°. Mix sugar, shortening, margarine, vanilla and egg in large bowl. Stir in flour, baking powder and salt.

Roll half of dough at a time 1/4 inch thick on lightly floured surface. Cut into 3-inch rounds. Place 2 inches apart on ungreased cookie sheet.

Bake 10 to 12 minutes or until light brown. Cool slightly; remove from cookie sheet.

Cool completely. Prepare Cream Cheese Spread. Spread about 2 teaspoons over each cookie. Arrange toppings on spread. Refrigerate any remaining cookies.

CREAM CHEESE SPREAD

1/2 cup sugar
1 teaspoon vanilla
1 package (8 ounces) cream cheese, softened

Mix ingredients until smooth.

Mint Ravioli Cookies

3 dozen cookies

(photograph on page 135)

1/2 cup margarine or butter, softened
1/2 cup shortening
1 cup sugar
1 egg
2 1/2 cups all-purpose flour
1 teaspoon baking powder
1/4 teaspoon salt
3 dozen rectangular chocolate mints

Mix margarine, shortening, sugar and egg in large bowl. Stir in flour, baking powder and salt. Cover and refrigerate about 1 hour or until firm.

Heat oven to 400°. Roll half of dough into rectangle, 13×9 inches, on floured surface. Place mints on dough, forming 6 uniform rows of 6. Roll remaining dough into rectangle, 13×9 inches, on floured waxed paper. Place over mint-covered dough and remove waxed paper. Cut between mints with pastry wheel or knife and press edges with fork to seal. Place on ungreased cookie sheet.

Bake 7 to 9 minutes or until light brown. Remove from cookie sheet.

Place mints on dough, forming six rows of 6.

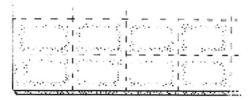

Place remaining dough over mint-covered dough; cut between mints.

Lemon Tea Biscuits

4 dozen sandwich cookies

Assemble these light wafers with the tart lemon filling no longer than an hour or two before serving—they soften on standing. Because they are quite English, we call them by the British name for cookie: "biscuit." Unfilled cookies can be frozen until needed.
(photograph on page 147)

1 cup margarine or butter
1/2 cup sugar
1 tablespoon grated lemon peel
1/4 teaspoon salt
1 egg
2 cups all-purpose flour
1/2 cup ground pecans
1 cup lemon curd or pie filling
Lemon Glaze (below)

Mix margarine, sugar, lemon peel, salt and egg in large bowl until well blended. Stir in flour and pecans. Cover and refrigerate 1 hour or until firm.

Heat oven to 350°. Roll half of dough at a time about 1/8 inch thick on floured surface. Cut into 2-inch rounds. Place on ungreased cookie sheet.

Bake 7 to 9 minutes or until edges are just barely brown. Remove from cookie sheet. Cool completely. Put cookies together in pairs using rounded teaspoonful lemon curd for filling. Prepare Lemon Glaze and brush on tops of cookies.

LEMON GLAZE

1/4 cup powdered sugar
1 teaspoon grated lemon peel
2 teaspoons lemon juice

Mix all ingredients.

Hazelnut Sablés (page 146)

Hazelnut Sablés

About 3 dozen cookies

Pronounced "sah-blay," sablés are French cookies that translate to "sandies." They are rich, short cookies with pronounced hazelnut flavor. (photograph on page 145)

3/4 cup margarine or butter, softened
3/4 cup powdered sugar
1/2 teaspoon vanilla
1 egg yolk
1 1/4 cups all-purpose flour
1/2 cup hazelnuts, toasted and ground
1 egg, beaten
1/4 cup chopped hazelnuts
1/4 cup sanding sugar

Beat margarine and powdered sugar in large bowl until light and fluffy. Stir in vanilla and egg yolk. Stir in flour and ground hazelnuts until well blended. Cover tightly and refrigerate 1 hour.

Heat oven to 350°. Roll one-fourth of dough at a time 1/4 inch thick on lightly floured surface. (Keep remaining dough refrigerated until ready to roll.) Cut into 2 1/2-inch rounds. Place about 2 inches apart on ungreased cookie sheet. Brush with egg. Sprinkle with chopped hazelnuts and sugar. Bake 8 to 10 minutes or until edges are light brown. Remove from cookie sheet.

Orange-Almond Pillows

2 dozen cookies

These little puffs really look like pillows. For crisp cookies, bake until light brown. For chewy cookies, bake just until set—not brown.

1 1/2 cups blanched almonds, ground
1 tablespoon grated orange peel
1 egg white
1/2 cup powdered sugar
Orange Glaze (below)

Heat oven to 350°. Grease and flour cookie sheet or line with cooking parchment paper. Mix almonds and orange peel; reserve. Beat egg white in medium bowl on high speed until stiff but not dry. Gradually beat in powdered sugar. Beat on high speed about 3 minutes or until slightly stiff. Fold almond mixture into egg white mixture (mixture will be stiff).

Roll dough into rectangle, 9 × 6 inches, on cloth-covered surface generously dusted with powdered sugar. Cut into 1 1/2-inch squares. Place 1 inch apart on cookie sheet. Bake 10 to 12 minutes or until set and very light brown. Remove from cookie sheet. Cool completely. Prepare Orange Glaze and drizzle on cookies.

ORANGE GLAZE

3/4 cup powdered sugar
3 to 4 teaspoons orange juice
1/4 teaspoon grated orange peel

Mix ingredients until smooth and of desired consistency.

Lemon Tea Biscuits (page 144), Orange-Almond Pillows

Pecan Crisps

About 4 dozen cookies

2 cups sugar
3/4 cup very finely chopped pecans
1/3 cup margarine or butter, softened
1 teaspoon vanilla
2 eggs
2 1/4 cups all-purpose flour
2 1/2 teaspoons baking powder
1/4 teaspoon salt

Heat oven to 375°. Mix sugar and pecans in large bowl. Reserve 3/4 cup of sugar mixture. Stir margarine, vanilla and eggs into remaining sugar mixture. Stir in flour, baking powder and salt.

Roll dough into rectangle, 18×13 inches, on floured surface. Sprinkle generously with reserved sugar mixture. Press sugar mixture into dough with rolling pin. Cut dough diagonally in both directions every 2 inches with pastry wheel or knife to form diamonds. Place about 2 inches apart on ungreased cookie sheet.

Bake 8 to 10 minutes or until golden brown. Immediately remove from cookie sheet.

Lemon Squares

64 squares

1 cup all-purpose flour*
1/2 cup margarine or butter, softened
1/4 cup powdered sugar
1 cup granulated sugar
2 eggs
2 teaspoons grated lemon peel, if desired
2 tablespoons lemon juice
1/2 teaspoon baking powder
1/4 teaspoon salt
Powdered sugar

Lemon Squares

Heat oven to 350°. Mix flour, margarine and 1/4 cup powdered sugar. Press in ungreased baking pan, 8×8×2 inches, building up 1/2-inch edges. Bake 20 minutes.

Beat granulated sugar, eggs, lemon peel, lemon juice, baking powder and salt until light and fluffy, about 3 minutes; pour over baked layer.

Bake just until no indentation remains when touched in center, about 25 minutes. Cool; sprinkle with powdered sugar. Cut into about 1-inch squares.

If using self-rising flour, omit baking powder and salt.

Sour Cream–Banana Bars

4 dozen bars

1 1/2 cups sugar
1 cup sour cream
1/2 cup margarine or butter, softened
2 eggs
1 1/2 cups mashed bananas (about 3 large)
2 teaspoons vanilla
2 cups all-purpose flour
1 teaspoon salt
1 teaspoon baking soda
1/2 cup chopped nuts
Browned Butter Frosting (page 251)

Heat oven to 375°. Grease and flour jelly roll pan, 15 1/2×10 1/2×1 inch. Mix sugar, sour cream, margarine and eggs in large mixer bowl on low speed, scraping bowl occasionally, 1 minute. Beat in bananas and vanilla on low speed 30 seconds. Beat in flour, salt and baking soda on medium speed, scraping bowl occasionally, 1 minute. Stir in nuts. Spread dough in pan.

Bake until light brown, 20 to 25 minutes. Cool; frost with Browned Butter Frosting. Cut into bars, about 2×1 1/2 inches.

TIP

Always check cookies at minimum bake times, as even one minute can make a difference with cookies, especially those high in sugar and fat.

Banana-Nut Bars

2 dozen bars

(photograph on page 151)

1 cup sugar
1 cup mashed ripe bananas (about 3 medium)
1/3 cup vegetable oil
2 eggs
1 cup all-purpose flour
1 teaspoon baking powder
1/2 teaspoon baking soda
1/2 teaspoon ground cinnamon
1/4 teaspoon salt
1/2 cup chopped nuts
Cream Cheese Frosting (below)

Heat oven to 350°. Grease rectangular pan, 13×9×2 inches. Beat sugar, bananas, oil and eggs in large bowl. Stir in flour, baking powder, baking soda, cinnamon and salt. Stir in nuts. Spread batter in pan.

Bake 25 to 30 minutes or until toothpick inserted in center comes out clean. Cool completely. Prepare Cream Cheese Frosting and spread on bars. Cover and refrigerate any remaining bars.

CREAM CHEESE FROSTING

1 package (3 ounces) cream cheese, softened
1/3 cup margarine or butter, softened
1 teaspoon vanilla
2 cups powdered sugar

Beat cream cheese, margarine and vanilla in medium bowl on low speed until smooth. Gradually beat in powdered sugar until smooth.

Zucchini Bars

2 dozen bars

2/3 cup packed brown sugar
1/4 cup margarine or butter, softened
1 egg
1/2 teaspoon vanilla
1 cup all-purpose flour
1 teaspoon baking soda
1/2 teaspoon ground cinnamon
1/2 teaspoon ground cloves
1 cup shredded zucchini, drained
1/2 cup chopped nuts
Spice Frosting (below)

Heat oven to 350°. Grease square pan, 8×8×2 inches or 9×9×2 inches. Mix brown sugar, margarine, egg and vanilla in large bowl. Stir in flour, baking soda, cinnamon and cloves. Stir in zucchini and nuts. Spread batter in pan.

Bake 25 to 30 minutes or until toothpick inserted in center comes out clean. Cool completely. Prepare Spice Frosting and spread on bars.

SPICE FROSTING

3/4 cup powdered sugar
1 tablespoon margarine or butter, softened
3 to 4 tablespoons milk
1/8 teaspoon ground cloves

Mix all ingredients until smooth and of spreading consistency.

Pumpkin-Spice Bars

About 4 dozen bars

4 eggs
2 cups sugar
1 cup vegetable oil
1 can (16 ounces) pumpkin
2 cups all-purpose flour
2 teaspoons baking powder
2 teaspoons ground cinnamon
1 teaspoon baking soda
3/4 teaspoon salt
1/2 teaspoon ground ginger
1/4 teaspoon ground cloves
1/2 cup raisins
Cream Cheese Frosting (below)
1/2 cup chopped nuts

Heat oven to 350°. Grease jelly roll pan, 15 1/2 ×10 1/2×1 inch. Beat eggs, sugar, oil and pumpkin. Stir in flour, baking powder, cinnamon, baking soda, salt, ginger and cloves. Mix in raisins. Pour batter into pan.

Bake until light brown, 25 to 30 minutes. Cool; frost with Cream Cheese Frosting. Sprinkle with nuts. Cut into bars, about 2× 1 1/2 inches. Refrigerate any remaining bars.

CREAM CHEESE FROSTING

1 package (3 ounces) cream cheese,
    softened
1/4 cup plus 2 tablespoons margarine or
    butter, softened
1 teaspoon vanilla
2 cups powdered sugar

Mix cream cheese, margarine, and vanilla. Gradually beat in powdered sugar until smooth and of spreading consistency.

Top to bottom: *Pumpkin-Spice Bars, Zucchini Bars, Banana-Nut Bars (page 149)*

Cream-Filled Oat Bars

2 dozen bars

Wonderfully creamy in the center, these golden brown bars are an exceptional treat.

1 can (14 ounces) sweetened condensed milk
2 teaspoons grated lemon peel
1/4 cup lemon juice
1 1/4 cups all-purpose flour
1 cup quick-cooking or regular oats
1/2 cup packed brown sugar
1/2 cup margarine or butter, softened
1/4 teaspoon salt
1/4 teaspoon baking soda

Heat oven to 375°. Grease square pan, 9×9×2 inches. Mix milk, lemon peel and lemon juice until thickened; reserve. Mix remaining ingredients until crumbly. Press half of the crumbly mixture in pan. Bake about 10 minutes or until set.

Spread milk mixture over baked layer. Sprinkle remaining crumbly mixture on milk mixture. Press gently into milk mixture.

Bake about 20 minutes or until edge is golden brown and center is set but soft. Cool completely.

Linzer Torte Bars

48 bars

For a heftier bar, cut into 18 pieces.

1 cup all-purpose flour
1 cup powdered sugar
1 cup ground walnuts
1/2 cup margarine or butter, softened
1/2 teaspoon ground cinnamon
2/3 cup red raspberry preserves

Heat oven to 375°. Mix all ingredients except preserves until crumbly. Press two-thirds of mixture in ungreased square pan, 9×9×2 inches. Spread with preserves. Sprinkle with remaining crumbs. Press gently into preserves.

Bake 20 to 25 minutes or until light golden brown. Cool completely.

Apricot Linzer Bars: *Substitute ground almonds for the ground walnuts and apricot preserves for the raspberry preserves.*

Tips for Bar Cookies

Use the pan size called for in the recipe. If you don't have the correct pan, choose a different type of cookie. Make sure that the cookie dough is spread to the sides and right into the corners of the pan. If you are not sure when the cookies are done, insert a toothpick into the center of the pan. If it comes out wet, they need more time. Let bar cookies cool completely in the pan unless the recipe directs otherwise.

Linzer Torte Bars

Coconut-Toffee Bars

Coconut-Toffee Bars

3 dozen bars

1/2 cup packed brown sugar
1/4 cup margarine or butter, softened
1/4 cup shortening
1 cup all-purpose flour*
Coconut-Almond Topping (below)

Heat oven to 350°. Mix brown sugar, margarine and shortening. Stir in flour. Press in ungreased baking pan, 13×9×2 inches. Bake 10 minutes.

Spread Coconut-Almond Topping over baked layer.

Bake until golden brown, about 2 minutes. Cool slightly; cut into bars, about 3×1 inch.

COCONUT-ALMOND TOPPING

2 eggs
1 cup packed brown sugar
1 cup shredded coconut
1 cup chopped almonds
2 tablespoons all-purpose flour
1 teaspoon baking powder
1 teaspoon vanilla
1/2 teaspoon salt

Beat eggs; stir in remaining ingredients.

If using self-rising flour, omit baking powder and salt from topping.

Chocolate Chip Bars

3 dozen bars

1/2 cup granulated sugar
1/3 cup packed brown sugar
1/2 cup margarine or butter, softened
1 teaspoon vanilla
1 egg
1 1/4 cups all-purpose flour
1/2 teaspoon baking soda
1/2 teaspoon salt
1/2 cup chopped nuts
1 package (6 ounces) semisweet chocolate
   chips

Heat oven to 375°. Grease and flour baking pan, 13×9×2 inches. Mix sugars, margarine and vanilla. Beat in egg. Stir in flour, baking soda and salt. Mix in nuts and chocolate chips. Spread dough in pan.

Bake until light brown, 12 to 14 minutes. Cool; cut into bars, about 2×1/2 inches.

Peanut Butter–Chocolate Chip Bars: *Decrease margarine to 1/4 cup and mix in 1/3 cup peanut butter. Beat in 2 tablespoons water with the egg. Use 1/2 cup chopped peanuts. Bake 22 to 25 minutes.*

Quick Praline Bars

About 4 dozen bars

24 graham cracker squares
1/2 cup packed brown sugar
1/2 cup (1 stick) margarine or butter
1/2 teaspoon vanilla
1/2 cup chopped pecans

Heat oven to 350°. Arrange graham crackers in single layer in ungreased jelly roll pan, 15 1/2 ×10 1/2×1 inch. Heat brown sugar and margarine to boiling. Boil and stir 1 minute; remove from heat. Stir in vanilla. Pour over crackers; spread evenly. Sprinkle with pecans.

Bake 8 to 10 minutes or until bubbly. Cool slightly. Cut into 2 1/4×1 1/4-inch bars.

TIP

Cookies are best baked on a rack in the center of the oven. If two cookie sheets are in the oven at the same time (placed on one oven rack in the upper third and one oven rack in the lower third of the oven), switch their positions halfway through baking time.

Pecan Pie Squares

About 5 dozen squares

3 cups all-purpose flour
1/3 cup sugar
3/4 cup margarine or butter, softened
1/2 teaspoon salt
Filling (below)

Heat oven to 350°. Grease jelly roll pan, 15 1/2 ×10 1/2×1 inch. Beat flour, sugar, margarine and salt in large bowl on low speed until crumbly. (Mixture will be dry.) Press firmly in pan. Bake about 20 minutes or until light golden brown.

Prepare Filling and pour over baked layer; spread evenly.

Bake about 25 minutes or until filling is set. Cool completely.

FILLING
1 1/2 cups sugar
1 1/2 cups corn syrup
3 tablespoons margarine or butter, melted
1 1/2 teaspoons vanilla
4 eggs, slightly beaten
2 1/2 cups chopped pecans

Mix all ingredients except pecans in large bowl until well blended. Stir in pecans.

Cashew Triangles

About 2 dozen cookies

You can cut these cookies into squares or bars. We think the triangles add a unique look!

1/2 cup (1 stick) margarine or butter, softened
1/4 cup granulated sugar
1/4 cup packed brown sugar
1/2 teaspoon vanilla
1 egg, separated
1 cup all-purpose flour
1/8 teaspoon salt
1 teaspoon water
1 cup chopped salted cashews, macadamia nuts or toasted almonds
1 ounce unsweetened chocolate, melted and cooled

Heat oven to 350°. Mix margarine, sugars, vanilla and egg yolk in medium bowl. Stir in flour and salt. Press dough in ungreased rectangular pan, 13×9×2 inches, with floured hands. Beat egg white and water; brush over dough. Sprinkle with cashews; press lightly into dough.

Bake about 25 minutes or until light brown; cool 10 minutes. Cut into 3-inch squares. Cut each square diagonally in half. Immediately remove from pan; cool. Drizzle with chocolate. Let stand about 2 hours or until chocolate is set.

Brownies

3 dozen brownies

(photograph on page 162)

4 squares (1 ounce *each*) unsweetened
    chocolate
2/3 cup shortening
2 cups sugar
4 eggs
1 teaspoon vanilla
1 1/4 cups all-purpose flour*
1 cup chopped nuts, if desired
1 teaspoon baking powder
1 teaspoon salt
Glossy Chocolate Frosting (right)

Heat oven to 350°. Grease baking pan,
13×9×2 inches. Heat chocolate and shortening in 3-quart saucepan over low heat until
melted; remove from heat. Stir in sugar, eggs
and vanilla. Mix in remaining ingredients.
Spread in pan.

Bake until brownies begin to pull away
from side of pan, about 30 minutes. (Do not
overbake.) Cool slightly; spread with Glossy
Chocolate Frosting (right), if desired. Cool
completely; cut into bars, about 2×1 1/2
inches.

GLOSSY CHOCOLATE FROSTING

3 squares (1 ounce *each*) unsweetened
    chocolate
3 tablespoons shortening
2 cups powdered sugar
1/4 teaspoon salt
1/3 cup milk
1 teaspoon vanilla
1/2 cup finely chopped nuts, if desired

Heat chocolate and shortening over low heat
until melted. Stir in powdered sugar, salt,
milk and vanilla; beat until smooth. Place pan
of frosting in bowl of ice and water; continue
beating until smooth and of spreading consistency. Stir in nuts.

*If using self-rising flour, omit baking powder and
salt.*

Raspberry Marbled Brownies

About 5 dozen brownies

Cream Cheese Filling (right)
1 cup (2 sticks) margarine or butter
4 ounces unsweetened chocolate
2 cups sugar
2 teaspoons vanilla
4 eggs
1 1/2 cups all-purpose flour
1/2 teaspoon salt
1 cup coarsely chopped nuts, if desired
1/2 cup raspberry jam or preserves

Heat oven to 350°. Grease rectangular pan, 13×9×2 inches. Prepare Cream Cheese Filling. Heat margarine and chocolate over low heat, stirring occasionally, until melted; cool. Beat chocolate mixture, sugar, vanilla and eggs in medium bowl on medium speed 1 minute, scraping bowl occasionally. Beat in flour and salt on low speed 30 seconds, scraping bowl occasionally. Beat on medium speed 1 minute. Stir in nuts.

Spread half of the batter in pan. Spread with filling. Gently spread remaining batter over filling. Drop jam by scant teaspoonfuls randomly over batter. Gently swirl through batter, filling and jam with spoon in an over-and-under motion for marbled effect.

Bake 60 to 70 minutes or until toothpick inserted in center comes out clean; cool. Cut into about 1 1/2×1-inch bars.

CREAM CHEESE FILLING

1/2 cup sugar
1 teaspoon ground cinnamon
1 1/2 teaspoons vanilla
1 egg
2 packages (8 ounces *each*) cream cheese, softened

Beat all ingredients in small bowl on medium speed 2 minutes, scraping bowl occasionally.

Unbelievable Brownies

For brownies you can't wait to sink your teeth into, try these simple tricks.

1. Use a shiny metal or glass pan. Nonstick-coated pans cause brownies to be soggy and low in volume.

2. Line your pan with aluminum foil when making brownies. The cooled brownies lift right out, are easily cut into uniform squares, and there's no pan to wash!

3. To prevent crumbling, cut brownies when completely cool unless the recipe specifies otherwise.

Fruit-Filled Brownies

About 3 dozen brownies

Use your favorite flavor of preserves or spreadable fruit to personalize these brownies.

2/3 cup shortening
4 squares (1 ounce each) unsweetened chocolate
2 cups sugar
4 eggs
1 1/2 cups all-purpose flour
1 teaspoon baking powder
1 teaspoon salt
Apricot or peach preserves or orange marmalade
Quick Chocolate Frosting (right)

Heat oven to 350°. Line jelly roll pan, 15 1/2 ×10 1/2×1 inch, with aluminum foil; grease. Heat shortening and chocolate in 3-quart saucepan over low heat, stirring constantly, until melted. Remove from heat; beat in sugar and eggs until smooth. Stir in flour, baking powder and salt. Spread in pan.

Bake until slight indentation remains when touched, about 20 minutes; cool.

Remove brownies from pan; remove aluminum foil. Cut 1/4-inch strip from each long side of brownies; cut 3/4-inch strip from each end. Discard strips. Cut remaining piece crosswise into halves. Spread 1 half with preserves; top with remaining half. Spread top with Quick Chocolate Frosting. Cut into bars, about 2×1 inch.

QUICK CHOCOLATE FROSTING

1 bar (4 ounces) sweet cooking chocolate

Heat chocolate over low heat, stirring constantly, until melted.

TIP

Cut thoroughly cooled brownies with a plastic knife or table knife for smooth-sided bars.

Cocoa Brownies

About 1 1/2 dozen brownies

This is the one for all those people who like cakelike, tender brownies.

1 cup sugar
1/2 cup shortening
1 teaspoon vanilla
2 eggs
2/3 cup all-purpose flour
1/2 cup cocoa
1/2 teaspoon baking powder
1/4 teaspoon salt
1/2 cup chopped walnuts, if desired

Heat oven to 350°. Grease square pan, 9×9×2 inches. Mix sugar, shortening, vanilla and eggs in large bowl. Stir in remaining ingredients except nuts. Stir in nuts. Spread batter in pan.

Bake 20 to 25 minutes or until toothpick inserted in center comes out clean. Cool completely.

Turtle Brownies: *Omit walnuts. Sprinkle 1/2 cup coarsely chopped pecans over batter before baking. Bake as directed. Heat 12 vanilla caramels and 1 tablespoon milk over low heat, stirring frequently, until caramels are melted. Drizzle over warm brownies. Cool completely.*

Turtle Brownies

Amaretto Brownies

About 2 1/2 dozen brownies

For the sophisticated brownie lover!

2/3 cup blanched almonds, toasted
8 ounces semisweet chocolate
1/3 cup margarine or butter
1 1/4 cups all-purpose flour
1 cup sugar
2 tablespoons amaretto or 1 teaspoon almond extract
1 teaspoon baking powder
1/2 teaspoon salt
2 eggs
Amaretto Frosting (below)

Heat oven to 350°. Grease rectangular pan, 13×9×2 inches. Place 1/3 cup of the almonds in food processor. Cover and process, using quick on-and-off motions, until almonds are ground. Chop remaining almonds; reserve. Heat chocolate and margarine in 3-quart saucepan over low heat, stirring frequently, until melted; remove from heat. Stir in ground almonds and remaining ingredients except Amaretto Frosting and chopped almonds. Spread batter in pan.

Bake 22 to 27 minutes or until toothpick inserted in center comes out clean. Cool completely. Prepare Amaretto Frosting and spread on brownies; sprinkle with reserved chopped almonds.

AMARETTO FROSTING

2 cups powdered sugar
3 tablespoons margarine or butter, softened
1 tablespoon amaretto or 1/4 teaspoon almond extract
1 to 2 tablespoons milk

Mix all ingredients until smooth.

Oatmeal Brownies

4 dozen brownies

2 1/2 cups quick-cooking or regular oats
3/4 cup all-purpose flour
3/4 cup packed brown sugar
1/2 teaspoon baking soda
3/4 cup margarine or butter, melted
Brownies (page 157)

Heat oven to 350°. Grease baking pan, 13×9×2 inches. Mix oats, flour, brown sugar and baking soda; stir in margarine. Reserve 3/4 cup of the oatmeal mixture. Press remaining oatmeal mixture in pan. Bake 10 minutes; cool 5 minutes.

Prepare Brownies as directed—except omit nuts. Spread dough over baked layer. Sprinkle with reserved oatmeal mixture.

Bake until brownies begin to pull away from sides of pan, about 35 minutes. (Do not overbake.) Cool; cut into about 1 1/2-inch squares.

Brownies (page 157), Oatmeal Brownies

German Chocolate Brownies

About 2 1/2 dozen brownies

2 bars (4 ounces *each*) sweet cooking
   chocolate
1/2 cup margarine or butter
1 1/2 cups all-purpose flour
1 cup sugar
1/2 teaspoon baking powder
1/2 teaspoon vanilla
1/4 teaspoon salt
2 eggs
Coconut-Pecan Frosting (below)

Heat oven to 350°. Grease rectangular pan, 13×9×2 inches. Heat chocolate and margarine in 3-quart saucepan over low heat, stirring frequently, until melted; remove from heat. Stir in remaining ingredients except Coconut-Pecan Frosting. Spread batter in pan.

Bake 20 to 25 minutes or until toothpick inserted in center comes out clean. Cool completely. Prepare Coconut-Pecan Frosting and spread on brownies.

COCONUT-PECAN FROSTING

1/2 cup sugar
1/4 margarine or butter
1/3 cup evaporated milk
1/2 teaspoon vanilla
2 egg yolks
1 cup flaked coconut
2/3 cup chopped pecans

Mix sugar, margarine, milk, vanilla and egg yolks in 1 1/2-quart saucepan. (Margarine will remain lumpy.) Cook over medium heat about 12 minutes, stirring frequently, until thick. Stir in coconut and pecans. Beat until of spreading consistency.

Main and Side Dishes

Rustic Pizza Pie (page 172)

Continued on next page

Basic Pizza Dough

Everyone loves pizza! This dough is great for Classic Four Seasons Pizza (page 170) or to make pizza with your favorite toppings.

ONE CRUST

1 package active dry yeast
1/2 cup warm water (105° to 115°)
1 1/4 to 1 1/2 cups all purpose flour*
1 teaspoon olive oil
1/2 teaspoon salt
1/4 teaspoon sugar

TWO CRUSTS

2 packages active dry yeast
1 cup warm water (105° to 115°)
2 1/3 to 2 2/3 cups all-purpose flour*
2 teaspoons olive oil
1 teaspoon salt
1/2 teaspoon sugar

THREE CRUSTS

2 packages active dry yeast
1 1/2 cups warm water (105° to 115°)
3 3/4 to 4 cups all-purpose flour*
1 tablespoon olive oil
1 teaspoon salt
1/2 teaspoon sugar

Dissolve yeast in warm water in large bowl. Stir in half of the flour, the oil, salt and sugar. Stir in enough of the remaining flour to make dough easy to handle. Turn dough onto lightly floured surface; knead about 10 minutes or until smooth and elastic. Place in greased bowl; turn greased side up. Cover and let rise in warm place for 20 minutes.

Punch down dough. Cover and refrigerate for at least 2 hours but no longer than 48 hours. (Punch down dough as necessary.)

*If using self-rising flour, omit salt. One cup whole wheat flour can be substituted for 1 cup of the all-purpose flour if desired.

> **TIP**
>
> *One pizza too many? Wrap the partially baked extra pizza, label and freeze no longer than two months. Heat oven to 375°. Bake a thin-crust pizza on a greased cookie sheet uncovered about 25 minutes and a thick-crust pizza about 55 minutes.*

Cheese Pizza

2 pizzas

Pizza Crust (below)
1 can (8 ounces) pizza sauce
**1 can (4 ounces) sliced mushrooms or
   chopped green chiles, drained**
**3 cups shredded mozzarella, Cheddar or
   Monterey Jack cheese (12 ounces)**
1/4 cup grated Parmesan or Romano cheese

Prepare Pizza Crust. Spread pizza sauce over partially baked crusts. Sprinkle with mushrooms and cheeses.

Bake pizzas at 425° about 10 minutes, until cheese is melted and pizzas are bubbly.

Meat Pizza: *Cook 1 pound ground beef, bulk Italian sausage or ground turkey, 1 teaspoon Italian seasoning and 2 cloves garlic, finely chopped, in 10-inch medium skillet over medium heat, stirring occasionally, until beef is brown; drain. Sprinkle beef mixture over pizza sauce. Decrease mozzarella cheese to 2 cups.*

Pizza Crust

1 package regular or quick active dry yeast
1 cup warm water (105° to 115°)
2 1/2 cups all-purpose flour*
2 tablespoons olive or vegetable oil
1/2 teaspoon salt
Olive or vegetable oil
Cornmeal

Dissolve yeast in warm water in medium bowl. Stir in flour, 2 tablespoons oil and the salt. Beat vigorously 20 strokes. Cover and let rest 20 minutes. Move oven rack to lowest position.

Heat oven to 425°. Grease 2 cookie sheets or 12-inch pizza pans with oil. Sprinkle with cornmeal. Divide dough in half; pat each half onto 11-inch circle on cookie sheet with floured fingers. Prick dough thoroughly with fork. Bake about 10 minutes or until crust just begins to brown.

*If using self-rising flour, omit salt. One cup whole wheat flour can be substituted for 1 cup of the all-purpose flour, if desired.

Simple Pizza Sauce

About 3 cups sauce

**2 cans (28 ounces each) imported pear-
   shaped tomatoes, drained**
1 tablespoon chopped fresh basil
1 1/2 teaspoons dried oregano
1 teaspoon freshly grated Romano cheese
2 teaspoons extra-virgin olive oil
1/4 teaspoon salt
1/4 teaspoon pepper
4 cloves garlic

Place all ingredients in food processor or blender; cover and process until smooth. Use immediately or cover and refrigerate sauce up to 48 hours. Freeze up to 2 months. Thaw in refrigerator before using.

Triple Cheese Pesto Pita Pizzas

Triple Cheese Pesto Pita Pizzas

6 servings

1 package (8 ounces) cream cheese,
    softened
2 tablespoons milk
6 whole wheat or white pita breads (6 inches
    in diameter)
6 tablespoons Pesto (right)
1 can (2 1/4 ounces) sliced ripe olives,
    drained
1 cup shredded mozzarella cheese
    (4 ounces)
2 tablespoons grated Parmesan cheese
2 tablespoons chopped fresh parsley

Heat oven to 425°. Mix cream cheese and milk until smooth. Place pita breads on ungreased large cookie sheet. Spread cream cheese mixture on pita breads to within 1/4 inch of edge. Carefully spread pesto over cream cheese. Top with olives. Sprinkle with cheeses and parsley.

Bake 7 to 12 minutes or until thoroughly heated and cheese is melted.

PESTO

2 cups firmly packed fresh basil leaves
3/4 cup grated Parmesan cheese
3/4 cup olive or vegetable oil
1/4 cup pine nuts
3 cloves garlic

Place all ingredients in blender or food processor. Cover and blend on medium speed about 3 minutes, stopping occasionally to scrape sides, until smooth. Toss with hot cooked pasta, if desired.

Classic Four-Seasons Pizza

2 servings

The Classic Four-Seasons Pizza is an edible display of the year's seasons, with spring represented by fresh basil and chunks of tomato, summer by capers and anchovies, fall by cheese and winter by prosciutto, one of the more nourishing foods available in winter.

Basic Pizza Dough for One Crust (page 167)
1/2 cup Simple Pizza Sauce (page 168)
1 cup shredded mozzarella cheese
    (4 ounces)
1/3 cup shredded provolone cheese
    (about 1 1/2 ounces)
1/3 cup chopped prosciutto or fully cooked
    Virginia ham (about 2 ounces)
1/4 cup chopped fresh basil
2 teaspoons large capers, drained
4 marinated artichoke hearts, cut into
    fourths
4 flat fillets of anchovy in oil
3 fresh pear-shaped tomatoes, peeled
    and chopped*
1 teaspoon olive oil
12 imported Italian black olives, pitted

Prepare Basic Pizza Dough for One Crust and Simple Pizza Sauce.

Place oven rack in lowest position of oven. Heat oven to 500°. Press or roll dough into 12-inch circle on lightly floured surface. Place on ungreased pizza screen or in 12-inch perforated pizza pan. Press dough from center to edge so edge is thicker than center. Spread pizza sauce over dough to within 1/2 inch of edge. Mix cheeses; sprinkle over sauce. Place prosciutto, basil, capers, artichoke hearts, fillets of anchovy and tomatoes on cheese; drizzle with oil. Place olives on top.

Bake 8 to 10 minutes or until crust is golden and cheeses are melted.

*3 canned imported pear-shaped tomatoes, drained, can be substituted for the fresh tomatoes.

Classic Four-Seasons Pizza

Chunky Vegetable Pizza with Cornmeal Crust

1 pizza, 6 slices

Cornmeal Crust (below)
2 tablespoons olive or vegetable oil
1 clove garlic, finely chopped
1 teaspoon dried basil leaves
1 package (16 ounces) frozen broccoli, red bell peppers, onions and mushrooms, thawed
2 cups shredded mozzarella cheese (8 ounces)

Heat oven to 425°. Prepare Cornmeal Crust. Mix oil, garlic and basil. Sprinkle vegetables over partially baked crust. Sprinkle with cheese. Drizzle with oil mixture.

Bake 15 to 20 minutes or until cheese is melted and vegetables are hot.

CORNMEAL CRUST

2 1/3 cups water
1 cup yellow cornmeal
1 tablespoon margarine or butter
1/4 teaspoon salt
1/8 teaspoon ground red pepper (cayenne)

Heat oven to 425°. Grease 12-inch pizza pan with shortening. Heat water to boiling in 2-quart saucepan. Stir in remaining ingredients with wire whisk until mixture is smooth and thickens. Spoon onto pizza pan and spread evenly, mounding edge slightly.

Bake 5 to 7 minutes or until set and light brown.

Rustic Pizza Pie

2 pizzas

Rustic Pizza Pies, or focaccias, come from rural southern Italy. Focaccias are baked at a moderate heat to allow the ingredients inside to cook evenly, unlike pizza, which is cooked quickly at a high temperature. (photograph on page 164)

Basic Pizza Dough for Two Crusts (page 167)
1 cup Simple Pizza Sauce (page 168)
1/2 pound bulk Italian sausage, cooked and drained.
1 cup shredded mozzarella cheese (4 ounces)
1/2 cup shredded provolone cheese (2 ounces)
1/2 cup sliced fresh mushrooms
1/2 cup chopped Genoa salami (about 3 ounces)
1 medium onion, sliced
1 cup chopped fresh basil
1 tablespoon extra-virgin olive oil
1 egg, beaten

Prepare Basic Pizza Dough and Simple Pizza Sauce. Heat oven to 425°. Grease pie plate, 10×1 1/2 inches. Divide dough in half. Press or roll one half into 13-inch circle on lightly floured surface; place in pie plate. Sprinkle sausage over dough in pie plate. Mix cheeses; sprinkle over sausage. Top with Simple Pizza Sauce, mushrooms, salami, onion and basil; drizzle with oil.

Press or roll remaining dough into 11-inch circle on lightly floured surface; place over filling. Pinch edges of dough together to seal; roll edge of dough up, forming a rim. Prick top of dough thoroughly with fork; brush with egg.

Bake about 30 minutes or until golden brown. serve hot or cold.

Classic Cheese Soufflé

4 servings

Serve this fluffy soufflé with asparagus spears, sliced ham, whole-grain bread and fresh fruit for a delicious meal.

1/4 cup margarine or butter
1/4 cup all-purpose flour
1/2 teaspoon salt
1/4 teaspoon ground mustard (dry)
Dash of ground red pepper (cayenne)
1 cup milk
1 cup shredded Cheddar cheese (4 ounces)
3 eggs, separated
1/4 teaspoon cream of tartar

Heat oven to 350°. Butter 1-quart soufflé dish or casserole. Make a 4-inch band of triple-thickness aluminum foil 2 inches longer than circumference of dish. Butter one side of foil. Secure foil band, buttered side in, around top edge of dish.

Melt margarine in 2 quart saucepan over medium heat. Stir in flour, salt, mustard and red pepper. Cook over medium heat, stirring constantly, until smooth and bubbly; remove from heat. Stir in milk. Heat to boiling, stirring constantly. Boil and stir 1 minute. Stir in cheese until melted; remove from heat.

Beat egg whites and cream of tartar in medium bowl with electric mixer on high speed until stiff but not dry. Beat egg yolks on high speed about 3 minutes or until very thick and lemon colored; stir into cheese mixture. Stir about one-fourth of the egg whites into cheese mixture. Fold cheese mixture into remaining egg white. *Carefully* pour into soufflé dish.

Bake 50 or 60 minutes or until knife inserted halfway between center and edge comes out clean. *Carefully* remove foil band and *quickly* divide soufflé into sections with 2 forks. Serve immediately.

Classic Shrimp Soufflé: *Omit mustard, red pepper and cheese. Add 1 can (4 to 4 1/2 ounces) shrimp, rinsed and drained, and 1 tablespoon chopped fresh or 1 teaspoon dried tarragon to sauce before adding the beaten egg yolks.*

Cooking with Cheese

- Four ounces of shredded, crumbled or grated cheese equals 1 cup.

- Keep cooking temperature low and the cooking time short. High heat and overcooking cause cheese to become stringy and tough.

- When adding cheese to other ingredients, cut it into small pieces so it melts evenly and quickly.

- Cheeses with similar flavors and textures can be used interchangeably.

- Cheese microwaves well, but lower power settings work best for the most even heating. Soften cream cheese by removing foil wrapper and microwaving uncovered on medium (50 percent) until softened, a 3-ounce package for 30 to 45 seconds and an 8-ounce package 60 to 90 seconds.

Onion Soufflé with Asparagus

4 servings

1/2 cup olive oil

2 tablespoons butter

1 pound pearl onions, peeled and cut in half

1 package (10 ounces) frozen asparagus spears*

2 flat anchovy fillets in oil, drained

1/2 cup all-purpose flour

1/2 cup freshly grated Parmesan cheese

1 tablespoon chopped fresh tarragon

1 teaspoon freshly grated nutmeg

1 teaspoon salt

1/2 teaspoon pepper

4 eggs, separated

Heat oven to 375°. Butter 6-cup soufflé dish. Heat oil and butter in 10-inch skillet over medium-high heat. Sauté onions in oil mixture, gently mashing, until soft; cool.

Cook asparagus as directed on package; drain well. Sprinkle flour over asparagus; toss until coated. Remove asparagus from flour, shaking off excess.

Place asparagus, onions and fillets of anchovy in food processor or in blender; cover and process until smooth. Mix asparagus mixture and remaining ingredients except egg whites thoroughly.

Beat egg whites in large bowl on high speed until stiff but not dry. Fold asparagus mixture into egg whites. Carefully pour into soufflé dish.

Bake uncovered 30 to 40 minutes or until knife inserted halfway between center and edge comes out clean.

*1 1/2 pounds cooked fresh asparagus spears can be substituted for the frozen asparagus spears.

TIP

Soufflés stay fluffy and are easiest to serve when two forks or a fork and spoon are used to divide the servings.

Cheese Strata

6 servings

1/3 cup margarine or butter, softened
1/2 teaspoon ground mustard (dry)
1 clove garlic, crushed
10 slices white bread, crusts removed
2 cups shredded sharp Cheddar cheese
    (8 ounces)
2 tablespoons chopped parsley
2 tablespoons chopped onion
1 teaspoon salt
1/2 teaspoon Worcestershire sauce
1/8 teaspoon pepper
Dash of ground red pepper (cayenne)
4 eggs
2 1/2 cups milk

Mix margarine, mustard and garlic. Spread evenly over each slice bread. Cut each slice into thirds. Line bottom and sides of ungreased square baking dish, 8×8×2 inches, with half of the bread slices, buttered sides down, cutting to fit.

Mix cheese, parsley, onion, salt, Worcestershire sauce, pepper and red pepper. Spread evenly over bread slices in dish. Top with remaining bread slices, buttered sides up.

Beat eggs in medium bowl. Stir in milk. Pour over bread. Cover and refrigerate at least 2 hours but no longer than 24 hours.

Heat oven to 325°. Bake uncovered about 1 1/4 hour or until knife inserted in center comes out clean. Let stand 10 minutes before cutting.

TIP

To save time, use finely chopped garlic from a jar, and don't remove the crusts from the bread. Purchase the cheese already shredded in an 8-ounce package.

Vegetable Frittata

4 servings

Frittatas are Italian omelets that have the ingredients stirred into the egg before cooking rather than being folded inside after the eggs are set.

1 tablespoon vegetable oil
1 cup broccoli flowerets
1 medium carrot, shredded (1/2 cup)
1 medium onion, chopped (1/2 cup)
1/4 cup sliced ripe olives
4 large eggs
1/4 cup milk
1 tablespoon chopped parsley
1/4 teaspoon salt
1/4 teaspoon pepper sauce
1 cup shredded Cheddar cheese (4 ounces)
1 tablespoon grated Parmesan cheese

Heat oil in 10-inch skillet over medium-high heat. Cook broccoli, carrot, onion, and olives in oil about 5 minutes, stirring frequently, until vegetables are crisp-tender.

Meanwhile beat eggs, milk, parsley, salt and pepper sauce thoroughly with fork or wire whisk until a uniform yellow color. Pour egg mixture over vegetables. sprinkle with cheese, reduce heat to low.

Cover and cook about 10 minutes or until set in center. Cut into 4 wedges. Serve immediately.

TIP

Substitute 2 cups broccoli slaw for the broccoli flowerets and carrot. Pick up chopped onion and sliced ripe olives at the salad bar of your supermarket.

Quiche Lorraine

6 servings

Pastry for 9-inch One-Crust Pie (right)
8 slices bacon, crisply cooked and crumbled
1 cup shredded natural Swiss cheese
    (4 ounces)
1/3 cup finely chopped onion
4 large eggs
2 cups whipping (heavy) cream
1/4 teaspoon salt
1/4 teaspoon pepper
1/8 teaspoon ground red pepper (cayenne)

Heat oven to 425°. Prepare pastry. Ease into quiche dish, 9×1 1/2 inches, or pie plate, 9×1 1/4 inches. Sprinkle bacon, cheese and onion in pastry-lined quiche dish. Beat eggs slightly; beat in remaining ingredients. Pour into quiche dish.

Bake 15 minutes. Reduce oven temperature to 300°. Bake about 30 minutes longer or until knife inserted in center comes out clean. Let stand 10 minutes before cutting.

Mushroom Quiche: *Add 1 can (4 ounces) mushroom stems and pieces, drained, and 1 jar (2 ounces) diced pimientos, well drained, with the bacon.*

Seafood Quiche: *Substitute 1 cup chopped cooked crabmeat, shrimp, seafood sticks or salmon for the bacon and green onion for the onion. (Pat crabmeat dry.) Increase salt to 1/2 teaspoon.*

9-INCH ONE-CRUST PIE

1/3 cup plus 1 tablespoon shortening or
    1/3 cup lard
1 cup all-purpose* or unbleached flour
1/4 teaspoon salt
2 to 3 tablespoons cold water

Cut shortening into flour and salt, using pastry blender or crisscrossing 2 knives, until particles are size of coarse crumbs. Sprinkle with cold water, 1 tablespoon at a time, tossing with fork until all flour is moistened and pastry almost cleans side of bowl (1 to 2 teaspoons more water can be added if necessary).

Gather pastry into a ball. Shape into flattened round on lightly floured cloth-covered board.

Roll pastry into circle 2 inches larger than upside-down pie plate, 9×1 1/4 inches, or 2 inches larger than 10- or 11-inch tart pan, with floured cloth covered rolling pin. Fold pastry into fourths; place in pie plate. Unfold and ease into plate, pressing firmly against bottom and side. Trim overhanging edge of pastry.

*If using self-rising flour, omit salt. Pie crusts made with self-rising flour differ in flavor and texture from those made with all-purpose flour.

Quiche Lorraine

Supper Popover

6 servings

1 pound ground beef
1 can (15 ounces) tomato sauce
1/4 cup chopped green pepper
2 tablespoons all-purpose flour*
1/2 teaspoon salt
1/2 teaspoon pepper
1 teaspoon parsley flakes
2 cups shredded Cheddar cheese (about
    8 ounces)
2 eggs
1 cup milk
1 tablespoon vegetable oil
1 cup all-purpose flour*
1/2 teaspoon salt
2 tablespoons chopped green onions

Heat oven to 425°. Cook and stir ground beef in 10-inch skillet until brown; drain. Stir in tomato sauce, green pepper, 2 tablespoons flour, 1/2 teaspoon salt, the pepper and parsley. Heat to boiling. Boil and stir 1 minute. Pour into ungreased baking pan, 13×9×2 inches. Sprinkle cheese on top.

Beat eggs, milk, oil, 1 cup flour and 1/2 teaspoon salt with hand beater; pour over cheese. Sprinkle with onions.

Bake until puffy and golden brown, 25 to 30 minutes. Serve immediately.

Do not use self-rising flour in this recipe.

Wild Mushroom Pie

6 servings

2 cups all-purpose flour
3/4 cup butter, softened
1 jumbo egg
2 tablespoons butter
1 small onion, thinly sliced
2 cups sliced fresh mushrooms
2 cups sliced porcini mushrooms
1 cup whole morel mushrooms
1 cup Marsala or dry red wine
1 1/4 cups whipping (heavy) cream
1/2 teaspoon salt
1/4 teaspoon pepper
1 1/2 cups ricotta cheese
1 cup shredded Fontina cheese (4 ounces)
1/2 cup freshly grated Parmesan cheese

Mix flour, 3/4 cup butter and the egg in large bowl until dough forms. Turn dough onto lightly floured surface. Knead lightly 1 or 2 minutes or until smooth. Cover and refrigerate 30 minutes.

Heat 2 tablespoons butter in 10-inch skillet over medium-high heat. Sauté onion in butter. Reduce heat to medium; stir in mushrooms. Cook uncovered 5 minutes. Stir in wine; cook until wine is evaporated. Stir in whipping cream; sprinkle with salt and pepper. Heat to boiling over medium heat; reduce heat. Cover and simmer 10 minutes; cool.

Move oven rack to lowest position. Heat oven to 350°. Roll dough into 14-inch circle. Ease dough into pie plate, 10×1 1/2 inches, pressing firmly against bottom and side. Mix mushroom mixture and cheeses. Spoon into pie plate; spread to make even. Trim excess dough from edge of plate. Bake 35 to 40 minutes or until set and crust is golden brown. Cool 10 to 15 minutes before cutting.

Wild Mushroom Pie

Spinach Phyllo Pie

Spinach Phyllo Pie

6 servings

1 tablespoon olive or vegetable oil
1 medium onion, chopped (1/2 cup)
1 medium red bell pepper, chopped (1 cup)
1 clove garlic, finely chopped
2 packages (9 ounces *each*) frozen chopped
    spinach, thawed and squeezed to drain
1 package (8 ounces) cream cheese, softened
1/2 cup crumbled feta or Gorgonzola
    cheese (2 ounces)
2 large eggs
1 tablespoon chopped fresh or 1 teaspoon
    dried dill weed
1/2 teaspoon salt
1/4 teaspoon pepper
8 sheets frozen phyllo (18×14 inches), thawed
2 tablespoons stick margarine or butter,
    melted*

Heat oven to 375°. Grease bottom and side of pie plate, 9×1 1/4 inches with margarine. Heat oil in 10-inch skillet over medium-high heat. Cook onion, bell pepper and garlic in oil, stirring frequently, until vegetables are crisp-tender; remove from heat. Stir in spinach, cream cheese, feta cheese, eggs, dill weed, salt and pepper.

Cut stack of phyllo sheets into 12-inch square; discard extra phyllo. Cover with waxed paper, then with damp towel to prevent them from drying out. Brush each of 4 phyllo squares with margarine and layer in pie plate. Gently press into pie plate, allowing corners to drape over edge.

Spread spinach mixture evenly over phyllo. Fold ends of phyllo up and over filling so corners overlap on top. Brush with margarine and layer remaining 4 phyllo sheets over pie, allowing corners to drape over edge.

Gently tuck phyllo draping over top inside edge of pie plate. Cut through top phyllo layers into 6 wedges, using sharp knife or scissors.

Bake 35 to 45 minutes or until crust is golden brown and filling is hot. Let stand 10 minutes before serving.

We do not recommend using vegetable oil spreads.

Fold ends of phyllo up and over filling so corners overlap on top. Brush with margarine and layer remaining 4 phyllo sheets over pie, allowing corners to drape over edge.

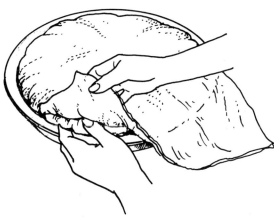

Carefully lift bottom layers of phyllo and tuck top corners between bottom layers and plate to seal.

Herbed Vegetable Bake

12 servings

This casserole can be prepared the day before. Cover and refrigerate, but plan to add 5 to 10 minutes to the cooking time.

1 small bunch broccoli (about 1 pound), cut
    into flowerets and 1-inch pieces
1 small head cauliflower (about
    1 1/4 pounds), cut into flowerets
5 or 6 carrots (about 1 pound), cut
    diagonally into 1/4-inch slices
1/3 cup margarine or butter, melted
Salt and pepper
1 tablespoon chopped fresh or 1 teaspoon
    dried basil leaves
1 tablespoon chopped fresh or 1 teaspoon
    dried tarragon leaves
2 cloves garlic, finely chopped
2 small onions, thinly sliced and separated
    into rings

Heat oven to 400°. Arrange broccoli along one long side of ungreased rectangular baking dish, 13×9×2 inches. Arrange cauliflower along other side of dish. Arrange carrots down center between broccoli and cauliflower. Drizzle with margarine. Sprinkle with salt, pepper, basil, tarragon and garlic. Arrange onions evenly over top.

Cover with aluminum foil and bake about 30 minutes or until vegetables are crisp-tender.

Three-Bean and Cornbread Casserole

8 servings

2 cans (21 ounces *each*) baked beans
2 cans (15 ounces *each*) kidney beans,
    drained
1 can (8 1/2 ounces) lima beans, drained
1 can (8 ounces) tomato sauce
1/4 cup catsup
2 tablespoons packed brown sugar
2 tablespoons instant minced onion
1/2 teaspoon dry mustard
1/2 teaspoon salt
1/4 teaspoon pepper
Cornbread Topping (below)

Heat oven to 425°. Mix all ingredients except Cornbread Topping; pour into ungreased baking dish, 13×9×2 inches. Prepare Cornbread Topping; spoon evenly over bean mixture to within 1 inch of edges.

Bake until topping is deep golden brown, 25 to 30 minutes.

CORNBREAD TOPPING

2/3 cup all-purpose flour*
1/3 cup yellow cornmeal
1/2 cup milk
2 tablespoons margarine or butter, softened
1 tablespoon sugar
1 teaspoon baking powder
1/2 teaspoon salt
1 egg

Beat all ingredients with hand beater until smooth.

If using self-rising flour, omit baking powder and salt.

Tamale Lentil Casserole

6 servings

1 tablespoon vegetable oil
1 large onion, chopped (1 cup)
1 medium green bell pepper, chopped
    (1 cup)
2 cloves garlic, finely chopped
3 cups water
1 1/4 cups dried lentils (10 ounces), sorted
    and rinsed
1 can (14 ounces) tomato sauce
1 package (1.25 ounces) taco seasoning mix
Cheese Cornbread Topping (below)

Heat oil in 3-quart saucepan over medium-high heat. Cook onion, bell pepper and garlic in oil, stirring frequently, until vegetables are tender. Stir in water, lentils, tomato sauce and seasoning mix; reduce heat to low. Partially cover and simmer 35 to 40 minutes or until lentils are tender.

Heat oven to 400°. Grease 2-quart casserole with shortening. Prepare Cheese Cornbread Topping. Spoon lentil mixture into casserole. Spread topping evenly over lentil mixture.

Bake uncovered 15 to 20 minutes until topping is golden brown.

CHEESE CORNBREAD TOPPING

1/2 cup shredded Cheddar cheese (2 ounces)
1/4 cup milk
1 package (8 1/2 ounces) cornbread muffin
    mix
1 can (8 1/2 ounces) cream-style corn
1 large egg

Mix all ingredients until moistened.

Three-Cheese Noodle Bake

8 servings

2 tablespoons margarine or butter
2 tablespoons all-purpose flour
1/2 teaspoon salt
1/8 teaspoon pepper
2 cups milk
1 cup shredded Fontina or mozzarella
    cheese (4 ounces)
1 cup shredded Gruyère or Swiss cheese
    (4 ounces)
1/2 cup grated Parmesan cheese
6 cups uncooked egg noodles (12 ounces)
3 tablespoons dry bread crumbs
1 tablespoon margarine or butter

Melt 2 tablespoons margarine in 2-quart saucepan over medium heat. Stir in flour, salt and pepper until blended. Cook, stirring constantly, until smooth and bubbly; remove from heat.

    Gradually stir in milk. Heat to boiling, stirring constantly. Boil and stir 1 minute. Stir in cheeses; keep warm over low heat.

    Heat oven to 350°. Meanwhile, cook and drain noodles as directed on package. Alternate layers of noodles and cheese mixture, ending with noodles, in ungreased 2-quart casserole.

    Heat bread crumbs and 1 tablespoon margarine over medium heat, stirring frequently, until crumbs are toasted. Sprinkle over noodles.

    Bake uncovered about 20 minutes or until hot and bubbly.

TIP

Use an 8-ounce package of a shredded cheese blend for the Fontina, Gruyère and Parmesan cheeses.

Macaroni and Cheese

5 servings

1 to 1 1/2 cups uncooked elbow macaroni
    (about 6 ounces)
1/4 cup (1/2 stick) margarine or butter
1/2 teaspoon salt
1/4 teaspoon pepper
1 small onion, chopped (about 1/4 cup)
1/4 cup all-purpose flour
1 3/4 cups milk
8 ounces process American loaf or sharp
    process American cheese loaf or process
    cheese spread loaf, cut into 1/2-inch
    cubes

Heat oven to 375°. Cook macaroni as directed on package; drain. Cook and stir margarine, salt, pepper, and onion in 2-quart saucepan over medium heat until onion is slightly tender. Stir in flour. Cook over low heat, stirring constantly until smooth and bubbly; remove from heat. Stir in milk. Heat to boiling, stirring constantly. Boil and stir 1 minute; remove from heat. Stir in cheese until melted. Mix macaroni and cheese sauce in ungreased 1/2-quart casserole. Bake uncovered 30 minutes.

Tomato Macaroni and Cheese: *Mix 1/4 cup sliced ripe olives into cheese sauce. Arrange 1 large tomato, cut into 5 slices, around edge of casserole before baking.*

Tuna-Macaroni Casserole

6 servings

1 package (7 ounces) elbow macaroni
    (2 cups)
2 cups grated Cheddar cheese (8 ounces)
1 medium onion, finely chopped (1/2 cup)
1 can (6 ounces) tuna, drained
1 can (10 3/4 ounces) condensed cream of
    mushroom or celery soup
1 soup can of milk

Heat oven 350°. Grease 2-quart casserole.

Cook and drain macaroni as directed on package.

Mix macaroni and remaining ingredients in casserole. Bake uncovered 30 to 40 minutes or until hot and bubbly.

Tuna-Broccoli Casserole

4 servings

1 1/2 cups uncooked small pasta shells
    (6 ounces)
1 package (10 ounces) frozen broccoli cuts,
    thawed
1 can (6 ounces) tuna, drained
1 can (10 3/4 ounces) condensed Cheddar
    cheese soup
1 soup can of milk
1 cup crushed potato chips

Heat oven to 350°.

Mix all ingredients except potato chips in casserole. Sprinkle with potato chips. Bake uncovered 30 to 40 minutes or until hot and bubbly.

Manicotti

7 servings

Try undercooking the manicotti shells by a few minutes—it will help prevent splitting when you fill them. The shells will cook completely when they are baked.

1 package (8 ounces) manicotti pasta shells
    (14 shells)
1 1/2 cups small curd creamed cottage
    cheese
1/4 cup grated Parmesan cheese
1/2 teaspoon salt
1/2 teaspoon garlic powder
1/8 teaspoon dried thyme leaves
2 eggs
1 small onion, chopped (about 1/4 cup)
1 package (10 ounces) frozen chopped
    spinach, thawed and squeezed to drain
1 can (8 ounces) tomato sauce
1 cup shredded mozzarella cheese
    (4 ounces)

Heat oven to 350°. Grease rectangular pan, 13×9×2 inches. Cook pasta shells as directed on package; drain. Mix remaining ingredients except tomato sauce and mozzarella cheese. Fill pasta shells with spinach mixture. Place in pan. Pour tomato sauce over shells. Sprinkle with mozzarella cheese. Cover and bake about 25 minutes or until hot and bubbly.

Overnight Lasagne

8 servings

Lasagne is an American favorite, always perfect for family meals, casual get-togethers and potluck suppers. While Americans use the word lasagne to mean a casserole made with lasagne noodles, cheese and tomato sauce, Italians use it to mean the wide noodles used in many kinds of Italian dishes.

1 pound ground beef
1 medium onion, chopped (about 1/2 cup)
1 clove garlic, crushed
1/3 cup chopped fresh or 2 tablespoons
     dried parsley leaves
1 tablespoon sugar
2 tablespoons chopped fresh or
     1 1/2 teaspoons dried basil leaves
1 teaspoon seasoned salt
1 can (16 ounces) whole tomatoes,
     undrained
1 can (10 3/4 ounces) condensed tomato
     soup
1 can (6 ounces) tomato paste
2 1/2 cups water
12 uncooked lasagne noodles (about
     12 ounces)
1 container (12 ounces) creamed cottage
     cheese
2 cups shredded mozzarella cheese
     (8 ounces)
1/4 cup grated Parmesan cheese

Cook and stir ground beef, onion and garlic in Dutch oven until beef is brown; drain. Stir in parsley, sugar, basil, seasoned salt, tomatoes, tomato soup, tomato paste and water; break up tomatoes. Heat to boiling, stirring occasionally; reduce heat. Simmer uncovered 20 minutes.

Spread 2 cups of the sauce mixture in ungreased rectangular baking dish, 13×9×2

inches. Top with 4 noodles. Spread half of the cottage cheese over noodles; spread with 2 cups of the sauce mixture. Sprinkle with 1 cup of the mozzarella cheese. Repeat with 4 noodles, the remaining cottage cheese, 2 cups of the sauce mixture and the remaining mozzarella cheese. Top with the remaining noodles and sauce mixture; sprinkle with Parmesan cheese. Cover and refrigerate up to 12 hours.

Heat oven to 350°. Bake covered 30 minutes. Uncover and bake until hot and bubbly, 30 to 40 minutes longer. Let stand 15 minutes before cutting.

Easy overnight lasagne: *Substitute 6 1/2 cups prepared spaghetti sauce for the parsley, sugar, basil, seasoned salt, canned tomatoes, tomato soup, tomato paste and water. Stir sauce into drained beef mixture. Do not simmer. Continue as directed.*

Pasta Casserole

8 servings

1 package (16 ounces) mostaccioli pasta
1 jar (26 to 30 ounces) spaghetti sauce
1 container (15 ounces) ricotta cheese
1 package (10 ounces) frozen chopped
     spinach, thawed and squeezed to drain
2 green onions, chopped
2 tablespoons sliced pimiento-stuffed olives
2 tablespoons grated Parmesan cheese
1 tablespoon chopped fresh parsley or
     1 teaspoon dried parsley flakes
1/8 teaspoon pepper

Heat oven to 375°. Cook pasta as directed on package; drain. Mix pasta and remaining ingredients. Spoon into ungreased rectangular baking dish, 13×9×2 inches. Cover and bake about 40 minutes or until hot and bubbly.

Lasagne Roll-ups

8 servings

6 uncooked dried lasagne noodles
6 uncooked dried spinach lasagne noodles
1 pound ground beef
1 large onion, chopped (about 1 cup)
1 jar (14 ounces) spaghetti sauce
1 can (8 ounces) mushroom stems and
    pieces, undrained
1 container (15 ounces) ricotta cheese or
    small curd creamed cottage cheese
    (about 2 cups)
1 package (10 ounces) frozen chopped
    spinach, thawed and squeezed to drain
1 cup shredded mozzarella cheese (4 ounces)
1/4 cup grated Parmesan cheese
1 teaspoon salt
1/4 teaspoon pepper
2 cloves garlic, crushed

Heat oven to 350°. Cook noodles as directed
on package; drain. Cover noodles with cold
water. Cook ground beef and onion in 10-
inch skillet, stirring occasionally, until beef is
brown; drain. Stir in spaghetti sauce and
mushrooms. Heat to boiling. Pour into rectangular baking dish. 11×7×1 1/2 inches.

Mix remaining ingredients. Drain noodles. Spread 3 tablespoons of the cheese mixture to edges of 1 noodle. Roll up; cut roll in
half to form 2 roll-ups. Place cut sides down in
beef mixture. Repeat with remaining noodles
and cheese mixture. Cover and bake about
30 minutes or until hot and bubbly. Serve with
grated Parmesan cheese, if desired.

Black Bean Lasagne

8 servings

9 uncooked lasagne noodles
1 tablespoon vegetable oil
1 medium onion, chopped (about 1/2 cup)
1 clove garlic, finely chopped
1 cup water
2 tablespoons chopped fresh cilantro
2 cans (15 ounces each) black beans, rinsed
    and drained
1 can (14 1/2 ounces) no-salt-added whole
    tomatoes, undrained
2 cans (6 ounces each) no-salt-added tomato
    paste
1 container (15 ounces) nonfat ricotta
    cheese
1/2 cup reduced-fat grated Parmesan-style
    cheese (2 ounces)
1/2 cup cholesterol-free egg product or
    4 egg whites
1/4 cup chopped fresh parsley
2 cups shredded reduced-fat Monterey Jack
    cheese (8 ounces)

Cook and drain noodles as directed on package. Rinse with hot water; drain. Heat oil in
12-inch nonstick skillet over medium-high
heat. Cook onion and garlic in oil, stirring
frequently, until onion is tender. Stir in water,
cilantro, beans, tomatoes and tomato paste,
breaking up tomatoes. Simmer uncovered 15
minutes, stirring occasionally. Mix remaining
ingredients except Monterey Jack cheese.

Heat oven to 350°. Layer 1/3 each of the
noodles, bean mixture, ricotta mixture and
Monterey Jack cheese in ungreased rectangular baking dish, 13×9×2 inches. Repeat
layers twice. Bake uncovered 30 to 35 minutes
or until hot and bubbly. Let stand 10 to 15
minutes before cutting.

Black Bean Lasagne

Chicken Jumbo Shells

4 servings

12 uncooked jumbo pasta shells
1 tablespoon olive or vegetable oil
2 medium tomatoes, seeded and chopped
    (about 1 1/2 cups)
1 medium stalk celery, thinly sliced
    (about 1/2 cup)
1 medium carrot, finely chopped
    (about 1/2 cup)
1 clove garlic, finely chopped
1 cup diced cooked chicken
1 tablespoon dry white wine or chicken
    broth
1 container (15 ounces) ricotta cheese
1 cup seasoned croutons
1 teaspoon chopped fresh parsley
1/4 teaspoon salt
1/4 teaspoon pepper

Cook pasta shells as directed on package; drain. Heat oven to 400°. Grease square pan, 8×8×2 inches. Heat oil in 10-inch skillet over medium-high heat. Cook tomatoes, celery, carrot and garlic in oil 5 to 7 minutes, stirring frequently, until celery and carrot are crisp-tender. Stir in chicken and wine. Cook 5 minutes until wine is evaporated.

Stir remaining ingredients into chicken mixture. Fill cooked shells with chicken mixture. Place filled sides up in pan. Bake uncovered about 10 minutes or until filling is golden brown.

Mexi Shells

6 servings

Jumbo pasta shells are a fun change of pace, especially when stuffed with the Mexican-inspired filling here.

18 uncooked jumbo pasta shells
4 cans (8 ounces each) no-salt-added
    tomato sauce
2 tablespoons all-purpose flour
1 teaspoon chile powder
2 teaspoons ground cumin
3/4 pound extra-lean ground beef
1 small onion, chopped (about 1/4 cup)
1 teaspoon ground cumin
1 tablespoon chopped fresh cilantro
1 can (4 ounces) chopped green chiles,
    drained
1 can (15 ounces) chile beans in sauce,
    undrained
1 cup shredded part-skim mozzarella cheese
    (4 ounces)

Heat oven to 350°. Cook and drain pasta shells as directed on package. While pasta is cooking, mix tomato sauce, flour, chile powder and 2 teaspoons cumin; reserve. Cook ground beef and onion in 2-quart saucepan over medium heat, stirring occasionally, until beef is brown; drain. Stir in 1 teaspoon cumin, the cilantro, green chiles and chile beans.

Pour 1 cup of the reserved tomato sauce mixture into ungreased rectangular baking dish, 13×9×2 inches. Spoon about 1 1/2 tablespoons beef mixture into each pasta shell. Place filled sides up on sauce in dish. Pour remaining tomato sauce mixture over shells. Sprinkle with cheese. Cover and bake 30 minutes. Let stand uncovered 10 minutes.

Pastitsio

8 servings

1 package (16 ounces) rigatoni pasta
1/2 pound extra-lean ground beef
1 medium onion, chopped (about 1/2 cup)
1/4 teaspoon salt
1/4 teaspoon ground allspice
1/4 teaspoon ground cinnamon
1/4 teaspoon ground nutmeg
1/2 cup dry white wine or water
1 can (6 ounces) no-salt-added tomato paste
1 tablespoon margarine
1/4 cup all-purpose flour
2 cans (12 ounces each) evaporated
    skimmed milk
1 can (14 1/2 ounces) 1/3-less-salt clear
    chicken broth
1/4 teaspoon pepper
1 cup crumbled feta cheese (4 ounces)
1/4 cup chopped fresh parsley

Heat oven to 350°. Grease rectangular baking dish, 13×9×2 inches. Cook and drain pasta as directed on package. While pasta is cooking, cook ground beef and onion in 10-inch nonstick skillet over medium heat, stirring occasionally, until beef is brown; drain. Stir in salt, allspice, cinnamon, nutmeg, wine and tomato paste; remove from heat and reserve.

Melt margarine in 3-quart saucepan over medium heat. Stir in flour. Cook, stirring frequently, until bubbly. Stir in milk, broth and pepper. Cook, stirring frequently with wire whisk, until mixture begins to thicken (do not boil). Stir in cheese and parsley until cheese is melted. Stir in pasta.

Spread half of the pasta mixture in baking dish. Spread beef mixture evenly over pasta mixture. Spread remaining pasta mixture over beef mixture. Bake uncovered 30 minutes.

Pepperoni Pizza–Hamburger Pie

6 servings

Ring a new change on a family favorite! This pie has the flavors of traditional pizza—but with a ground beef crust!

1 pound lean ground beef
1/3 cup dry bread crumbs
1 large egg
1 1/2 teaspoons chopped fresh or
    1/2 teaspoon dried oregano leaves
1/4 teaspoon salt
1/2 cup sliced mushrooms
1 small green bell pepper
1/3 cup chopped pepperoni (2 ounces)
1/4 cup sliced ripe olives
1 cup spaghetti sauce
1 cup shredded mozzarella cheese
    (4 ounces)

Heat oven to 400°. Mix beef, bread crumbs, egg, oregano and salt; press evenly against bottom and side of ungreased pie plate, 9× 1 1/4 inches. Sprinkle mushrooms, bell pepper, pepperoni and olives into meat-lined plate. Pour spaghetti sauce over toppings.

Bake uncovered 25 minutes or until beef is no longer pink in center and juice is clear; carefully drain. Sprinkle with cheese. Bake about 5 minutes longer or until cheese is light brown. Let pie stand 5 minutes before cutting.

Pizza Casserole

6 servings

4 cups uncooked wagon wheel pasta
    (8 ounces)
1/2 pound bulk Italian sausage
1/4 cup sliced ripe olives
1 can (4 ounces) mushroom stems and
    pieces, drained
1 jar (28 ounces) spaghetti sauce
1 cup shredded mozzarella cheese
    (4 ounces)

Heat oven to 350°.

Cook and drain pasta as directed on package.

While pasta is cooking, cook sausage in 10-skillet over medium-high heat, stirring occasionally, until no longer pink; drain. Mix pasta, sausage and remaining ingredients except cheese in ungreased 2 1/2-quart casserole.

Cover and bake about 30 minutes or until hot and bubbly. Sprinkle with cheese. Bake uncovered about 5 minutes or until cheese is melted.

Pizza Casserole

Hearty Shepherd's Pie

6 to 8 servings

Eggplant adds a new twist to this updated favorite.

1/2 pound extra-lean ground beef
1 large onion, chopped (about 1 cup)
1 clove garlic, finely chopped
1 medium eggplant (about 12 ounces), cut
    into 1/2-inch cubes (about 3 cups)
1 package (16 ounces) frozen broccoli,
    cauliflower and carrots
1 can (15 to 16 ounces) great northern
    beans, rinsed and drained
1 can (14 1/2 ounces) no-salt-added whole
    tomatoes, undrained
2 teaspoons Italian seasoning
1/2 teaspoon salt
1/4 teaspoon pepper
2 tablespoons water
2 tablespoons all-purpose flour
4 cups hot mashed potatoes

Heat oven to 350°. Spray rectangular baking dish, 13×9×2 inches, with nonstick cooking spray. Cook ground beef, onion and garlic in 12-inch nonstick skillet over medium heat, stirring occasionally, until beef is brown and onion is tender; drain. Stir in remaining ingredients except water, flour and potatoes, breaking up tomatoes. Heat to boiling; reduce heat. Simmer uncover 15 minutes, stirring occasionally.

Shake water and flour in tightly covered container; stir into beef mixture. Spoon beef mixture into baking dish. Spoon potatoes evenly over beef mixture; spread to edges of dish. Bake uncovered about 30 minutes or until heated through. Let stand 5 minutes before serving.

Hamburger-Cabbage Casserole

6 servings

All the taste of stuffed cabbage, without all the work!

1 pound lean ground beef
1 large onion, chopped (1 cup)
1/2 cup uncooked instant rice
1/2 teaspoon salt
1/2 teaspoon pepper
1 can (10 3/4 ounces) condensed tomato soup
1/4 cup water
4 cups coleslaw mix or shredded cabbage

Heat oven to 400°.

Cook beef and onion in 10-inch skillet over medium heat 8 to 10 minutes, stirring occasionally, until beef is brown; drain. Stir in remaining ingredients. Spoon into ungreased 2-quart casserole. Cover and bake 45 minutes or until hot and bubbly.

Favorite Meat Loaf

6 servings

This midwestern meat loaf, seasoned with mustard, pepper and sage, surely upholds country cooking's reputation as hearty and delicious. Soft bread crumbs replace the dry crackers that were typical of the loves popular at nineteenth-century lunches. Meat loaf is, of course, delicious for dinner, but we suspect that some people bake it just to have the leftovers in a sandwich! Still popular today, meat loaf sandwiches have been popular bring-along lunches since the Industrial Revolution.

1 1/2 pounds ground beef
1 cup milk
1 tablespoon Worcestershire sauce
1 teaspoon salt
1/2 teaspoon dry mustard
1/4 teaspoon pepper
1/4 teaspoon rubbed sage
3 slices soft bread, torn into small pieces
1 clove garlic, finely chopped or 1/8 teaspoon garlic powder
1 small onion, chopped (about 1/4 cup)
1 egg
1/2 cup ketchup, chile sauce or barbecue sauce

Heat oven to 350°. Mix all ingredients except ketchup. Spread in ungreased loaf pan, 8 1/2 ×4 1/2 or 9×5×3 inches, or shape into loaf in ungreased rectangular pan, 13×9×2 inches. Spoon ketchup over top. Bake uncovered until done, 1 to 1 1/4 hours. Remove from pan.

Individual meat loaves: *Shape meat mixture into 6 small loaves; place in ungreased rectangular pan, 13× 9× 2 inches. Bake as directed—except decrease baking time to 45 minutes.*

Favorite Meat Loaf

Western Meat Loaf

8 servings

With the pungent flavor of horseradish and dry mustard, our Western Meat Loaf recipe reflects its frontier heritage. This hearty meaty loaf has been a favorite of western ranch hands through the years.

1 can (8 ounces) tomato sauce
1 1/2 pounds ground beef
1/2 pound ground pork
2 cups soft bread crumbs
2 to 4 tablespoons prepared horseradish
1 teaspoon dry mustard
1/2 teaspoon salt
1/4 teaspoon pepper
1 medium onion, finely chopped
    (about 1/2 cup)
2 eggs, slightly beaten
1 tablespoon packed brown sugar
1/4 teaspoon dry mustard

Heat oven to 350°. Reserve 1/4 cup of the tomato sauce. Mix the remaining tomato sauce and remaining tomato sauce and remaining ingredients except brown sugar and 1/4 teaspoon dry mustard. Spread in ungreased loaf pan. 8 1/2×4 1/2×2 1/2 or 9×5×3 inches, or shape mixture into loaf in ungreased rectangular pan, 13×9×2 inches.

Mix reserved tomato sauce, brown sugar and 1/4 teaspoon dry mustard; spread over loaf. Bake uncovered until done, 1 to 1 1/4 hours. Cover loosely with aluminum foil; let stand 10 minutes. Remove from pan.

Cornbread Beef Bake

6 servings

A cast-iron skillet works well for this casserole. However, if you don't have one, any ovenproof skillet works just fine.

1 pound lean ground beef
1 medium onion, chopped (1/2 cup)
1 can (14 1/2 ounces) Mexican-style stewed
    tomatoes, undrained
1 can (15 ounces) black beans, rinsed and
    drained
1 can (8 ounces) tomato sauce
1/2 cup frozen corn
2 teaspoons chile powder
1 can (11 1/2 ounces) refrigerated
    cornbread twists

Heat oven to 350°.

Cook beef and onion in 10-inch ovenproof skillet over medium heat 8 to 10 minutes, stirring occasionally, until beef is brown; drain.

Stir in tomatoes, beans, tomato sauce, corn and chile powder; heat to boiling. Immediately top with cornbread twists left in round shape (do not unwind), pressing down gently. Bake uncovered 35 to 40 minutes or until cornbread is golden brown.

Cornbread Beef Bake

Beef Enchiladas

Beef Enchiladas

4 servings

1 pound lean ground beef
1 medium onion, chopped (1/2 cup)
1/2 cup sour cream
1 cup shredded Cheddar cheese (4 ounces)
2 tablespoons chopped fresh parsley
1/4 teaspoon pepper
1/3 cup chopped green bell pepper
2/3 cup water
1 tablespoon chile powder
1 1/2 teaspoons chopped fresh or
    1/2 teaspoon dried oregano leaves
1/4 teaspoon ground cumin
2 whole green chiles, chopped, if desired
1 clove garlic, finely chopped
1 can (15 ounces) tomato sauce
8 corn tortillas (6 inches in diameter)
Shredded cheese, sour cream and chopped
    onions, if desired

Heat oven to 350°. Cook beef in 10-inch skillet over medium heat 8 to 10 minutes, stirring occasionally, until brown; drain. Stir in onion, sour cream, 1 cup cheese, the parsley and pepper. Cover and set aside.

Heat bell pepper, water, chile powder, oregano, cumin, chiles, garlic and tomato sauce to boiling, stirring occasionally; reduce heat to low. Simmer uncovered 5 minutes. Pour into ungreased pie plate, 9×11 1/4 inches.

Dip each tortilla into sauce to coat both sides. Spoon about 1/4 cup beef mixture onto each tortilla; roll tortilla around filling. Place in ungreased rectangular baking dish, 11×7×1 1/2 inches. Pour remaining sauce over enchiladas.

Bake uncovered about 20 minutes or until bubbly. Garnish with shredded cheese, sour cream and chopped onion.

Cheese Enchiladas: *Substitute 2 cups shredded Monterey Jack cheese (8 ounces) for the beef. Mix with onion, sour cream, 1 cup cheese, the parsley, salt and pepper. Sprinkle 1/4 cup shredded Cheddar cheese (1 ounce) on enchiladas before baking.*

Taco Casserole

6 servings

1 pound ground beef
1 can (15 ounces) chili beans
1 can (8 ounces) tomato sauce
2 tablespoons taco sauce, picante sauce
    or salsa
2 to 4 teaspoons chile powder
1 teaspoon garlic powder
2 cups coarsely broken tortilla chips
1 cup sour cream
1/2 cup sliced green onions (5 medium)
1 medium tomato, chopped (3/4 cup)
1 cup shredded Cheddar or Monterey Jack
    cheese (4 ounces)
Shredded lettuce and taco sauce, if desired

Heat oven to 350°. Cook beef in 10-inch skillet over medium-high heat, stirring occasionally, until brown; drain. Stir in beans, tomato sauce, 2 tablespoons taco sauce, the chile powder and garlic powder. Heat to boiling, stirring occasionally.

Place tortilla chips in ungreased 2-quart casserole. Top with beef mixture. Spread with sour cream. Sprinkle with onions, tomato and cheese.

Bake uncover 20 to 30 minutes or until hot and bubbly. Arrange additional tortilla chips around edge of casserole if desired. Serve with lettuce and taco sauce.

Spicy Mexican Torte

8 servings

Chorizo is a coarsely ground pork sausage highly seasoned with garlic, chile powder and other spices.

1/2 pound chorizo or spicy Italian sausage
    links
2 medium onions, chopped (1 cup)
2 cloves garlic, finely chopped
1 can (4 ounces) chopped green chiles,
    drained
8 flour tortillas (10 inches in diameter)*
2 cups shredded Monterey Jack cheese
    (8 ounces)
1 can (16 ounces) refried beans
1 jar (7 ounces) roasted red bell peppers,
    drained
Salsa, sour cream or guacamole, if desired

Remove casings from sausage links. Cut sausages into 1/4-inch slices. Cook sausage, onions and garlic in 10-inch skillet over medium heat, stirring occasionally, until sausage is brown; drain. Stir in chiles; set aside.

Heat oven to 400°. Grease pie plate, 10× 1 1/2 inches, with shortening. Place 2 tortillas in pie plate. Spread with half of the sausage mixture; sprinkle with half of the cheese. Place 2 tortillas on cheese; spread with beans. Place 2 tortillas on beans; place peppers on tortillas. Place 2 tortillas on peppers; spread with remaining sausage mixture. Sprinkle with remaining cheese.

Cover and bake 40 minutes. Uncover and bake about 15 minutes longer or until cheese is melted and center is hot. Cool 10 minutes before cutting. Serve with salsa. 8 servings.

*16 corn tortillas (6 inches in diameter) can be substituted for the flour tortillas. Overlap 4 tortillas for each layer.

Harvest Bean Casserole

6 servings

Use either spicy or regular sausage—whichever suits your household—for this hearty casserole.

**1 pound bulk turkey or pork breakfast
   sausage
1 can (28 ounces) baked beans
2 baking apples, thinly sliced
1 can (18 ounces) vacuum-packed sweet
   potatoes
3 medium green onions, sliced (1/3 cup)**

Heat oven to 375°.

Cook sausage in 10-inch skillet over medium heat 8 to 10 minutes, stirring occasionally, until no longer pink; drain.

Place sausage in ungreased rectangular baking dish, 11×7×1 1/2 inches. Stir in baked beans. Arrange apple slices over sausage mixture. Slice sweet potatoes over apples.

Cover and bake 30 to 35 minutes or until apples are tender. Sprinkle with onions.

Fruit-stuffed Pork Roast

12 servings

**1/2 teaspoon ground cinnamon
1/4 teaspoon ground cloves
15 dried apricot halves (about 3 ounces)
9 pitted prunes (about 3 ounces)
4-pound pork boneless top loin roast
   (double)
3/4 teaspoon salt
1/4 teaspoon pepper
1 1/4 cups apple cider or juice
1 tablespoon cornstarch
1 tablespoon cold water**

Sprinkle cinnamon and cloves over apricots and prunes; toss to coat. Stuff fruit lengthwise between the 2 pieces of pork roast in ribbon about 2 inches wide (work from both ends of roast). Sprinkle with salt and pepper.

Heat oven to 325°. Place pork, fat side up, on rack in shallow roasting pan. Insert meat thermometer so tip is in center of thickest part of pork and does not rest in fat or fruit mixture. Roast uncovered until thermometer registers 170°, about 3 hours. After 1 1/2 hours, brush occasionally with 1/4 cup of the apple cider.

Remove pork and rack from pan; keep pork warm. Pour remaining cider into roasting pan; stir to loosen brown particles. Mix cornstarch and water; stir into cider mixture. Heat to boiling, stirring constantly. Boil and stir 1 minute. Serve with pork.

Fruit-stuffed Pork Roast

Pork Roast with Rosemary

12 servings

2 1/2- to 3-pound pork loin roast
2 tablespoons chopped fresh rosemary
   leaves
4 cloves garlic, finely chopped
1 teaspoon salt
1/2 teaspoon pepper
1 tablespoon margarine or butter
1 small onion, chopped (about 1/4 cup)
2 tablespoons olive or vegetable oil

Heat oven to 350°. Trim fat from pork roast. Mix rosemary and garlic. Make 8 to 10 deep cuts about 2 inches apart in pork with sharp knife. Insert small amounts of garlic mixture in cuts. Sprinkle pork with salt and pepper.

Melt margarine in shallow roasting pan in oven; sprinkle with onion. Place pork in pan; drizzle with oil. Insert meat thermometer so that tip is in center of thickest part of pork and does not touch fat. Roast uncovered 1 3/4 to 2 hours or until thermometer reads 160°. Let stand 15 minutes before slicing.

Cajun Pork Tenderloin with Vegetables

4 servings

If you'd like a milder flavor, just reduce the amount of Cajun spice.

2 teaspoons Cajun or Creole seasoning
1 pound pork tenderloin
2 medium sweet potatoes or yams
   (3/4 pound)
4 small zucchini (1 pound)
1 1/2 cups frozen small whole onions
2 tablespoons margarine, butter or spread,
   melted
1/2 teaspoon dried thyme leaves
1/4 teaspoon salt

Heat oven to 425°.

Rub Cajun seasoning into pork. Place in ungreased jelly roll pan, 15 1/2×10 1/2×1 inches. Insert meat thermometer horizontally into center of thickest part of pork.

Cut sweet potatoes and zucchini lengthwise into halves. Place sweet potatoes, zucchini and onions around pork. Drizzle margarine over vegetables. Sprinkle with thyme and salt.

Roast uncovered about 35 minutes or until thermometer reads 160°. Loosely cover pan with aluminum foil and let stand 10 minutes. Cut pork into thin slices. Serve with vegetables.

Pork Roast with Rosemary

Glazed Baked Ham

10 servings

1/4 cup packed brown sugar
1/4 teaspoon ground cloves
1/4 teaspoon ground cinnamon
1 can (6 ounces) frozen orange juice
    concentrate, thawed
5- to 7-pound fully cooked smoked ham
Whole cloves, if desired
Raisin Sauce (below)

Heat oven to 325°, Mix brown sugar, cloves, cinnamon and orange juice concentrate. Place ham, fat side up, on rack in shallow roasting pan. Insert meat thermometer so tip is in thickest part of ham and does not touch bone or rest in fat. Spoon or spread half of the juice mixture onto ham. Roast uncovered until meat thermometer registers 135°, 1 1/2 to 2 hours.

About 30 minutes before ham is done, remove from oven; pour droppings from pan. Cut fat surface of ham in uniform diamond pattern 1/4 inch deep. Insert whole clove in each diamond, if desired. Spoon or spread remaining juice mixture on ham; continue baking 30 minutes. Remove from oven. Cover and let stand 10 minutes. Serve with Raisin Sauce.

RAISIN SAUCE

2 cups apple cider or juice
3 tablespoons cornstarch
1 cup raisins
2 tablespoons margarine or butter

Gradually stir apple cider into cornstarch in 1-quart saucepan. Add raisins and margarine. Heat over medium heat, stirring constantly, until mixture thickens and boils. Boil and stir 1 minute. Serve warm.

Ham and Swiss Casserole

4 servings

When it's a chilly night and time for comfort food, this flavorful, creamy casserole really fills the bill. If no-salt-added mushrooms are available in your area, use them to reduce sodium even further.

1 tablespoon margarine
2 tablespoons all-purpose flour
1 1/4 cups skim milk
2 cups cooked brown or white rice
1 1/4 cups cut-up fully cooked smoked
    reduced-fat ham (about 10 ounces)
1 cup shredded reduced-fat Swiss cheese
    (4 ounces)
1/4 cup chopped fresh parsley
1/2 teaspoon dried marjoram leaves
1 can (4 ounces) mushroom stems and
    pieces, drained

Heat oven to 350°. Spray 2-quart casserole with nonstick cooking spray. Melt margarine in 3-quart saucepan over low heat. Cook flour in margarine, stirring constantly, until thickened; remove from heat.

Stir milk into flour mixture. Heat to boiling, stirring constantly with wire whisk. Boil and stir 1 minute. Stir in remaining ingredients. Spoon into casserole. Bake uncovered 30 to 35 minutes or until hot and bubbly.

Parsley Pinwheels and Ham Bake

6 to 8 servings

2 cups cut-up fully cooked smoked ham
1 can (10 3/4 ounces) condensed cream of
    chicken soup
1/2 cup chopped green pepper
1/2 cup chopped onion
1 jar (2 ounces) chopped pimiento, drained
1/2 teaspoon dry mustard
1/3 cup shortening
1 3/4 cups all-purpose flour*
2 1/2 teaspoons baking powder
3/4 teaspoon salt
3/4 cup milk
1/2 cup snipped parsley

Parsley Pinwheels and Ham Bake

Heat oven to 425°. Mix ham, soup, green pepper, onion, pimiento and mustard; pour into ungreased baking dish, 8×8×2 inches.

Cut shortening into flour, baking powder and salt with pastry blender until mixture resembles fine crumbs. Stir in just enough milk so dough leaves side of bowl and rounds up into a ball.

Turn dough onto lightly floured surface. Knead lightly 10 times. Roll into rectangle, 12×9 inches; sprinkle with parsley. Roll up, beginning at narrow end; pinch edge to seal. Cut into 1-inch slices. Arrange slices, cut sides up, on ham mixture.

Bake until biscuits are golden brown, 20 to 30 minutes.

*If using self-rising flour, omit baking powder and salt.

Ham and Egg Bake

8 servings

This is a perfect dish to make ahead. Just cover and refrigerate no longer than 24 hours; increase bake time to 55 to 60 minutes.

**6 cups frozen (not thawed) hash brown
    potatoes
2 cups diced, fully cooked smoked ham
2 cups shredded Swiss cheese (8 ounces)
1 jar (7 ounces) roasted red bell peppers,
    drained and chopped
1 jar (4 1/2 ounces) sliced mushrooms,
    drained
6 large eggs
1/3 cup milk
1 cup small curd, creamed cottage cheese
1/4 teaspoon pepper**

Heat oven to 350°. Grease rectangular baking dish, 13×9×2 inches, with shortening. Sprinkle 3 cups of the potatoes evenly in baking dish. Layer with ham, Swiss cheese, bell peppers and mushrooms. Sprinkle remaining potatoes over mushrooms.

Beat eggs, milk, cottage cheese, and pepper with fork or wire whisk until blended. Pour egg mixture over potatoes.

Bake uncovered 45 to 50 minutes or until light golden brown and set in center.

TIP

For less fat and fewer calories per serving, use extra-lean ham and reduced-fat Swiss cheese. Substitute 1 1/2 cups fat-free cholesterol-free egg product for the eggs.

Sausage Pie

6 servings

**1 1/2 pounds bulk pork sausage
1 medium onion, chopped (about 1/2 cup)
1 tablespoon sugar
1 1/2 teaspoons salt
1 medium head green cabbage (1 3/4 pounds),
    cut into large chunks and cored
1 can (16 ounces) whole tomatoes, undrained
Pastry for 9-inch One-Crust Pie (below)
2 tablespoons all-purpose flour
1/4 cup cold water**

Cook and stir sausage and onion in Dutch oven until sausage is done; drain. Stir in sugar, salt, cabbage, and tomatoes. Heat to boiling; reduce heat. Cover and simmer 10 minutes.

Heat oven to 400°. Prepare pastry; shape into flattened round on lightly floured cloth-covered board, Roll to fit top of 2-quart casserole. Fold into fourths; cut slits so steam can escape.

Mix flour and water; stir into hot sausage mixture. Pour into ungreased casserole. Place pastry over top and unfold; seal pastry to edge of casserole. Bake until crust is brown, 25 to 30 minutes.

ONE-CRUST PIE PASTRY

**1/3 cup plus 1 tablespoon shortening
    or 1/3 cup lard
1 cup all-purpose flour
1/2 teaspoon salt
2 to 3 tablespoons cold water**

Cut shortening into flour and salt until particles are size of small peas. Sprinkle in water, 1 tablespoon at a time, tossing with fork until all flour is moistened and pastry almost cleans side of bowl (1 to 2 teaspoons water can be added if necessary).

Saucy Ribs

6 servings

4 1/2 pounds pork loin back ribs, pork spareribs or beef short ribs or 3 pounds pork country-style ribs
Spicy Barbecue Sauce (below), Mustard Sauce or Sweet-Savory Sauce (right)

Heat oven to 325°. Prepare Spicy Barbecue Sauce. Use sauce as directed in chart below. Cut ribs into serving pieces. Place meaty sides up in pan listed in chart. Cook as directed in chart below.

SPICY BARBECUE SAUCE

1/3 cup margarine or butter
2 tablespoons white vinegar
2 tablespoons water
1 teaspoon sugar
1/2 teaspoon garlic powder
1/2 teaspoon onion powder
1/2 teaspoon pepper
Dash of ground red pepper (cayenne)

Heat all ingredients in 1-quart saucepan over medium heat, stirring frequently, until margarine is melted.

MUSTARD SAUCE

1/2 cup molasses
1/3 cup Dijon mustard
1/3 cup cider vinegar

Mix molasses and mustard. Stir in vinegar.

SWEET-SAVORY SAUCE

1 cup chile sauce
3/4 cup grape jelly
1 tablespoon plus 1 1/2 teaspoons dry red wine or beef broth
1 teaspoon Dijon mustard

Heat all ingredients in 1-quart saucepan over medium heat, stirring occasionally, until jelly is melted.

Saucy Ribs Cooking Chart

Kind of Ribs	Pan	Cooking Directions	Serving Tips
Pork loin back ribs	Rack in shallow roasting pan	Bake uncovered 1 1/2 hours; brush with sauce. Bake uncovered about 45 minutes longer, brushing frequently with sauce, until tender.	Heat any remaining sauce to boiling, stirring constantly, boil and stir 1 minute. Serve sauce with ribs.
Pork spareribs	Rack in shallow roasting pan	Bake uncovered 1 hour; brush with sauce. Bake uncovered about 45 minutes longer, brushing frequently with sauce, until tender.	Heat any remaining sauce to boiling, stirring constantly; boil and stir 1 minute. Serve sauce with ribs.
Pork country-style ribs	Rectangular pan, 13×9×2 inches	Cover and bake about 2 hours or until tender; drain. Pour sauce over ribs. Bake uncovered 30 minutes longer.	Spoon sauce from pan over ribs.
Beef short ribs	Rectangular pan, 13×9×2 inches	Pour sauce over ribs. Cover and bake about 2 1/2 hours or until tender.	Spoon sauce from pan over ribs.

Chili Dog Wraps

5 servings

This Mexican-inspired casserole gives you another great way to serve the always popular hot dog.

10 corn or flour tortillas (6 to 8 inches in diameter)
10 hot dogs
1 can (15 to 16 ounces) chili
2 cups salsa
1 cup shredded Cheddar or Monterey Jack cheese (4 ounces)

Heat oven to 350°. Grease rectangular baking dish. 13×9×2 inches.

Soften tortillas as directed on package. Place 1 hot dog and 3 tablespoons chili on each tortilla. Roll up tortillas; place seam side down in baking dish. Spoon salsa over tortillas.

Cover and bake 20 minutes. Sprinkle with cheese. Bake uncovered about 5 minutes longer or until cheese is melted.

Chicken with Gingered Brown Rice Stuffing

4 servings

Crystallized ginger adds a spicy flavor to this easy chicken and rice dish.

1 tablespoon orange juice
1 small onion, finely chopped (about 1/4 cup)
2 cups cooked brown or white rice
3 tablespoons finely chopped crystallized ginger
2 tablespoons chopped fresh parsley or 2 teaspoons dried parsley flakes
1 teaspoon orange juice
3/4 teaspoon chopped fresh or 1/4 teaspoon dried thyme leaves
4 skinless, boneless chicken breast halves (1 pound)
1 tablespoon orange juice
1/4 teaspoon cinnamon

Heat oven to 350°. Heat 1 tablespoon orange juice to boiling in 2-quart saucepan over medium heat. Cook onion in orange juice, stirring frequently, until crisp-tender. Stir in rice, ginger, parsley, 1 tablespoon orange juice and the thyme. Spoon rice mixture into greased square baking dish, 8×8×2 inches.

Place chicken breasts over rice mixture; brush with 1 tablespoon orange juice; sprinkle with cinnamon. Cover and bake 30 minutes. Remove cover; bake 15 to 20 minutes longer or until juice of chicken is no longer pink when centers of thickest pieces are cut.

Chicken with Gingered Brown Rice Stuffing

Chicken Pot Pie

6 servings

1 package (10 ounces) frozen peas and
    carrots
1/3 cup margarine or butter
1/3 cup all-purpose flour
1/3 cup chopped onion
1/2 teaspoon salt
1/4 teaspoon pepper
1 3/4 cups chicken broth
2/3 cup milk
2 1/2 to 3 cups cut-up cooked chicken
    or turkey
Pastry for 9-inch Two-Crust Pie (page 259)

Rinse frozen peas and carrots in cold water to separate; drain. Melt margarine in 2-quart saucepan over medium heat. Stir in flour, onion, salt and pepper. Cook, stirring constantly, until mixture is bubbly; remove from heat. Stir in broth and milk. Heat to boiling, stirring constantly. Boil and stir 1 minute. Stir in chicken and peas and carrots; remove from heat.

Heat oven to 425°. Prepare pastry. Roll two-thirds of the pastry into 13-inch square. Ease into ungreased square pan, 9×9×2 inches. Pour chicken mixture into pastry-lined pan.

Roll remaining pastry into 11-inch square. Cut out designs with 1-inch cookie cutter. Place square over chicken mixture. Arrange cutouts on pastry. Turn edges of pastry under and flute.

Bake about 35 minutes or until golden brown.

Chicken-Rice Casserole

6 servings

For a crunchy topping, don't mix the almonds in with the other ingredients. Instead, sprinkle the almonds over the casserole 10 minutes before it's done baking.

1/4 cup margarine or butter
1/3 cup all-purpose flour
3/4 teaspoon salt
1/8 teaspoon pepper
1 1/2 cups milk
1 cup chicken broth
2 cups cut-up cooked chicken
1 1/2 cups cooked white rice
3 ounces mushrooms, sliced (about 1 cup)*
1/3 cup chopped green bell pepper
1/4 cup slivered almonds
2 tablespoons chopped pimientos

Heat oven to 350°. Melt margarine in 2-quart saucepan over medium heat. Stir in flour, salt and pepper. Cook, stirring constantly, until bubbly; remove from heat. Stir in milk and broth. Heat to boiling, stirring constantly. Boil and stir 1 minute. Stir in remaining ingredients. Pour into ungreased 2-quart casserole or square baking dish, 8×8×2 inches.

Bake uncovered 40 to 45 minutes or until bubbly. Garnish with parsley sprig, if desired.

1 can (4 ounces) mushroom stems and pieces, drained, can be substituted for the fresh mushrooms.

Turkey–Wild Rice Casserole: *Substitute 2 cups cut-up cooked turkey for the chicken, and wild rice for the white rice.*

Tuscan Chicken Rolls with Pork Stuffing

6 servings

**6 boneless, skinless chicken breast halves
   (about 1 1/2 pounds)**
1/2 pound ground pork
**1 small onion, finely chopped
   (about 1/4 cup)**
1 clove garlic, finely chopped
1 egg, beaten
1/2 cup soft bread crumbs
1/2 teaspoon salt
**1/4 teaspoon ground savory or crushed
   dried savory leaves**
1/4 teaspoon pepper
2 tablespoons margarine or butter, melted
1/2 teaspoon salt
1/2 cup dry white wine or chicken broth
1/2 cup cold water
2 teaspoons cornstarch
1/2 teaspoon chicken bouillon granules
Chopped fresh parsley

Heat oven to 400°. Grease rectangular baking dish, 11 × 7 × 1 1/2 inches. Flatten each chicken breast half to 1/4-inch thickness between sheets of plastic wrap or waxed paper. Cook ground pork, onion and garlic in 10-inch skillet over medium heat, stirring occasionally, until pork is no longer pink; drain. Stir in egg, bread crumbs, 1/2 teaspoon salt, the savory and pepper.

Place about 1/3 cup pork mixture and each chicken breast half to within 1/2 inch of edges. Roll up tightly; secure with toothpicks. Place in greased dish. Drizzle rolls with margarine. Sprinkle with 1/2 teaspoon salt. Pour wine into dish. Bake uncovered 35 to 40 minutes or until chicken is no longer pink when center of thickest pieces are cut.

Remove chicken to warm platter; remove toothpicks. Keep chicken warm. Pour liquid from dish into 1-quart saucepan. Stir cold water into cornstarch; pour into liquid in saucepan. Stir bouillon granules. Heat to boiling over medium heat, stirring constantly. Boil and stir 1 minute. Pour gravy over chicken. Sprinkle with parsley.

Baked Chicken and Rice

6 servings

This hearty favorite is based on a traditional Spanish recipe, Arroz con Pollo, "chicken with rice." A specialty of Mexico and Puerto Rico, this classic dish is especially popular in the southwestern United States.

2 1/2- to 3-pound cut-up broiler-fryer
   chicken
3/4 teaspoon salt
1/4 to 1/2 teaspoon paprika
1/4 teaspoon pepper
2 1/2 cups chicken broth
1 cup uncooked regular long grain rice
1 medium onion, chopped (about 1/2 cup)
1 clove garlic, finely chopped
1/2 teaspoon salt
1 1/2 teaspoons chopped fresh or
   1/2 teaspoon dried oregano leaves
1/8 teaspoon ground turmeric
1 bay leaf
2 cups shelled fresh green peas*
Pimiento strips
Pitted ripe olives

Heat oven to 350°. Place chicken, skin sides up, in ungreased rectangular baking dish, 13×9×2 inches. Sprinkle with salt, paprika and pepper. Bake uncovered 30 minutes.

Heat broth to boiling. Remove chicken and drain fat from dish. Mix broth, rice, onion, garlic, salt, oregano, turmeric, bay leaf and peas in baking dish. Top with chicken. Cover with aluminum foil and bake until rice and thickest pieces of chicken are done and liquid is absorbed, about 30 minutes. Remove bay leaf. Top with pimiento strips and olives.

*1 package (10 ounces) frozen green peas, thawed and drained, can be substituted for the fresh green peas.

Chicken with Orange-Pecan Rice

4 servings

1 package (6.25 ounces) fast-cooking long
   grain and wild rice
2 cups orange juice
1/4 cup chopped pecans
1 jar (2 ounces) diced pimientos, drained
4 skinless boneless chicken breast halves
   (about 1 pound)
Chopped fresh parsley, if desired

Heat oven to 350°. Grease square pan, 8×8×2 inches.

Mix rice, seasoning packet included in rice mix, orange juice, pecans and pimientos in pan. Place chicken on rice.

Cover and bake 35 to 45 minutes or until liquid is absorbed and juice of chicken is no longer pink when center of thickest pieces are cut. Sprinkle with parsley.

Chicken with Orange-Pecan Rice

Baked Barbecued Chicken

6 servings

1/4 cup (1/2 stick) margarine or butter
2 1/2- to 3-pound cut-up broiler-fryer
    chicken
1 cup ketchup
1/2 cup water
1/4 cup lemon juice
1 tablespoon Worcestershire sauce
2 teaspoons paprika
1/2 teaspoon salt
1 medium onion, finely chopped (about
    1/2 cup)
1 clove garlic, finely chopped

Heat oven to 375°. Heat margarine in rectangular pan, 13×9×2 inches, in oven. Place chicken in margarine, turning to coat. Arrange skin side down in pan. Bake uncovered 30 minutes.

Mix remaining ingredients in 1-quart saucepan. Heat to boiling; remove from heat. Drain fat from chicken. Bake uncovered until thickest pieces are done and juices of chicken run clear, about 30 minutes longer.

Grilled Barbecue Chicken: *Cover and grill chicken, bone sides down, 4 to 5 inches from medium coals, 25 minutes. Prepare sauce as directed. Turn chicken. Grill until thickest pieces are done, turning and brushing frequently with sauce, 30 to 40 minutes.*

Zesty Roasted Chicken and Potatoes

6 servings

Serve this family favorite with a super-quick salad. Simply pick up prepared salad greens at your local fast-food restaurant or supermarket, toss them with your favorite dressing, and you'll have a meal on the table in a snap!

6 skinless boneless chicken breast halves
1 pound small red potatoes, cut in quarter
1/3 cup mayonnaise or salad dressing
3 tablespoons Dijon mustard
1/2 teaspoon pepper
2 cloves garlic, crushed
Chopped fresh chives, if desired

Heat oven to 350°. Grease jelly roll pan, 15 1/2 ×10 1/2×1 inch.

Place chicken and potatoes in pan. Mix remaining ingredients except chives; brush over chicken and potatoes.

Bake uncovered 30 to 35 minutes or until potatoes are tender and juice of chicken is no longer pink when centers of thickest pieces are cut. Sprinkle with chives.

Zesty Roasted Chicken and Potatoes

Country Captain

6 servings

1/2 cup all-purpose flour
1 teaspoon salt
1/4 teaspoon pepper
2 1/2- to 3-pound cut-up broiler-fryer
    chicken
1/4 cup vegetable oil
1 1/2 teaspoons curry powder
1 1/2 teaspoons chopped fresh or
    1/2 teaspoon dried thyme leaves
1/4 teaspoon salt
1 large onion, chopped (about 1 cup)
1 large green bell pepper, chopped (about
    1 1/2 cups)
1 clove garlic, finely chopped, or
    1/8 teaspoon garlic powder
1 can (16 ounces) whole tomatoes,
    undrained
1/4 cup currants or raisins
1/3 cup slivered almonds, toasted
3 cups hot cooked rice

Heat oven to 350°. Mix flour, 1 teaspoon salt and the pepper. Coat chicken with flour mixture. Heat oil in 10-inch skillet until hot. Cook chicken in oil over medium heat until light brown, 15 to 20 minutes. Place chicken in ungreased 2 1/2 quart casserole. Drain oil from skillet.

Add curry powder, thyme, 1/4 teaspoon salt, the onion, bell pepper, garlic and tomatoes to skillet. Heat to boiling; stirring frequently to loosen brown particles from skillet.

Pour over chicken. Cover and bake until thickest pieces are done and juices of chicken run clear, about 40 minutes. Skim fat from liquid if necessary; add currants. Bake uncovered 5 minutes. Sprinkle with almonds. Serve with rice, and if desired, grated fresh coconut and chutney.

Sole Parmesan

4 servings

8 thin sole or orange roughly fillets (about
    2 1/2 pounds)
1/2 cup all-purpose flour
2 tablespoons margarine or butter
2 green onions, thinly sliced
1/2 teaspoon salt
1/2 teaspoon pepper
1 cup dry white wine or chicken broth
3 tablespoons lemon juice
1/2 cup freshly grated Parmesan cheese

Heat oven to 375°. Coat fish fillets with flour; set aside. Melt margarine in 12-inch oven-proof skillet over medium-low heat. Cook onions in margarine 3 to 5 minutes, stirring occasionally, until crisp-tender. Add fish and cook uncovered 4 minutes turn fish carefully. Cook 4 minutes longer. Sprinkle with salt and pepper. Pour wine and lemon juice into skillet. Sprinkle with cheese. Bake uncovered 15 minutes or until hot and bubbly.

Venetian Scallops

4 servings

This dish is best made with sea scallops, which are large, rather than small bay scallops.

1 tablespoon margarine or butter
1 small onion, thinly sliced
1 pound sea scallops, cut in half
1/2 cup dry white wine or chicken broth
1/2 cup whipping (heavy) cream
1/4 teaspoon freshly grated nutmeg
1/4 cup seasoned dry bread crumbs
1/4 cup freshly grated Parmesan cheese

Heat oven to 400°. Melt margarine in 10-inch ovenproof skillet over medium-low heat. Cook onion in margarine, stirring occasionally, until tender. Add scallops. Cook 5 minutes. Stir in wine. Cook uncovered until liquid is evaporated. Stir in whipping cream and nutmeg. Mix bread crumbs and cheese; sprinkle over scallops. Bake uncovered 12 to 15 minutes or until hot and bubbly.

Twice-Baked Potatoes

8 servings

4 large baking potatoes (8 to 10 ounces each)
1/4 to 1/2 cup milk
1/4 cup margarine or butter, softened
1/4 teaspoon salt
Dash of pepper
1 cup shredded Cheddar cheese (4 ounces)
1 tablespoon chopped fresh chives

Pierce potatoes; bake at 375° for 1 1/4 to 1 1/2 hours or until tender.

Cut potatoes lengthwise in half; scoop out inside, leaving a thin shell. Mash potato in medium bowl until no lumps remain. Add milk in small amounts, beating after each addition (amount of milk needed to make potatoes smooth and fluffy depends on kind of potatoes used.)

Add margarine, salt and pepper; beat vigorously until potato is light and fluffy. Stir in cheese and chives. Fill potato shills with mashed potato. Place on ungreased cookie sheet.

Heat oven to 400°. Bake about 20 minutes or until hot.

TIP

To microwave, arrange filled potatoes in circle on 10-inch microwavable plate. Cover with waxed paper and microwave on High 8 to 10 minutes, rotating plate 1/2 turn after 5 minutes, until hot.

Au Gratin Potatoes

6 servings

**6 medium boiling or baking potatoes
     (2 pounds)**
1/4 cup margarine or butter
1 medium onion, chopped (1/2 cup)
1 tablespoon all-purpose flour
1 teaspoon salt
1/4 teaspoon pepper
2 cups milk
**2 cups shredded natural sharp Cheddar
     cheese (8 ounces)**
1/4 cup fine dry bread crumbs
Paprika

Heat oven to 375°. Scrub potatoes but do not peel, if desired. Cut into 1/8-inch slices to measure about 4 cups.

Melt margarine in 2-quart saucepan over medium heat. Cook onion in margarine about 2 minutes, stirring occasionally, until tender. Stir in flour, salt and pepper. Cook, stirring constantly, until bubbly; remove from heat. Stir in milk and 1 1/2 cups of the cheese. Heat to boiling, stirring constantly. Boil and stir 1 minute.

Spread potatoes in ungreased 1 1/2-quart casserole. Pour cheese sauce over potatoes.

Bake uncovered 1 hour. Mix remaining cheese and the bread crumbs; sprinkle over potatoes. Sprinkle with paprika. Bake uncovered 15 to 20 minutes longer or until top in brown and bubbly.

TIP

To save time, use frozen chopped onions and purchase already shredded cheese.

Sun-Dried Tomato au Gratin Potatoes: *Increase milk to 2 1/2 cups. Mix 1 package (3 ounces) sun-dried tomatoes (not oil-packed), cut up, with the potatoes.*

Garlic-Parmesan Potatoes

8 servings

This is fancy enough for entertaining, yet so easy! You'll want to serve it to company, and it's also a great time-saving idea for holiday meals.

**1 package (1.25 pounds) refrigerated
     mashed potatoes (2 2/3 cups)**
1 cup sour cream
1/3 cup grated Parmesan cheese
2 large cloves garlic, finely chopped
**20 frozen potato wedges with skins (from
     24-ounce package)**
2 tablespoons grated Parmesan cheese
Chopped fresh chives, if desired

Heat oven to 400°. Spray quiche dish, 9×1 1/2 inches, with nonstick cooking spray.

Mix mashed potatoes, sour cream, 1/3 cup cheese and the garlic in quiche dish; spread evenly. Arrange potato wedges in spoke fashion with 2 wedges in center on mashed potato mixture. Sprinkle with 2 tablespoons cheese.

Bake 25 to 30 minutes or until hot. Sprinkle with chives. Cut into wedges.

Garlic-Parmesan Potatoes

Potato Skins Olé

8 servings (2 shells each)

In this Tex-Mex version of a popular appetizer, the potato skins are baked, not fried.

4 large potatoes (about 2 pounds), baked
2 tablespoons margarine or butter, melted
1 cup shredded Colby-Monterey Jack cheese (4 ounces)
1/2 cup sour cream
1/2 cup sliced green onions (5 medium)
1/4 cup salsa

Let potatoes stand until cool enough to handle. Cut potatoes lengthwise into fourths; carefully scoop out pulp, leaving 1/4-inch shells. Save potato pulp for another use.

Set oven control to broil. Place potato shells, skin sides down, in broiler pan. Brush potato flesh with margarine. Broil 4 to 5 inches from heat 8 to 10 minutes or until crisp and brown.

Sprinkle cheese over potato shells. Broil about 30 seconds or until cheese is melted. Mix sour cream and onions; spoon onto potatoes. Top with salsa.

Baked Rice with Green Chiles

5 servings

3 cups cooked white rice
1 cup sour cream
1/2 cup shredded Monterey Jack cheese (2 ounces)
1/2 cup shredded Cheddar cheese (2 ounces)
1 to 2 teaspoons chile powder
2 cans (4 ounces each) chopped green chiles, drained

Heat oven to 350°. Mix all ingredients in ungreased 2-quart casserole. Bake uncovered 30 minutes.

TIP

Want to reduce fat and calories? Use low-fat or fat-free sour cream and reduced-fat cheeses.

Polenta with Cheese

6 servings

Serve this satisfying polenta with grilled chicken.

1 cup yellow cornmeal
3/4 cup water
3 1/4 cups boiling water
2 teaspoons salt
1 tablespoon margarine or butter
1 cup grated Parmesan cheese
1/3 cup shredded Swiss cheese

Heat oven to 350°. Grease 1 1/2 -quart casserole. Mix cornmeal and 3/4 cup water in 2-quart saucepan. Stir in 3 1/4 cups boiling water and the salt. Cook over medium-high heat, stirring constantly, until mixture thickens and boils; reduce heat. Cover and simmer 10 minutes, stirring occasionally; remove from heat. Stir until smooth.

Spread one-third of the polenta in casserole; dot with one-third of the margarine and sprinkle with 1/3 cup of the Parmesan cheese. Repeat twice. Sprinkle with Swiss cheese. Bake uncovered 15 to 20 minutes or until hot and bubbly.

Cheesy Grits

8 servings

2 cups milk
2 cups water
1 teaspoon salt
1/4 teaspoon pepper
1 cup hominy quick grits
**1 1/2 cups shredded Cheddar cheese
    (6 ounces)**
1/4 cup sliced green onions
2 eggs, slightly beaten
1 tablespoon margarine or butter
1/4 teaspoon paprika

Heat oven to 350°. Grease 1 1/2-quart casserole. Heat milk, water, salt and pepper to boiling in 2-quart saucepan. Gradually add grits, stirring constantly; reduce heat. Simmer uncovered, stirring frequently, until thick, about 5 minutes. Stir in cheese and onions. Stir 1 cup of the hot mixture into eggs; stir into remaining hot mixture in saucepan.

Pour hot mixture into casserole. Dot with margarine; sprinkle with paprika. Bake uncovered until set, 35 to 40 minutes. Let stand 10 minutes.

Scalloped Corn

4 servings

4 ears corn
2 tablespoons margarine or butter
1 small onion, chopped (1/4 cup)
1/4 cup chopped green bell pepper
2 tablespoons all-purpose flour
1/2 teaspoon salt
1/2 teaspoon paprika
1/4 teaspoon ground mustard (dry)
Dash of pepper
3/4 cup milk
1 large egg, slightly beaten
1/3 cup fine dry cracker crumbs
1 tablespoon margarine or butter, melted

Prepare corn. Boil ears in enough unsalted cold water to cover. Add 1 tablespoon sugar and 1 tablespoon lemon juice to each gallon of water, if desired. Heat to boiling. Boil uncovered 2 minutes; remove from heat. Let stand uncovered 10 minutes. Or steam ears 6 to 9 minutes or until tender. Cut enough kernels from ears to measure 2 cups.

Heat oven to 350°.

Melt 2 tablespoons margarine in 1-quart saucepan over medium heat. Cook onion and bell pepper in margarine about 2 minutes, stirring occasionally, until onion is tender; remove from heat.

Stir in flour, salt, paprika, mustard and pepper. Cook, stirring constantly, until mixture is bubbly; remove from heat. Gradually stir in milk. Heat to boiling, stirring constantly. Boil and stir 1 minute. Stir in corn and egg. Pour into ungreased 1-quart casserole.

Mix cracker crumbs and 1 tablespoon melted margarine. Sprinkle over corn mixture. Bake uncovered 30 to 35 minutes or until bubbly.

Chile Scalloped Corn: *Omit paprika and mustard. Add 1/2 teaspoon chile powder and 1/2 teaspoon ground cumin with the flour. Stir in 1 can (4 ounces) chopped green chiles drained, with the egg.*

TIP

Substitute 1 package (10 ounces) frozen whole kernel corn, cooked and drained, or 1 can (16 ounces) whole kernel corn, drained, for the cooked fresh corn.

Corn Pudding

8 servings

Corn on the cob is a time-honored American favorite. And corn off the cob can be just as wonderful! In the summer, use just-picked corn to make this simple and creamy pudding. Be sure to scrape all the pulp and milk from the cob.

4 medium ears corn*
2 tablespoons sugar
2 tablespoons all-purpose flour
1/2 teaspoon salt
Dash of pepper
2 eggs
1 1/4 cups milk
2 tablespoons margarine or butter, melted
1/2 teaspoon ground nutmeg

Heat oven to 350°. Grease 1-quart casserole or soufflé dish. Cut enough kernels from corn to measure 2 cups. (Scrape ears with knife to extract all pulp and milk.) Mix the corn, sugar, flour, salt and pepper in 2-quart bowl. Stir in eggs. Stir in milk and margarine; pour into casserole. Sprinkle with nutmeg.

Set casserole in baking pan on middle oven rack. Pour hot water into pan on middle oven rack. Pour hot water into pan until about 1 1/2 inches deep. Bake until knife inserted halfway between center and edge comes out clean, about 50 to 55 minutes.

*2 cups frozen whole kernel corn, thawed, or 1 can (16 ounces) whole kernel corn, drained, can be substituted for the fresh corn.

Eggplant Acapulco

8 servings

Here's and out-of-the-ordinary eggplant dish that is great for a buffet supper.

1 small eggplant (1 pound), peeled and cut into 1/2-inch cubes
1 1/2 cups coarsely crushed corn chips (3 ounces)
1 cup shredded Cheddar cheese (4 ounces)
1 can (15 ounces) chunky Mexican-style tomato sauce

Heat over to 350°. Grease square baking dish, 8×8×2 inches. Heat 1/2 inch water to boiling in 2-quart saucepan. Add eggplant. Cover and heat to boiling; reduce heat to medium-high. Cook 5 minutes; drain.

Mix corn chips and cheese. Spread half of the eggplant in baking dish; spoon half of the tomato sauce over eggplant. Sprinkle with half of the corn chip mixture. Repeat with remaining eggplant, tomato sauce and corn chip mixture. Bake uncovered about 30 minutes or until bubbly around edges.

Favorite Green Bean Casserole

Makes 6 servings, about 3/4 cup each

2 packages (16 ounces each) frozen cut
    green beans
1 can (10 3/4 ounces) condensed cream of
    celery, cream of chicken or cream of
    mushroom soup
1/2 cup milk
1 jar (2 ounces) diced pimientos, drained
1/8 teaspoon pepper
1 can (2.8 ounces) French fried onions

Heat oven to 350°.

Cook green beans as directed on package
for the minimum amount of time; drain.

Mix soup, milk, pimientos and pepper in
2-quart casserole or square baking dish,
8×8×2 inches. Stir in beans. Sprinkle with
onions. Bake uncovered 30 to 40 minutes or
until hot in center.

TIP

*Substitute 2 cans (16 ounces each) cut green
beans, drained, for the frozen green beans,
but do not cook. To microwave, use microwavable casserole. Decrease milk to 1/4 cup.
Stir beans into soup mixture. Cover and
microwave on High 5 minutes; stir. Sprinkle
with onions. Microwave uncovered 3 to
5 minutes or until hot.*

Cinnamon Squash Rings

6 servings

2 tablespoons packed brown sugar
2 tablespoons milk
1 egg
3/4 cup soft bread crumbs (about
    2 1/2 slices bread)
1/4 cup cornmeal
2 teaspoons ground cinnamon
1 large acorn squash (1 1/2 pounds), cut
    crosswise into 1/2-inch slices and seeded
1/3 cup margarine or butter, melted

Heat oven to 400°. Mix brown sugar, milk and
egg. Mix bread crumbs, cornmeal and cinnamon. Dip squash slices into egg mixture, then
coat with bread crumb mixture; repeat.

Place in ungreased rectangular pan, 13×9
×2 inches. Drizzle with margarine. Bake
uncovered 30 to 35 minutes or until squash is
tender.

Cinnamon Squash Rings

Glazed Acorn Squash

4 servings

2 acorn squash (1 to 1 1/2 pounds each)
4 tablespoons maple-flavored syrup
4 tablespoons whipping (heavy) cream or
    margarine or butter

Heat oven to 350°.

Cut each squash lengthwise in half; remove seeds and fibers. Place squash, cut sides up, in ungreased pan. Spoon 1 tablespoon syrup and 1 tablespoon whipping cream into each half. Bake uncovered about 1 hour or until tender.

Lighter Glazed Acorn Squash: *For less fat and fewer calories, omit whipping cream.*

Apple-Stuffed Acorn Squash: *Bake squash 30 minutes. Mix 1 large tart red apple, diced, 2 tablespoons chopped nuts, 2 tablespoons packed brown sugar and 1 tablespoon margarine or butter, melted. Spoon apple mixture into squash halves. Bake about 30 minutes longer or until tender.*

Rutabaga Casserole

6 servings, about 3/4 cup each

2 medium rutabagas* (about 2 pounds)
2 eggs, beaten
1/4 cup dry bread crumbs
1/4 cup half-and-half
2 teaspoons sugar or corn syrup
1 teaspoon salt
1/4 teaspoon ground nutmeg
2 tablespoons margarine or butter

Wash rutabagas; peel thinly. Cut into 1/2-inch cubes or 2-inch pieces. Boil cubes 20 to 25 minutes; boil pieces 30 to 40 minutes or until tender. Or steam 25 to 28 minutes or until tender.

Heat oven to 350°. Grease 1 1/2-quart casserole.

Drain rutabagas, reserving 1/4 cup cooking liquid. Mash rutabagas with reserved liquid. Stir remaining ingredients except margarine into rutabagas. Pour into casserole; dot with margarine.

Bake 45 to 50 minutes until top is light brown.

*6 medium turnips (about 2 pounds) can be substituted for the rutabagas.

Stuffed Zucchini

8 servings

4 medium zucchini (about 2 pounds)
1 medium onion, chopped (about 1/2 cup)
1/4 cup (1/2 stick) margarine or butter
1 can (4 ounces) chopped green chiles,
    drained
1 jar (2 ounces) diced pimientos, drained
1 1/2 cups herb-seasoned stuffing mix (dry)
3/4 cup shredded mozzarella or Monterey
    Jack cheese

Heat 2 inches water (salted if desired) to boiling. Add zucchini. Heat to boiling; reduce heat. Cover and simmer just until tender, 8 to 10 minutes; drain. Cool slightly; cut each zucchini lengthwise in half. Spoon out pulp; chop coarsely. Place zucchini, cut sides up, in ungreased baking dish, 13×9×2 inches.

Heat oven to 350°. Cook and stir onion in margarine in 10-inch skillet until onion is tender. Stir in chopped pulp, chiles, pimientos and stuffing mix. Divide stuffing mixture among zucchini halves. Sprinkle each with about 1 tablespoon cheese. Bake uncovered until hot, 30 to 35 minutes.

Mixed Roasted Vegetables

8 servings

This also makes a tasty meatless main dish; just toss roasted vegetables with 8 ounces of cooked pasta.

1 medium eggplant (1 1/2 pounds), cut into
    1 1/2-inch chunks
1 medium green bell pepper, cut into 1-inch
    pieces
1 medium red bell pepper, cut into 1-inch
    pieces
1 medium onion, cut into 8 wedges and
    separated
2 medium zucchini, cut into 1-inch pieces
1/2 pound whole mushrooms
1/3 cup chopped fresh or 2 tablespoons
    dried basil leaves
3 tablespoons olive or vegetable oil
2 tablespoons red wine vinegar
1 teaspoon dried oregano leaves
1/2 teaspoon salt
1/4 teaspoon pepper
1 medium tomato, seeded and cut into
    2-inch pieces
Grated Parmesan cheese, if desired

Heat oven to 350°.

Place eggplant, bell peppers, onion, zucchini and mushrooms in 3-quart casserole. Sprinkle evenly with basil.

Mix oil, vinegar, oregano, salt and pepper. Drizzle evenly over vegetables.

Bake uncovered 30 minutes. Add tomatoes; toss to coat. Bake uncovered about 15 minutes longer or until vegetables are tender. Serve with cheese.

Desserts

Caramel-Chocolate Pie (page 274)

About Cakes

Cakes play many roles—all of them delicious! There are cakes for celebrations and cakes for busy days; and—for folks looking for fat-free desserts—there's exceptional homemade Angel Food Cake. Frosting and glazes add the finishing touch and also give you a wonderful variety of combinations. So have some fun, and bake a cake!

Pans and Pan Preparation

- Use pans of the size called for in the recipe. To check the width of the pan, measure across the top from inside edge to inside edge. Baking a cake in too large of a pan will result in a pale, flat and shrunken cake. Too small or too shallow a pan will result in a bulge and a loss of shape.

- Shiny metal pans are preferred for baking cakes. They reflect heat away from the cake and produce a tender, light brown crust.

- Dark nonstick or glass baking pans should be used following the manufacturer's directions. These pans readily absorb heat, and a better result may be achieved if the baking temperature is reduced by 25°.

- Fill cake pans no more than half full. If using an unusually shaped pan (heart, star, bell), measure the capacity by filling the pan with water, then measure the water and use half that amount of batter. Cupcakes can be made from any remaining batter.

Mixing Cakes

- The cake recipes in this book have been tested with electric hand-held mixers. Because mixers vary in power, you may need to adjust the speed, particularly during the initial step of combining ingredients. If using a powerful stand mixer, be careful not to overmix. Overmixing can result in tunnels (large air holes) or cause the cake to sink in the center.

- The one-bowl cake-mixing method was developed using the electric mixer, but mixing also can be done by hand. Stir the ingredients to moisten, and combine them well. Beat 150 strokes for each minute of beating time (3 minutes equals 450 strokes). If a cake is not beaten enough, the volume will be lower.

- We recommend that stick margarine or butter be used for cakes when margarine or butter is specified. Vegetable oil spreads (also in stick form) with at least 65 percent fat can be substituted and the baked result will be satisfactory, although the batter may have a slightly softer consistency.

- We do not recommend using vegetable oil spreads with less than 65 percent fat (either in stick form or tubs), tub margarines or whipped products (whether butter, margarine or spreads). Because these products contain more water and less fat, using them can result in poor quality overall (thinner or softer consistency when mixing; less tender or wet and gummy texture after baking).

Baking Cakes

- Except where noted, bake cakes on the oven rack placed in the center of the oven.

- Cakes are done when a toothpick stuck in the center comes out clean.

- Do not place cakes directly from the oven in a drafty place to cool. They tend to mold quickly when covered and stored at room temperature.

Cutting Cakes

- For layer cakes, use a sharp, long, thin knife.

- For angel food, chiffon and pound cakes, use a long serrated knife or an electric knife.

- If the frosting sticks to the knife, dip the knife into hot water and wipe with a damp towel after cutting each slice.

- For fruitcake, use a thin, nonserrated or electric knife. For easiest slicing and a mellow flavor, make fruitcake three to four weeks ahead of time, then wrap and store in the refrigerator. It can be occasionally brushed with rum, brandy or bourbon for a rich mellow flavor.

Baking Cupcakes

Cupcakes are great to make for easy individual servings, especially at parties or picnics. They can be made from any of the cake batters and will yield 24 to 36 cupcakes.

- Line medium muffin cups, 2 1/2 × 1 1/4 inches, with paper baking cups.

- Fill each cup about 1/2 full. Bake 20 to 25 minutes or until toothpick inserted in center comes out clean.

- If you have only one 12-cup muffin pan, cover and refrigerate the remaining batter while the first cupcakes are baking. Then bake the remaining batter, adding 1 or 2 minutes to the baking time.

Baking with Confidence

PERFECT SHORTENING CAKES ARE:

High, golden brown
Slightly rounded, smooth top
Fine-grained, even texture, not crumbly
Soft, velvety, slightly moist, light, tender

Problem	Possible Cause
Pale	• too little sugar • too short baking time
Does not rise properly	• too much liquid • too much fat • too large pan • oven too cool
Peaked or cracked on top	• too much flour • too hot oven
Coarse grained	• too much shortening • underbeaten
Crumbly	• too much shortening • too much sugar • underbeaten
Dry	• too much baking powder • too long baking time
Heavy	• too much liquid • too much shortening • too much flour
Batter overflows	• too much batter in pan • pan too small • too much leavening

Starlight Yellow Cake

16 servings

Jazz up this favorite cake by stirring in 1/2 cup chopped nuts, dried cherries or flaked coconut before pouring into pans.

2 1/4 cups all-purpose flour*
1 1/2 cups sugar
1/2 cup shortening
1 1/4 cups milk
3 1/2 teaspoons baking powder
1 teaspoon salt
1 teaspoon vanilla
3 large eggs
Chocolate Buttercream Frosting (right)
or Peanut Butter Buttercream Frosting
(right), if desired

Heat oven to 350°. Grease bottom and sides of rectangular pan, 13×9×2 inches, 2 round pans, 9×1 1/2 inches, or 3 round pans, 8×1 1/2 inches, with shortening; lightly flour.

Beat all ingredients except Chocolate Buttercream Frosting with electric mixer on low speed 30 seconds, scraping bowl constantly. Beat on high speed 3 minutes, scraping bowl occasionally. Pour into pan(s).

Bake rectangle 40 to 45 minutes, 9-inch rounds 30 to 35 minutes, 8-inch rounds 20 to 25 minutes, or until toothpick inserted in center comes out clean or until cake springs back when touched lightly in center. Cool rectangle in pan on wire rack. Cool rounds 10 minutes; remove from pans to wire rack. Cool completely.

Frost rectangle or fill and frost layers with Chocolate Buttercream Frosting.

If using self-rising flour, omit baking powder and salt.

Peanut Butter Marble Cake: *Substitute peanut butter for the shortening. Pour two-thirds of the batter (about 3 cups) into pan(s). Stir 3 tablespoons baking cocoa and 1/8 teaspoon baking soda into remaining batter. Drop chocolate batter by generous tablespoonfuls randomly in mounds onto peanut butter batter. Pull knife through batters in S-shaped curves in one continuous motion for marbled design. Turn pan one-fourth turn; repeat marbling. Bake and cool as directed above. Frost with Peanut Butter Buttercream Frosting (below). If desired, drop about 1/4 cup prepared fudge topping by teaspoonfuls randomly over the top and marble as directed for the batter.*

Poppy Seed Cake: *Stir in 1/4 cup poppy seed with the sugar.*

CHOCOLATE BUTTERCREAM FROSTING

3 cups powdered sugar
1/3 cup *stick* margarine or butter, softened*
2 teaspoons vanilla
3 ounces unsweetened baking chocolate, melted and cooled
2 to 3 tablespoons milk

Mix all ingredients except milk in medium bowl.

Stir in milk until smooth and spreadable. Frosts one 13×9-inch cake generously or fills and frosts one 8- or 9-inch two-layer cake.

We do not recommend using vegetable oil spreads.

Note: *To fill and frost one 8-inch three-layer cake, use 4 1/2 cups powdered sugar, 1/2 cup stick margarine or butter, softened, 3 teaspoons vanilla and about 1/4 cup milk.*

Peanut Butter Marble Cake

PEANUT BUTTER BUTTERCREAM FROSTING

3 cups powdered sugar
1/3 cup peanut butter
1 1/2 teapoons vanilla
1/4 cup milk

Mix powdered sugar and peanut butter in medium bowl. Stir in vanilla and milk.

Beat until smooth and spreadable. Frosts one 13×9-inch cake or fills and frosts one 8- or 9-inch two-layer cake.

TIP

Place all ingredients in food processor. Cover and process, stopping, occasionally to scrape sides, until smooth and spreadable.

Maple-Pecan Cake

14 to 16 servings

Maple-Buttermilk Cake (below)
Maple-Butter Frosting (right)
1 cup finely chopped pecans
Chocolate Twigs (right), if desired
Malted-milk balls, if desired

Bake Maple-Buttermilk Cake as directed. Fill layers and frost side only with Maple-Butter Frosting. Place pecans on waxed paper. Hold cake as shown in diagram; roll side carefully in pecans to coat. Frost top of cake with remaining frosting in spiral design using large spatula. Garnish with Chocolate Twigs and malted-milk balls.

MAPLE-BUTTERMILK CAKE

2 1/2 cups all-purpose flour or 2 3/4 cups
    cake flour
1 1/2 cups sugar
1/2 cup (1 stick) margarine or butter, softened
1/4 cup shortening
1 1/2 cups buttermilk
1 1/2 teaspoons baking soda
3/4 teaspoon salt
1 1/2 teaspoons maple flavoring
3 eggs

Heat oven to 350°. Grease and flour 2 round pans, 9×1 1/2 inches, or 3 round pans, 8× 1 1/2 inches. Beat all ingredients in large bowl on medium speed 30 seconds, scraping bowl constantly. Beat on high speed 3 minutes, scraping bowl occasionally. Pour batter into pans.

    Bake 30 to 35 minutes or until toothpick inserted in center comes out clean. Cool 10 minutes; remove from pans. Cool completely.

COATING SIDES OF CAKES

Two filled cake layers can be rolled in chopped nuts, candies or flaked coconut to coat sides. Place nuts on waxed paper. Hold cake as shown in illustration. Roll side carefully in nuts to coat. (See photo of Maple-Pecan Cake.)

Storing Cakes

- Unfrosted cakes should be cooled completely before storing. They will become sticky if covered while warm.

- Foam-type cakes will stay fresh overnight stored in their baking pan and covered with waxed paper. Remove from pan and frost that day.

- Cakes with creamy-type frosting can be stored in a cake safe or under a large inverted bowl. They can also be loosely covered with aluminum foil, plastic wrap or waxed paper.

- Cakes with fluffy frosting should be served the same day they are made. If it is necessary to store this type of cake, use a cake safe or inverted bowl, with a knife slipped under the edge, so the container is not airtight.

- Refrigerate cakes with whipped cream toppings, cream fillings or cream cheese frostings. Cover with cake safe or large inverted bowl, or cover loosely with aluminum foil, plastic wrap or waxed paper.

MAPLE BUTTER FROSTING

3 cups powdered sugar
1/3 cup margarine or butter, softened
1/3 cup maple-flavored syrup

Mix all ingredients. Beat until frosting is smooth and of spreading consistency. If necessary, stir in additional syrup, 1/2 teaspoon at a time.

CHOCOLATE TWIGS

2 ounce white chocolate (white baking bar)
**   or semisweet chocolate**
1 teaspoon shortening

Melt chocolate and shortening. Pour into decorating bag with small writing tip. Squeeze melted chocolate onto waxed paper into twig shapes; sprinkle with white decorator's sugar, if desired. Let dry. Peel twigs from waxed paper; arrange on cake.

Maple Pecan Cake

Decadent Chocolate Cake with Raspberry Sauce

12 servings

1 cup semisweet chocolate chips
1/2 cup margarine or butter
1/2 cup all-purpose flour or cake flour
4 eggs, separated
1/2 cup sugar
1/2 cup semisweet chocolate chips
2 tablespoons margarine or butter
2 tablespoons corn syrup
Raspberry Sauce (right)

Heat oven to 325°. Grease springform pan, 8 × 2 1/2 inches, or round pan, 9 × 1 1/2 inches. Heat 1 cup chocolate chips and 1/2 cup margarine in 2-quart heavy saucepan over medium heat until chocolate chips are melted; cool 5 minutes. Stir in flour until smooth. Stir in egg yolks until well blended.

Beat egg whites in large bowl on high speed until foamy. Beat in sugar, 1 tablespoon at a time, until soft peaks form. Fold chocolate mixture into egg whites. Spread in pan.

Bake springform 35 to 40 minutes, round 30 to 35 minutes (top will appear dry and cracked) or until toothpick inserted in center comes out clean; cool 10 minutes.

Run knife along side of cake to loosen; remove side of springform pan. Invert cake onto wire rack; remove bottom of springform pan and cool cake completely. Place on serving plate.

Heat 1/2 cup chocolate chips, 2 tablespoons margarine and the corn syrup over medium heat until chocolate chips are melted. Spread over top of cake, allowing some to drizzle down side. Serve with Raspberry Sauce. Garnish with fresh raspberries and sweetened whipped cream, if desired.

RASPBERRY SAUCE

1 package (10 ounces) frozen raspberries, thawed, drained and juice reserved
1/4 cup sugar
2 tablespoons cornstarch
1 to 2 tablespoons orange- or raspberry-flavored liqueur, if desired

Add enough water to reserved juice to measure 1 cup. Mix sugar and cornstarch in 1-quart saucepan. Stir in juice and raspberries. Heat to boiling over medium heat. Boil and stir 1 minute; strain. Stir in liqueur.

Lemon Meringue Cake

8 to 10 servings

Meringue Cake (right)
1 package (4-serving size) lemon pudding and pie filling (not instant)
1/2 cup whipped cream

Bake Meringue Cake as directed. Prepare pudding and pie filling as directed on package. Refrigerate about 1 1/2 hours or until chilled. Stir pudding; spread 1 1/4 cups over meringue on 1 cake layer. Place remaining layer, meringue side up, on pudding. Spread with remaining pudding.

Place whipped cream in decorating bag with star tip. Pipe on whipped cream or garnish with whipped cream as desired. Serve within 30 minutes.

Lemon Meringue Cake and Strawberries and Cream Cake (page 245)

MERINGUE CAKE

1 1/2 cups cake flour
3/4 cup sugar
1 1/2 teaspoons baking powder
1/2 teaspoon salt
3/4 cup shortening
2/3 cup milk
1 1/2 teaspoons vanilla
4 eggs, separated
1 cup sugar

Heat oven to 325°. Grease sides of 2 round pans, 9×1 1/2 inches or 8×1 1/2 inches. Line bottoms of pans with cooking parchment paper or waxed paper circles. Beat flour, 3/4 cup sugar, the baking powder, salt, shortening, milk, vanilla and egg yolks in medium bowl on low speed 30 seconds, scraping bowl constantly. Beat on high speed 2 minutes, scraping bowl occasionally (batter will be stiff). Spread evenly in pans.

Beat egg whites in small bowl on medium speed until foamy. Beat in 1 cup sugar, 1 tablespoon at a time, on high speed until stiff peaks form. Spread half of the egg white mixture over batter in each pan.

Bake 30 to 35 minutes or until meringue looks set and dry. Cool 10 minutes. Loosen meringues from edges of pans with knife point if necessary. Carefully remove from pans and peel off paper. Place layers, meringue sides up, on wire racks. Cool completely.

Lemon-filled Coconut Cake

16 servings

Lemon Filling (right)
2 1/4 cups all-purpose flour
1 2/3 cups granulated sugar
2/3 cup shortening
1 1/4 cups milk
3 1/2 teaspoons baking powder
1 teaspoon salt
1 teaspoon vanilla
5 egg whites
1 cup flaked or shredded coconut
1 cup whipping (heavy) cream
1/4 cup powdered sugar

Prepare Lemon Filling; press plastic wrap onto hot filling. Refrigerate until set, about 1 hour.

Heat oven to 350°. Grease and flour 2 round pans, 8×1 1/2 or 9×1 1/2 inches. Beat flour, granulated sugar, shortening, milk, baking powder, salt and vanilla in 3-quart bowl on low speed, scraping bowl constantly, 30 seconds. Beat on high speed, scraping bowl occasionally, 2 minutes. Beat in egg whites on high speed, scraping bowl occasionally, 2 minutes. Stir in coconut. Pour into pans.

Bake until toothpick inserted in center comes out clean or top springs back when touched lightly, 30 to 35 minutes. Cool 10 minutes; remove from pans. Cool completely on wire rack.

Beat whipping cream and powdered sugar in chilled 1 1/2-quart bowl until stiff. Fill layers with Lemon Filling and frost with whipped cream; refrigerate. Immediately refrigerate any remaining cake.

LEMON FILLING

3/4 cup sugar
3 tablespoons cornstarch
1/4 teaspoon salt
3/4 cup water
1 tablespoon margarine or butter
1 teaspoon finely grated lemon peel
1/3 cup lemon juice
2 to 4 drops yellow food color, if desired

Mix sugar, cornstarch and salt in 1 1/2-quart saucepan. Gradually stir in water. Cook over medium heat, stirring constantly, until mixture thickens and boils. Boil and stir 5 minutes; remove from heat. Stir in margarine and lemon peel until margarine is melted. Gradually stir in lemon juice and food color.

Raspberry Jam Cake

16 servings

Southwesterners are particularly fond of traditional southern cakes, such as this spice-laden jam cake. You'll find that blackberry is the jam of choice in Texas and the western states, but in the Appalachian Mountain region, raspberry is the favorite. One thing everyone agrees on is that the buttery caramel frosting is just perfect! This rich dense cake keeps well for several days, so it's easy to have on hand when neighbors and friends drop by to chat over a cup of coffee.

1 cup (2 sticks) margarine or butter, softened
1/2 cup granulated sugar
1/2 cup packed brown sugar
4 eggs
1 jar (10 ounces) red raspberry preserves
  (about 1 cup)
3 1/4 cups all-purpose flour
1 teaspoon baking powder
1 teaspoon baking soda
1 teaspoon ground nutmeg
1 teaspoon ground cinnamon
1/2 teaspoon salt
1/4 teaspoon ground cloves
1 cup buttermilk
1 cup chopped pecans
Caramel Frosting (right)

Heat oven to 350°. Grease and flour tube pan, 10×4 inches. Beat margarine and sugars in 3-quart bowl on medium speed, scraping bowl constantly, until blended. Beat on high speed 1 minute. Beat in eggs and preserves until well blended. (Mixture will appear curdled.) Beat in flour, baking powder, baking soda, nutmeg, cinnamon, salt and cloves alternately with buttermilk, beginning and ending with flour mixture, until well blended. Stir in pecans. Pour into pan.

Bake until toothpick inserted in center comes out clean and top springs back when touched lightly, 70 to 75 minutes. Cool 10 minutes; remove from pan. Cool completely on wire rack. Frost with Caramel Frosting.

CARAMEL FROSTING
1/2 cup (1 stick) margarine or butter
1 cup packed brown sugar
1/4 cup milk
2 cups powdered sugar

Heat margarine in 2-quart saucepan until melted. Stir in brown sugar. Heat to boiling, stirring constantly. Boil and stir over low heat 2 minutes; stir in milk. Heat to boiling; remove from heat. Cool to lukewarm. Gradually stir in powdered sugar; beat until smooth and of spreading consistency. If frosting becomes too stiff, stir in additional milk, 1 teaspoon at a time.

Best Chocolate Cake with Fudge Frosting

1 cake

A chocolate treat that's a satisfying ending to any meal. For a quicker cake, try the sheet cake in the 13×9×2-inch pan.

2 cups all-purpose flour
2 cups sugar
1/2 cup shortening
3/4 cup water
3/4 cup buttermilk
1 teaspoon baking soda
1 teaspoon salt
1 teaspoon vanilla
1/2 teaspoon baking powder
2 eggs
4 ounces unsweetened chocolate, melted and cooled
Fudge Frosting (right)

Heat oven to 350°. Grease and flour rectangular pan, 13×9×2 inches, 3 round pans, 8×1 1/2 inches, or 2 round pans, 9×1/2 inches. Beat all ingredients except Fudge Frosting in large bowl on low speed 30 seconds, scraping bowl constantly. Beat on high speed 3 minutes, scraping bowl occasionally. Pour into pan(s).

Bake rectangular pan 40 to 45 minutes, round pans 30 to 35 minutes or until toothpick inserted in center comes out clean. Cool rounds 10 minutes; remove from pans. Cool completely. Prepare Fudge Frosting; frost cake. (Fill layers with 1/3 cup frosting; frost side and top with remaining frosting.)

FUDGE FROSTING

2 cups sugar
1/2 cup shortening
2/3 cup milk
1/2 teaspoon salt
3 ounces unsweetened chocolate
2 teaspoons vanilla

Mix all ingredients except vanilla in 2 1/2-quart saucepan. Heat to rolling boil, stirring occasionally. Boil 1 minute without stirring. Place saucepan in bowl of ice and water. Beat until frosting is smooth and of spreading consistency; stir in vanilla.

Best Chocolate Cake with Fudge Frosting

Angel Food Cake Deluxe

16 servings

Angel food cake is thought to have originated in St. Louis, Missouri, in the mid-nineteenth century. Some people believe that the recipe was brought by slaves from the South up the Mississippi River to St. Louis. Others believe that angel food cake can be traced to the Pennsylvania Dutch.

1 cup cake flour
1 1/2 cups powdered sugar
1 1/2 cups egg whites (about 12)
1 1/2 teaspoons cream of tartar
1 cup granulated sugar
1 1/2 teaspoons vanilla
1/2 teaspoon almond extract
1/4 teaspoon salt

Heat oven to 375°. Mix flour and powdered sugar. Beat egg whites and cream of tartar in large bowl on medium speed until foamy. Beat in granulated sugar on high speed, 2 tablespoons at a time, adding vanilla, almond extract and salt with the last addition of sugar; continue beating until meringue holds stiff peaks. Do not underbeat.

Sprinkle flour-sugar mixture, 1/4 cup at a time, over meringue, folding in gently just until mixture disappears. Spread in ungreased tube pan, 10×4 inches. Gently cut through batter with spatula.

Bake 30 to 35 minutes or until cracks feel dry and top springs back when touched lightly. Immediately invert pan onto heatproof funnel; let hang until cake is completely cool.

Gingerbread

9 servings

For a smooth and creamy treat, add a spoonful of whipped cream cheese before topping with sauce, or serve with whipped cream and a sprinkle of cinnamon.

2 1/3 cups all-purpose flour*
1/2 cup shortening
1/3 cup sugar
1 cup molasses
3/4 cup hot water
1 teaspoon baking soda
1 teaspoon ground ginger
1 teaspoon ground cinnamon
3/4 teaspoon salt
1 large egg
Divine Caramel Sauce (right) or
    Lemon Sauce (right), if desired

Heat oven to 325°. Grease bottom and sides of square pan, 9×9×2 inches, with shortening; lightly flour.

Beat all ingredients except Divine Caramel Sauce with electric mixer on low speed 30 seconds, scraping bowl constantly. Beat on medium speed 3 minutes, scraping bowl occasionally. Pour into pan.

Bake 50 to 55 minutes or until toothpick inserted in center comes out clean. Serve warm with Divine Caramel Sauce.

*Do not use self-rising flour in this recipe.

DIVINE CARAMEL SAUCE

2 cups sugar
3/4 cup *stick* margarine or butter*
2 cups whipping (heavy) cream
1 cup light corn syrup
Pinch of salt
1 teaspoon vanilla

Heat all ingredients except vanilla to boiling in heavy Dutch oven over medium heat, stirring constantly; reduce heat slightly. Boil about 30 minutes, stirring frequently, until sugar is dissolved and mixture is caramel colored.

Stir in vanilla. Serve hot or warm. Store in refrigerator up to 2 months.

We do not recommend using vegetable oil spreads.

LEMON SAUCE

1/2 cup sugar
2 tablespoons cornstarch
3/4 cup water
1 tablespoon grated lemon peel
1/4 cup lemon juice
2 tablespoons *stick* margarine or butter*

Mix sugar and cornstarch in 1-quart saucepan. Gradually stir in water. Cook over medium heat, stirring constantly, until mixture thickens and boils. Boil and stir 1 minute; remove from heat.

Stir in remaining ingredients. Serve warm or cool. Cover and refrigerate any remaining sauce.

Spreads with at least 65% vegetable oil can be substituted.

TIP

To microwave, mix sugar and cornstarch in 4-cup microwavable measure. Gradually stir in water. Microwave uncovered on high 3 to 4 minutes, stirring every minute, until thickened and clear. Stir in remaining ingredients.

Pound Cake

1 cake

1 1/2 cups margarine or butter, softened
2 3/4 cups sugar
5 eggs
1 teaspoon vanilla
3 cups all-purpose flour*
1 teaspoon baking powder
1/4 teaspoon salt
1 cup evaporated milk

Heat oven to 350°. Grease and flour tube pan, 10×4 inches, or 12-cup bundt pan. Beat margarine, sugar, eggs and vanilla in large mixer bowl on low speed, scraping bowl constantly, 30 seconds. Beat on high speed, scraping bowl occasionally, 5 minutes. Beat in flour, baking powder and salt alternately with milk on low speed. Pour into pan.

Bake until toothpick inserted in center comes out clean, 70 to 80 minutes. Cool in pan about 20 minutes; remove from pan.

Do not use self-rising flour in this recipe.

Carrot Cake

16 servings

This cake is mixed without an electric mixer. Use a food processor to shred the carrots and put the cake together even faster.

1 1/2 cups sugar
1 cup vegetable oil
3 large eggs
2 cups all-purpose flour*
1 1/2 teaspoons ground cinnamon
1 teaspoon baking soda
1 teaspoon vanilla
1/2 teaspoon salt
1/4 teaspoon ground nutmeg
3 cups shredded carrots (5 medium)
1 cup coarsely chopped nuts
Cream Cheese Frosting (right), if desired

Heat oven to 350°. Grease bottom and sides of rectangular pan, 13×9×2 inches, or 2 round pans, 8×1 1/2 or 9×1 1/2 inches, with shortening; lightly flour.

Mix sugar, oil and eggs in large bowl until blended; beat 1 minute. Stir in remaining ingredients except carrots, nuts and Cream Cheese Frosting; beat 1 minute. Stir in carrots and nuts. Pour into pan.

Bake rectangle 40 to 45 minutes, rounds 30 to 35 minutes, or until toothpick inserted in center comes out clean. Cool in pan on wire rack.

Frost rectangle or fill and frost layers with Cream Cheese Frosting.

If using self-rising flour, omit baking soda and salt.

Lighter Carrot Cake: *For less fat and fewer calories per serving, substitute 1/2 cup unsweetened applesauce for 1/2 cup of the oil and 1 egg plus 4 egg whites for the eggs. Decrease the chopped nuts to 1/2 cup.*

CREAM CHEESE FROSTING

1 package (8 ounces) cream cheese, softened
1/4 cup *stick* margarine or butter, softened*
2 teaspoons milk
1 teaspoon vanilla
4 cups powdered sugar

Beat cream cheese, margarine, milk and-vanilla inmedium bowl with electric mixer on low speed until smooth.

Gradually beat in powdered sugar on low speed, 1 cup at a time, until smooth and spreadable. Frosts one 13×9-inch cake generously, or fills and frosts one 8- or 9-inch two-layer cake. Refrigerate any remaining frosting.

We do not recommend using vegetable oil spreads.

Chocolate Cream Cheese Frosting: *Add 2 ounces unsweetened baking chocolate, melted and cooled, with the margarine.*

Black Forest Cherry Torte

Bonnie Butter Cake (page 250)
Cherry Filling (below)
1 1/2 cups chilled whipping cream
1/4 cup powdered sugar
1/3 bar (4-ounce size) sweet cooking chocolate, grated

Bake Bonnie Butter Cake in 9-inch layers as directed. Cool 10 minutes; remove from pans. Cool completely. Prepare Cherry Filling; refrigerate until chilled.

To assemble cake, place 1 layer, top side down, on serving plate. Beat whipping cream and powdered sugar in chilled bowl until very stiff. Form thin rim of whipped cream around edge of layer with decorators' tube or spoon. Fill center with Cherry Filling. Place other layer, top side up, on filling. Gently spread whipped cream on side and top of cake. Gently press chocolate by teaspoonfuls onto side of cake.

Place remaining whipped cream in decorators' tube with star tip. Pipe border of whipped cream around top edge of cake. Beginning from center of cake, outline individual portions in spoke design. Place desired number of reserved dipped cherries in each portion. Store torte in refrigerator.

CHERRY FILLING

2 tablespoons cornstarch
2 tablespoons sugar
1 can (16 ounces) pitted dark sweet cherries
1 tablespoon brandy flavoring

Mix cornstarch and sugar in 1-quart saucepan. Drain cherries, reserving syrup. Add enough water to reserved cherry syrup to measure 1 cup; stir into sugar-cornstarch mixture. Cook, stirring constantly, until mixture thickens and boils. Boil and stir 1 minute. Cool to lukewarm.

Stir in brandy flavoring. Dip 36 cherries into thickened syrup; reserve for top of cake. Cut remaining cherries into fourths and stir into thickened syrup.

Black Forest Cherry Torte

Caramel-Pecan Torte

18 servings

Caramel Cake (below)
Caramel Frosting (right)
1 to 2 teaspoons milk
Chopped pecans or chocolate-covered pecan
    halves

Bake Caramel Cake as directed. Cut cake horizontally into 3 layers. Reserve 1/2 cup Caramel Frosting. Fill layers with remaining frosting. Stir milk into reserved frosting until of drizzling consistency; drizzle over cake. Garnish with chopped pecans.

CARAMEL CAKE

2 1/4 cups all-purpose flour
1 3/4 cups packed brown sugar
1/2 cup shortening
1 cup milk
3 teaspoons baking powder
1/2 teaspoon salt
1 teaspoon vanilla
2 eggs
1/2 cup chopped pecans

Heat oven to 350°. Grease and flour 12-cup bundt cake pan. Beat all ingredients except pecans in large bowl on low speed 30 seconds, scraping bowl constantly. Beat on high speed 3 minutes, scraping bowl frequently. Stir in pecans. Pour batter into pan.

Bake 35 to 40 minutes or until toothpick inserted in center comes out clean. Cool 20 minutes; invert onto wire rack. Cool completely.

CARAMEL FROSTING

1/2 (1 stick) margarine or butter
1 cup packed brown sugar
1/4 cup milk
2 cups powdered sugar

Heat margarine over medium heat in 2-quart saucepan until melted. Stir in brown sugar. Heat to boiling, stirring constantly. Reduce heat to low. Boil and stir 2 minutes. Stir in milk. Heat to boiling; remove from heat. Cool to lukewarm. Gradually stir in powdered sugar. Place saucepan of frosting in bowl of cold water. Beat until smooth and of spreading consistency. If frosting becomes too stiff, stir in additional milk, 1 teaspoon at a time.

Strawberries and Cream Cake

16 servings

Do you love raspberries or peaches? Any berries or cut-up fruit can be substituted for the strawberries in this luscious cake.

Whipped Cream Cake (below)
Whipped Cream Cheese Frosting (right)
1 pint strawberries, sliced

Bake Whipped Cream Cake as directed. Spread 1 layer with 1/2 cup of the Whipped Cream Cheese Frosting; top with layer of sliced strawberries. Place remaining cake layer on top. Spread thin layer of frosting on side of cake.

Place remaining frosting in decorating bag with large open star tip #4B. Pipe vertical rows on side of cake. Pipe shell border around top edge of cake. Arrange sliced strawberries on top of cake. Refrigerate remaining cake.

WHIPPED CREAM CAKE

2 cups all-purpose flour or 2 1/4 cups cake flour
1 1/2 cups sugar
2 teaspoons baking powder
1/2 teaspoon salt
1 1/2 cups whipping (heavy) cream
3 eggs
1 1/2 teaspoons vanilla

Heat oven to 350°. Grease and flour 2 round pans, 8×1 1/2 or 9×1 1/2 inches. Mix flour, sugar, baking powder and salt.

Beat whipping cream in chilled large bowl until stiff. Beat eggs in small bowl about 5 minutes or until very thick and lemon colored. Fold eggs and vanilla into whipped cream. Add flour mixture, about 1/2 cup at a time, folding gently after each addition until blended. Pour batter into pans.

Bake 30 to 35 minutes or until toothpick inserted in center comes out clean. Cool 10 minutes; remove from pans. Cool completely.

WHIPPED CREAM CHEESE FROSTING

1 package (3 ounces) cream cheese, softened
1 tablespoon milk
2 cups whipping (heavy) cream
2/3 cup powdered sugar

Beat cream cheese and milk in chilled bowl on low speed until smooth; beat in whipping cream and powdered sugar. Beat on high speed, scraping bowl occasionally, until stiff peaks form.

TIP

Substitute 1 package (18.25 ounces) yellow cake mix with pudding for the Whipped Cream Cake. Prepare and bake as directed on package.

Fudge Tart

10 servings

5 ounces bittersweet chocolate, chopped
1/2 cup (1 stick) margarine or butter
1 1/2 cups sugar
3/4 cup all-purpose flour
4 eggs, beaten
Chocolate Glaze (right)
2 ounces white chocolate (white baking bar), chopped
1 tablespoon whipping (heavy) cream
Creamy Almond Sauce (right)

Heat oven to 350° Grease 11-inch tart pan with removable bottom. Heat chocolate and margarine in 1-quart saucepan over low heat until melted; cool slightly. Mix sugar, flour and eggs in large bowl until well blended. Stir in chocolate mixture; pour into tart pan.

Bake 30 to 35 minutes or until edges are set. Cool completely on wire rack.

Prepare Chocolate Glaze. Reserve 2 tablespoons for plate design, if desired. Spread remaining warm glaze over tart, melt white chocolate and whipping cream; drizzle over warm glaze. Pull knife through glaze for marble effect. Let stand until glaze is set. remove rim of pan before serving. Serve with Creamy Almond Sauce.

CHOCOLATE GLAZE

1 ounce unsweetened chocolate
1 teaspoon margarine or butter
1 cup powdered sugar
5 teaspoons boiling water

Heat chocolate and margarine over low heat until melted. Blend in powdered sugar and water until smooth. Stir in additional boiling water, 1/2 teaspoon at a time, until of drizzling consistency.

CREAMY ALMOND SAUCE

1/4 cup sugar
1 tablespoon cornstarch
1 1/2 cups milk
2 eggs, beaten
1/4 teaspoon almond extract

Mix sugar and cornstarch in 2-quart saucepan. Gradually stir in milk. Cook over medium heat, stirring constantly, until mixture thickens. Gradually stir at least half of the hot mixture into eggs; then stir back into hot mixture in saucepan. Boil and stir 1 minute; remove from heat. Stir in almond extract. Serve warm or chilled. Cover and refrigerate any remaining sauce.

TIP

You can drizzle the melted white chocolate randomly over the Chocolate Glaze, or follow a specific design.

Fudge Tart

Lemon Chiffon Cake

1 cake

2 cups all-purpose flour*
1 1/2 cups sugar
3 teaspoons baking powder
1 teaspoon salt
1/2 cup vegetable oil
7 egg yolks
3/4 cup cold water
2 teaspoons grated lemon peel
2 teaspoons vanilla
1 cup egg whites (7 or 8)
1/2 teaspoon cream of tartar
Lemon Butter Frosting (below)

Heat oven to 325°. Mix flour, sugar, baking powder and salt in bowl. Make a well and add in order: oil, egg yolks, water, lemon peel and vanilla. Beat with spoon until smooth. Beat egg whites and cream of tartar in large mixer bowl on high speed until stiff peaks form. Pour egg yolk mixture gradually over beaten whites, gently folding with rubber spatula just until blended. Pour into ungreased tube pan, 10×4 inches.

Bake until top springs back when touched lightly, about 1 1/4 hours. Invert pan on funnel; let hang until cake is cold. Remove from pan. Frost with Lemon Butter Frosting.

If using self-rising flour, omit baking powder and salt.

LEMON BUTTER FROSTING

1/3 cup margarine or butter, softened
3 cups powdered sugar
1/2 teaspoon grated lemon peel
About 2 tablespoons lemon juice

Mix margarine and powdered sugar. Beat in lemon peel and lemon juice until of spreading consistency.

Sour Cream–Chocolate Cake

1 cake

2 cups all-purpose flour*
2 cups sugar
1/4 cup shortening
1 cup water
3/4 cup dairy sour cream
1 1/4 teaspoons baking soda
1 teaspoon salt
1/2 teaspoon baking powder
1 teaspoon vanilla
2 eggs
4 ounces melted unsweetened chocolate
    (cool)
Chocolate Butter Frosting (right)

Heat oven to 350°. Grease and flour rectangular pan, 13×9×2 inches, or 2 round pans, 9×1 1/2 inches. Beat all ingredients except frosting in large mixer bowl on low speed, scraping bowl constantly, 30 seconds. Beat on high speed, scraping bowl occasionally, 3 minutes. Pour into pan(s).

Bake until top springs back when touched lightly, rectangular 40 to 45 minutes, layers 30 to 35 minutes. Cool layers 10 minutes; remove from pans. Cool completely. Frost rectangular or fill and frost layers with Chocolate Butter Frosting.

If using self-rising flour, decrease baking soda to 1/4 teaspoon and omit salt and baking powder.

CHOCOLATE BUTTER FROSTING

1/3 cup margarine or butter, softened
2 ounces melted unsweetened chocolate
**   (cool)**
2 cups powdered sugar
1 1/2 teaspoons vanilla
About 2 tablespoons milk

Mix margarine and chocolate. Mix in powdered sugar. Beat in vanilla and milk until smooth and of spreading consistency.

Chocolate Roll

10 servings

3/4 cup all-purpose flour*
1/4 cup cocoa
1 teaspoon baking powder
1/4 teaspoon salt
3 eggs
1 cup granulated sugar
1/3 cup water
1 teaspoon vanilla
Powdered sugar
1 quart chocolate mint or vanilla ice cream,
**   slightly softened**
French Silk Frosting (right)

Heat oven to 375°. Line jelly roll pan, 15 1/2 ×10 1/2×1 inch, with aluminum foil or waxed paper; grease. Mix flour, cocoa, baking powder and salt. Beat eggs in small mixer bowl until very thick and lemon colored, about 5 minutes. Pour eggs into large mixer bowl. Beat in granulated sugar gradually. Beat in water and vanilla on low speed. Mix in dry ingredients gradually, beating just until batter is smooth. Pour into pan, spreading batter to corners.

Bake until toothpick inserted in center comes out clean, 12 to 15 minutes.

Loosen cake from edges of pan; invert on towel sprinkled with powdered sugar. Carefully remove foil; trim off stiff edges if necessary. While hot, roll cake and towel from narrow end. Cool on wire rack. Unroll cake; remove towel. Spread with ice cream. Roll up; wrap in plastic wrap. Freeze until firm, about 6 hours. Frost with French Silk Frosting.

If using self-rising flour, omit baking powder and salt.

FRENCH SILK FROSTING

1/3 cup margarine or butter, softened
1 1/3 cups powdered sugar
1 ounce melted unsweetened chocolate
**   (cool)**
1/2 teaspoon vanilla
1 tablespoon milk

Beat margarine, powdered sugar, chocolate and vanilla on low speed until blended. Gradually beat in milk until fluffy.

Chocolate-Almond Roll: *Omit ice cream. Beat 1 cup chilled whipping cream, 1/4 cup powdered sugar and 2 tablespoons cocoa in chilled bowl until stiff. Beat in 1/2 teaspoon vanilla. Fold in 1/4 cup toasted sliced almonds. Spread roll with whipped cream mixture. Roll up; frost with French Silk Frosting. Refrigerate any remaining cake roll.*

Bonnie Butter Cake

1 cake

2/3 cup margarine or butter, softened
1 3/4 cups sugar
2 eggs
1 1/2 teaspoons vanilla
2 3/4 cups all-purpose flour*
2 1/2 teaspoons baking powder
1 teaspoon salt
1 1/4 cups milk
Chocolate Butter Frosting (page 249)

Heat oven to 350°. Grease and flour rectangular pan, 13×9×2 inches, or 2 round pans, 9×1 1/2 inches. Mix margarine, sugar, eggs and vanilla in large mixer bowl until fluffy. Beat on high speed, scraping bowl occasionally, 5 minutes. Beat in flour, baking powder and salt alternately with milk on low speed. Pour into pan(s).

Bake until toothpick inserted in center comes out clean, rectangular 45 to 50 minutes, layers 30 to 35 minutes. Cool layers 10 minutes; remove from pan. Cool completely. Frost rectangular or fill and frost layers with Chocolate Butter Frosting.

*If using self-rising flour, omit baking powder and salt.

Peach-Almond Shortcake

6 to 8 servings

2 cups all-purpose flour
2 tablespoons sugar
3 teaspoons baking powder
1 teaspoon salt
1/3 cup shortening
3/4 cup milk
1 tablespoon margarine or butter, softened
1/4 cup packed brown sugar
1/2 cup slivered almonds
Almond Whipped Cream (below)
4 cups sweetened sliced peeled peaches

Heat oven to 450°. Grease round pan, 9×1 1/2 inches. Mix flour, 2 tablespoons sugar, the baking powder and salt. Cut in shortening. Stir in milk. Spread in pan; brush with margarine. Sprinkle with brown sugar and almonds.

Bake until golden brown, about 20 minutes. Remove from pan; cool slightly. Split shortcake to make 2 layers. Fill layers with half of the Almond Whipped Cream and peaches. Top each serving with remaining whipped cream and peaches.

ALMOND WHIPPED CREAM

1 cup whipping (heavy) cream, chilled
3 tablespoons sugar
1/2 teaspoon almond extract

Beat all ingredients in chilled bowl until soft peaks form.

Applesauce-Spice Cake

1 cake

2 1/2 cups all-purpose flour*
2 cups sugar
1 cup raisins
1/2 cup chopped walnuts
1/2 cup shortening
1 1/2 cups applesauce
1/2 cup water
1 1/2 teaspoons baking soda
1 1/2 teaspoons salt
3/4 teaspoon ground cinnamon
1/2 teaspoon ground cloves
1/2 teaspoon ground allspice
1/4 teaspoon baking powder
2 eggs
Browned Butter Frosting (right)

Heat oven to 350°. Grease and flour rectangular pan, 13×9×2 inches, or 2 round pans, 8 or 9×1 1/2 inches. Beat all ingredients except Browned Butter Frosting in large mixer bowl on low speed, scraping bowl constantly, 30 seconds. Beat on high speed, scraping bowl occasionally, 3 minutes. Pour into pan(s).

Bake until toothpick inserted in center comes out clean, rectangular 60 to 65 minutes, layers 50 to 55 minutes or. Cool layers 10 minutes; remove from pans. Cool completely. Frost rectangular or fill and frost layers with Browned Butter Frosting.

Do not use self-rising flour in this recipe.

TIP

Carefully wipe the knife blade with vegetable oil before chopping the raisins, to prevent sticking.

BROWNED BUTTER FROSTING

1/3 cup margarine or butter
3 cups powdered sugar
1 1/2 teaspoons vanilla
About 2 tablespoons milk

Heat margarine over medium heat until delicate brown. Mix in powdered sugar. Beat in vanilla and milk until smooth and of spreading consistency.

Dinette Cake

1 cake

1 1/4 cups all-purpose flour*
1 cup sugar
1 1/2 teaspoons baking powder
1/2 teaspoon salt
3/4 cup milk
1/3 cup shortening
1 egg
1 teaspoon vanilla
French Silk Frosting (page 249)

Heat oven to 350°. Grease and flour square pan, 8×8×2 or 9×9×2 inches, or round pan 9×1 1/2 inches. Beat all ingredients except frosting in large mixer bowl on low speed, scraping bowl constantly, 30 seconds. Beat on high speed, scraping occasionally, 3 minutes. Pour into pan.

Bake until toothpick inserted in center comes out clean, square 35 to 50 minutes, round 35 minutes; cool. Frost with French Silk Frosting.

If using self-rising flour, omit baking powder and salt.

Hot Fudge Pudding Cake

9 servings

1 cup all-purpose flour*
3/4 cup granulated sugar
2 tablespoons cocoa
2 teaspoons baking powder
1/4 teaspoon salt
1/2 cup milk
2 tablespoons vegetable oil
1 teaspoon vanilla
1 cup chopped nuts, if desired
1 cup packed brown sugar
1/4 cup cocoa
1 3/4 cups hottest tap water
Ice cream

Heat oven to 350°. Mix flour, granulated sugar, 2 tablespoons cocoa, the baking powder and salt in ungreased baking pan, 9×9×2 inches. Mix in milk, oil and vanilla with fork until smooth. Stir in nuts. Spread in pan. Sprinkle with brown sugar and 1/4 cup cocoa. Pour hot water over batter.

Bake 40 minutes. Let stand 15 minutes; spoon into dessert dishes or cut into squares and invert on dessert plates. Top with ice cream and spoon sauce over each serving.

If using self-rising flour, omit baking powder and salt.

Hot Fudge–Butterscotch Pudding Cake: *Substitute 1 package (6 ounces) butterscotch chips for the nuts. Decrease brown sugar to 1/2 cup and the 1/4 cup cocoa to 2 tablespoons.*

Tips for Cheesecakes

- Cheesecakes are baked at low temperatures to prevent excess shrinkage. The center may look slightly soft but will set while chilling. Refrigerate cheesecakes for at least three hours (or as directed in recipe) before serving.

- To check for doneness, do not insert a knife in the center, because the hole could cause cheesecake to crack. Touch lightly or gently shake the pan. Center may jiggle slightly but will set while refrigerated.

- Let cheesecake stand at room temperature no longer than 15 minutes after baking and before refrigerating. Then refrigerate up to 3 hours uncovered. If covered immediately, moisture may condense and drip on cheesecake top. Cover cheesecake for remaining refrigeration to prevent drying out or picking up other food odors.

- Run metal spatula along side of cheesecakes with side crusts to loosen after baking and after refrigerating. Otherwise, cheesecake could pull away from crust as it cools if not loosened from side of pan.

- Cheesecakes cut easily when a wet knife is used, cleaning after each cut. Or use a piece of dental floss.

Lindy's Cheesecake

20 servings

1 cup all-purpose flour
1/2 cup margarine or butter, softened
1/4 cup sugar
1 tablespoon grated lemon peel
1 egg yolk
5 packages (8 ounces each) cream cheese, softened
1 3/4 cups sugar
3 tablespoons all-purpose flour
1 tablespoon grated orange peel
1 tablespoon grated lemon peel
1/4 teaspoon salt
5 eggs
2 egg yolks
1/4 cup whipping (heavy) cream
3/4 cup whipping (heavy) cream
1/3 cup toasted slivered almonds, if desired

Move oven rack to lowest position. Heat oven to 400°. Lightly grease springform pan, 9×3 inches; remove bottom. Mix 1 cup flour, the margarine, 1/4 cup sugar, 1 tablespoon lemon peel and 1 egg yolk with hands. Press one-third of the mixture evenly on bottom of pan. Place on cookie sheet.

Bake 8 to 10 minutes or until golden brown; cool. Assemble bottom and side of pan; secure side. Press remaining mixture all the way up side of pan.

Heat oven to 475°. Beat cream cheese, 1 3/4 cups sugar, 3 tablespoons flour, the orange peel, 1 tablespoon lemon peel, the salt and 2 eggs in large bowl until smooth. Continue beating, adding remaining eggs and 2 egg yolks, one at a time, until blended. Beat in 1/4 cup whipping cream on low speed. Pour into pan.

Bake 15 minutes. Reduce oven temperature to 200°. Bake 1 hour. Turn off oven and leave cheesecake in oven 15 minutes. Run metal spatula along side of cheesecake to loosen before and after refrigerating. Cover and refrigerate at least 12 hours.

Remove cheesecake from side of pan. Beat 3/4 cup whipping cream in chilled bowl until stiff. Spread whipped cream over top of cheesecake. Decorate with almonds. Refrigerate any remaining cheesecake.

Lindy's Cheesecake Squares: *Heat oven to 400°. Lightly grease rectangular pan, 13×9×2 inches. Press crust mixture on bottom of pan. Do not place pan on cookie sheet. Bake 15 minutes; cool. Heat oven to 475°. Pour cream cheese mixture into pan. Bake 15 minutes. Reduce oven temperature to 200°. Bake about 45 minutes or until center is set. Turn off oven and leave cheesecake in oven 15 minutes; cool 15 minutes. Cover and refrigerate at least 12 hours.*

Continue as directed—except increase almonds to 1/2 cup.

Pumpkin Cheesecake

20 servings

A wonderful variation on cheesecake, which could easily become a favorite Thanksgiving dessert.

1 1/2 cups graham cracker crumbs
1/2 finely chopped pecans
1/3 cup packed brown sugar
1/2 cup margarine or butter, melted
3 packages (8 ounces each) cream cheese, softened
1/2 cup sour cream
1 cup packed brown sugar
2 teaspoons ground cinnamon
1/2 teaspoon ground nutmeg
1/2 teaspoon ground ginger
1/4 teaspoon ground allspice
1 can (16 ounces) pumpkin
3 eggs
Caramelized Sugar (right)

Mix graham cracker crumbs, pecans, 1/3 cup brown sugar and the margarine. Press evenly on bottom and side of ungreased springform pan, 9×3 inches. Refrigerate 20 minutes.

Heat oven to 300°. Beat cream cheese, sour cream, 1 cup brown sugar and the spices in large bowl on medium speed until smooth. Add pumpkin. Beat in eggs on low speed. Pour over crumb mixture.

Bake about 1 hour 15 minutes or until center is firm. Cover and refrigerate at least 3 hours but no longer than 48 hours.

Prepare Caramelized Sugar; drizzle with fork over top of chilled cheesecake. Loosen cheesecake from side of pan; remove side of pan. Place cheesecake on plate. Refrigerate any remaining cheesecake immediately.

CARAMELIZED SUGAR

1 cup sugar
3 tablespoons water

Combine sugar and water in small saucepan. Boil mixture over medium heat, stirring until sugar is dissolved. Boil syrup, without stirring, until golden brown. Remove from heat and gently swirl until syrup stops cooking. Let caramel cool about 1 minute or until thick enough to drizzle from fork.

Bittersweet Chocolate Cheesecake with White Truffle Sauce

12 servings

2 packages (8 ounces each) cream cheese, softened
1 teaspoon vanilla
2/3 cup sugar
1 tablespoon all-purpose flour
3 eggs
8 ounces bittersweet chocolate, melted and cooled
White Truffle Sauce (right)

Heat oven to 275°. Lightly grease springform pan, 9×3 inches. Beat cream cheese and vanilla on medium speed in medium bowl until smooth. Gradually add sugar, beating until fluffy. Beat in flour. Beat in eggs, one at a time. Beat in chocolate; pour into pan.

Bake about 1 hour 15 minutes or until center is firm. Cool 15 minutes. Run metal spatula along side of cheesecake to loosen before and after refrigerating. Cover and refrigerate about 3 hours or until chilled. Meanwhile, prepare White Truffle Sauce.

Remove cheesecake from side of pan. Let cheesecake stand at room temperature 15 minutes before cutting. Serve cheesecake with sauce and, if desired, fresh raspberries or strawberries. Refrigerate any remaining cheesecake.

WHITE TRUFFLE SAUCE

1 package (6 ounces) white chocolate (white baking bar), chopped
2 tablespoons margarine or butter
1/2 cup whipping (heavy) cream

Heat baking bar and margarine in heavy 2-quart saucepan over low heat, stirring constantly, until melted (mixture will be thick and grainy); remove from heat. Stir in whipping cream until smooth. Cover and refrigerate about 2 hours or until chilled.

Chocolate Terrine

16 servings

This luscious dessert takes its name from the pan it was cooked in. We use a loaf pan for this elegant treat with wonderful results.

1 package (3 1/2 ounces) almond paste
1 1/2 cups half-and-half
4 squares (1 ounce each) semisweet chocolate, coarsely chopped
4 ounces white chocolate (vanilla-flavored candy coating), coarsely chopped
4 eggs, slightly beaten
2 tablespoons brandy or 2 teaspoons brandy extract
Chocolate Glaze (right)

Line loaf pan, 8 1/2×4 1/2×2 1/2 inches, with aluminum foil, leaving about 2 inches overhanging sides. Roll almond paste between 2 sheets waxed paper into rectangle, 8×4 inches; cover with plastic wrap and set aside.

Heat oven to 350°. Heat half-and-half, semisweet chocolate and white chocolate over low heat, stirring constantly, until chocolates are melted and mixture is smooth; cool slightly. Gradually stir eggs and brandy into chocolate mixture. Pour into lined pan. Place pan in pan of very hot water (1 inch deep) in oven.

Bake until knife inserted halfway between edge and center comes out clean, 40 to 50 minutes. Remove from water. Remove waxed paper from almond paste and immediately place on hot terrine; cool 1 hour. Cover and refrigerate at least 6 hours but no longer than 24 hours.

Reserve Chocolate Glaze; reserve 1/4 cup. Remove terrine from pan by inverting on serving plate. Carefully remove foil. Spread remaining glaze evenly and smoothly over sides and top of terrine.

Stir 1 to 2 tablespoons powdered sugar into reserved chocolate glaze until smooth and of desired consistency. Place in decorating bag with small writing tip or small sturdy plastic storage bag. (If using plastic bag, cut off very small corner of bag, about 1/8 inch in diameter.) Write *Terrine* on top and decorate around edges of top with remaining chocolate. To serve, cut into 8 slices, about 1 inch each; cut slices into halves. Refrigerate any remaining terrine.

CHOCOLATE GLAZE

1 cup semisweet chocolate chips
1/4 cup margarine to butter
2 tablespoons corn syrup

Heat chocolate chips, margarine and corn syrup over low heat, stirring constantly, until chocolate is melted; cool.

About Pies and Pastry

Enjoy the collection of pies and pastries here, from luscious fruit pies to creamy custard-based favorites. Have fun experimenting with pretty crusts—everything you need to know is right here!

Pans and Preparation

- Choose heat-resistant glass pie plates or dull-finish (anodized) aluminum pie pans. Never use a shiny pan because the pan reflects heat and the pie will have a soggy bottom crust.

- The most common pie size is 9 inches. Even though pie plates and pans on the market may be labeled 9 inches, they can vary in capacity. Our pie recipes were developed with pie plates that hold about 5 cups. However, we often use 8 cups of fruit for 2-crust pies for a full baked pie, as the fruit does cook down during baking.

- Because of the amount of fat in pastry and crusts, pie plates and pans usually are not greased.

- Nonstick pie pans can cause pastry to shrink excessively when baking one-crust pie shells. Be sure pastry is securely hooked over the edge of the pan.

Mixing and Rolling Pastry

- A pastry blender is a great help to cut the shortening evenly into the flour. If you don't own one, use two knives; with the knife blades almost touching each other, move the knives back and forth in opposite directions in a parallel cutting motion. The side of a fork or a wire whisk also can be used. The shortening melts during baking, producing a flaky texture throughout.

- Don't overwork pastry or it will become tough.

- If using self-rising flour, omit the salt. Pastry made with self-rising flour will be slightly different—mealy and tender instead of flaky and tender.

- Unbleached flour works especially well for pastry, as shrinkage is diminished and the baked pastry color is more golden.

- To roll out pastry, choose the method that works best for you. (See "How to Shape Pastry," page 258.) We like the following method best because the pastry does not stick to the flat surface or the rolling pin. Anchor a pastry cloth or kitchen towel (not terry cloth) around a large cutting board (at least 12×12 inches) with masking tape, and use a cloth cover (stockinet) for your rolling pin to keep the dough from sticking. Rub flour into both cloths; this will prevent sticking, yet the flour won't be absorbed by the dough.

    If a pastry cloth or rolling pin cover is not available, rub flour into a large cutting board (at least 12×12 inches) and into the rolling pin.

    Begin rolling from the center out, lifting and turning the pastry occasionally. This will help prevent sticking. If the dough begins to stick, rub more flour into the flat surface and rolling pin a little at a time.

- To make rolling and shaping even easier, wrap flattened round of pastry tightly and refrigerate at least 15 minutes. This allows the moisture to be evenly absorbed, the shortening to solidify and the gluten to relax for easier rolling.

Baking Pies and Pastry

- Bake pies and pie crusts on the oven shelf located in the center of the oven. In some electric ovens, placing the oven shelf on the lowest rack puts the pie closer to the heating element, resulting in a drier, flakier bottom crust. You may also find the top of the pie may not have to be shielded with aluminum foil to prevent overbrowning.

- To give a special, more finished look to the top crust of two-crust pies, try one of the following before baking:
  Shiny crust—brush with milk.
  Sugary crust—moisten with water, then sprinkle with granulated sugar.
  Glazed crust—brush the crust lightly with a beaten egg or an egg yolk mixed with a little water.

- To glaze a two-crust pie after baking, brush with a mixture of 1/2 cup powdered sugar, 2 teaspoons finely shredded orange or lemon peel and 1 tablespoon orange or lemon juice (Do not allow glaze to run over edge of pie.)

- Pies are baked at higher temperatures (375° to 425°) than cakes so the rich pastry dries and becomes flaky and golden brown while the filling cooks throughout.

- To prevent excessive browning, add aluminum foil. (See "How to Prevent Excessive Browning of Pastry Edges," page 264.) Bake as directed, removing foil 15 minutes before end of baking time to allow edge to brown.

- Prevent an unbaked unfilled one-crust pie shell from puffing up as it bakes by pricking the pastry thoroughly with a fork just before baking to allow steam to escape. For one-crust pies such as pumpkin or pecan pie where the filling is baked in the shell, do not prick the crust because the filling would seep under the crust during baking.

- Shape crumb crusts evenly and make them firm and smooth by pressing another pie plate of the same diameter firmly into the crust. Do this after pressing the crumbs in by hand.

Pie Yields and Storage

- Most of the pies in this book make 8 servings. Very rich pies make 10 to 12 servings.

- Refrigerate pies that contain eggs, such as pumpkin and cream pies.

- Pie shells can be frozen either unbaked or baked. Frozen unbaked shells will keep two months and baked shells four months. To thaw baked pie shells, unwrap and let stand at room temperature, or heat in 350° oven about 6 minutes. Do not thaw unbaked shells; immediately bake after removing from freezer.

- Do not freeze custard or cream pies with meringue topping.

- Baked fruit pies can be frozen. They are easiest to wrap if frozen uncovered first, then wrapped tightly or placed in plastic freezer bags. Baking before freezing prevents soggy crusts or the possible texture breakdown of raw fruit. Frozen baked pies will keep up to four months.

- To serve frozen two-crust pies, unwrap and thaw at room temperature 1 hour. Heat in 375° oven on lowest rack 35 to 40 minutes or until warm.

How To Shape Pastry

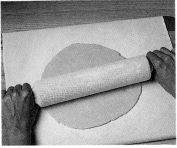

1. Roll pastry from center to outside in all directions, occasionally giving it a quarter turn. For even thickness, lift the rolling pin as it approaches the edge.

2. Push edge of pastry in gently with sides of hands to keep it circular when rolling it out. Lift pastry occasionally to prevent it from sticking to cloth.

3. Fold pastry into quarters, place in pie plate with point in center. Unfold and gently ease into plaste, being careful not to stretch pastry. Trim.

4. For two-crust pie, cut slits or special design in top pastry before folding. Carefully place folded pastry over filling and unfold. Let top pastry overhang 1 inch beyond edge of pie plate. Fold and roll overhanging pastry under edge of bottom pastry, pressing to seal.

5. Form a stand-up rim on the edge of the pie plate while pinching the top and bottom edges together.

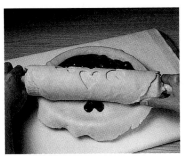

For pastry top with lots of cutouts, be sure bottom of pastry is floured well. Roll onto rolling pin and unroll over filling. Or slide flat end of cookie sheet under pastry and gently slide over filling, shaking pan if needed.

Favorite Pastry

8 servings per pie pastry

ONE-CRUST PIE, 9 INCHES

1 cup all-purpose flour
1/2 teaspoon salt
1/3 cup lard or 1/3 cup plus 1 tablespoon
shortening
2 to 3 tablespoons cold water

ONE-CRUST PIE, 10 INCHES

1 1/3 cups all-purpose flour
1/2 teaspoon salt
1/4 cup plus 3 tablespoons lard or 1/2 cup
shortening
3 to 4 tablespoons cold water

TWO-CRUST PIE, 9 INCHES

2 cups all-purpose flour
1 teaspoon salt
2/3 cup lard or 2/3 cup plus 2 tablespoons
shortening
4 to 5 tablespoons cold water

TWO-CRUST PIE, 10 INCHES

2 2/3 cups all-purpose flour
1 teaspoon salt
3/4 cup plus 2 tablespoons lard or 1 cup
shortening
7 to 8 tablespoons cold water

Mix flour and salt. Cut in lard until particles are size of small peas. Sprinkle with water, 1 tablespoon at a time, tossing with fork until all flour is moistened and pastry almost cleans side of bowl (1 to 2 teaspoons water can be added if necessary).

Gather pastry into ball; shape into flattened round on lightly floured cloth-covered surface. (For Two-Crust Pie, divide pastry in half and shape into 2 rounds.)

Roll pastry 2 inches larger than inverted pie plate with floured cloth-covered rolling pin. Fold pastry into fourths; unfold and ease into plate, pressing firmly against bottom and side.

For One-Crust Pie: Trim overhanging edge of pastry 1 inch from rim of plate. Fold and roll pastry under, even with plate. Flatten pastry evenly on rim of pie plate. Press firmly around edge with tines of fork, dipping fork into flour occasionally to prevent sticking. Or build up edge of pastry. Place index finger on inside of pastry edge and knuckles (or thumb and index finger) on outside. Pinch pastry into V shape; pinch again to sharpen. Fill and bake as directed in recipe.

For Baked Pie Shell: Heat oven to 475°. Prick bottom and side thoroughly with fork. Bake 8 to 10 minutes or until light brown; cool.

For Two-Crust Pie: Turn desired filling into pastry-lined pie plate. Trim overhanging edge of pastry 1/2 inch from rim of plate. Roll other round of pastry. Fold into fourths; cut slits so steam can escape.

Place over filling and unfold. Trim overhanging edge of pastry 1 inch from rim of plate. Fold and roll top edge under lower edge, pressing on rim to seal. Flatten pastry evenly on rim of pie plate. Press firmly around edge with tines of fork, dipping fork into flour occasionally to prevent sticking. Or build up edge of pastry. Place index finger on inside of pastry edge and knuckles (or thumb and index finger) on outside. Pinch pastry into V shape; pinch again to sharpen.

Deep-Dish Cherry-Berry Pie

9 servings

**Favorite Pastry for 9-inch one-crust pie
    (page 259)**
3/4 cup sugar
1/2 cup all-purpose flour
2 1/3 cups fresh red tart cherries, pitted*
2 cups fresh strawberries, cut in half**
1 teaspoon grated orange peel
1 tablespoon orange juice
Red food color, if desired
1 tablespoon butter or margarine

Heat oven to 425°. Generously grease square pan, 9×9×2 inches, or deep-dish pie plate, 9 1/2×1 3/4 inches. Prepare pastry as directed—except roll into 10-inch square. Make cutouts near center so steam can escape. Mix sugar and flour in medium bowl; stir in cherries, strawberries, orange peel, orange juice and red food color. Turn into pan. Dot with butter. Fold pastry in half; place over fruit mixture. Fold edges of pastry just under inside edges of pan; press pastry to edges of pan.

Bake about 55 minutes or until juice begins to bubble through cutouts in crust. Serve warm with whipping (heavy) cream if desired.

*2 cans (about 16 ounces each) pitted red tart cherries, drained, can be substituted for the fresh cherries.
**2 cups frozen strawberries, thawed, drained and cut in half, can be substituted for the fresh strawberries.

Country Apple Pie

8 servings

Apple pie is particularly nice when served with ice cream or a slice of Cheddar cheese.

**Favorite Pastry for 10-inch two-crust pie
    (page 259)**
1 cup sugar
1/4 cup all-purpose flour
3/4 teaspoon ground cinnamon
1/2 teaspoon ground nutmeg
Dash of salt
**8 cups thinly sliced peeled tart cooking
    apples (about 8 medium)**
4 tablespoons whipping (heavy) cream

Heat oven to 425°. Prepare pastry. Mix sugar, flour, cinnamon, nutmeg and salt. Stir in apples. Turn into pastry-lined deep-dish pie plate, 9×1 1/2 inches, or pie plate, 10×1 1/2 inches. Drizzle with 3 tablespoons of the whipping cream.

Cover with top crust that has slits cut in it; seal and flute. Brush with remaining whipping cream. Top with leaf or other shapes cut from pastry scraps if desired.

Bake 40 to 45 minutes or until crust is brown and juice begins to bubble through slits in crust.

Berry Pie

1 pie

Lattice Top (below)
1 cup sugar
1/3 cup all-purpose flour*
4 cups fresh berries (raspberries,
    blackberries, boysenberries)
2 tablespoons margarine or butter
Milk

Heat oven to 425°. Prepare Lattice Top. Mix sugar and flour; gently stir in berries. Turn into pastry-lined pie plate; dot with margarine. Arrange pastry strips on filling as directed; trim ends. Seal and flute, building up high edge. Brush pastry with milk; sprinkle with sugar if desired. Cover edge with 2- to 3-inch strip of aluminum foil to prevent excessive browning; remove foil during last 15 minutes of baking.

Bake until crust is golden brown, 35 to 40 minutes.

*Self-rising flour can be used in this recipe.

LATTICE TOP

Favorite Pastry for 9-inch Two-Crust Pie
    (page 259)

Prepare pastry for 9-inch Two-Crust Pie as directed—except leave 1 inch overhang on lower crust. After rolling pastry for top crust, cut into 10 strips, about 1/2 inch wide. (Pastry wheel can be used for more decorative strips.) Place 5 strips across filling. Weave a cross-strip through center by first folding back every other strip going the other way. Continue weaving until lattice is complete, folding back alternate strips each time cross-strip is added.

Blueberry Pie: *Decrease sugar to 1/2 cup, add 1/2 teaspoon ground cinnamon and use 4 cups fresh blueberries. Sprinkle blueberries with 1 tablespoon lemon juice before dotting with margarine.*

Berry Pie

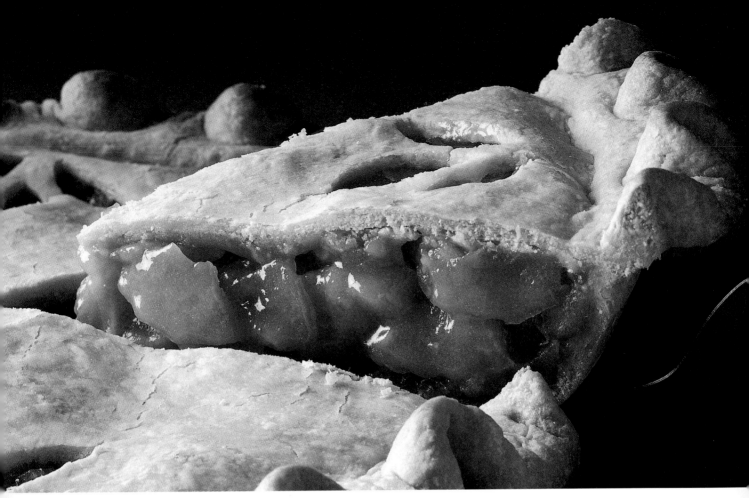

Applescotch Pie

Applescotch Pie

1 pie

5 cups thinly sliced peeled tart apples
   (about 5 medium)
1 cup packed brown sugar
1/4 cup water
1 tablespoon lemon juice
1/4 cup all-purpose flour*
2 tablespoons granulated sugar
3/4 teaspoon salt
1 teaspoon vanilla
3 tablespoons margarine or butter
Favorite Pastry for 9-inch Two-Crust Pie
   (page 259)

Mix apples, brown sugar, water and lemon juice in 2-quart saucepan. Heat to boiling; reduce heat. Cover and simmer just until apples are tender, 7 to 8 minutes. Mix flour, granulated sugar and salt; stir into apple mixture. Cook, stirring constantly, until mixture thickens and boils. Boil and stir 1 minute; remove from heat. Stir in vanilla and margarine; cool.

Heat oven to 425°. Prepare pastry. Turn apple mixture into pastry-lined pie plate. Cover with top crust that has slits cut in it; seal and flute. Cover edge with 2- to 3-inch strip of aluminum foil to prevent excessive browning; remove foil during last 15 minutes of baking.

Bake until crust is golden brown, 40 to 45 minutes.

*If using self-rising flour, omit salt.

Bake until crust is golden brown and juice begins to bubble through slits in crust, 40 to 50 minutes.

*Self-rising flour can be used in this recipe.

Blushing Peach Pie

1 pie

**Favorite Pastry for 9-inch Two-Crust Pie
   (page 259)**
**2 cans (29 ounces each) sliced peaches,
   drained**
1/2 cup sugar
1/4 cup all-purpose flour*
1/4 cup red cinnamon candies
2 tablespoons margarine or butter

Heat oven to 425°. Prepare pastry. Mix peaches, sugar, flour and candies; turn into pastry-lined pie plate. Dot with margarine. Cover with top crust that has slits cut in it; seal and flute. Cover edge with 2- to 3-inch strip of aluminum foil to prevent excessive browning; remove foil during last 15 minutes of baking.

Bake until crust is golden brown and juice begins to bubble through slits in crust, 40 to 50 minutes.

*Self-rising flour can be used in this recipe.

Cranberry-Apple Pie

Cranberry-Apple Pie

**Favorite Pastry for 9-inch Two-Crust Pie
   (page 259)**
1 3/4 cups sugar
1/4 cup all-purpose flour*
**3 cups sliced peeled tart apples (about
   3 medium)**
2 cups fresh or frozen (thawed) cranberries
2 tablespoons margarine or butter

Heat oven to 425°. Prepare pastry. Mix sugar and flour. Alternate layers of apples, cranberries and sugar mixture in pastry-lined pie plate, beginning and ending with apples. Dot with margarine. Cover with top crust that has slits cut in it; seal and flute. Cover edge with 2- to 3-inch strip of aluminum foil to prevent excessive browning; remove foil during last 15 minutes of baking.

How to Prevent Excessive Browning of Pastry Edges

Cover edge of a two-crust pie with a 2- to 3-inch strip of aluminum foil and gently mold to edge of pie.

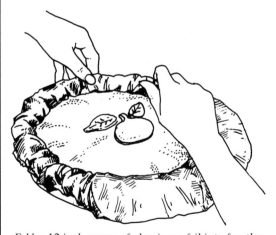

Fold a 12-inch square of aluminum foil into fourths; trim the open corner to make a 12-inch circle. Cut a 3-inch strip from the curved edge. Unfold and gently mold to edge of pie.

Spicy Walnut-Raisin Pie

1 pie

Love nuts? Then this is the pie for you!

Favorite Pastry for 9-inch One-Crust Pie (page 259)
3 eggs
2/3 cup sugar
1/2 teaspoon salt
1/2 teaspoon ground cinnamon
1/2 teaspoon ground nutmeg
1/2 teaspoon ground cloves
1 cup light or dark corn syrup
1/3 cup margarine or butter, melted
1/2 cup coarsely chopped walnuts
1/2 cup raisins

Heat oven to 375°. Prepare pastry. Beat eggs, sugar, salt, cinnamon, nutmeg, cloves, corn syrup and margarine with hand beater until blended. Stir in walnuts and raisins. Pour into pastry-lined pie plate.

Bake until set, 40 to 50 minute.

Apple Dumplings

Apple Dumplings

6 dumplings

**Favorite Pastry for 9-inch Two-Crust Pie
    (page 259)**
**6 baking apples (each about 3 inches in
    diameter), peeled and cored**
3 tablespoons raisins
3 tablespoons chopped nuts
2 1/2 cups packed brown sugar
1 1/3 cups water

Heat oven to 425°. Prepare pastry. Gather into
a ball. Roll two-thirds of the pastry into 14-inch
square on lightly floured cloth-covered board
with floured stockinet-covered rolling pin;
cut into 4 squares. Roll remaining pastry into
rectangle, 14×7 inches; cut into 2 squares.
Place apple on each square.

   Mix raisins and nuts; fill each apple.
Moisten corners of each pastry square; bring
2 opposite corners up over apple and pinch.
Repeat with remaining corners; pinch edges
of pastry to seal. Place dumplings in ungreased baking dish, 13×9×2 inches.

   Heat brown sugar and water to boiling;
carefully pour around dumplings. Bake,
spooning or basting syrup over dumplings
2 or 3 times, until crust is golden and apples
are tender, about 40 minutes. Serve warm or
cool with cream or sweetened whipped cream
if desired.

Baking with Confidence

PERFECT PASTRY IS:

Golden brown and blistered on top
Crisp, brown under crust
Tender, cuts easily and holds its shape
    when served
Flaky and crisp

Problem	Possible Cause
Pale color	• baked in shiny, not dull pan
	• underbaked
Pastry looks smooth	• dough was handled too much
Bottom crust is soggy	• baked in shiny, not dull pan
	• baking temperature too low
Tough	• too much water
	• too much flour
	• too much mixing
Too tender; falls apart	• too little water
	• too much shortening
Dry and mealy, not flaky	• shortening was cut in too fine
	• too little water

Classic French Silk Pie

1 pie

We have a new method for making this classic pie—cooking the eggs—which gives the filling a soft texture. Freezing the pie makes it easier to cut, yet it still retains its rich, smooth texture and great chocolate flavor.

Favorite Pastry for 9-inch One-Crust Pie Shell (page 259)
1/4 cup (1/2 stick) margarine or butter, softened
3 ounces unsweetened chocolate
1 cup sugar
2 tablespoons cornstarch
3 eggs
1 teaspoon vanilla
1 cup chilled whipping (heavy) cream
Whipped cream, if desired

Prepare and bake pie shell; cool. Heat margarine and chocolate in 2-quart saucepan over low heat until melted. Remove from heat. Mix sugar and cornstarch; stir into chocolate mixture. Meanwhile, beat eggs in small bowl on medium speed until thick and lemon colored; stir into chocolate mixture. Cook mixture over medium heat 5 minutes, stirring constantly, until thick and glossy; stir in vanilla. Cool 10 minutes, stirring occasionally.

Beat whipping cream in chilled medium bowl until stiff. Fold chocolate mixture into whipped cream; pour into pie shell.

Cover and freeze about 4 hours or until firm. Garnish with whipped cream, if desired. Freeze any remaining pie.

Classic French Silk Pie

Pumpkin-Cheese Pie

1 pie

Favorite Pastry for 9-inch One-Crust Pie (page 259)
1 package (8 ounces) cream cheese, softened
3/4 cup sugar
2 tablespoons all-purpose flour*
1 teaspoon ground cinnamon
1 teaspoon grated lemon peel
1 teaspoon grated orange peel
1/4 teaspoon ground nutmeg
1/4 teaspoon ground ginger
1/4 teaspoon vanilla
3 eggs
1 can (16 ounces) pumpkin
Sour Cream Topping (below)

Heat oven to 350°. Prepare pastry. Beat cream cheese, sugar and flour in large mixer bowl until blended. Add remaining ingredients except topping; beat on medium speed until smooth. Pour into pastry-lined pie plate.

Bake until knife inserted in center comes out clean, 50 to 55 minutes. Immediately spread with Sour Cream Topping; cool. Refrigerate at least 4 hours.

Self-rising flour can be used in this recipe.

Sour Cream Topping

3/4 cup dairy sour cream
1 tablespoon sugar
1/4 teaspoon vanilla

Mix all ingredients.

Pecan Pie

8 servings

Favorite Pastry for One-Crust Pie (page 259)
2/3 cup sugar
1/3 cup stick margarine or butter, melted*
1 cup corn syrup
1/2 teaspoon salt
3 large eggs
1 cup pecan halves or broken pecans

Heat oven to 375°. Prepare pastry.

Beat sugar, margarine, corn syrup, salt and eggs in medium bowl with wire whisk or hand beater until well blended. Stir in pecans. Pour into pastry-lined pie plate.

Bake 40 to 50 minutes or until center is set.

Spreads with at least 65% vegetable oil can be substituted.

Lighter Pecan Pie: *For less fat and fewer calories per serving, decrease the margarine to 1/4 cup. Substitute 1 egg plus 4 egg whites for the 3 eggs. Add 1 teaspoon vanilla with the egg. Substitute 1/2 cup quick-cooking or old-fashioned oats and 1/2 cup chopped pecans for the 1 cup pecan halves.*

Kentucky Pecan Pie: *Add 2 tablespoons bourbon with the corn syrup. Stir in 1 package (6 ounces) semisweet chocolate chips (1 cup) with the pecans.*

Chocolate Pie Deluxe

Chocolate Pie Deluxe

8 to 10 servings

Favorite Pastry for 9-Inch One-Crust Pie
   (page 259)
1 1/2 cups miniature marshmallows
   or 16 large marshmallows
1/2 cup milk
1 bar (8 ounces) milk chocolate candy
1 cup whipping cream, chilled

Bake pie shell. Heat marshmallows, milk and chocolate over low heat, stirring constantly, just until chocolate and marshmallows are melted and mixture is smooth. Refrigerate, stirring occasionally, until mixture mounds slightly when dropped from a spoon.

Beat whipping cream in chilled bowl until stiff. Fold chocolate mixture into whipped cream. Pour into pie shell.

Refrigerate until set, about 8 hours. Spread with sweetened whipped cream and garnish with chocolate curls if desired.

Sweet Potato Pie

8 servings

Pastry for 9-inch one-crust pie (page 259)
2 eggs
3/4 cup sugar
1 teaspoon ground cinnamon
1/2 teaspoon salt
1/2 teaspoon ground ginger
1/4 teaspoon ground cloves
1 can (23 ounces) sweet potatoes, drained
  and mashed (1 3/4 to 2 cups)
1 can (12 ounces) evaporated milk
Whipped Cream, if desired

Heat oven to 425°. Prepare Pastry. Beat eggs slightly in 2-quart bowl with hand beater; beat in remaining ingredients except whipped cream. Place pastry-lined pie plate on oven rack; pour sweet potato mixture into plate. Cover edge with 2-inch strip of aluminum foil to prevent excessive browning; remove foil last 15 minutes of baking. Bake 15 minutes.

Reduce oven temperature to 350°. Bake until knife inserted in center comes out clean, 45 to 50 minutes. Refrigerate until chilled, at least 4 hours. Serve with whipped cream, if desired. Immediately refrigerate remaining pie.

Praline Sweet Potato Pie: *Decrease second baking time to 35 minutes. Mix 1/3 cup packed brown sugar, 1/3 cup chopped pecans and 1 tablespoon margarine or butter, softened; sprinkle over pie. Bake until knife inserted in center comes out clean, about 10 minutes longer.*

Key Lime Pie

8 servings

Key Lime Pie hails from the Florida Keys, which is the only place where the special yellow Key limes will grow. But you don't have to go to Florida to pick your own limes; regular lemons and limes will also make a delicious pie. Sweetened condensed milk is the "key" to the wonderful creamy texture of this nationwide favorite.

1 can (14 ounces) sweetened condensed milk
1 tablespoon grated lemon peel
1/2 teaspoon grated lime peel
1/4 cup lemon juice
1/4 cup lime juice
3 or 4 drops green food color
3 eggs, separated
1/4 teaspoon cream of tartar
9-inch baked pie shell (right)

Mix milk, lemon peel, lime peel, lemon juice, lime juice and food color. Beat egg yolks slightly; stir in milk mixture. Beat egg whites and cream of tartar in 2 1/2-quart bowl until stiff and glossy. Fold egg yolk mixture into egg whites; mound in pie shell. Refrigerate until set, at least 2 hours. Garnish with sweetened whipped cream and grated lime peel, if desired. Immediately refrigerate any remaining pie.

BAKED ONE-CRUST PIE SHELL

1/3 cup plus 1 tablespoon shortening or
   1/3 cup lard
1 cup all-purpose flour
1/2 teaspoon salt
2 to 3 tablespoons cold water

Heat oven to 475°. Cut shortening into flour and salt until particles are size of small peas. Sprinkle in water, 1 tablespoon at a time, tossing with fork until all flour is moistened and pastry almost cleans side of bowl (1 to 2 teaspoons water can be added if necessary).

Gather pastry into a ball; shape into flattened round on lightly floured cloth-covered board. Roll pastry 2 inches larger than inverted pie plate. Fold pastry into fourths and place in pie plate with point in center; unfold. Trim overhanging edge of pastry 1 inch from rim of pie plate. Fold and roll pastry under even with pie plate; flute. Prick bottom and side thoroughly with fork to prevent puffing while baking. Bake 8 to 10 minutes or until light brown; cool.

Lemon Cake Pie

1 pie

Favorite Pastry for 9-inch One-Crust Pie (page 259)
3 eggs, separated
2 tablespoons grated lemon peel
2/3 cup lemon juice
1 cup milk
1 1/4 cups sugar
1/3 cup all-purpose flour*
1/4 teaspoon salt

Heat oven to 350°. Prepare pastry. Beat egg whites in large mixer bowl until stiff peaks form; reserve. Beat egg yolks; beat in lemon peel, lemon juice and milk. Add sugar, flour and salt; beat until smooth. Beat lemon mixture into egg whites on low speed until blended, about 1 minute. Pour into pastry-lined pie plate.

Bake until golden brown, 45 to 50 minutes. Serve with sweetened whipped cream, if desired.

*Do not use self-rising flour in this recipe.

Banana Cream Pie

1 pie

Favorite Pastry for 9-inch One-Crust Pie (page 259)
3 medium bananas
1 package (8 ounces) cream cheese, softened
1 can (14 ounces) sweetened condensed milk
1/3 cup lemon juice
1 teaspoon vanilla

Bake pie shell. Slice 2 of the bananas; arrange in pie shell. Beat cream cheese in small mixer bowl on medium speed until light and fluffy. Gradually beat in milk until well blended. Beat in lemon juice and vanilla. Pour into pie shell.

Refrigerate until firm, at least 2 hours. Slice remaining banana; arrange on pie.

Crunchy Nut Ice Cream Pie

8 servings

1 1/2 cups ground pecans, walnuts or almonds
3 tablespoons sugar
2 tablespoons margarine or butter, softened
1 quart coffee, chocolate or vanilla ice cream
Rich Chocolate Sauce (below)

Heat oven to 400°. Mix pecans, sugar and margarine. Press firmly and evenly against bottom and side of ungreased pie plate, 9× 1 1/4 inches.

Bake 6 to 8 minutes; cool.

Spoon or scoop ice cream into pie shell. Freeze until firm, about 4 hours. Remove from freezer 10 to 15 minutes before serving. Cut into wedges; spoon Rich Chocolate Sauce over each serving.

RICH CHOCOLATE SAUCE

8 ounces sweet cooking chocolate or 1 package (6 ounces) semisweet chocolate chips (1 cup)
1/4 cup sugar
1/4 cup water
1/4 cup half-and-half

Heat chocolate, sugar and water in saucepan over low heat, stirring constantly, until chocolate and sugar are melted. Remove from heat; blend in half-and-half. Serve warm or cool.

Baked Alaska Pumpkin Pie

Favorite Pastry for 9-inch One-Crust Pie
    (page 259)
3/4 cup sugar
1 teaspoon ground cinnamon
1/2 teaspoon salt
1/2 teaspoon ground ginger
1/4 teaspoon ground cloves
3 egg yolks, slightly beaten
1 can (16 ounces) pumpkin
1 can (13 ounces) evaporated milk
1 pint vanilla or toffee chip ice cream
Brown Sugar Meringue (below)

Heat oven to 425°. Prepare pastry. Mix remaining ingredients except ice cream and meringue. Pour into pastry-lined pie plate.

Bake 15 minutes. Reduce oven temperature to 350°. Bake until knife inserted in center comes out clean, about 45 minutes longer.

Refrigerate baked pie at least 1 hour. Soften ice cream slightly; press into waxed paper-lined pie plate, 8×1 1/2 inches. Freeze until solid.

Just before serving, heat oven to 500°. Prepare Brown Sugar Meringue. Unmold ice cream and invert on pie; remove waxed paper. Spoon meringue onto pie, covering ice cream completely and sealing meringue to edge of crust. Bake until golden brown, 2 to 3 minutes. Serve immediately.

BROWN SUGAR MERINGUE

3 egg whites
1/4 teaspoon cream of tartar
6 tablespoons packed brown sugar
1/2 teaspoon vanilla

Beat egg whites and cream of tartar until foamy. Beat in brown sugar, 1 tablespoon at a time; continue beating until stiff and glossy. Do not underbeat. Beat in vanilla.

Baked Alaska Pumpkin Pie

Caramel-Chocolate Pie

12 servings

(photograph on page 226)

1 1/2 cups vanilla wafer crumbs (about 25 wafers)
1/4 cup (1/2 stick) margarine or butter, melted
30 vanilla caramels
2 tablespoons margarine or butter
2 tablespoons water
1/2 cup chopped pecans, toasted
2 packages (3 ounces each) cream cheese, softened
1/3 cup powdered sugar
1 bar (4 ounces) sweet cooking chocolate
3 tablespoons hot water
1 teaspoon vanilla
2 cups whipping (heavy) cream
2 tablespoons powdered sugar
Easy Chocolate curls, if desired (right)

Heat oven to 350°. Mix crumbs and 1/4 cup margarine. Press mixture firmly against side and bottom of pie plate, 9×1 1/4 inches. Bake 10 minutes; cool.

Heat caramels, 2 tablespoons margarine and 2 tablespoons water over medium heat, stirring frequently, until caramels are melted. Pour into crust. Sprinkle with pecans. Refrigerate about 1 hour until chilled.

Beat cream cheese and 1/3 cup powdered sugar until smooth. Spread over caramel layer; refrigerate.

Heat chocolate and 3 tablespoons hot water over low heat, stirring constantly, until chocolate is melted. Cool to room temperature. Stir in vanilla. Beat whipping cream and 2 tablespoons powdered sugar in chilled medium bowl until stiff. Reserve 1 1/2 cups. Fold chocolate mixture into remaining whipped cream. Spread over cream cheese mixture. Top with reserved whipped cream and Easy Chocolate Curls. Refrigerate any remaining pie.

EASY CHOCOLATE CURLS

Place a bar or block of chocolate on waxed paper. Make chocolate curls by pulling a vegetable peeler toward you across the flattest side of the chocolate, pressing firmly in long, thin strokes. Small curls can be made by using the side of the chocolate bar. Transfer each curl carefully with a toothpick to a waxed paper–lined cookie sheet or directly onto frosted cake, pie or other dessert.

The curl will be easier to make if the chocolate is slightly warm, so let the chocolate stand in a warm place for about 15 minutes before making curls. Semisweet chocolate can be used but the curls will be small. Also, the thicker the bar of chocolate, the larger your curls will be.

Chocolate Brownie Pie

1 pie

**Favorite Pastry for 9-inch One-Crust Pie
   (page 259)**
**2 squares (1 ounce each) unsweetened
   chocolate**
2 tablespoons margarine or butter
3 eggs
1/2 cup sugar
3/4 cup dark corn syrup
1 cup pecan halves

Heat oven to 375°. Prepare pastry. Heat chocolate and margarine over low heat until melted; cool. Beat chocolate mixture, eggs, sugar and corn syrup with hand beater. Stir in pecans. Pour into pastry-lined pie plate.

Bake just until set, 40 to 50 minutes. Serve with sweetened whipped cream, if desired.

Chocolate Cheese Eclairs

8 eclairs

3/4 cup plus 2 tablespoons all-purpose flour
2 tablespoons cocoa
1 tablespoon sugar
1 cup water
1/2 cup margarine or butter
4 eggs
Chocolate Cheese Filling (right)
Cocoa Glaze (right)

Heat oven to 400°. Mix flour, cocoa and sugar. Heat water and margarine in 3-quart saucepan to a rolling boil. Stir in flour mixture. Stir vigorously over low heat until mixture forms a ball, about 1 minute. Remove from heat. Beat in eggs; continue beating until smooth. Drop dough by about 1/4 cupfuls 3 inches apart onto ungreased cookie sheet. With spatula, shape each into finger 4 1/2 inches long and 1 1/2 inches wide.

Bake until puffed and darker brown on top, 35 to 40 minutes; cool.

Cut off tops; pull out any filaments of soft dough. Fill eclairs with Chocolate Cheese Filling; replace tops. Spread with Cocoa Glaze just before serving. Refrigerate any remaining eclairs.

CHOCOLATE CHEESE FILLING

1/4 cup semisweet chocolate chips
**1 package (3 ounces) cream cheese,
   softened**
1/3 cup packed brown sugar
1/4 cup milk
1/2 teaspoon vanilla
1 cup chilled whipping (heavy) cream

Heat chocolate chips in small heavy saucepan over low heat, stirring occasionally, until melted; cool. Beat cream cheese, sugar, milk and vanilla until smooth and creamy. Stir in chocolate. Beat whipping cream in chilled bowl until soft peaks form. Fold in chocolate mixture.

COCOA GLAZE

1 cup powdered sugar
2 tablespoons cocoa
2 tablespoons milk

Mix powdered sugar and cocoa. Stir in milk until smooth. If necessary, stir in additional milk, 1/2 teaspoon at a time, until of desired consistency.

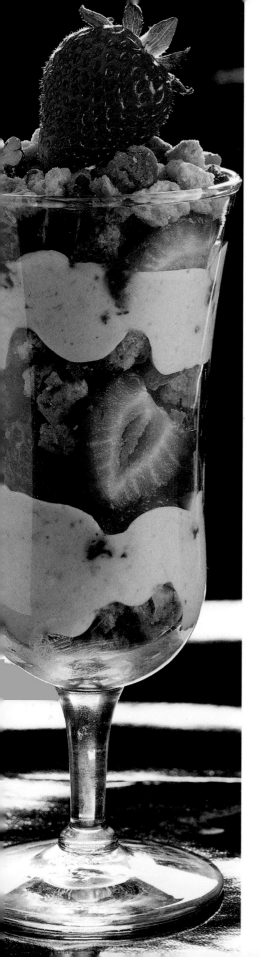

Butter Crunch Desserts

2 1/2 cups crunch

1 cup all-purpose flour*
1/2 cup butter
1/4 cup packed brown sugar
**1/2 cup chopped pecans, chopped walnuts or flaked
    coconut**

Heat oven to 400°. Mix all ingredients with hands. Spread in ungreased baking pan, 13×9×2 inches. Bake 15 minutes; stir. Cool; cover and store in refrigerator.

**Do not use self-rising flour in this recipe.*

Berry Parfaits: *For each serving, alternate layers of 1 tablespoon Butter Crunch, 2 tablespoons fruit-flavored yogurt and 2 tablespoons fresh berries; repeat. Top with 1 tablespoon Butter Crunch. Garnish with berries. (Suggested combinations: lemon-flavored yogurt and blueberries, strawberry-flavored yogurt and strawberry halves, raspberry-flavored yogurt and raspberries.)*

Cinnamon-Applesauce Dessert: *Mix 2 cups applesauce and 1 teaspoon cinnamon. Top with 1 cup sweetened whipped cream and sprinkle with 1 cup Butter Crunch. 6 servings*

Fruit-Custard Dessert: *For each serving, pour chilled soft custard over fresh berries or fruit (oranges, bananas, peaches, strawberries). Sprinkle with Butter Crunch.*

Pudding Dessert: *Prepare your favorite flavor pudding and pie filling as directed on package for pudding—except pour into shallow serving dish. After refrigerating, sprinkle with 1 cup Butter Crunch. Serve with cream. 6 servings*

Butter-Crunch Desserts

Cream Puffs

12 cream puffs

1 cup water
1/2 cup margarine or butter
1 cup all-purpose flour*
4 eggs
Ice cream
Chocolate Fudge Sauce (below)

Heat oven to 400°. Heat water and margarine to rolling boil in 1-quart saucepan. Stir in flour. Stir vigorously over low heat until mixture forms a ball, about 1 minute. Remove from heat; cool 10 minutes. Beat in eggs, all at once; continue beating until smooth. Drop dough by scant 1/4 cupfuls about 3 inches apart onto ungreased cookie sheet. Bake until puffed and golden, 35 to 40 minutes. Cool away from draft. Cut off tops; pull out any filaments of soft dough. Fill puffs with ice cream; replace tops. Drizzle with Chocolate Fudge Sauce.

*Self-rising flour can be used in this recipe.

CHOCOLATE FUDGE SAUCE

1 package (12 ounces) semisweet chocolate
 chips or 4 bars (4 ounces *each*) sweet
 cooking chocolate
1/2 cup sugar
1/2 cup water
1/2 cup half-and-half or evaporated milk

Heat chocolate, sugar and water over low heat, stirring constantly, until chocolate and sugar are melted; remove from heat. Stir in half-and-half.

Cream Puffs

Baking with Kids

Bumblebees (page 298), Super Snack Bars (page 306)

Baker's Corner

Let's Get Started!

Before You Start

- Check with an adult to make sure that it's a good time to bake. Also, always let an adult know when the recipe uses the range (stove top).

- If your hair is long, tie it back so it won't get in the way.

- Wash your hands and wear an apron.

- Read the recipe all the way through before starting to cook. Ask an adult about anything you don't understand.

- Gather all the ingredients and utensils before starting to make sure that you have everything. Measure all the ingredients carefully. Put everything you need on a tray. When the tray is empty, you'll know you haven't left anything out!

- Many baked recipes use baking *soda* or baking *powder*, or some of each, as a leavening to make the recipe rise. Pay close attention when reading your recipes so that you do not get these ingredients mixed up.

- Reread the recipe to make sure that you haven't left anything out.

While You Bake

- Clean up as you bake— it makes less work at the end! As you finish using a utensil (except for sharp knives), put it in warm soapy water to soak. Wash sharp knives separately, and be careful of the sharp blades.

Finishing Up

- Wash and dry all the utensils you have used, and put them away. Wash the counters, and leave the kitchen neat and clean.

- Check the range, oven and any other appliances to be sure that you have turned them off. Put away any appliances you have used.

- Leaving the kitchen clean will make sure everyone is glad to have you bake again. Now, enjoy your creation!

Playing It Safe in the Kitchen

Preparing the Food

- Before you use a sharp knife, can opener, blender, electric mixer or the range or oven, be sure that someone older is in the kitchen to help you and to answer questions. Watch for "Adult help" signs throughout the recipes.

- Always dry your hands after you wash them to avoid slippery fingers.

- Wipe up any spills right away to avoid slippery floors.

- When slicing or chopping ingredients, be sure to use a cutting board.

- Always turn the sharp edge of a knife or vegetable peeler away from you and your hand when you chop or peel foods.

- Turn off the electric mixer or blender before you scrape the sides of the bowl or container so the scraper won't get caught in the blades.

- Turn off the electric mixer and make sure that it's unplugged whenever you put the beaters in or take them out.

- Put large pans on large burners, small pans on small burners. Turn the handles of pots and pans so that they don't stick out over the edge of the range, where they might accidentally be bumped, and make sure that they're not over another burner either.

When You're Baking

- If the racks need to be adjusted higher or lower, be sure to arrange them before you turn on the oven.

- Allow plenty of air space around foods you're baking—no pans or dishes should touch.

- Arrange foods on oven racks so that one isn't placed directly over another.

- Use a tight-fitting lid or aluminum foil when the recipe calls for covering. Uncover cooked foods away form you, and keep your face away from the steam.

- Always use thick, dry holders to avoid burns, not thin or wet ones.

- Ask an adult to help you put pans into and take pans out of the oven.

- Ask an adult to help when checking if a recipe is done. Close the oven door quickly when you have finished looking in, so that heat wont be lost.

- Be careful where you put hot pans. Put them only on a surface that is dry and can withstand heat.

For the Baker's Adult Helper

Preparing food for themselves and others is a very satisfying endeavor for children, and children love to bake! There are precautions that must be taught. Your supervision along with some simple rules can make it fun and, more important, safe for boys and girls to fix their own snacks and help prepare meals. You are the best judge of the age at which a child should be allowed to use the range, oven, other appliances or sharp knives. Follow these simple steps to help children cook safely:

- Read the recipe all the way through with the child before they start to cook. Explain anything they don't understand.

- We recommend adult supervision whenever children use sharp knives, the range, the oven or small appliances.

- Children should be taught how to correctly set the controls on the range and oven.

- Provide pot holders in a size that's easy for smaller, less adept hands to use.

- Teach children safe foods-preparation techniques and how to handle hot foods.

Kitchen Computing

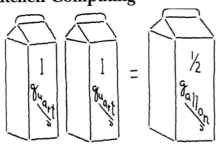

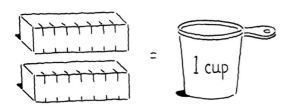

Baker's Talk

Beat: Make smooth with a vigorous stirring motion using a spoon, wire whisk, eggbeater or electric mixer.

Boil: Heat liquid until bubbles keep rising and breaking on the surface.

Chop: Cut food into small, uneven pieces; a sharp knife, food chopper or food processor may be used.

Core: Cut out the stem end and remove the seeds.

Cut in: Mix fat into a flour mixture with a pastry blender using a rolling motion or by cutting with a fork or two knives until particles are size specifies.

Dice: Cut into cubes smaller than 1/2 inch.

Drain: Pour off liquid or let it run off through the holes in a strainer or colander, as when draining cooked pasta or ground beef. Or remove pieces of food from a fat or liquid and set them on paper towels to soak up excess moisture.

Flute: Flatten pastry evenly on rim of pie plate and press firmly around rim with tines of fork.

Grate: Rub against grater to cut into small pieces.

Grease: Spread the bottom and side of a dish with butter or shortening using a pastry brush or paper towel.

Knead: Curve your fingers and fold dough toward you, then push it away with the heels of your hands, using a quick, rocking motion.

Mix: Combine to distribute ingredients evenly using a spoon, fork, blender or an electric mixer.

Peel: Cut off the skin with a knife or peel with fingers.

Pipe: Press out frosting from a decorating bag using steady pressure to form a design or write a message. To finish a design, stop the pressure and lift the point up and away.

Roll or pat: Flatten and spread with a floured rolling pin or hands.

Utensils You Should Have

For Preparation

Apple corer

Kitchen scissors

Covered rolling pin and board

Biscuit or doughnut cutter

Cookie cutters

Vegetable peeler

Potato masher

Can opener

Decorating bag

Pizza cutter

Pastry blender

Grater

Pastry brush

Sharp knife

Juicer

Ice-cream scoop

Small sharp knife

Long serrated knife

Cutting board

Mixing bowls (set of 3)

Ruler

Custard cups (6- and 10-ounce)

Timer

Eggbeater

Colander

Strainer

Wire whisk

Electric mixer

For Measuring

Liquid measuring cup (1 cup)

Rubber scraper

Small spatula

Dry-ingredient measuring cups (1-, 1/2-, 1/3-, 1/4-cup)

Measuring spoons (1/4-, 1/2-, 1-teaspoon, 1-tablespoon)

For Top-of-Range Cooking

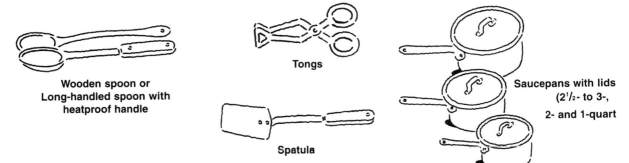

**Wooden spoon or
Long-handled spoon with
heatproof handle**

Tongs

Spatula

Saucepans with lids
($2^1/2$- to 3-,
2- and 1-quart)

For Baking

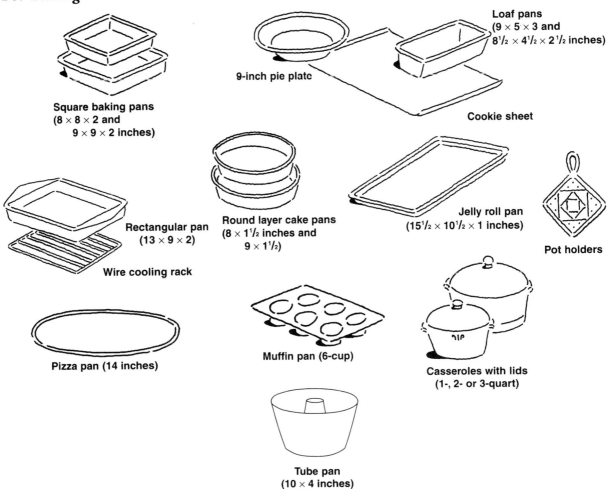

Square baking pans
($8 \times 8 \times 2$ and
$9 \times 9 \times 2$ inches)

9-inch pie plate

Loaf pans
($9 \times 5 \times 3$ and
$8^1/2 \times 4^1/2 \times 2^1/2$ inches)

Cookie sheet

Rectangular pan
($13 \times 9 \times 2$)

Wire cooling rack

Round layer cake pans
($8 \times 1^1/2$ inches and
$9 \times 1^1/2$)

Jelly roll pan
($15^1/2 \times 10^1/2 \times 1$ inches)

Pot holders

Pizza pan (14 inches)

Muffin pan (6-cup)

Casseroles with lids
(1-, 2- or 3-quart)

Tube pan
(10×4 inches)

"Gingerpop" Cookies

About 18 cookies

¶¶/ Utensils You Will Need

Large Bowl • Liquid measuring cup • Wooden spoons • Plastic wrap •
18 flat wooden ice-cream sticks • Cookie sheet • Glass • Pot holders •
Spatula • Wire cooling rack • Small bowl • Knife

1 Mix in large bowl with a
wooden spoon ▬ ▬ ▬ ▬ ▶

> **1 package (14.5 ounces) gingerbread
> cake and cookie mix
> 1/3 cup lukewarm water**

2 Cover dough with plastic wrap
and refrigerate about 15 minutes
or until slightly firm.

3 Heat oven to 375°.

4 Shape dough into eighteen 1 1/4-inch balls. Poke 1 ice-cream stick into
the side of each ball until tip of stick is in center of ball. Put balls about
2 inches apart on cookie sheet.

5 Flatten balls gently with bottom
of glass dipped in ▬ ▬ ▬ ▶

> **Sugar**

6 Bake 8 to 10 minutes or until edges are firm. Cool cookies on cookie sheet
1 minute, then remove with spatula to wire rack. Cool completely.

7 Mix in small bowl with wooden
spoon ▬ ▬ ▬ ▬ ▶

> **1 cup vanilla ready-to-spread frosting
> 2 drops red food color**

8 Spread frosting over each cookie with knife, then immediately make face or decorate as you like with ■ ■ ■ ■ ■ ■ ➤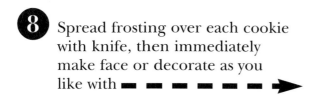

Assorted candies (candy-coated chocolate candies, candy corn, licorice or gumdrops

TIP

If dough is too soft to shape into balls, cover with plastic wrap and refrigerate about 1 hour. When flattening balls of dough with a glass, you may want to lightly grease the bottom of the glass with shortening to help the sugar stick to the glass.

Holiday Honey Cookies

About 42 cookies
(photograph on page 290)

¡¡/ Utensils You will Need

Cookie Sheet • Pastry brush • Large bowl • Dry-ingredient measuring cups •
Small sharp knife • Measuring spoons • Wooden spoon • Rolling pin •
Ruler • 2-inch cookie cutters • Pot holders • Spatula • Wire cooking rack

1 Heat oven to 375°.

2 Lightly grease cookie sheet
with ━ ━ ━ ━ ━ ▶ | **Shortening**

3 Mix in large bowl
with wooden spoon ━ ━ ━ ▶

| 1/3 cup powdered sugar
1/3 cup margarine or butter, softened
2/3 cup honey
1 teaspoon almond extract
1 large egg

4 Stir in ━ ━ ━ ━ ━ ▶

| 2 3/4 cups all-purpose flour
1 teaspoon baking soda
1/2 teaspoon salt

5 Sprinkle a clean surface (such as a kitchen counter or breadboard) with flour. Put dough on surface. Roll dough until 1/8 inch thick. Cut with cookie cutters. Put cookies about 1 inch apart on cookie sheet.

6 Bake 6 to 8 minutes or until light brown. Watch carefully because cookies brown quickly. Immediately remove cookies from cookie sheet with spatula to wire rack. Cool completely.

7 Frost cookies with ■ ■ ■ ■ ➤ | **Glaze (below)**

8 Decorate cookies with ■ ■ ■ ➤ | **Decorator's Frosting (below)**

GLAZE

Medium bowl • Dry-ingredient measuring cup • Measuring spoons •
Wooden spoon

1 Mix in medium bowl with wooden spoon until smooth ■ ■ ■ ■ ➤

2 cups powdered sugar
1/4 teaspoon almond extract
2 tablespoons water

2 Stir in, 1 teaspoon at a time, until spreadable ■ ■ ■ ➤

2 to 4 teaspoons water

DECORATOR'S FROSTING

Small bowl • Dry-ingredient measuring cup • Measuring spoons •
Wooden spoon

1 Mix in small bowl with wooden spoon, adding the water 1 teaspoon at a time, until frosting is thin enough to drizzle or thick enough to be used in a decorating bag ■ ■ ■ ■ ➤

1 cup powdered sugar
3 or 4 drops food color
3 to 5 teaspoons water

Easy Sugar Cookies

About 48 cookies

¶¶ Utensils You Will Need

Large Bowl • Dry-ingredient measuring cups • Measuring spoons •
Wooden spoon • Cookie sheet • Teaspoon • Glass • Pot holders • Spatula •
Wire cooling rack • Small bowl

1 Heat oven to 375°.

2 Beat in large bowl with wooden
spoon until smooth ■ ■ ■ ➔

> **1 cup sugar**
> **1 cup (2 sticks) margarine or butter,**
> **softened**
> **1/2 teaspoon vanilla**
> **1 large egg**

3 Stir in ■ ■ ■ ■ ➔   **2 1/4 cups all-purpose flour**

4 Shape dough by teaspoonfuls into balls. Place balls about 2 inches apart on
cookie sheet.

5 Flatten balls gently with bottom
of glass dipped in ■ ■ ■ ➔

> **Sugar, colored sugar or**
> **candy sprinkles**

6 Bake 10 to 12 minutes or until set and edges just begin to brown. Cool
cookies on cookie sheet 1 minute, then remove with spatula to wire rack.
Cool.

TIP

If dough is too soft to shape, cover with plastic wrap and refrigerate about 1 hour.

Holiday Honey Cookies (page 288)

Giant Colorful Candy Cookies

About 18 cookies

♨ **Utensils You Will Need**

Large Bowl • Dry-ingredient measuring cups • Electric mixer •
Measuring spoons • Wooden spoon • Cookie sheet • Ruler • Fork •
Pot holders • Spatula • Wire cooling rack

1 Heat oven to 375°.

2 Beat in large bowl with electric
mixer on medium speed about
5 minutes or until fluffy ▪ ▪ ▪ ➤

> **1 cup packed brown sugar**
> **3/4 cup granulated sugar**
> **1 cup (2 sticks) margarine or
> butter, softened**

3 Beat in ▪ ▪ ▪ ▪ ▪ ▪ ➤

> **1 teaspoon vanilla**
> **2 large eggs**
> **2 1/2 cups all-purpose flour**
> **3/4 teaspoon salt**
> **3/4 teaspoon baking soda**

4 Stir in ▪ ▪ ▪ ▪ ▪ ➤

> **2 cups candy-coated
> chocolate candies**

5 Drop dough by 1/4 cupfuls about
2 inches apart onto cookie sheet. Flatten dough gently with fork.

6 Bake 11 to 14 minutes or until edges are light brown. Cool cookies 3 to 4 minutes on cookie sheet, then carefully remove with spatula to wire rack. Cool.

Here's another idea. . . Make **Giant Chocolate Chip Cookies:** *Leave out candy-coated chocolate candies. Stir in 2 cups semisweet chocolate chips instead.*

Rocky Road Cookies

About 48 cookies

♨ Utensils You Will Need

1-quart saucepan • Dry-ingredient measuring cups • Wooden spoons •
Small sharp knife • Large bowl • Measuring spoons • Teaspoon • Cookie
sheet • Ruler • Pot holders • Spatula • Wire cooling rack

1 Melt in saucepan over low
heat, stirring a few times,
then remove from heat and
cool slightly ➤

> **1/2 cup semisweet chocolate chips**
> **1/2 cup (1 stick) margarine or butter**

2 Heat oven to 400°.

3 Mix in large bowl with
wooden spoon ➤

> **1 1/2 cups all-purpose flour**
> **1 cup sugar**
> **1/2 teaspoon baking powder**
> **1/2 teaspoon vanilla**
> **1/4 teaspoon salt**
> **2 large eggs**
> **1 cup chopped nuts**
> **1/2 cup semisweet chocolate chips**
> **The melted chocolate mixture**

4 Drop dough by rounded
teaspoonfuls about 2 inches
apart onto cookie sheet.

5 Press into center of each
cookie 1 of ➤

> **About 48 miniature marshmallows**

6 Bake 8 to 12 minutes or until almost no mark stays when cookie is touched.
Immediately remove cookies from cookie sheet with spatula to wire rack.
Cool.

Peanut Butter Cookies

About 36 cookies

🍴 Utensils You Will Need

Large Bowl • Dry-ingredient measuring cups • Small sharp knife •
Wooden spoon • Measuring spoons • Plastic wrap • Ruler • Cookie sheet •
Fork • Pot holders • Spatula • Wire cooling rack

1 Heat oven to 375°.

2 Mix in large bowl with wooden spoon ▬ ▬ ▬ ▬ ▶

> 1/2 cup granulated sugar
> 1/2 cup packed brown sugar
> 1/2 cup peanut butter
> 1/4 cup shortening
> 1/4 cup (1/2 stick) margarine or
> butter, softened
> 1 large egg

3 Stir in ▬ ▬ ▬ ▬ ▬ ▶

> 1 1/4 cups all-purpose or
> whole wheat flour
> 3/4 teaspoon baking soda
> 1/2 teaspoon baking powder
> 1/4 teaspoon salt

4 Shape dough into 1 1/4-inch balls. Put balls about 3 inches apart on cookie sheet. Flatten balls gently in crisscross pattern with fork dipped in sugar.

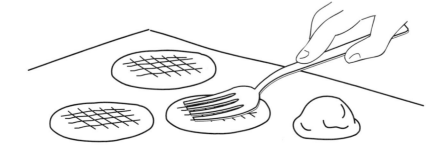

Bake 9 to 10 minutes or until light brown. Cool cookies 2 minutes on cookie sheet, then remove with spatula to wire rack. Cool.

---

*Here's another idea. . . Make **Quick Peanut Butter Sticks:** Divide dough into fourths. Shape fourths into strips, 10 inches long by 11/2 inches wide, on cookie sheets. (Two strips can fit on 1 cookie sheet.) Flatten strips to 3 inches wide with fork dipped in sugar. Bake 10 to 12 minutes or until golden brown. Cool 2 minutes, then cut each strip crosswise into 1-inch slices. Remove cookies from cookie sheet with spatula to wire rack. Cool. About 42 cookies.*

TIP

If dough is too soft to shape into balls, cover with plastic wrap and refrigerate about 1 hour.

Caramel-Nut Cookies

About 32 cookies

ⓎⓎⓎ Utensils You Will Need

Large Bowl • Dry-ingredient measuring cups • Measuring spoons • Wooden spoons • Cookie sheet • Sharp knife • Cutting board • Teaspoon • Pot holders • Spatula • Wire cooling rack • 1-quart saucepan • Knife

1 Mix in large bowl with wooden spoon ▪ ▪ ▪ ▪ ▪ ▪ ➤

> **1/2 cup packed brown sugar**
> **1/2 cup (1 stick) margarine or butter, softened**
> **2 tablespoons water**
> **1 teaspoon vanilla**

2 Stir in until dough holds together (if dough is dry, stir in 1 to 2 teaspoons water) ▪ ▪ ▪ ▪ ▪ ➤

> **1 1/2 cups all-purpose flour**
> **1/8 teaspoon salt**

3 Heat oven to 350°.

4 To assemble cookies, you will need about ▪ ▪ ▪ ▪ ▪ ➤

> **160 pecan halves (about 2 1/4 cups)**
> **8 vanilla caramels, unwrapped**

5 **Adult help:** Cut each caramel into 4 pieces with sharp knife.

6 For each cookie, group 5 pecan halves on cookie sheet (for legs and head of turtle). Shape 1 teaspoon dough around each caramel piece to form a ball. Press ball firmly onto center of each turtle.

7 Bake 12 to 15 minutes or until set but not brown. Immediately remove cookies from cookie sheet with spatula to wire rack. Cool completely.

8 Melt in saucepan over low heat, stirring a few times, then remove from heat ▬ ▬ ▬ ▬ ▬ ➤

> **1 ounce unsweetened chocolate**

9 Beat into chocolate with wooden spoon, adding the water 1 teaspoon at a time, until smooth ▬ ▬ ▬ ▬ ➤

> **1 cup powdered sugar**
> **1 teaspoon vanilla**
> **2 to 4 teaspoons water**

10 Spread tops of cookies with chocolate glaze.

Bumblebees

About 48 cookies

(*photograph on page 278*)

♨ Utensils You Will Need

Large Bowl • Dry-ingredient measuring cups • Liquid measuring cup •
Wooden spoon • Measuring spoons • Plastic wrap • Ruler • Cookie sheet •
Pot holders • Spatula • Wire cooling rack

1) Mix in large bowl with wooden spoon ▪ ▪ ▪ ▪ ▪ ▶

> 1/2 cup peanut butter
> 1/2 cup shortening
> 1/3 cup packed brown sugar
> 1/3 cup honey
> 1 large egg

2 Stir in ▪ ▪ ▪ ▪ ▪ ▶

> 1 3/4 cups all-purpose flour
> 3/4 teaspoon baking soda
> 1/2 teaspoon baking powder

3 Cover dough with plastic wrap and refrigerate about 2 hours or until firm.

4 Heat oven to 350°.

5 Shape dough into 1-inch balls. (Dough will be slightly sticky.)

6 To assemble cookies, you will need about ▪ ▪ ▪ ▪ ▪ ▶

> 8 dozen pretzel twists
> 8 dozen pretzel sticks

7 For each cookie, put 2 pretzel twists side by side on cookie sheet, with rounded sides touching. Put 1 ball of dough in center, and flatten gently.

8 Break 2 pretzel sticks in half. Gently press 3 pretzel stick halves into dough for stripes on bee. Break last pretzel piece in half. Poke pieces in one end of dough for antennae.

9 Bake 11 to 13 minutes or until light golden brown. Immediately remove cookies from cookie sheet with spatula to wire rack. Cool.

Multigrain Cutouts

About 70 cookies

🍴 Utensils You Will Need

Large Bowl • Dry-ingredient measuring cups • Liquid measuring cups •
Measuring spoons • Wooden spoon • Rolling pin • Ruler • Cookie cutters •
Cookie sheet • Decorating bag • Pot holders • Spatula • Wire cooling rack

1 Heat oven to 350°.

2 Mix in large bowl with wooden spoon ■ ■ ■ ■ ■ ➤

> **1 cup sugar**
> **2/3 cup shortening**
> **3 1/4 cups whole wheat flour**
> **1/4 cup cornmeal**
> **1/4 cup wheat germ**
> **3/4 cup milk**
> **1 teaspoon baking powder**
> **1/2 teaspoon salt**
> **1/2 teaspoon vanilla**

3 Sprinkle a clean surface (such as a kitchen counter or bread board) with flour. Put dough on surface. Divide dough into 3 parts. Roll 1 part of dough at a time until 1/8 inch thick. Cut dough with cookie cutters. Put cookies on cookie sheet.

4 Put Baked-on Frosting in decorating bag with #5 writing tip and outline or decorate unbaked cookies with ■ ■ ➤

> **Baked-on Frosting (right)**

5 Bake 12 to 14 minutes or until edges are light brown. Cool 1 minute on cookie sheet, then remove with spatula to wire rack. Cool.

BAKED-ON FROSTING

🍴 Utensils You Will Need
Small bowl • Dry-ingredient measuring cup • Small sharp knife •
Wooden spoon • Measuring spoon

1 Mix in small bowl with wooden spoon until smooth ➡

> 2/3 cup all-purpose flour
> 2/3 cup margarine or butter, softened

2 Stir in, 1 teaspoon at a time, until spreadable ➡

> 3 to 4 teaspoons hot water

TIP

If you don't have a decorating bag, you can make one with a plastic bag or paper envelope. Put frosting in the corner of a plastic bag and seal or put frosting in the corner of an envelope and fold the other end over. Snip a small piece off the corner of the bag or envelope to make a writing tip.

The Best Brownies

24 brownies

🍴 Utensils You Will Need

Square pan, 9×9×2 inches • Pastry brush • 1-quart saucepan • Small sharp
knife • Wooden spoons • Large bowl • Dry-ingredient measuring cups •
Measuring spoons • Electric mixer • Pot holders • Wire cooling rack • Ruler

1 Heat oven to 350°.

2 Grease square pan with ➔ **Shortening**

3 Melt in saucepan over low heat, stirring a few times, then remove from heat and cool slightly ➔ **5 ounces unsweetened chocolate
2/3 cup margarine or butter**

4 Beat in large bowl with electric mixer on high speed 5 minutes ➔ **1 3/4 cups sugar
2 teaspoons vanilla
3 large eggs**

5 Beat the melted chocolate mixture into sugar mixture with electric mixer on low speed.

6 Beat in until mixed ➔ **1 cup all-purpose flour**

7 Stir in ➔ **1 cup chopped nuts
1 cup (6 ounces) semisweet chocolate chips, if you like**

8 Spread batter in pan.

9 Bake 40 to 45 minutes or just until brownies begin to pull away from side of pan. Cool completely on wire rack.

10 Make ▬ ▬ ▬ ▬ ▬ ▬ ➤ | **Chocolate Frosting (below)** |

11 Frost brownies with frosting. Cut into 2 1/4×1 1/2-inch bars.

CHOCOLATE FROSTING

🍴 Utensils You Will Need
2-quart saucepan • Small sharp knife • Wooden spoon • Dry-ingredient measuring cup • Measuring spoon

1 Melt in saucepan over low heat, stirring a few times, then remove from heat ▬ ▬ ▬ ➤ | **2 ounces unsweetened chocolate**
2 tablespoons (from a stick)
margarine or butter |

2 Stir until smooth ▬ ▬ ▬ ➤ | **2 cups powdered sugar**
3 tablespoons hot water |

Double Apple Bars

24 bars

Utensils You Will Need

Large Bowl • Dry-ingredient measuring cups • Wooden spoon • Measuring spoons • Tablespoon • Square pan, 9×9×2 inches • Toothpick • Pot holders • Wire cooling rack • Ruler • Sharp knife

1 Heat oven to 350°.

2 Grease square pan with - - ➤ | **Shortening** |

3 Mix in large bowl with wooden spoon - - - ➤

| **3/4 cup packed brown sugar** |
| **3/4 cup applesauce** |
| **1/4 cup vegetable oil** |
| **1 large egg** |

4 Stir in - - - - ➤

| **1 1/4 cups all-purpose flour** |
| **1/2 teaspoon baking soda** |
| **1/2 teaspoon ground cinnamon** |
| **1/4 teaspoon salt** |

5 Stir in - - - - ➤ | **1/2 cup chopped unpeeled all-purpose apple** |

6 Spread batter in pan.

7 Bake 25 to 30 minutes or until toothpick poked in center comes out clean. Cool completely on wire rack.

8 If you like, sprinkle with - ➤ | **Powdered sugar** |

9 Cut into 2 1/4×1 1/2-inch bars.

Double Apple Bars

Super Snack Bars

32 bars

(photograph on page 278)

🍴 Utensils You Will Need

Large Bowl • Dry-ingredient measuring cups • Small sharp knife •
Measuring spoons • Wooden spoon • Rectangular pan, 13×9×2 inches •
Pot holders • Wire cooling rack • Ruler • Sharp knife

1 Heat oven to 350°.

2 Grease rectangular pan with ■ ➤ | **Shortening**

3 Mix in large bowl with wooden spoon ■ ■ ■ ■ ➤

> **3/4 cup granulated sugar**
> **3/4 cup packed brown sugar**
> **3/4 cup (1 1/2 sticks) margarine or butter, softened**
> **1 teaspoon vanilla**
> **2 large eggs**

4 Stir in ■ ■ ■ ■ ■ ➤

5 Spread batter in pan.

> **2 cups all-purpose flour**
> **1 teaspoon baking soda**
> **1/2 teaspoon baking powder**
> **1/2 teaspoon salt**
> **1 cup whole-grain wheat flake cereal, slightly crushed**
> **3/4 cup quick-cooking oats**
> **3/4 cup chopped pecans**
> **2/3 cup candy-coated chocolate candies**

6 Sprinkle with ■ ■ ■ ■ ➤

> **1/3 cup candy-coated chocolate candies**
> **1/4 cup chopped pecans**

7 Bake 30 to 40 minutes or until golden brown. Cool completely on wire rack. Cut into about 2×1 1/4-inch bars.

Candy Bar Cupcakes

About 20 cupcakes

Utensils You Will Need

Muffin pan with medium cups, 2 1/2 × 1 1/4 inches • Pastry brush • Cutting board • Sharp knife • Large Bowl • Liquid measuring cup • Electric mixer • Pot holders • Wire cooling rack

1 **Adult help:** Coarsely chop all the candy, then finely chop enough to measure 3/4 cup ▪ ▪ ▪ ▪ ▪ ▪ ➤

> **8 bars (2.1 oz *each*) chocolate-covered crispy peanut-buttery candy**

2 Make and bake cupcakes as directed on package—except after beating, gently stir in the 3/4 cup finely chopped candy ▪ ▪ ▪ ▪ ▪ ➤

> **1 package (1 lb 2.25 oz) white cake mix with pudding**

3 **Adult help:** Immediately remove cupcakes from pan to wire rack. Cool completely.

4 Frost cupcakes with ▪ ▪ ▪ ➤

> **1 tub (1 lb) milk chocolate ready-to-spread frosting**

5 Put coarsely chopped candy pieces on tops of cupcakes. Store loosely covered at room temperature.

TIP

Candy bars are easier to cut if refrigerated about 1 hour.

Heart Cake

12 servings

🍴 Utensils You Will Need

Round pan, 8×1 1/2 inches • Square pan, 8×8×2 inches • Pastry brush •
Liquid measuring cup • Large Bowl • Electric mixer • Pot holders • Wire
cooling racks • Large tray or covered cardboard, 18×15 inches • Sharp knife

1 Heat oven to 350°.

2 Grease round and square pans
with ▪ ▪ ▪ ▪ ▪ ▪ ➤

| **Shortening** |

3 Put small amount in pans and
shake to coat, then pour out
any extra ▪ ▪ ▪ ▪ ▪ ➤

| **All-purpose flour** |

4 Make and bake as directed on
package for 8-inch round pan,
dividing batter between round
and square pans ▪ ▪ ▪ ▪ ➤

| **1 package (1 lb 2.25 oz) white or sour cream white cake mix with pudding** |

5 **Adult help:** Cool cakes in pan
10 minutes, then remove from
pans to wire rack. Cool completely.

6 Cut round cake in half, as shown in drawing. Put square cake on tray with one point toward you. Put cut side of each half of round cake against one of the top sides of square cake, as shown in drawing, to make a heart.

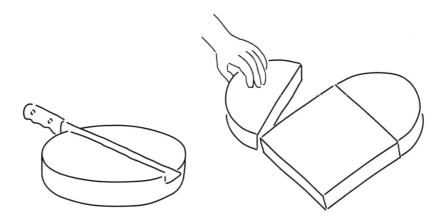

7 Make as directed on package with electric mixer ▬ ▬ ▬ ➤ | **1 package (7.2 oz) fluffy white frosting mix**

8 Beat into frosting to tint pink ▬ ▬ ▬ ▬ ▬ ▬ ➤ | **Few drops of red food color**

9 Frost cake with frosting. Be sure to cover top of cake well, especially over the cut sections.

10 Decorate cake with ▬ ▬ ▬ ➤ | **Red candies or red sugar**

Mystery Cake

9 servings

Utensils You Will Need

Square pan, 9×9×2 inches • Pastry Brush • Large Bowl • Dry-ingredient measuring cups • Measuring spoons • Electric mixer • Rubber scraper • toothpick • 1 1/2-quart saucepan • Small spatula

1 Heat oven to 325°.

2 Grease square pan with ■ ■ ➤ | **Shortening**

3 Put small amount in pan and shake to coat, then pour out any extra ■ ■ ■ ■ ➤ | **All-purpose flour**

4 Beat in large bowl with electric mixer on medium speed about 30 seconds, scraping the bowl all the time, until mixed ■ ➤

1 1/2 cups all-purpose flour
1 cup granulated sugar
2 tablespoons margarine or butter, softened
1 teaspoon ground cinnamon
1 teaspoon baking soda
1/2 teaspoon salt
1/2 teaspoon ground nutmeg
1/4 teaspoon ground cloves
1 large egg
1 can (10 3/4 ounces) condensed tomato soup

5 Beat batter with electric mixer on high speed 3 minutes, scraping bowl a few times.

6 If you like, stir into batter ■ ➤

1/2 cup raisins
1/2 cup chopped nuts

7 Spread batter in pan.

8 **Adult help:** Bake 37 to 43 minutes or until toothpick poked in center comes out clean. Cool on wire rack.

9 **Adult help:** Heat in 1 1/2-quart saucepan over medium heat until light brown ■ ■ ■ ➡

3 tablespoons margarine or butter

10 Beat in ■ ■ ■ ■ ➡

3/4 cup powdered sugar
1 teaspoon vanilla
3 to 4 teaspoons milk

11 Frost cake with frosting.

TIP

Beat in enough milk to make frosting spreadable. If frosting becomes too stiff to spread, stir in more milk, 1/2 teaspoon at a time.

Chocolate Gift Loaf

14 servings
(*photograph on page 314*)

♈ Utensils You Will Need

Sharp knife • Cutting board • 1-quart saucepan • Loaf pan,
9×5×3 inches • Pastry brush • 2 Large bowls • Dry-ingredient measuring
cups • Liquid measuring cup • Measuring spoons • Electric mixer •
Rubber scraper • Toothpick • Pot holders • Wire cooling rack •
Small sharp knife • Small spatula • Kitchen scissors

1 Heat oven to 350°.

2 Melt in saucepan over low heat,
stirring a few times, then remove
from heat and cool slightly ■ ►

| **2 ounces unsweetened chocolate, chopped** |

3 Grease loaf pan with ■ ■ ►

| **Shortening** |

4 Put small amount in pan and
shake to coat, then pour out
any extra ■ ■ ■ ■ ►

| **All-purpose flour** |

5 Beat in large bowl with electric
mixer on medium speed about
30 seconds, scraping bowl all
the time, until mixed ■ ■ ►

| **1 1/2 cups all-purpose flour**
1 cup sugar
1/2 cup shortening
3/4 cup milk
2 teaspoons baking powder
1 teaspoon vanilla
1/2 teaspoon salt
2 large eggs
The melted chocolate |

6 Beat batter with electric mixer on high speed 3 minutes, scraping bowl a few times. Spread batter in pan.

7 Bake 1 hour 5 minutes to 1 hour 10 minutes or until toothpick poked in center comes out clean. **Adult help:** Cool cake in pan 10 minutes, then remove from pan to wire rack. Cool completely.

8 Beat in second large bowl with electric mixer on medium speed until smooth and spreadable (if necessary, add more water, 1/2 teaspoon at a time) ━ ━ ➤

**3 cups powdered sugar
1/3 cup (from a stick) margarine
or butter, softened
1 teaspoon vanilla
1 tablespoon water**

9 Frost cake with frosting.

10 Cut into strips with scissors, and put on cake to look like ribbon on a wrapped package, looping strips on top for bow ━ ━ ➤

2 rolls cherry or strawberry chewy fruit snack (from 4-ounce package)

Banana Oatmeal Cake

15 servings

⟨🍴⟩ Utensils You Will Need

Rectangular pan, 13×9×2 inches • Pastry brush • Large Bowl • Liquid measuring cup • Dry-ingredient measuring cups • Fork • Measuring spoons • Wooden spoon • Pot holders • Toothpick • Wire cooling rack

1 Heat oven to 350°.

2 Grease rectangular pan with ▪ ▪ ▪ ▪ ▶ | **Shortening** |

3 Beat in large bowl with wooden spoon ▪ ▪ ▪ ▶

> **1 1/2 cups mashed very ripe bananas (4 medium)**
> **3/4 cup sugar**
> **2/3 cup vegetable oil**
> **2/3 cup buttermilk**
> **1 teaspoon vanilla**
> **1 large egg**

4 Mix in ▪ ▪ ▪ ▪ ▪ ▶

> **1 1/3 cups all-purpose flour**
> **1 cup quick-cooking or regular oats**
> **2 teaspoons baking soda**
> **1 1/2 teaspoons ground cinnamon**
> **1 teaspoon baking powder**
> **1/2 teaspoon ground cloves**

5 Stir in ▪ ▪ ▪ ▪ ▶

> **2/3 cup chopped nuts**
> **2/3 cup raisins**

6 Spread batter in pan.

7 Bake 30 to 35 minutes or until toothpick poked in center comes out clean. Cool completely on wire rack.

Chocolate Gift Loaf (page 312)

Cookie–Sour Cream Cake

8 servings

Utensils You Will Need

Round pan, 8×1 1/2 or 9×1 1/2 inches • Pastry Brush • Sharp knife • Cutting board • Large Bowl • Dry-ingredient measuring cup • Small sharp knife • Liquid measuring cup • Measuring spoons • Electric mixer • Rubber scraper • Wooden spoon • Pot holders • Wire cooling rack

1 Heat oven to 350°.

2 Grease round pan with ➡ | **Shortening**

3 Put small amount in pan and shake to coat, then pour out any extra ➡ | **All-purpose flour**

4 **Adult help:** Coarsely chop with knife, then set aside ➡ | **8 creme-filled sandwich cookies**

5 Beat in large bowl with electric mixer on low speed 30 seconds, scraping bowl all the time ➡

6 Beat batter with electric mixer on high speed 2 minutes, scraping bowl a few times. Stir the chopped cookies into batter. Spread batter in pan.

> 1 cup all-purpose flour
> 3/4 cup sugar
> 1/2 cup sour cream
> 1/4 cup (1/2 stick) margarine
> or butter, softened
> 1/4 cup water
> 1/2 teaspoon baking soda
> 1/2 teaspoon baking powder
> 1 large egg

7 Bake 30 to 35 minutes or until cake springs back when touched lightly in center. **Adult help:** Cool cake in pan 10 minutes, then remove from pan to wire rack. Cool completely.

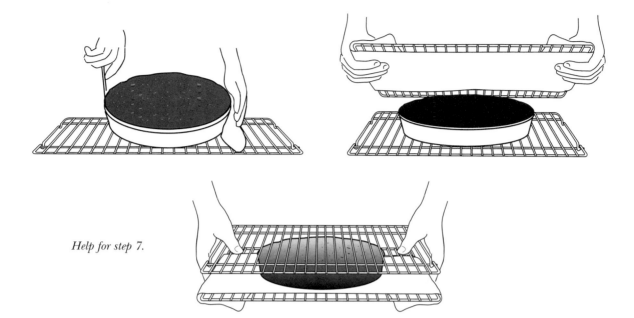

Help for step 7.

8 Frost cake with ■ ■ ■ ■ ➤   **Sweetened Whipped Cream (below)**

9 If you like, decorate cake with more cookies.

SWEETENED WHIPPED CREAM

🍴 Utensils You Will Need

Medium bowl • Liquid measuring cup • Measuring spoon • Egg beater

1 Chill medium bowl in freezer about 15 minutes or until cold.

2 Beat in chilled bowl with
eggbeater until stiff ■ ■ ■ ➤   **3/4 cup whipping (heavy) cream
2 tablespoons granulated or
powdered sugar**

Dinosaur Cakes

14 cakes
(photograph on page 360)

℣℣ **Utensils You Will Need**

Jelly roll pan, 15 1/2×10 1/2×1 inch • Pastry brush • Large bowl •
Dry-ingredient measuring cups • Measuring spoons • Liquid measuring cup •
Electric mixer • Rubber scraper • Fork • Pot holders • Toothpick • Wire
cooling rack • Dinosaur-shaped cookie cutters • Spatula

1 Heat oven to 350°.

2 Grease jelly roll pan with ➡ | **Shortening**

3 Put small amount in pan and
shake to coat, then pour out
any extra ➡ | **All-purpose flour**

4 Beat in large bowl with electric
mixer on low speed 30 seconds,
scraping bowl all the time ➡ |
2 1/3 cups all-purpose flour
1 1/3 cups sugar
1/2 cup shortening
1 1/4 cups orange juice
3 1/2 teaspoons baking powder
1 teaspoon vanilla
1/2 teaspoon salt
3 large eggs

5 Beat batter with electric
mixer on high speed 3 minutes,
scraping bowl a few times.

6 Add ➡ | 1/4 cup multicolored candy
decorations

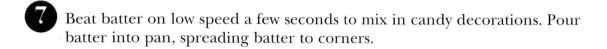

7 Beat batter on low speed a few seconds to mix in candy decorations. Pour batter into pan, spreading batter to corners.

8 Bake 20 to 25 minutes or until toothpick poked in center comes out clean. Cool completely on wire rack.

9 Freeze cake uncovered about 1 hour. Cut cake into dinosaur shapes with cookie cutters. Remove dinosaur cakes from pan with spatula.

10 Frost tops of cakes with frosting and sprinkle with dinosaur candies from ➤

1 tub (1 lb) chocolate ready-to-spread frosting with dinosaur candy bit sprinkles

---

*Here's another idea. . . Make **Shaped Cakes:** Cut cake into shapes using your favorite cookie cutters and frost with any ready-to-spread frosting with candy bit sprinkles.*

Chocolate Malt Cakes

12 cakes

Utensils You Will Need

Muffin pan with medium cups, 2 1/2×1 1/4 inches, or rectangular
pan, 13×9×2 inches • Medium bowl • Dry-ingredient measuring cups •
Measuring spoons • Wooden spoon • Small bowl • Liquid measuring cup •
Wire whisk • Pot holders • Toothpick • Wire cooling rack • Straws •
Kitchen scissors • Ice-cream scoop

1 Heat oven to 350°.

2 Put in muffin cups or pan ➡ | 12 to 16 ice-cream cones with flat bottoms

3 Mix in medium bowl
with wooden spoon ➡

1 1/4 cups all-purpose flour
3/4 cup sugar
1/3 cup malted milk powder,
if you like
1/4 cup cocoa
1 teaspoon baking soda
1/4 teaspoon salt

4 Mix in small bowl with
wire whisk ➡

1/4 cup vegetable oil
1 teaspoon vinegar
1/2 teaspoon vanilla

5 Stir hard into flour mixture
with wire whisk about 1 minute
or until well mixed ➡

The oil mixture
2/3 cup cold water

6 Immediately pour batter into cones, filling each to within about 1 inch of top of cone.

7 Bake about 30 minutes or until toothpick poked in centers of cakes comes out clean. **Adult help:** Remove cones from muffin cups or pans to wire rack. Cool completely.

8 Top each cake with small scoop of, then freeze until ready to serve ━ ━ ━ ━ ➤

Chocolate or vanilla ice cream

9 Just before serving, cut in half, then poke closed ends into ice cream ━ ━ ━ ━ ➤

12 to 16 candy powder straws or plastic straws

10 Squirt each "malt" with desired amount of whipped cream and top with cherry ━ ━ ━ ━ ➤

**1 can (7 ounces) whipped cream topping
12 to 16 maraschino cherries**

Upside-Down Pineapple Cake

9 servings
(photograph on page 324)

Utensils You Will Need

Square pan, 9×9×2 inches • Small sharp knife • Pot holders • Dry-ingredient measuring cups • Can opener • Large Bowl • Liquid measuring cup • Measuring spoons • Electric mixer • Rubber scraper • Toothpick • Heatproof serving plate

1 Heat oven to 350°.

2 Melt in square pan in oven ▶
| 1/4 cup (1/2 stick) margarine or butter |

3 Sprinkle over margarine ▶
| 2/3 cup packed brown sugar |

4 Put on top of brown sugar mixture ▶
| 1 can (about 16 ounces) sliced pineapple, drained |

5 If you like, put in centers of pineapple slices ▶
| Maraschino cherries |

6 Beat in large bowl with electric mixer on low speed 30 seconds, scraping bowl all the time ▶

7 Beat batter with electric mixer on high speed 3 minutes, scraping bowl a few times. Pour batter over fruit mixture in pan.

| 1 1/3 cups all-purpose flour |
| 1 cup granulated sugar |
| 1/3 cup shortening |
| 3/4 cup milk |
| 1 1/2 teaspoons baking powder |
| 1/2 teaspoon salt |
| 1 large egg |

8 Bake 55 to 60 minutes or until toothpick poked in center comes out clean. **Adult help:** Immediately turn pan upside down onto heatproof serving plate. Let pan remain over cake a few minutes, then remove pan.

9 Serve warm and, if you like, with ■ ■ ■ ■ ■ ■ ■ ➤

**Sweetened Whipped Cream
(page 317)**

TIP

*If any pieces of pineapple or cherries stick to the pan when you remove it,
just pick them off and place on cake where they go.*

Apple Crisp

4 servings

Utensils You Will Need

Square pan, 8×8×2 inches • Cutting board • Sharp knives • Dry-ingredient measuring cups • Small bowl • Measuring spoons • Liquid measuring cup • Medium bowl • Pot holders • Wire cooling rack

1 Heat oven to 375°.

2 **Adult help:** Cut into fourths, then core, peel and slice to measure 4 cups ➝ | **About 5 medium cooking apples**

3 Put apple slices in square pan.

4 Mix in small bowl, then sprinkle over apples ➝ | **1/4 cup granulated or packed brown sugar**
1/2 teaspoon ground cinnamon

5 Pour over apples ➝ | **1/4 cup water**

6 Mix with hands in medium bowl until crumbly, then sprinkle over apples ➝ | **1 cup all-purpose flour**
2/3 cup granulated sugar
1/2 cup (1 stick) margarine or butter, softened

7 Bake 45 to 50 minutes or until apples are tender and topping is golden brown. Cool on wire rack.

8 If you like, serve with ➝ | **Sweetened Whipped Cream (page 317) or ice cream**

Upside-Down Pineapple Cake (page 322)

Quick Blueberry Cobbler

6 servings

⚑ Utensils You Will Need

1 1/2-quart casserole • Can opener • Wooden spoon • Small bowl • Dry-ingredient measuring cup • Measuring spoons • Liquid measuring cup • Small sharp knife • Tablespoon • Pot holders • Wire cooling rack

1 Heat oven to 400°.

2 Mix in casserole with wooden spoon ▪ ▪ ▪ ▪ ▪ ▪ ▶

> **1 can (21 ounces) blueberry pie filling**
> **1 teaspoon grated orange peel, if you like**

3 Bake uncovered about 15 minutes or until hot and bubbly.

4 While blueberry mixture is baking, stir in small bowl to make a soft dough ▪ ▪ ▪ ▶

> **1 cup Bisquick Original baking mix**
> **1 tablespoon sugar**
> **1/4 cup orange juice**
> **1 tablespoon (from a stick) margarine or butter, softened**

5 **Adult help:** Drop dough by 6 spoonfuls onto hot blueberry mixture. Bake uncovered 20 to 25 minutes or until topping is light brown. Cool slightly on wire rack. Serve warm.

---

*Here's another idea. . . Make **Quick Cherry-Almond Cobbler:** Use 1 can (21 ounces) cherry pie filling in place of the blueberry pie filling, 1/2 teaspoon almond extract in place of the orange peel and 1/4 cup milk in place of the orange juice. Stir 2 tablespoons toasted slivered almonds into the dough in Step 4.*

Quick Blueberry Cobbler

Strawberry Pie

8 servings

Utensils You Will Need

2 Medium bowls • Dry-ingredient measuring cups • Measuring spoons •
Fork • Pastry blender • Pastry cloth and cloth cover for rolling pin •
Rolling pin • Pie plate, 9×1 1/2 inches • Colander • Sharp knife •
Potato masher • Pot holders • Wire cooling rack • 1 1/2-quart saucepan •
Liquid measuring cup • Wooden spoon

1 Heat oven to 475°.

2 Mix in medium bowl with fork ➡

> **1 cup all-purpose flour**
> **1/2 teaspoon salt**

3 Cut into flour mixture with pastry blender until pieces are the size of small peas ➡

> **1/3 cup plus 1 tablespoon shortening**

4 Sprinkle in, 1 tablespoon at a time, tossing with fork until all the flour is wet and pastry almost leaves side of bowl ➡

> **2 to 3 tablespoons cold water**

5 Cover a breadboard with a pastry cloth. Sprinkle flour lightly over cloth. Shape pastry into a ball on floured cloth. Shape ball into a flattened round. Roll pastry with floured cloth-covered rolling pin until pastry is 2 inches larger than pie plate turned upside down.

6 Fold pastry into fourths. Put pastry into pie plate, 9×1 1/2 inches. Unfold and fit pastry into plate, pressing firmly against bottom and side. Trim edge of pastry that hangs over pie plate to 1 inch from rim of plate. Fold and roll pastry under, even with pie plate, then press around edge with fork dipped in flour. Poke bottom and side of pastry many times with fork.

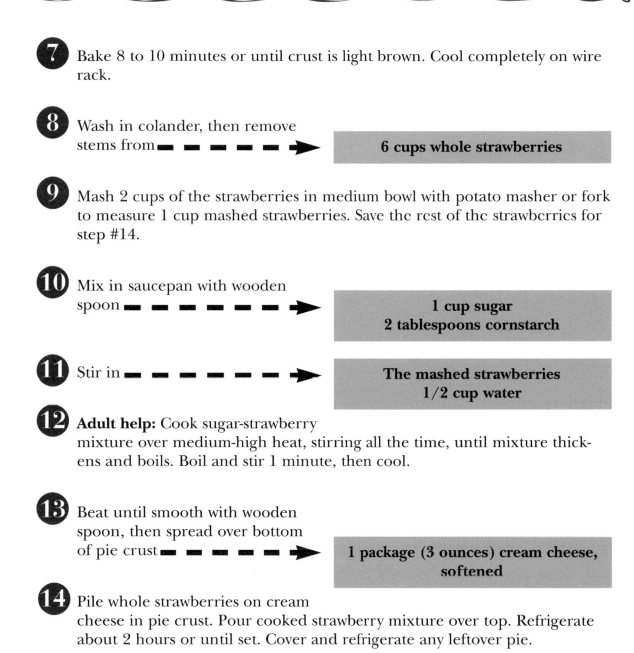

7 Bake 8 to 10 minutes or until crust is light brown. Cool completely on wire rack.

8 Wash in colander, then remove stems from ▬ ▬ ▬ ▬ ▬ ➤

6 cups whole strawberries

9 Mash 2 cups of the strawberries in medium bowl with potato masher or fork to measure 1 cup mashed strawberries. Save the rest of the strawberries for step #14.

10 Mix in saucepan with wooden spoon ▬ ▬ ▬ ▬ ▬ ➤

1 cup sugar
2 tablespoons cornstarch

11 Stir in ▬ ▬ ▬ ▬ ▬ ➤

The mashed strawberries
1/2 cup water

12 **Adult help:** Cook sugar-strawberry mixture over medium-high heat, stirring all the time, until mixture thickens and boils. Boil and stir 1 minute, then cool.

13 Beat until smooth with wooden spoon, then spread over bottom of pie crust ▬ ▬ ▬ ▬ ▬ ➤

1 package (3 ounces) cream cheese, softened

14 Pile whole strawberries on cream cheese in pie crust. Pour cooked strawberry mixture over top. Refrigerate about 2 hours or until set. Cover and refrigerate any leftover pie.

Here's another idea. . . Make **Raspberry Pie:** *Use 6 cups raspberries in place of the strawberries.*

Lemon–Cream Cheese Dessert

9 servings

♈ Utensils You Will Need

Plastic bag with zipper top • Dry-ingredient measuring cups • Rolling pin •
Small bowl • Measuring spoons • Wooden spoon • Square pan, 8×8×2
inches • Wire cooling rack • Large Bowl • Electric mixer • Can opener •
Liquid measuring cup • Plastic wrap

1 Heat oven to 350°.

2 Put in plastic bag ▪ ▪ ▪ ▶

> **3 cups toasted whole-grain oat cereal**

3 Press air out of plastic bag, then
seal. Roll cereal with rolling pin or jar until finely crushed.

4 Mix in small bowl with
wooden spoon, then save
2 tablespoons ▪ ▪ ▪ ▶

> **The crushed cereal**
> **1/3 cup (from a stick) margarine**
> **or butter, melted**
> **1/4 cup sugar**
> **1 teaspoon ground cinnamon**

5 Press the rest of the cereal
mixture in square pan, 8×8×2
inches. Bake 12 minutes.
Cool on wire rack.

6 Beat in large bowl with electric
mixer on medium speed until
light and fluffy ▪ ▪ ▪ ▶

> **1 package (8 ounces) cream cheese, softened**

7 Beat in, a little at a time ▬ ▬ ▶

> **1 can (14 ounces) sweetened condensed milk**

8 Stir in ▬ ▬ ▬ ▬ ▬ ▬ ▶

> **1/4 cup lemon juice
> 1 teaspoon vanilla**

9 Pour cream cheese mixture over baked cereal mixture in pan. Sprinkle saved cereal mixture over top. Cover with plastic wrap and refrigerate 3 to 4 hours or until firm.

10 If you like, top with ▬ ▬ ▬ ▶

> **Fresh fruit**

11 Cover and refrigerate any leftover dessert.

Strawberry Shortcakes

6 shortcakes
(photograph on page 334)

🍴 Utensils You Will Need

Colander • Small sharp knife • Paper towel • Cutting board • Medium
bowl • Wooden spoon • Dry-ingredient measuring cups • Large Bowl • Liquid
measuring cup • Measuring spoons • Rolling pin • Ruler • 3-inch round cookie
cutter • Cookie sheet • Pot holders • Spatula • Wire cooling rack • Spoon

1 Rinse in colander ■ ■ ■ ➡ | **1 quart whole strawberries** |

2 Gently pat strawberries dry with paper towel. Remove stems from strawberries. **Adult help:** Cut strawberries in half. Put strawberries in medium bowl.

3 Stir in, then cover and refrigerate ■ ■ ■ ■ ➡ | **1/2 cup sugar** |

4 Heat oven to 425°.

5 Mix in large bowl with wooden spoon to make a soft dough ■ ■ ■ ■ ■ ➡

> **2 1/3 cups Bisquick Original baking mix**
> **1/2 cup half-and-half**
> **3 tablespoons sugar**
> **3 tablespoons (from a stick) margarine or butter, melted**

6 Sprinkle a clean surface (such as a kitchen counter or bread board) with flour or Bisquick. Put dough on surface. Roll ball of dough around 3 or 4 times. Knead dough quickly and lightly by folding, pressing and turning. Repeat 10 times.

7 Roll or pat dough until 1/2 inch thick. Cut dough with cookie cutter dipped in flour. Carefully put dough on cookie sheet.

8 Bake 12 to 15 minutes or until golden brown.

9 While shortcakes are baking, make ▬ ▬ ▬ ▬ ▬ ▬ ➤

> **Sweetened Whipped Cream (page 317)**

10 **Adult help:** Remove shortcakes from cookie sheet with spatula to wire rack. Split shortcakes horizontally in half with knife, then put on dessert plates. Spoon strawberries between shortcake halves and over tops. Top with the whipped cream.

TIP

Cut 3 nicely shaped strawberries with green tops in half lengthwise and use to top shortcakes.

Mini Pineapple Desserts

6 servings

♈ Utensils You Will Need

Pie plate, 9×1 1/2 inches • Fork • Dry-ingredient measuring cups •
Measuring spoons • Small sharp knife • Pot holders • 1 1/2-quart saucepan •
Can opener • Grater • Six 6-ounce custard cups

1 Heat oven to 400°.

2 Mix in pie plate with fork until crumbly ▬ ▬ ▬ ▬ ▶

3 Bake 8 to 10 minutes or until light and dry. Stir with fork.

> 1/2 cup Bisquick Original
> baking mix
> 3 tablespoons sugar
> 2 tablespoons finely chopped nuts
> 2 tablespoons (from a stick)
> margarine or butter, softened
> 1/4 teaspoon ground cinnamon

4 Heat in saucepan, stirring a few times, until hot ▬ ▬ ▬ ▬ ▶

> 1 can (21 ounces) apple pie filling
> 1 can (8.25 ounces) crushed
> pineapple in syrup, undrained
> 1 teaspoon grated orange peel

5 Spoon apple mixture into 6-ounce custard cups. Sprinkle with baked topping. Store any
leftover topping in tightly covered container in refrigerator.

Strawberry Shortcakes (page 332)

Yummy Yogurt Cups

4 servings

⟨⟨⟨ Utensils You Will Need

Medium bowl • Dry-ingredient measuring cups • Small sharp knife •
Measuring spoons • Fork • Tablespoon • Four 6-ounce custard cups •
Pot holders • Small metal spatula • Wire cooling rack • Spoon

1 Heat oven to 375°.

2 Mix in medium bowl with fork until crumbly ▬ ▬ ▬ ▬ ➤

> 3/4 cup all-purpose flour
> 1/4 cup (1/2 stick) margarine or butter, softened
> 3 tablespoons powdered sugar

3 Sprinkle in, 1 teaspoon at a time, stirring to make a dough ▬ ➤

> 2 to 3 teaspoons cold water

4 Press about 3 tablespoons of the dough in bottom and up side of each 6-ounce custard cup to within 1/2 inch of top.

5 Bake 10 to 12 minutes or until golden brown. Cool 10 minutes.
Adult help: Carefully remove shells from custard cups with small metal spatula to wire rack. Cool completely.

6 Spoon evenly into shells ▬ ➤

> 1 1/3 cups yogurt (any flavor)

7 If you like, top with ▬ ▬ ▬ ➤

> Fresh fruit

TIP

Keep edges of dough even when pressing it into custard cups.

Cinnamon-Sugar Muffins

12 muffins

🍴 Utensils You Will Need

Muffin pan with medium cups, 2 1/2×1 1/4 inches • Pastry brush • Medium bowl • Fork • Dry-ingredient measuring cups • Wooden spoon • Small bowl • Measuring spoons • Liquid measuring cup • Pot holders • 1-quart saucepan

1 Heat oven to 350°.

2 Grease bottoms only of 12 muffin cups with ➜ **Shortening**

3 Beat in medium bowl with fork ➜
1/2 cup sugar
1/2 cup milk
1/3 cup vegetable oil
1 large egg

4 Stir into milk mixture just until all the flour is wet (do not stir too much—batter will be lumpy) ➜
1 1/2 cups all-purpose flour
1 1/2 teaspoons baking powder
1/2 teaspoon salt
1/4 teaspoon ground nutmeg

5 Spoon batter into muffin cups until 2/3 full. Bake 20 to 25 minutes or until golden brown.

6 While muffins are baking, mix in small bowl, then set aside ➜
1/2 cup sugar
1 teaspoon ground cinnamon

7 Melt in saucepan over low heat, then remove from heat ➜ 1/2 cup (1 stick) margarine or butter

8 **Adult help:** Immediately remove muffins from pan. Roll hot muffins in the melted margarine, then in the cinnamon-sugar mixture. Serve hot.

Blueberry Streusel Muffins

12 muffins

(photograph on page 350)

¶♨ Utensils You Will Need

Small bowl • Dry-ingredient measuring cups • Measuring spoons •
Fork • Small sharp knife • Wooden spoon • Muffin pan with medium cups,
2 1/2 × 1 1/4 inches • Pastry brush • Medium bowl • Liquid measuring cup •
Pot holders • Wire cooling rack

1 Heat oven to 400°.

2 For topping, mix in small bowl with fork until crumbly, then set aside ▬ ▬ ▬ ▬ ➤

> 1/4 cup all-purpose flour
> 2 tablespoons packed brown sugar
> 2 tablespoons firm margarine
> or butter
> 1/4 teaspoon ground cinnamon

3 Grease bottoms only of 12 medium muffin cups with (or line muffin cups with paper baking cups) ▬ ▬ ▬ ▬ ➤

> **Shortening**

4 Beat in medium bowl with fork ▬ ▬ ▬ ▬ ➤

> 1 cup milk
> 1/4 cup vegetable oil
> 1/2 teaspoon vanilla
> 1 large egg

5 Stir into milk mixture just until all the flour is wet (do not stir too much—batter will be lumpy) ▬ ▬ ▬ ▬ ➤

> 2 cups all-purpose or whole wheat flour
> 1/3 cup granulated sugar
> 3 teaspoons baking powder
> 1/2 teaspoon salt

6 Gently stir in ■ ■ ■ ■ ➤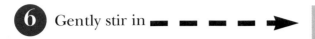

1 cup fresh or drained canned blueberries or 3/4 cup frozen blueberries, thawed and well drained

7 Spoon batter into muffin cups until 2/3 full. Sprinkle each with about 2 teaspoons of topping mixture.

8 Bake 20 to 25 minutes or until golden brown. **Adult help:** Immediately remove muffins from pan to wire rack. Serve warm or cool.

Here's another idea. . . Make **Apple Muffins:** *Leave out blueberries. Stir in 1 cup grated apple with the milk, and stir in 1/2 teaspoon ground cinnamon with the flour in Step 5. Bake 25 to 30 minutes.*

Easy Pumpkin Nut Pie

8 servings

⚔️ Utensils You Will Need

2 large bowls • Dry-ingredient measuring cups • Wooden spoons •
Measuring spoons • Pie plate, 9×1 1/2 inches • Fork • Can opener •
Aluminum foil • Pot holders • Knife • Wire cooling rack • Medium bowl •
Liquid measuring cup • Eggbeater

1 Mix in large bowl with wooden spoon ━ ━ ━ ➤

> 1/2 cup (1 stick) margarine or butter, softened
> 1/3 cup packed brown sugar

2 Stir in just until crumbly ━ ━ ━ ━ ➤

3 Press mixture against bottom and up side of pie plate, 9×1 1/2 inches, building up a 1/2-inch edge above top of pie plate. (A high edge is necessary to keep filling from running over.)

> 1 1/4 cups all-purpose or whole wheat flour
> 1/2 cup chopped nuts
> 1/2 teaspoon vanilla
> 1/4 teaspoon salt
> 1/4 teaspoon baking soda

4 Heat oven to 425°.

5 Beat slightly in large bowl with fork ━ ━ ━ ━ ➤

> 2 large eggs

6 Stir in until smooth ━ ━ ━ ➤

> 1 cup mashed pumpkin (about half of a 16-ounce can)
> 3/4 cup packed brown sugar
> 1 teaspoon ground cinnamon
> 1/2 teaspoon salt
> 1/4 teaspoon ground cloves
> 1/4 teaspoon ground ginger
> 1/4 teaspoon freshly ground nutmeg

7 Stir in, a little at a time ▬ ▬ ➤   **1 can (12 ounces) evaporated milk**

8 Pour pumpkin mixture into pie crust. Cover edge of crust with 2- to 3-inch strip of aluminum foil to keep crust from browning too much.

9 Bake 15 minutes. Turn oven temperature down to 350°. Bake 45 to 55 minutes longer or until knife poked in pie near center comes out clean. Cool completely on wire rack.

10 Chill medium bowl in freezer about 15 minutes or until cold.

11 Beat in chilled bowl with eggbeater until stiff ▬ ▬ ▬ ➤   **1 cup whipping (heavy) cream**
3 tablespoons packed brown sugar

12 Serve pie with the whipped cream.
Cover and refrigerate any leftover pie and whipped cream.

Elephant Ears

4 servings

🍴 Utensils You Will Need

Cookie sheet • Pastry brush • 1-quart saucepan • Small sharp knife • Medium bowl • Dry-ingredient measuring cups • Measuring spoons • Wooden spoon • Liquid measuring cup • Rolling pin • Ruler • Small bowl • Sharp knife • Pot holders • Spatula • Wire cooling rack

1 Heat oven to 425°.

2 Grease cookie sheet with ➡ **Shortening**

3 Melt in saucepan over low heat, then set aside ➡ **1/4 cup (1/2 stick) margarine or butter**

4 Mix in medium bowl with wooden spoon ➡

**1 cup all-purpose flour
2 tablespoons sugar
1/2 teaspoon baking powder
1/2 teaspoon salt**

5 Stir to make a dough ➡

**3 tablespoons of the melted margarine or butter
1/3 cup milk**

6 Sprinkle a clean surface (such as a kitchen counter or bread board) with flour. Put dough on surface. Roll ball of dough around 3 or 4 times. Knead dough quickly and lightly by folding, pressing and turning. Repeat 10 times. Roll or pat dough into 9×5-inch rectangle.

7 Mix in small bowl ➡

**2 tablespoons sugar
1 teaspoon ground cinnamon**

8 Brush dough with the rest of the melted margarine or butter, then sprinkle with the sugar-cinnamon mixture.

9 Roll dough up tightly, beginning at short end of rectangle. Pinch edge of dough into roll to seal. **Adult help:** Cut roll into 4 equal pieces with sharp knife. Put pieces, cut sides up, on cookie sheet, then pat into 6-inch circles.

10 Sprinkle circles with ━ ━ ➤ **Sugar**

11 Bake 8 to 10 minutes or until edges are golden brown. Immediately remove elephant ears from cookie sheet with spatula to wire rack. Cool.

TIP

Dip hands in sugar to keep them from sticking to dough when patting circles on cookie sheet.

Apple-Cinnamon Bread

1 loaf (16 slices)

♈ Utensils You Will Need
Loaf pan, 9×5×3 inches • Pastry brush • Cutting board • Sharp knives •
Large Bowl • Dry-ingredient measuring cups • Measuring spoons • Wooden
spoon • Small bowl • Pot holders • Toothpick • Wire cooling rack

1 Heat oven to 350°.

2 Grease bottom only of loaf
pan with ► **Shortening**

3 **Adult help:** Cut apples into
fourths, then core, peel and
chop to measure 2 cups ► **About 2 medium cooking apples**

4 Mix in large bowl with
wooden spoon ►
**1 cup sugar
1/2 cup shortening
1 teaspoon vanilla
2 large eggs**

5 Stir in until smooth (batter will
be thick) ►
**2 cups all-purpose flour
1 teaspoon baking powder
1 teaspoon baking soda
1 teaspoon ground cinnamon
1/2 teaspoon salt**

6 Stir in ▬ ▬ ▬ ▬ ▬ ➤

> **The chopped apples**
> **1/2 cup chopped walnuts**
> **1/2 cup raisins**

7 Spread batter in pan.

8 Mix in small bowl, then sprinkle over batter ▬ ▬ ▬ ▬ ▬ ➤

> **1 tablespoon sugar**
> **1/4 teaspoon ground cinnamon**

9 Bake 50 to 55 minutes or until toothpick poked about 1 inch from center comes out clean. **Adult help:** Immediately remove bread from pan to wire rack. Cool. Store bread tightly covered.

Pull-Apart Coffee Cake

16 servings

🍴 Utensils You Will Need

1-quart saucepan • Liquid measuring cup • 2 large bowls • Kitchen scissors •
Wooden spoon • Dry-ingredient measuring cups • Small sharp knife •
Measuring spoons • Kitchen towel • Ruler • Small bowl • Tube pan,
10×4 inches • Pastry brush • Pot holders • Serving plate • 2 forks

1 Mix in large bowl with wooden spoon ▬ ▬ ▬ ▬ ➤

> **2 cups all-purpose flour**
> **1/3 cup sugar**
> **1 teaspoon salt**
> **1 package regular or quick-acting**
> **active dry yeast**

2 Heat in saucepan until very warm ▬ ▬ ▬ ▬ ➤

> **1/2 cup milk**
> **1/2 cup warm water**

3 Stir into yeast mixture, then beat with wooden spoon until smooth ▬ ▬ ▬ ▬ ➤

> **The warm milk mixture**
> **1/3 cup shortening or margarine**
> **or butter (from a stick), softened**
> **1 egg**

4 Mix in enough to make dough easy to handle ▬ ▬ ▬ ▬ ➤

> **1 1/2 to 2 cups all-purpose flour**

5 Sprinkle a clean surface (such as a kitchen counter or bread board) with flour. Put dough on surface. Roll ball of dough around 3 or 4 times. Knead dough quickly and lightly by folding, pressing and turning. Continue kneading about 5 minutes or until dough is smooth and elastic.

6 Grease large bowl with ▬ ▬ ➤

> **Shortening**

7 Put dough in bowl, then turn greased side up. Cover dough with towel and let rise in warm place about 1 1/2 hours or until dough doubles. (Dough is ready if a mark stays when dough is touched.)

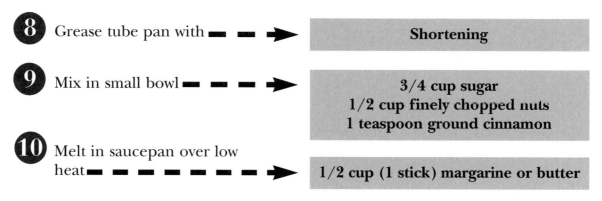

8 Grease tube pan with ➤ **Shortening**

9 Mix in small bowl ➤
3/4 cup sugar
1/2 cup finely chopped nuts
1 teaspoon ground cinnamon

10 Melt in saucepan over low heat ➤ **1/2 cup (1 stick) margarine or butter**

11 Punch down dough with fist. Shape dough into 1 1/2-inch balls.

12 Dip each ball in margarine, then in sugar-nut mixture. Put a single layer of balls in pan so they just touch. (If pan has removable bottom, line with aluminum foil.) Top with another layer of balls. Cover and let rise in warm place about 40 minutes or until balls double.

13 Heat oven to 375°.

14 Bake 35 to 40 minutes or until golden brown. (If coffee cake browns too quickly, cover loosely with aluminum foil.) **Adult help:** Loosen coffee cake from pan. Immediately turn pan upside down onto serving plate. Let pan stay a minute so margarine-sugar mixture can drizzle over coffee cake, then remove pan. Serve coffee cake while warm by pulling it apart with fingers or breaking apart with 2 forks.

Cheesy Pretzels

16 pretzels
(photograph on page 350)

Utensils You Will Need

Cookie sheet • Pastry brush • Medium bowl • Fork • Dry-ingredient measuring cups • Liquid measuring cup • Measuring spoons • Rolling pin • Ruler • Knife • Small bowl • Pot holders • Spatula • Wire cooling rack

1 Heat oven to 400°.

2 Generously grease cookie sheet with ▪ ▪ ▪ ▪ ➤

Shortening

3 Mix in medium bowl with fork to make a dough ▪ ▪ ▪ ➤

1 1/2 cups all-purpose flour
1/2 cup shredded Cheddar cheese (2 ounces)
2/3 cup milk
2 tablespoons (from a stick) margarine or butter
2 teaspoons baking powder
1 teaspoon sugar
1/2 teaspoon salt

4 Sprinkle a clean surface (such as a kitchen counter or bread board) with flour. Put dough on surface. Roll ball of dough around 3 or 4 times. Knead dough quickly and lightly by folding, pressing and turning. Repeat 10 times.

5 Divide dough in half. Roll or pat half of the dough into 12×8-inch rectangle. **Adult help:** Cut dough lengthwise into eight 1-inch-wide strips. Fold each strip lengthwise in half to make it more narrow. Pinch the edges to seal.

6 Twist each strip into a pretzel shape. Put pretzels, seam sides down, on cookie sheet.

7 Beat in small bowl with fork ▪ ▪ ▪ ▪ ▪ ▪ ▪ ➤

1 large egg

8 Brush pretzels with the beaten egg, then sprinkle lightly with ▪ ▪ ▪ ▪ ▪ ➤

Coarse salt

9 Bake 10 to 15 minutes or until golden brown. Remove pretzels from cookie sheet with spatula to wire rack. Cool. Repeat making pretzels with the rest of the dough.

Here's another idea. . . Make **Peanutty Pretzels:** *Leave out the cheese. Use 2 tablespoons crunchy peanut butter in place of the margarine. Use 2 tablespoons chopped salted peanuts in place of the coarse salt.*

TIP

A pizza cutter makes quick work of cutting the dough into strips.

Pizza Bites

6 servings

Utensils You Will Need
Toaster • Small bowl • Small sharp knife • Measuring spoons •
Spoon • Sharp knife • Cutting board • Cookie sheet • Dry-ingredient
measuring cup • Pot holders

1 Heat oven to 425°.

2 Split with fork, then toast ➤ **3 English muffins**

3 Mix in small bowl with spoon, then spread on muffin halves ➤ **2 tablespoons margarine or butter, softened
1/8 teaspoon instant minced garlic**

4 Cut each muffin half into 4 wedges. Put wedges, with sides touching, on cookie sheet.

5 Put 1 slice on each muffin wedge ➤ **About 1/2 package (3 1/2-ounce size) thinly sliced pepperoni**

6 Sprinkle over muffin wedges ➤ **1 cup shredded mozzarella cheese (4 ounces)
1/2 teaspoon dried oregano leaves**

7 Bake 8 to 10 minutes or until cheese is melted. Separate into wedges.

Cheesy Pretzels (page 348), Blueberry Streusel Muffins (page 338)

Top-It-Your-Way Pizza

4 servings

♨️ Utensils You Will Need

Cookie sheet or pizza pan, 15 inches • Pastry brush • Ruler • Can opener • Rubber scraper • sharp knife • Cutting board • Dry-ingredient measuring cups • Pot holders • Wire cooling rack • Pizza cutter

1 Move oven rack to lowest position. Heat oven to 350°.

2 Grease cookie sheet or pizza pan with ➡️ **Shortening**

3 Thaw pizza dough as directed on package, then shape into 14×11-inch rectangle on cookie sheet or 14-inch circle on pizza pan ➡️ **1 loaf (1 pound) frozen pizza dough**

4 Spread over dough with rubber scraper ➡️ **1 can (8 ounces) pizza sauce**

5 Choose 2 or 3 of your favorite toppings and sprinkle them over the sauce ➡️

> **1 cup sliced mushrooms**
> **1/2 cup chopped green bell pepper**
> **1/4 cup sliced ripe olives**
> **A few thinly sliced onion rings**
> **1/2 package (3 1/2-ounce size) thinly sliced pepperoni**
> **1/4 pound hamburger or sausage, cooked**
> **Other favorite topping**

6 Sprinkle over the toppings ➡️ **1 1/2 cups shredded mozzarella cheese (6 ounces)**

7 Bake 25 to 35 minutes or until cheese is melted and light brown. Cut pizza into wedges.

Top-It-Your-Way Pizza

Pocket Pizza

2 servings

❦ Utensils You Will Need

Cookie sheet • Pastry brush • Small bowl • Dry-ingredient measuring cups •
Liquid measuring cup • Measuring spoons • Wooden spoon • Rolling pin •
Ruler • Scissors • Fork • Pot holders

1 Stir hard in small bowl with wooden spoon until dough leaves side of bowl (if dough seems dry, add 1 to 2 tablespoons milk) ▪ ▪ ▪ ➤

> **1 cup all-purpose flour**
> **1/3 cup milk**
> **2 tablespoons vegetable oil**
> **1 teaspoon baking powder**
> **1/2 teaspoon salt**

2 Sprinkle a clean surface (such as a kitchen counter or bread board) with flour. Put dough on surface. Roll ball of dough around 3 or 4 times. Knead dough quickly and lightly by folding, pressing and turning. Repeat 10 times. Cover dough with bowl and let stand 15 minutes.

3 Heat oven to 425°.

4 Grease cookie sheet with ▪ ▪ ▪ ➤   **Shortening**

5 Roll or pat dough into 12-inch circle on lightly floured surface. Fold dough loosely in half. Put dough on cookie sheet, then unfold.

6 Brush dough lightly, using pastry brush, with ▪ ▪ ➤   **Vegetable oil**

7 Layer on half of the dough circle in the order listed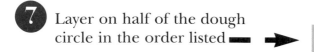

8 Fold dough over filling. Turn edge of lower dough over edge of top dough, then pinch edge to seal. Poke top with fork.

9 Bake 20 to 25 minutes or until golden brown. Cut pizza in half.

1/4 cup pizza sauce
1/2 cup shredded mozzarella cheese (2 ounces)
1 tablespoon finely chopped onion or 1/4 teaspoon onion powder
1/8 to 1/4 teaspoon garlic powder
About 1/2 package (3 1/2-ounce size) thinly sliced pepperoni
2 to 3 tablespoons pizza sauce
Another 1/2 cup shredded mozzarella cheese (2 ounces)

Quick Cheeseburger Pie

6 servings

🍴 Utensils You Will Need

Pie plate, 10×1 1/2 inches • Pastry brush • Sharp knife • Cutting board •
10-inch skillet • Wooden spoon • Measuring spoons • Strainer • Blender •
Liquid measuring cup • Dry-ingredient measuring cups • Pot holders • Knife

1 Heat oven to 400°.

2 Grease pie plate with ▬ ▬ ▬ ➤
Shortening

3 **Adult help:** Wash, then chop with sharp knife ▬ ▬ ▬ ➤
2 medium onions

4 Cook in skillet over medium heat about 10 minutes, stirring often, until beef is brown ▬ ➤
The chopped onions **1 pound ground beef** **1/4 teaspoon pepper**

5 Pour beef mixture into strainer to drain off any fat. Spread beef mixture in pie plate.

6 Put in blender, cover and blend on high speed 15 seconds (or use eggbeater or wire whisk), then pour over beef in pie plate ▬ ➤
1 1/2 cups milk **3 large eggs** **3/4 cup Bisquick Original** **baking mix**

7 Bake 25 minutes.

8 **Adult help:** Meanwhile, wash, then cut into slices ▬ ▬ ▬ ➤ | **2 medium tomatoes**

9 **Adult help:** Carefully remove pie from oven. Top with tomatoes, then sprinkle with ▬ ▬ ▬ ➤ | **1 cup shredded Cheddar or process American cheese (4 ounces)**

10 Bake 5 to 8 minutes longer or until knife poked in center of pie comes out clean. Cool 5 minutes.

Dinosaur Calzones

10 servings
(*photograph on page 360*)

🍴 Utensils You Will Need
10-inch skillet • Wooden spoon • Colander • Cutting board • Sharp knife •
Dry-ingredient measuring cup • Liquid measuring cup • Large bowl •
Measuring spoons • Rolling pin • Ruler • 2 cookie sheets • Small bowl •
Fork • Pastry brush • Pot holders

1 Heat oven to 450°.

2 **Adult help:** Cook in skillet over medium heat about 10 minutes, stirring often, until brown ➡

| **1 pound ground beef** |

3 Pour beef into colander to drain off any fat. Put beef back in skillet.

4 Stir into beef, then set aside ➡

| **1 medium onion, chopped (1/2 cup)** |
| **2/3 cup pizza sauce** |

5 Mix in large bowl to make a dough (using hands to shape into ball, if necessary) ➡

| **5 cups Bisquick Original baking mix** |
| **3/4 cup water** |
| **3 tablespoons vegetable oil** |

6 Cut off and save about 1/4 of the dough. Divide the rest of the dough in half.

7 Sprinkle a clean surface (such as a kitchen counter or breadboard) with flour or baking mix. Put dough on surface. Roll or pat each dough half into 12-inch circle. Put each circle on cookie sheet.

8 Top half of each circle (1/2 cup for each circle) **- - - -** ➤

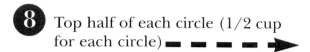

**1 cup shredded Cheddar cheese
(4 ounces)**

9 Top cheese with beef mixture to within 1 inch of edge of dough. Fold dough over filling, then press edge with fork to seal.

10 Beat in small bowl with fork **-** ➤

1 egg white

11 Make fourteen 3/4-inch balls from some of the saved dough. Press 10 of the balls into triangle shapes. Press 5 triangles into sealed edge of each calzone for spikes on the backs of the dinosaurs, using egg white as glue. (Use the photo on page 360 as a guide.)

12 Roll the rest of the balls between your hands to make legs with feet. Press 2 legs into folded edge of each calzone, using egg white as glue. Divide the rest of the saved dough into 4 pieces. Roll pieces between your hands to make tails and heads with necks. Press into calzones, using egg white as glue.

13 If you like, press into each head for eye 1 of **- - -** ➤

2 whole peppercorns

14 Bake 15 to 20 minutes or until golden brown (it may be necessary to cover small dough pieces with pieces of aluminum foil during the last few minutes of baking).

TIP

If your oven does not hold 2 cookie sheets side by side, make one calzone with half the dough and beef mixture. Bake that one while you make the second calzone.

Reuben Pitas

4 sandwiches

Utensils You Will Need
Cutting board • Sharp knife • Medium bowl • Can opener •
Dry-ingredient measuring cups • Liquid measuring cups • Measuring spoon •
Wooden spoon • Cookie sheet • Spatula

1 Heat oven to 425°.

2 **Adult help:** Cut in half around
edge with knife ➤

2 pita breads (about 6 inches across)

3 Mix in medium bowl with
wooden spoon ➤

**6 ounces thinly sliced corned beef,
coarsely chopped
1 can (8 ounces) sauerkraut,
rinsed and well drained
1 cup shredded Swiss cheese
(4 ounces)
1/3 cup Thousand Island dressing
2 teaspoons caraway seed, if you like**

4 Spread beef mixture on pita
bread halves. Put on cookie
sheet.

5 Bake 5 to 7 minutes or until
cheese is melted. Remove
sandwiches from cookie sheet
with spatula.

Dinosaur Calzones (page 358), Dinosaur Cakes (page 318)

Holidays

Bûche de Noël (page 396)

Continued on next page

Gingerbread Cookies

About 2 1/2 dozen 5-inch gingerbread cookies or about 5 dozen 2 1/2-inch cookies

1 cup packed brown sugar
1/3 cup shortening
1 1/2 cups dark molasses
2/3 cup cold water
7 cups all-purpose flour
2 teaspoons baking soda
2 teaspoons ground ginger
1 teaspoon salt
1 teaspoon ground allspice
1 teaspoon ground cloves
1 teaspoon ground cinnamon
Creamy Frosting (below)

Mix brown sugar, shortening, molasses and water in large bowl. Stir in remaining ingredients except Creamy Frosting. Cover and refrigerate about 2 hours or until firm.

Heat oven to 350°. Lightly grease cookie sheet. Roll one-fourth of dough at a time 1/4 inch thick on floured surface. Cut with floured gingerbread cookie cutter or other favorite shaped cutter. Place about 2 inches apart on cookie sheet.

Bake 10 to 12 minutes or until almost no indentation remains when touched in center. Remove from cookie sheet. Cool completely. Prepare Creamy Frosting and spread on cookies.

CREAMY FROSTING

4 cups powdered sugar
5 tablespoons half-and-half
1 teaspoon vanilla
Food color, if desired

Mix all ingredients until smooth.

Decorating Cookies

Below you'll find fun cookie decorating ideas:

- Sprinkle frosted or iced cookies with chopped nuts. Press the nuts into the topping while it is still wet; that way, the nuts will hold fast to the cookies.

- Arrange raisins, currants or candied cherry halves or cherry cutouts on pale-frosted cookies before the frosting or icing sets.

- Press cinnamon candies into cookie-dough cutouts before baking. Although the candies soften with heating, they don't melt enough to spread. The design you make with the candies will be unchanged when the cookies come out of the oven.

- Christmas cookies just wouldn't be the same without red- and green-colored sugars. Dust unbaked cookies with sugar or sprinkle it over frosted or iced cookies.

- Jimmies, sprinkles and chocolate shots are colorful ways to decorate unbaked or frosted cookies without any fuss—just sprinkle!

- Turn rolled cookies into hanging ornaments. Use a drinking straw to poke a hole in the dough at the top of the cookie before baking. When the baked cookie has cooled, slip a length of yarn through the hole.

Gingerbread Cookie Tree

1 cookie tree (60 servings)

This "tree" is an edible centerpiece that can be made from stars, hearts, fluted circles or rings. Ten cutters, ranging from 2 to 8 3/4 inches (increasing by 3/4 inch from one size to the next) are required. Nested cookie-cutter sets are available in specialty shops, but homemade patterns work just as well.

2 recipes Gingerbread Cookies (page 365)
4 cups powdered sugar
1 teaspoon vanilla
4 to 5 tablespoons half-and-half
Assorted candies, if desired

Prepare and refrigerate recipes individually as directed. Heat oven to 350°. Lightly grease cookie sheet.

Roll half of 1 recipe of dough at a time 1/4 inch thick on floured surface. Cut 3 cookies of each size with floured cutter or patterns. Place about 2 inches apart on cookie sheet.

Bake large cookies 12 to 14 minutes and small cookies 8 to 10 minutes or until no indentation remains when touched. Cool slightly; remove from cookie sheet. Cool completely.

Beat powdered sugar, vanilla and half-and-half until smooth and of spreading consistency. Assemble tree on serving plate or foil-covered cardboard: Starting with largest cookies, stack cookies as frosted, or stack unfrosted cookies together with small dab of frosting in center of each. Let layers dry or hold cookies in place with bamboo skewers if necessary. Use remaining frosting to pipe "snow" on the tree with decorating bag. Decorate with assorted candies.

Gingerbread Cookie Tree

Deluxe Sugar Cookies

About 5 dozen 2-inch cookies

These are our favorite sugar cookies! If using cookie cutters with imprints, cut the amount of baking soda and cream of tartar in half—you'll get a more distinctive design. (photograph on page 371)

1 1/2 cups powdered sugar
1 cup (2 sticks) margarine or butter, softened
1 teaspoon vanilla
1/2 teaspoon almond extract
1 egg
2 1/2 cups all-purpose flour
1 teaspoon baking soda
1 teaspoon cream of tartar
Creamy Decorator's Frosting (below)
    or Chocolate Frosting (right)

Mix powdered sugar, margarine, vanilla, almond extract and egg in large bowl. Stir in flour, baking soda and cream of tartar. Cover and refrigerate at least 2 hours.

Heat oven to 375°. Grease cookie sheet lightly. Divide dough in half. Roll each half 1/4 inch thick on lightly floured surface. Cut into desired shapes with cookie cutters. Place on cookie sheet.

Bake 7 to 8 minutes or until edges are light brown. Remove from cookie sheet. Cool on wire rack. Frost with Creamy Decorator's Frosting and decorate as desired.

CREAMY DECORATOR'S FROSTING

1 cup powdered sugar
1 tablespoon water or 1 to 2 tablespoons
    half-and-half
1/2 teaspoon vanilla
Few drops food color, if desired

Beat ingredients until smooth and of spreading consistency.

CHOCOLATE FROSTING

2 ounces unsweetened chocolate
2 tablespoons margarine or butter
3 tablespoons water
About 2 cups powdered sugar

Heat chocolate and margarine in 1 1/2-quart saucepan over low heat, stirring until melted; remove from heat. Stir in water and powdered sugar until smooth and of spreading consistency.

Stained Glass Cookies

1 recipe Deluxe Sugar Cookies (left)
Food colors

Prepare dough for Deluxe Sugar Cookies. Before refrigerating, divide dough in half. Divide one half into 3 to 5 parts. Tint each part with a different food color. Wrap each tinted dough and the plain dough separately. Refrigerate at least 2 hours.

Heat oven to 375°. Grease cookie sheet lightly. Roll plain dough 1/8 inch thick on lightly floured surface. Cut with bell, star, tree or other decorative cookie cutter. Place on cookie sheet. Roll each tinted dough 1/8 inch thick; cut out different shapes and arrange on plain dough shapes.

Bake 7 to 8 minutes or until edges are light brown. Remove from cookie sheet. Cool on wire rack.

Magic Window Cookies

About 6 dozen 3-inch cookies

If you like, you can use tiny round hard candies in place of the ring-shaped candy, but you'll need more tubes of the round candies. (photograph on page 371)

1 cup sugar
**3/4 cup shortening (part margarine or
    butter, softened)**
**1 teaspoon vanilla or 1/2 teaspoon lemon
    extract**
2 eggs
2 1/2 cups all-purpose flour
1 teaspoon baking powder
1 teaspoon salt
**About 4 rolls (about 0.9 ounce each) ring-
    shaped hard candy**

Mix sugar, shortening, vanilla and eggs in large bowl. Stir in flour, baking powder and salt. Cover and refrigerate at least 1 hour.

Heat oven to 375°. Line cookie sheet with aluminum foil. Roll dough 1/8 inch thick on lightly floured surface. Cut into desired shapes with cookie cutters. Place on cookie sheet. Cut out designs from cookies using smaller cutters or your own patterns. Place whole or partially crushed candy in cutouts, depending on size and shape of design. (To crush candy, place in heavy plastic bag and tap lightly with rolling pin. Because candy melts easily, leave pieces as large as possible.) If cookies are to be hung as decorations, make a hole in each, 1/4 inch from top with end of plastic straw.

Bake 7 to 9 minutes or until cookies are very light brown and candy is melted. If candy has not completely spread within cutout design, immediately spread with metal spatula. Cool completely before removing from cookie sheet. Remove cookies gently.

Candy Cane Cookies

About 4 1/2 dozen cookies

While red and white are the traditional colors for candy canes, feel free to create candy canes of different colors. Paste food color will give you more intense colors.

2 tablespoons crushed peppermint candies
2 tablespoons sugar
1 recipe Chocolate-Nut Fingers (page 372)
1 teaspoon peppermint extract
1/2 teaspoon red food color

Heat oven to 375°. Mix candies and sugar; reserve. Prepare dough for Chocolate-Nut Fingers—except substitute peppermint extract for the almond extract. Divide dough in half. Tint one half with food color. For each cookie, shape 1 teaspoon dough from each half into 4-inch rope side by side; press together lightly and twist. Place on ungreased cookie sheet, and curve one end of cookie to form handle of cane.

Bake 9 to 12 minutes or until set and very light brown. Immediately sprinkle reserved sugar mixture over cookies. Remove from cookie sheet. Cool on wire rack.

Santa Claus Cookies

About 1 1/2 dozen cookies

1 cup granulated sugar
1/2 cup shortening
2 tablespoons milk
1 teaspoon grated lemon peel
1 egg
2 cups all-purpose flour
1 teaspoon baking powder
1/2 teaspoon baking soda
1/2 teaspoon salt
Creamy Frosting (right) or Chocolate
   Frosting (page 368)
Miniature marshmallows
Red sugar
Currants or semisweet chocolate chips
Red cinnamon candies
Shredded coconut

Heat oven to 400°. Mix granulated sugar, shortening, milk, lemon peel and egg. Stir in flour, baking powder, baking soda and salt. Shape dough into 1 1/4-inch balls. Place about 2 inches apart on ungreased cookie sheet. Flatten to about 2 1/2-inches in diameter with greased bottom of glass dipped in sugar.

Bake until edges are light brown, 8 to 10 minutes. Cool on wire rack.

Spread 1 cookie with small amount of Creamy Frosting. (Frost and decorate cookies one at a time.) Sprinkle top third of cookie with red sugar. Press on miniature marshmallow for tassel of cap. Press 2 currants for the eyes and 1 red cinnamon candy for nose into center third of cookie. Sprinkle coconut over bottom third for beard.

CREAMY FROSTING

1 1/2 cups powdered sugar
2 to 3 tablespoons water
1/2 teaspoon vanilla

Mix all ingredients until of desired consistency.

Santa Claus Cookie Pops: *After shaping dough into balls, insert wooden ice-cream sticks halfway into balls; continue as directed.*

TIP

To divide dough easily, press dough evenly in the bottom of a loaf pan lined with waxed paper. Lift out the dough using the waxed paper. Cut 3 strips lengthwise and five strips crosswise, then shape into balls.

Magic Window Cookies (page 369), Deluxe Sugar Cookies (page 368) Santa Claus Cookies

Berliner Kranzer

About 6 dozen cookies

We have made these German wreath-shaped cookies a bit easier than the traditional shaping method, to speed your holiday baking.

1 cup sugar
3/4 cup (1 1/2 sticks) margarine or butter, softened
3/4 cup shortening
2 teaspoons grated orange peel
2 eggs
4 cups all-purpose flour
1 egg white
2 tablespoons sugar
Red candied cherries
Green candied citron

Heat oven to 400°. Mix 1 cup sugar, the margarine, shortening, orange peel and eggs in large bowl. Mix in flour. Shape dough by rounded teaspoonfuls into ropes, 6 inches long. Form each rope into a circle, crossing ends and tucking under. (This shaping method is easier than the traditional method of tying knots.) Place on ungreased cookie sheet.

Beat egg white and 2 tablespoons sugar until foamy; brush over tops of cookies. Press bits of red candied cherries on center of knot for holly berries. Add "leaves" cut from green candied citron.

Bake 10 to 12 minutes or until set but not brown. Immediately remove from cookie sheet. Cool on wire rack.

Chocolate-Nut Fingers

About 8 dozen cookies

For a different look, dip cookies halfway into the chocolate or brush the entire top of the cookie before dipping into the nuts.

1 cup sugar
1 cup (2 sticks) margarine or butter, softened
1/2 cup milk
1 teaspoon vanilla
1 teaspoon almond extract
1 egg
3 1/2 cups all-purpose flour
1 teaspoon baking powder
1/4 teaspoon salt
1/2 cup semisweet chocolate chips
1/2 cup chopped nuts

Mix sugar, margarine, milk, vanilla, almond extract and egg in large bowl. Stir in flour, baking powder and salt. Cover and refrigerate at least 4 hours.

Heat oven to 375°. For each cookie, shape 1 teaspoon dough into 4-inch rope. (For smooth, even ropes, roll back and forth on sugared surface.) Place on ungreased cookie sheet.

Bake 9 to 12 minutes or until set and very light brown. Remove from cookie sheet. Cool on wire rack.

Heat chocolate chips until melted. Dip ends of cookies into chocolate, then into nuts. Place cookies on waxed paper. Let stand about 10 minutes or until chocolate is set.

Berliner Kranzer, Chocolate-Nut Fingers

Peppernuts

About 8 dozen cookies

These spicy, crunchy morsels are Christmas favorites. The traditional German spelling is Pfeffernusse, *and many people like to call them by this name.*

3/4 cup packed brown sugar
1/2 cup shortening
1/2 cup light molasses
1 tablespoon hot water
1 egg
3 drops anise oil or 1/2 teaspoon anise extract
3 1/3 cups all-purpose flour
1/2 teaspoon baking soda
1/2 teaspoon ground cinnamon
1/2 teaspoon ground cloves
1/4 teaspoon salt
1/8 teaspoon white pepper

Heat oven to 350°. Mix brown sugar, shortening, molasses, water, egg and anise oil in large bowl. Stir in remaining ingredients. Knead dough until stiff enough to mold. Shape dough into 3/4-inch balls. Place about 1 inch apart on ungreased cookie sheet.

Bake about 12 minutes or until bottoms are golden brown. Remove from cookie sheet. Cool on wire rack.

Note: *For traditionally hard Peppernuts, store in airtight container. For softer cookies, store with an apple or orange slice in airtight container, replacing fruit slice frequently.*

Holiday Cookie Mix

15 to 16 cups cookie mix

This multipurpose mix makes quite a large batch, but it can be easily mixed in a large roasting pan, a plastic dishpan, the vegetable bin from your refrigerator or a 6-quart mixing bowl.

8 cups all-purpose flour
4 cups packed brown sugar
1 tablespoon salt
1 1/2 teaspoons baking soda
1 1/2 cups shortening

Mix flour, sugar, salt and baking soda. Cut in shortening with pastry blender or 2 knives until mixture resembles fine crumbs. Place desired amounts of mix in storage containers (plastic containers or jars or large plastic bags). Seal tightly, label and refrigerate up to 10 weeks. To measure, dip dry-ingredient measuring cup into cookie mix; level with straight-edged spatula.

Chocolate Bonbon Cookies

About 5 dozen cookies

These little gems are even more tempting when topped with festive treats such as flaked or shredded coconut, edible glitter, chopped candied fruit or chopped maraschino cherries. (photograph on page 377)

4 cups Holiday Cookie Mix (left)
1 cup chopped nuts
1/4 cup (1/2 stick) margarine or butter, softened
1 teaspoon vanilla
1/2 teaspoon almond extract
2 eggs
2 ounces unsweetened chocolate, melted and cooled
Powdered sugar
Easy Frosting (right)

Heat oven to 375°. Mix Holiday Cookie Mix, nuts, margarine, vanilla, almond extract, eggs and chocolate. Shape dough into 1-inch balls. Place about 1 inch apart on ungreased cookie sheet.

Bake 10 to 12 minutes or until set. Cool slightly before removing from cookie sheet.

Roll about 30 cookies in powdered sugar while warm; cool on wire rack. Roll in powdered sugar again. Frost remaining cookies with Easy Frosting. Decorate frosted cookies with coconut.

EASY FROSTING

1 cup powdered sugar
About 1 tablespoon milk
1/2 teaspoon almond extract

Mix all ingredients until smooth and of spreading consistency.

Toffee Bars

4 dozen bars

(photograph on page 381)

4 cups Holiday Cookie Mix (left)
1/2 cup (1 stick) margarine or butter, softened
1 teaspoon vanilla
1 egg
4 ounces milk chocolate candy, broken into pieces
1/2 cup chopped nuts, if desired

Heat oven to 350°. Grease rectangular pan, 13×9×2 inches. Mix Holiday Cookie Mix, margarine, vanilla and egg. Press in pan.

Bake 25 to 30 minutes or until very light brown (layer will be soft). Remove from oven; immediately place chocolate candy on baked layer. Let stand until soft; spread evenly. Sprinkle with nuts. Cut into about 2×1-inch bars while warm.

Storing Cookies and Bars

- Keep different kinds of cookies and bars in separate containers to maintain the best flavor.

- Store crisp cookies loosely covered. If they become soft, heat in a 300° oven for 3 to 5 minutes or until warm. (In humid weather, they'll keep best tightly covered.)

- Store soft cookies tightly covered. If replaced often, a piece of bread or apple in the container will help keep the cookies soft.

- Store brownies and bars in tightly covered containers, or leave them in the pan and cover tightly with foil.

Cherry-Coconut Bars

4 dozen bars

The crackly top on these bars is easiest to cut with a wet, sharp knife.

4 cups Holiday Cookie Mix (page 374)
1/2 cup (1 stick) margarine or butter, softened
1 1/2 cups sugar
3/4 cup flaked coconut
1/3 cup all-purpose flour
3/4 cup chopped maraschino cherries, drained
1 teaspoon vanilla
3/4 teaspoon baking powder
1/2 teaspoon salt
3 eggs, beaten
1 cup chopped nuts

Heat oven to 350°. Mix Holiday Cookie Mix and margarine. Press in ungreased rectangular pan, 13×9×2 inches. Bake 25 minutes.

Mix remaining ingredients except nuts; spread over baked layer. Sprinkle with nuts.

Bake about 25 minutes or until center is set. Cool completely. Cut into about 2×1-inch bars.

Chocolate Bonbon Cookies (page 375), Cherry-Coconut Bars

Mincemeat Bars

About 3 1/2 dozen bars

1 cup packed brown sugar
1/2 cup (1 stick) margarine or butter,
    softened
1/4 cup shortening
1 1/2 cups all-purpose flour
1 cup quick-cooking oats
1 teaspoon salt
1/2 teaspoon baking soda
1 jar (27 ounces) prepared mincemeat
    (about 3 cups)
1/2 cup chopped walnuts or almonds
Powdered sugar

Heat oven to 400°. Grease rectangular pan, 13×9×2 inches. Mix brown sugar, margarine and shortening in large bowl. Stir in flour, oats, salt and baking soda until crumbly. Press half of the crumbly mixture in pan. Mix mincemeat and walnuts; spread over layer in pan. Sprinkle with remaining crumbly mixture; press lightly.

Bake 25 to 30 minutes or until light brown. While warm, make a diagonal cut from corner to corner. Continue making cuts parallel to first cut, spacing them about 1 1/2 inches apart. Repeat, cutting diagonally in opposite direction. Sprinkle with powdered sugar.

Apricot-Date Bars: *Omit mincemeat and walnuts. Mix 1 1/2 cups chopped dried apricots, 1 1/4 cups chopped dates, 1/2 cup sugar and 1 1/2 cups water in 2-quart saucepan. Cook over medium-low heat about 10 minutes, stirring constantly, until thickened. Substitute for the mincemeat and walnut mixture.*

Fudge Melt-Away Squares

36 squares

1/2 cup margarine or butter
1 1/2 squares unsweetened chocolate
1 3/4 cups graham cracker crumbs
1 cup flaked coconut
1/2 cup chopped nuts
1/4 cup granulated sugar
2 tablespoons water
1 teaspoon vanilla
2 cups powdered sugar
1/4 cup margarine or butter, softened
2 tablespoons milk
1 teaspoon vanilla
1 1/2 squares unsweetened chocolate

Line square pan, 9×9×2 inches, with aluminum foil. Heat 1/2 cup margarine and 1 1/2 squares chocolate in 3-quart saucepan over low heat, stirring occasionally, until melted; remove from heat. Stir in graham cracker crumbs, coconut, nuts, granulated sugar, water and 1 teaspoon vanilla. Press in pan. Refrigerate.

Mix remaining ingredients except 1 1/2 squares unsweetened chocolate. Spread over refrigerated crumb mixture. Refrigerate 15 minutes.

Heat chocolate until melted. Drizzle over frosted bars. Refrigerate 2 hours or until almost hard. Remove squares, along with foil, from pan. Fold foil back to cut squares. Cover and refrigerate any remaining squares.

Fudge Melt-Away Squares

Mousse Bars

16 bars

1 1/2 cups vanilla wafer crumbs
   (about 40 wafers)
1/4 cup margarine or butter, melted
3/4 cup whipping (heavy) cream
1 package (6 ounces) semisweet chocolate
   chips (1 cup)
3 eggs
1/3 cup sugar
1/8 teaspoon salt
Chocolate Topping (below)

Heat oven to 350°. Mix wafer crumbs and margarine. Press in ungreased square pan, 8×9×2 inches or 9×9×2 inches. Bake 10 minutes.

Heat whipping cream and chocolate chips over low heat, stirring frequently, until chocolate is melted; remove from heat. Cool about 5 minutes. Beat eggs, sugar and salt in large bowl until foamy. Pour chocolate mixture into egg mixture, stirring constantly. Pour over baked layer in pan.

Bake 25 to 35 minutes or until center springs back when touched lightly. Cool 15 minutes. Prepare Chocolate Topping and spread on bars. Refrigerate uncovered 2 hours or until chilled.

CHOCOLATE TOPPING

1/2 cup semisweet chocolate chips
1 tablespoon shortening

Heat chocolate chips and shortening over low heat, stirring frequently, until melted.

Chocolate-Peppermint Refrigerator Cookies

4 dozen cookies

1 1/2 cups powdered sugar
1 cup margarine or butter, softened
1 egg
2 2/3 cups all-purpose flour
1/4 teaspoon salt
1/4 cup cocoa
1 tablespoon milk
1/4 cup finely crushed peppermint candy

Mix powdered sugar, margarine and egg in large bowl. Stir in flour and salt. Divide dough in half. Stir cocoa and milk into one half and peppermint candy into other half.

Shape chocolate dough into rectangle, 12×6 1/2 inches, on waxed paper. Shape peppermint dough into roll, 12 inches long; place on chocolate dough. Wrap chocolate dough around peppermint dough using waxed paper to help lift. Press edges together. Wrap and refrigerate about 2 hours or until firm.

Heat oven to 375°. Cut rolls into 1/4-inch slices. Place about 1 inch apart on ungreased cookie sheet.

Bake 8 to 10 minutes or until set. Remove from cookie sheet. Cool on wire rack.

Chocolate-Wintergreen Refrigerator Cookies:
Omit peppermint candies. Stir 1/4 cup chocolate shot, 1/4 teaspoon wintergreen extract and 4 drops green food color into plain dough. Continue as directed.

Mousse Bars, Toffee Bars (page 375)

Maple Nut Refrigerator Cookies

4 dozen cookies

3/4 cup packed brown sugar
3/4 cup margarine or butter, softened
1/4 teaspoon maple extract
1 1/2 cups all-purpose flour
1 cup chopped pecans
1 teaspoon baking powder
1/4 teaspoon salt

Mix brown sugar, margarine and maple extract in large bowl. Stir in remaining ingredients. Shape into roll, 12 inches long. Wrap and refrigerate about 2 hours or until firm.

Heat oven to 375°. Cut roll into 1/4-inch slices. Place 2 inches apart on ungreased cookie sheet.

Bake 8 to 10 minutes or until edges are golden brown. Remove from cookie sheet. Cool on wire rack.

Anise Biscotti

About 3 1/2 dozen cookies

(photograph on page 387)

1 cup sugar
1/2 cup margarine or butter, softened
2 teaspoons anise seed, ground
2 teaspoons grated lemon peel
2 eggs
3 1/2 cups all-purpose flour
1 teaspoon baking powder
1/2 teaspoon salt

Heat oven to 350°. Beat sugar, margarine, anise seed, lemon peel and eggs in large bowl. Stir in flour, baking powder and salt.

Shape half of dough at a time into rectangle, 10×3 inches, on ungreased cookie sheet.

Bake about 20 minutes or until toothpick inserted in center comes out clean. Cool on cookie sheet 15 minutes.

Cut crosswise into 1/2-inch slices. Place, cut sides down, on cookie sheet.

Bake about 15 minutes or until crisp and light brown. Remove from cookie sheet.

Orange Biscotti: *Omit anise seed and lemon peel. Add 1 tablespoon grated orange peel to the margarine mixture.*

Springerle

About 3 dozen cookies

A springerle rolling pin has recessed designs that make an imprint on the dough. These richly flavored cookies are very hard—excellent for dunking.

1 cup sugar
2 eggs
2 cups all-purpose flour
2 teaspoons anise seed

Heat oven to 325°. Beat sugar and eggs in large bowl about 5 minutes or until thick and lemon colored. Stir in flour and anise seed.

Roll half of dough at a time 1/4 inch thick on floured cloth-covered surface. Roll well-floured springerle rolling pin over dough to emboss with designs. Cut out cookies. Place about 1 inch apart on ungreased cookie sheet.

Bake 12 to 15 minutes or until light brown. Immediately remove from cookie sheet. Cool on wire rack.

Maple Nut Refrigerator Cookies

Bittersweet Chocolate Cream Cheese Cookies

About 6 dozen 2 1/2-inch cookies

1 cup sugar
1/2 cup (1 stick) margarine or butter, softened
1 1/2 teaspoons vanilla
1 egg
1 package (3 ounces) cream cheese, softened
3 ounces bittersweet or semisweet chocolate, melted and cooled
2 1/2 cups all-purpose flour
1/2 teaspoon baking powder
1/2 teaspoon salt
6 ounces vanilla-flavored candy coating, melted
3/4 cup finely crushed peppermint candies or finely chopped pistachio nuts

Heat oven to 375°. Mix sugar, margarine, vanilla, egg, cream cheese and chocolate in large bowl until smooth. Mix flour, baking powder and salt; stir into margarine mixture.

Divide dough in half. Roll each half 1/8 inch thick on lightly floured cloth-covered surface with cloth-covered rolling pin. Cut into desired shapes with cookie cutters. Place about 1 inch apart on ungreased cookie sheet.

Bake 8 to 10 minutes or until dry and set. Remove from cookie sheet. Cool on wire rack.

Roll edge of cookies about 1/4 inch deep in candy coating; immediately roll in candies. Place on waxed paper. Let stand about 10 minutes or until coating is set.

Lebkuchen

About 5 dozen cookies

This cakelike cookie comes from Germany and is especially popular in Nuremberg. They are often baked in decorative molds, but our version is faster, and just as tasty.

1/2 cup honey
1/2 cup molasses
3/4 cup packed brown sugar
1 teaspoon grated lemon peel
1 tablespoon lemon juice
1 egg
2 3/4 cups all-purpose flour
1 teaspoon ground allspice
1 teaspoon ground cinnamon
1 teaspoon ground cloves
1 teaspoon ground nutmeg
1/2 teaspoon baking soda
1/3 cup chopped citron
1/3 cup chopped nuts
Cookie Glaze (right)

Mix honey and molasses in 3-quart saucepan. Heat to boiling, stirring occasionally; remove from heat. Cool completely. Stir in brown sugar, lemon peel, lemon juice and egg. Stir in four, allspice, cinnamon, cloves, nutmeg and baking soda. Stir in citron and nuts. Cover and refrigerate at least 8 hours.

Heat oven to 400°. Grease cookie sheet. Roll about one-fourth of the dough at a time 1/4 inch thick on lightly floured surface (keep remaining dough refrigerated). Cut dough into rectangles, 2 1/2×1 1/2 inches. Place 1 inch apart on cookie sheet.

Bake 10 to 12 minutes or until no indentation remains when touched lightly. Immediately remove from cookies sheet. Cool on wire rack. Brush Cookie Glaze over cookies.

Cookie Glaze

1 cup granulated sugar
1/2 cup water
1/4 cup powdered sugar

Mix granulated sugar and water in 1-quart saucepan. Cook over medium heat to 230° on candy thermometer or just until small amount of mixture spins a 2-inch thread when dropped from a spoon; remove from heat. Stir in powdered sugar. (If glaze becomes sugary while brushing cookies, heat slightly, adding a little water, until clear again.)

Christmas Cookie Pizza

16 servings

1/2 cup (1 stick) margarine or butter, softened
1/2 cup packed brown sugar
1/4 cup granulated sugar
1 teaspoon vanilla
1 egg
1 1/4 cups all-purpose flour
1/2 teaspoon baking soda
Chocolate Pizza Sauce (right)
1/2 cup pecan halves
1/2 cup red and green candy-coated chocolate candies
1/4 cup shredded coconut, toasted, if desired
2 ounces vanilla-flavored candy coating, melted

Heat oven to 350°. Mix margarine, sugars, vanilla and egg in large bowl. Stir in flour and baking soda (dough will be stiff). Spread or pat dough in ungreased 12-inch pizza pan or on cookie sheet.

Bake about 15 minutes or until golden brown; cool.

Prepare Chocolate Pizza Sauce; spread over baked layer. Immediately sprinkle with pecan halves, candies and coconut; press lightly. Drizzle with candy coating. Let stand until set. Remove from pan if desired. Cut into wedges.

Chocolate Pizza Sauce

1 package (6 ounces) semisweet chocolate chips (1 cup)
2 tablespoons margarine or butter
3 tablespoons milk
1 cup powdered sugar

Heat chocolate chips, margarine and milk over low heat, stirring occasionally, just until chocolate is melted; remove from heat. Stir in powdered sugar. Beat with wire whisk until smooth, glossy and of spreading consistency. (If not glossy, stir in a few drops hot water.)

Palmiers

About 2 1/2 dozen cookies

Palmiers ("palm leaves" in French) are very easy to make from commercial puff pastry. The dusting of granulated sugar caramelizes in the oven. To make sixty palmiers, use one whole package of puff pastry dough.

1/2 package (17 1/4-ounce size) frozen puff pastry dough
1/2 cup sugar
1 ounce semisweet chocolate, melted

Heat oven to 375°. Lightly grease cookie sheet. Roll dough into 1/8-inch-thick rectangle, 12×9 1/2 inches, on sugared surface. Mark a line lengthwise down center of dough. Fold long sides toward center line, leaving 1/4 inch at center. Fold dough in half lengthwise to form strip, 12×2 1/2 inches, pressing dough together.

Cut dough strip crosswise into 1/4-inch slices. Coat slices with sugar. Place about 2 inches apart on cookie sheet.

Bake 8 to 10 minutes, turning after 5 minutes, until cookies begin to turn golden brown. Immediately remove from cookie sheet. Cool completely. Dip ends of cookies into melted chocolate. Place on waxed paper until chocolate is firm.

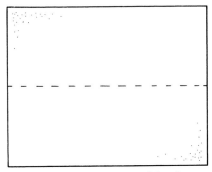

Mark a line lengthwise down center of dough.

Fold long sides toward center line, leaving 1/4 inch at center.

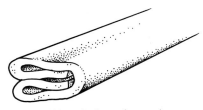

Fold dough in half lengthwise to form strip.

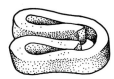

Cut dough strip crosswise into slices.

Anise Biscotti (page 382), Palmiers

Florentines

About 4 1/2 dozen cookies

Want festive, professional-looking cookies? Make wavy lines with the tines of a table fork in the chocolate before it is set.

3/4 cup whipping (heavy) cream
1/4 cup sugar
1/2 cup very finely chopped blanched almonds
4 ounces candied orange peel, very finely chopped
1/4 cup all-purpose flour
2 bars (4 ounces each) sweet cooking chocolate or bittersweet chocolate

Heat oven to 350°. Grease and flour cookie sheet. Mix whipping cream and sugar in medium bowl until well blended. Stir in almonds, orange peel and flour. (Dough may thicken as it stands.) Drop dough by rounded teaspoonfuls about 2 inches apart onto cookie sheet. Spread to form 2-inch circles. (Dough may be sticky.)

Bake 10 to 12 minutes or until edges are light brown. Cool 2 minutes; remove from cookie sheet to wire rack.

Heat chocolate until melted. Turn cookies over; spread with chocolate. Dry several hours at room temperature until chocolate becomes firm.

Lacy Cookie Cups

About 6 cookie cups

These cups are versatile as well as delicious. Try filing them with pudding, mousse or ice cream; then top with your favorite sauces—the combinations can take you through the 12 days of Christmas, and then some!

1/2 cup powdered sugar
1/4 cup (1/2 stick) butter softened*
1/2 teaspoon vanilla
2 egg whites
1/4 cup all-purpose flour
1/4 teaspoon ground cinnamon
2 cups mixed fresh strawberries and raspberries
1/3 cup raspberry jam, melted

Heat oven to 400°. Generously grease cookie sheet. Beat powdered sugar, butter and vanilla in medium bowl on medium speed until well blended. Beat in egg whites on low speed until mixture is well blended but not foamy. Fold in flour and cinnamon.

Drop dough by about 1 1/2 tablespoonfuls 6 inches apart onto cookie sheet. Flatten into 5-inch rounds using back of spoon dipped into cold water.

Bake 5 to 6 minutes or until golden brown. Let stand 30 seconds or until firm; remove from cookie sheet. Immediately shape each cookie over inverted 6-ounce custard cup. Cool completely. Fill each cookie cup with about 1/3 cup berries. Drizzle with jam.

*Do not use margarine in this recipe.

Fruit Jumbles

About 6 dozen cookies

4 cups Holiday Cookie Mix (page 374)
3/4 cup sour cream
1 teaspoon vanilla
2 eggs
1 1/2 cups candied cherries, cut in half
1 1/2 cups chopped dates
1 cup chopped pecans
Pecan halves, if desired

Heat oven to 375°. Mix Holiday Cookie Mix, sour cream, vanilla and eggs in large bowl. Stir in cherries, dates and chopped pecans. Drop dough by rounded teaspoonfuls about 2 inches apart onto ungreased cookie sheet. Place pecan half on each cookie.

Bake about 8 minutes or until almost no indentation remains when touched. Immediately remove from cookie sheet. Cool on wire rack.

TIP

A miniature spring-handled ice-cream scoop (#40) makes shaping these cookies quick work.

Festive Fruitcake Bars

3 dozen bars

1 cup all-purpose flour
3/4 cup packed brown sugar
1/2 cup (1 stick) margarine or butter, softened
1 teaspoon grated orange peel
1/2 teaspoon baking soda
1/2 teaspoon ground cinnamon
1/4 teaspoon salt
1 egg
1/4 cup all-purpose flour
16 ounces fruitcake mix
8 ounces dates, cut up
1 cup chopped pecans or chopped filberts
Orange Glaze (below)

Heat oven to 350°. Grease and flour rectangular pan, 13×9×2 inches. Mix 1 cup flour, the brown sugar, margarine, orange peel, baking soda, cinnamon, salt and egg in large bowl. Mix 1/4 cup flour, the fruitcake mix, dates and pecans; stir into brown sugar mixture. Spread in pan.

Bake about 35 minutes or until toothpick inserted in center comes out clean; cool. Drizzle with Orange Glaze. Cut into about 2×1/2-inch bars.

ORANGE GLAZE

1/3 cup sugar
2 tablespoons orange juice

Heat sugar and juice in 1-quart saucepan over medium heat, stirring occasionally, until mixture thickens slightly.

Raspberry–White Chocolate Cream Cake

1 cake

Raspberry Filling (right)
3 ounces white baking bar, chopped
2 1/4 cups all-purpose flour
1 1/2 cups sugar
2 1/4 teaspoons baking powder
1/2 teaspoon salt
1 2/3 cups whipping (heavy) cream
3 eggs
1 teaspoon almond extract
White Chocolate Frosting (right)

Prepare Raspberry Filling. Heat oven to 350°. Grease and flour 2 round pans, 8×1 1/2 inches or 9×1 1/2 inches. Heat white baking bar over low heat, stirring occasionally, until melted; cool. Mix flour, sugar, baking powder and salt; reserve. Beat whipping cream in chilled large bowl until stiff; reserve. Beat eggs about 5 minutes or until thick and lemon colored; beat in melted baking bar and almond extract.

Fold egg mixture into whipped cream. Add flour mixture, about 1/2 cup at a time, folding gently after each addition until blended. Pour into pans.

Bake 8-inch rounds 35 to 40 minutes, 9-inch rounds 30 to 35 minutes or until toothpick inserted in center comes out clean. Cool 10 minutes; remove from pans. Cool completely on wire racks.

Fill layers with Raspberry Filling. Prepare White Chocolate Frosting; spread over side and top of cake.

RASPBERRY FILLING

1/4 cup sugar
2 tablespoons cornstarch
1/8 teaspoon salt
1 cup raspberry-flavored wine cooler
    or sparkling raspberry juice
1 tablespoon margarine or butter
1/8 teaspoon almond extract
2 or 3 drops red food color, if desired

Mix sugar, cornstarch and salt in 1 1/2-quart saucepan. Stir in wine cooler. Cook over medium heat, stirring constantly, until mixture thickens and boils. Boil and stir 1 minute; remove from heat. Stir in remaining ingredients. Cover and refrigerate until chilled.

WHITE CHOCOLATE FROSTING

3 ounces white baking bar, chopped
3 1/2 cups powdered sugar
1/4 cup margarine or butter, softened
3 to 4 tablespoons plus 2 teaspoons
    raspberry-flavored wine cooler
    or water
1/2 teaspoon almond extract

Heat white baking bar over low heat, stirring occasionally, until melted; cool. Beat melted baking bar and remaining ingredients in medium bowl on medium speed until smooth and of spreading consistency. If necessary, stir in additional wine cooler, 1 teaspoon at a time.

Raspberry–White Chocolate Cream Cake

Black and Gold Fruitcake

2 loaves (16 slices each)

3 cups Bisquick Original baking mix
1 cup sugar
6 eggs
1 teaspoon almond extract
1 1/2 cups dried apricots (about 8 ounces)
1 cup candied pineapple
1 cup golden raisins
1 teaspoon ground cinnamon
2 teaspoons vanilla
3 ounces semisweet chocolate, melted
    and cooled
1 cup candied cherries
2 packages (8 ounces each) pitted dates

Heat oven to 300°. Grease and flour two 6-cup bundt cake pans or ring molds, or 2 loaf pans, 8 1/2×4 1/2×2 1/2 inches or 9×5×3 inches. Beat baking mix, sugar and eggs in large bowl on low speed until blended. Beat on medium speed 2 minutes. Pour half of the batter into large bowl; beat in almond extract until smooth. Stir in apricots, pineapple and raisins.

Beat cinnamon, vanilla and chocolate into remaining half of batter, using same beaters, until smooth. Stir in cherries and dates. Divide chocolate batter between pans, spread evenly. Divide gold batter between pans, carefully spooning over chocolate batter; spread evenly.

Bake bundt pans about 1 hour 20 minutes to 1 hour 30 minutes, loaf pans about 1 hour 30 minutes to 1 hour 40 minutes or until toothpick inserted in center comes out clean. Cool 5 minutes. Invert bundt cakes onto wire rack; turn loaves out of pans and place top sides up on wire rack. Cool completely. Wrap tightly and refrigerate 1 day before slicing.

Christmas Coconut Cake

16 servings

Tutti-Frutti Filling (right)
2 cups all-purpose flour
1 1/2 cups granulated sugar
1/2 cup shortening
1 cup milk
3 1/2 teaspoons baking powder
1 teaspoon salt
1 teaspoon vanilla
4 egg whites
2/3 cup flaked coconut
1 cup whipping (heavy) cream
1/4 cup powdered sugar
3/4 teaspoon almond extract

Prepare Tutti-Frutti Filling. Heat oven to 350°. Grease and flour 2 round pans, 9×1 1/2 inches. Beat flour, granulated sugar, shortening, milk, baking powder, salt and vanilla in large bowl on low speed 30 seconds, scraping bowl constantly. Beat on high speed 2 minutes, scraping bowl occasionally. Add egg whites; beat on high speed 2 minutes, scraping bowl occasionally. Stir in coconut. Pour into pans.

Bake 30 to 35 minutes or until toothpick inserted in center comes out clean. Remove from pans; cool on wire rack.

Fill layers and frost top of cake to within 1 inch of edge with Tutti-Frutti Filling. Beat whipping cream, powdered sugar and almond extract in chilled medium bowl until stiff. Spread over side and top edge of cake. Refrigerate until serving time. Refrigerate any remaining cake.

TUTTI-FRUTTI FILLING

2 egg yolks
2/3 cup sour cream
2/3 cup sugar
1 cup finely chopped pecans
2/3 cup flaked coconut
1/2 to 1 cup finely chopped raisins
**1/2 to 1 cup finely chopped candied
    cherries**

Mix egg yolks and sour cream in 2-quart saucepan. Stir in sugar. Cook over low heat, stirring constantly, until mixture begins to simmer. Simmer, stirring constantly, until mixture begins to thicken; remove from heat. Stir in remaining ingredients; cool.

Espresso-Praline Torte

12 servings

4 egg whites
1/4 teaspoon cream of tartar
1 cup sugar
Almond Praline (right)
1 1/2 cups whipping (heavy) cream
1 tablespoon sugar
1 teaspoon instant espresso coffee (dry)
1/4 teaspoon almond extract

Cover 3 cookie sheets with cooking parchment paper or heavy brown paper. Heat oven to 225°. Beat egg whites and cream of tartar in large bowl on medium speed until foamy.

Beat in 1 cup sugar, 1 tablespoon at a time on high speed; continue beating until stiff and glossy. Do not underbeat. Shape meringue into three 8-inch circles on brown paper.

Bake 1 hour. Turn oven off and leave meringues in oven with door closed 1 hour. Finish cooling at room temperature. Remove from paper to wire rack with spatula.

Prepare Almond Praline. Beat whipping cream, 1 tablespoon sugar, the espresso and almond extract in chilled medium bowl until stiff. Reserve 1 to 2 tablespoons praline for garnish. Fold remaining praline into whipped cream. Stack meringues, spreading whipped cream mixture between layers and over top. Sprinkle with reserved praline. Refrigerate at least 2 hours. Cover and refrigerate any remaining torte.

ALMOND PRALINE

1/2 cup sliced almonds
1/4 cup sugar

Grease cookie sheet. Cook almonds and sugar in 1-quart saucepan over low heat, stirring occasionally, until sugar is melted and golden brown. Pour onto cookie sheet; cool. Crush coarsely in blender or place in plastic bag and crush with wooden mallet.

Hazelnut-Chocolate Torte

16 servings

6 eggs, separated
1 tablespoon grated orange peel
3/4 teaspoon ground cinnamon
1/2 cup granulated sugar
1 teaspoon cream of tartar
1/2 cup granulated sugar
3 cups very finely ground hazelnuts (filberts)
1/2 cup all-purpose flour
Chocolate Butter Frosting (right)
1 cup whipping (heavy) cream
1/2 cup powdered sugar
1/4 cup cocoa
2 teaspoons grated orange peel
1/2 cup finely chopped hazelnuts (filberts)

Heat oven to 325°. Grease bottom only of springform pan, 9×3 inches. Line bottom with waxed paper; grease generously. Beat egg yolks, 1 tablespoon orange peel and the cinnamon in small bowl on high speed about 6 minutes or until very thick and light colored. Gradually beat in 1/2 cup granulated sugar, 1 tablespoon at a time; reserve. Wash beaters.

Beat egg whites and cream of tartar in large bowl on high speed until soft peaks form. Gradually beat in 1/2 cup granulated sugar, 1 tablespoon at a time; continue beating until stiff peaks form. Fold egg yolk mixture into meringue.

Mix 3 cups ground hazelnuts and the flour. Sprinkle about one-third of the hazelnut mixture over meringue; fold in. Repeat twice with remaining hazelnut mixture. Spread in pan. Bake 55 to 60 minutes or until toothpick inserted in center comes out clean. Cool in pan on wire rack 15 minutes. Loosen side of cake from pan with metal spatula. Carefully remove side of pan. Invert cake onto wire rack; remove bottom of pan. Turn cake right side up. Cool cake completely. Wrap tightly and refrigerate at least 4 hours.

Prepare Chocolate Butter Frosting; reserve 1 cup for decorating. Beat whipping cream, powdered sugar and cocoa in chilled small bowl until stiff. Fold in 2 teaspoons orange peel. Carefully split cake horizontally to make 3 layers. (To split, mark side of cake with toothpicks and cut with long, thin straight-edged knife.) Spread 1 layer with half of the whipped cream mixture. Top with second layer; spread with remaining whipped cream mixture. Top with remaining layer. Frost side and top of torte with Chocolate Butter Frosting. Press chopped hazelnuts around side.

Place reserved 1 cup frosting in decorating bag with large open star tip (#4B). Or place frosting in strong plastic bag; cut off a tip from one corner of bag. Pipe rosettes on top of cake. Garnish with whole hazelnuts if desired. Refrigerate at least 8 hours. Cut with sharp, straight-edged knife. Refrigerate any remaining torte.

CHOCOLATE BUTTER FROSTING

1/2 cup (1 stick) margarine or butter, softened
3 ounces unsweetened chocolate, melted and cooled, or 1/2 cup cocoa
3 cups powdered sugar
About 3 tablespoons milk
1 tablespoon brandy, if desired
2 teaspoons vanilla

Mix margarine and chocolate in large bowl. Beat in remaining ingredients until mixture is smooth and of spreading consistency.

Hazelnut Chocolate Torte

Bûche de Noël

10 servings

(photograph on page 362)

3 eggs
1 cup sugar
1/3 cup water
1 teaspoon vanilla
3/4 cup all-purpose flour
1 teaspoon baking powder
1/4 teaspoon salt
1 cup whipping (heavy) cream
2 tablespoons sugar
1 1/2 teaspoons freeze-dried or powdered
    instant coffee (dry)
Chocolate Buttercream Frosting (right)
Meringue Mushrooms (right)

Heat oven to 375°. Line jelly roll pan, 15 1/2
×10 1/2×1 inch, with aluminum foil or waxed
paper; grease. Beat eggs in small bowl on high
speed about 5 minutes or until very thick and
lemon colored. Pour eggs into large bowl;
gradually beat in 1 cup sugar. Beat in water
and vanilla on low speed. Gradually add flour,
baking powder and salt, beating just until batter is smooth. Pour into pan, spreading batter
to corners.

Bake 12 to 15 minutes or until toothpick
inserted in center comes out clean. Immediately loosen cake from edges of pan; invert onto
towel generously sprinkled with powdered
sugar. Carefully remove foil. Trim off stiff
edges of cake if necessary. While hot, carefully roll cake and towel from narrow end.
Cool on wire rack at least 30 minutes.

Beat whipping cream, 2 tablespoons sugar
and the coffee in chilled medium bowl until
stiff. Unroll cake; remove towel. Spread
whipped cream mixture over cake. Roll up
cake. For tree stump, cut off a 2-inch diagonal
slice from one end. Attach stump to one
long side using 1 tablespoon frosting. Frost
with Chocolate Buttercream Frosting. Make
strokes in frosting to resemble tree bark,
using tines of fork. Garnish with Meringue
Mushrooms.

CHOCOLATE BUTTERCREAM FROSTING

1/3 cup cocoa
1/3 cup margarine or butter, softened
2 cups powdered sugar
1 1/2 teaspoons vanilla
1 to 2 tablespoons hot water

Thoroughly mix cocoa and margarine in
medium bowl. Beat in powdered sugar on low
speed. Stir in vanilla and hot water. Beat until
smooth and of spreading consistency.

MERINGUE MUSHROOMS

2 egg whites
1/4 teaspoon cream of tartar
1/2 cup sugar
Cocoa
Chocolate Decorator's Frosting (right)

Cover 2 cookie sheets with cooking parchment paper or heavy brown paper. Beat egg
whites and cream of tartar in small bowl on
medium speed until foamy. Beat in sugar on
high speed, 1 tablespoon at a time; continue
beating about 5 minutes or until stiff and
glossy. Do not underbeat.

Heat oven to 200°. Place meringue in decorating bag with plain tip with 1/4-inch open-
ing (#10 or #11). Or place meringue in
strong plastic bag; cut off a tiny tip from one
corner of bag. Pipe meringue in about
55 mushroom-cap shapes, each 1 to 1 1/4
inches in diameter, onto 1 cookie sheet. Sift
cocoa over mushroom caps.

Bake 45 to 50 minutes or until firm. Immediately turn mushroom caps upside down and make an indentation in bottom of each cap. Brush off excess cocoa with soft-bristled brush.

Pipe about fifty-five 3/4-inch upright cone shapes onto second cookie sheet for mushroom stems. Stems should have peaks that fit into indentations in mushrooms caps. Bake 40 to 45 minutes or until firm; cool. Prepare Chocolate Decorator's Frosting.

To assemble mushrooms, spread small amount frosting in indentation of each mushroom cap; insert peak end of stem into frosting. Place upside down to dry. Store uncovered at room temperature. About 55 candies.

CHOCOLATE DECORATOR'S FROSTING

1 ounce unsweetened chocolate
1 teaspoon margarine or butter
1 cup powdered sugar
1 tablespoon hot water

Heat chocolate and margarine until melted; remove from heat. Beat in powdered sugar and hot water until smooth and of spreading consistency. If necessary, stir in additional hot water, 1 teaspoon at a time.

TIP

Instead of taking the time to make the tree stump and Meringue Mushrooms, garnish the "log" with chopped pistachio nuts and candied red cherries.

Fudge-Pecan Torte

24 servings

1 1/2 cups pecan shortbread cookie crumbs (about twelve 2-inch cookies)
1 1/2 cups sugar
1 cup (2 sticks) margarine or butter
1 cup water
1 pound semisweet chocolate, cut into pieces
8 eggs
1/2 cup all-purpose flour
1 cup chopped pecans
Soft Cream (below)

Heat oven to 350°. Press cookie crumbs on bottom of ungreased springform pan 9×3 inches.* Bake 10 to 12 minutes or until light golden brown.

Heat sugar, margarine, water and chocolate in 3-quart saucepan over low heat, stirring constantly, until melted and smooth. Beat eggs slightly in large bowl. Gradually stir chocolate mixture into eggs. Stir in flour and pecans. Pour over crust in pan.

Bake 1 hour to 1 1/4 hours or until toothpick inserted in center comes out clean. Cool 30 minutes. Loosen torte from side of pan with knife if necessary; remove side of pan. Cover with plastic wrap and refrigerate about 4 hours or until chilled. Serve with Soft Cream. Refrigerate any remaining torte.

*If springform pan does not seal tightly, wrap aluminum foil around outside bottom of pan.

SOFT CREAM

1 cup whipping cream
2 tablespoons packed brown sugar
1 tablespoon praline liqueur or bourbon, if desired

Beat all ingredients in chilled medium bowl until soft peaks form.

Chocolate Swirl Cheesecake with Raspberry Topping

12 servings

The remaining Thick Yogurt is delicious spread on toast or bagels or to top fresh fruit.

2 cups Thick Yogurt (right)
4 chocolate wafers, crushed (about 1/4 cup)
1 package (8 ounces) cream cheese, softened
2/3 cup sugar
1/4 cup milk
2 tablespoons all-purpose flour
2 teaspoons vanilla
3 egg whites
1 tablespoon cocoa
1 teaspoon chocolate extract
Raspberry Topping (right)

Prepare Thick Yogurt. Heat oven to 300°. Spray springform pan, 9×3 inches, with nonstick cooking spray. Sprinkle chocolate wafer crumbs on bottom of pan. Beat Thick Yogurt and cream cheese in medium bowl on medium speed until smooth. Add sugar, milk, flour, vanilla and egg whites. Beat on medium speed about 2 minutes or until smooth.

Place 1 cup batter in small bowl. Beat in cocoa and chocolate extract until blended. Carefully spread vanilla batter over crumbs in pan. Drop chocolate batter by spoonfuls onto vanilla batter. Swirl through batter with metal spatula for marbled effect, being careful not to touch bottom.

Bake 1 hour. Turn off oven; leave cheesecake in oven 30 minutes. Prepare Raspberry Topping; spread over cheesecake. Cover and refrigerate at least 3 hours. Loosen cheesecake from side of pan; remove side of pan. Refrigerate any remaining cheesecake.

THICK YOGURT

Line 6-inch strainer with basket-style paper coffee filter or double-thickness cheesecloth. Place strainer over bowl. Spoon yogurt into strainer. Cover strainer and bowl and refrigerate at least 12 hours, draining liquid from bowl occasionally.

RASPBERRY TOPPING

1 package (10 ounces) frozen raspberries, thawed, drained and juice reserved
1/4 cup sugar
2 tablespoons cornstarch

Add enough water to reserved juice to measure 1 1/4 cups. Mix sugar and cornstarch in 1 1/2-quart saucepan. Stir in juice mixture and raspberries. Heat to boiling over medium heat, stirring frequently. Boil and stir 1 minute; cool.

Pumpkin Pecan Cheesecake

16 servings

1 1/4 cups pecan shortbread cookie crumbs (about ten 2-inch cookies)
2 tablespoons margarine or butter, melted
3 packages (8 ounces each) cream cheese, softened
1 cup sugar
1 teaspoon ground cinnamon
1 teaspoon ground ginger
1/2 teaspoon ground cloves
1 can (16 ounces) pumpkin
4 eggs
2 tablespoons sugar
16 pecan halves
3/4 cup whipping (heavy) cream

Heat oven to 350°. Mix cookie crumbs and margarine. Press evenly on bottom of ungreased springform pan, 9×3 inches. Bake 10 minutes; cool. Reduce oven temperature to 300°.

Beat cream cheese, 1 cup sugar, the cinnamon, ginger and cloves in large bowl on medium speed until smooth and fluffy. Beat in pumpkin. Beat in eggs, one at a time, on low speed. Pour over baked layer.

Bake about 1 1/4 hours or until center is firm. Cover and refrigerate at least 3 hours until chilled.

Cook 2 tablespoons sugar and the pecan halves over medium heat, stirring frequently, until sugar is melted and pecans are coated. Immediately spread on dinner plate or aluminum foil; cool. Carefully break nuts apart to separate if necessary.

Loosen cheesecake from side of pan; remove side of pan. Beat whipping cream in chilled small bowl until stiff. Serve cheesecake with whipped cream and garnish with pecans. Refrigerate any remaining cheesecake.

Classic Pumpkin Pie

8 servings

Favorite Pastry for 9-inch One-Crust Pie
   (page 259)
2 eggs
1/2 cup sugar
1 teaspoon ground cinnamon
1/2 teaspoon salt
1/2 teaspoon ground ginger
1/8 teaspoon ground cloves
1 can (16 ounces) pumpkin
1 can (12 ounces) evaporated milk

Heat oven to 425°. Prepare pastry. Beat eggs slightly with hand beater or wire whisk in medium bowl. Beat in remaining ingredients.

To prevent spilling, place pastry-lined pie plate on oven rack. Pour filling into pie plate.

Bake 15 minutes. Reduce oven temperature to 350°. Bake about 45 minutes longer or until knife inserted in center comes out clean. Refrigerate about 4 hours or until chilled. Serve with whipped cream or ice cream if desired. Refrigerate any remaining pie.

Storing Pies

- Pies containing eggs should be refrigerated.

- Pie shells can be frozen unbaked or baked. Frozen unbaked shells will keep two months and baked shells four months. To thaw baked pie shells, unwrap and let stand at room temperature or heat in 350° oven about 6 minutes. Do not thaw unbaked shells; immediately bake after removing from freezer.

- Baked pies can be frozen. They are easiest to wrap if frozen uncovered, then wrapped tightly or placed in freezer plastic bags. Bake pies before freezing to prevent soggy crusts or possible texture breakdown of raw fruit. Frozen baked pies will keep up to four months.

- To serve frozen two-crust pies, unwrap and thaw at room temperature 1 hour. Heat in 375° oven on lowest rack for 35 to 40 minutes until warm.

Chocolate Nesselrode Pie

8 servings

Favorite Pastry for 9-inch Pie Shell (page 259)
6 egg yolks, slightly beaten
1/2 cup sugar
1/4 cup cornstarch
2 cups milk
4 teaspoons unflavored gelatin
1/2 teaspoon salt
1 bar (4 ounces) sweet cooking chocolate, grated
1 teaspoon vanilla
1/2 teaspoon rum flavoring
1 jar (10 ounces) Nesselrode
3 cups whipping (heavy) cream

Bake pie shell; cool. Mix egg yolks, sugar, cornstarch, milk, gelatin and salt in 2-quart saucepan. Cook over medium heat, stirring constantly, until mixture thickens and boils. Boil and stir 1 minute. Pour 1 1/2 cups of the hot mixture into a bowl; cool completely. Reserve 2 tablespoons of the chocolate for topping. Stir remaining chocolate and the vanilla into hot mixture in saucepan; cool.

Line pie plate, 9×1 1/4 inches, with waxed paper. Stir rum flavoring and Nesselrode into 1 1/2-cup mixture in bowl. Beat 2 cups of the whipping cream in chilled medium bowl until stiff. Fold half of the whipped cream into Nesselrode mixture and half into chocolate mixture. Pour chocolate mixture into baked pie shell. Pour Nesselrode mixture onto waxed paper in pie plate. Refrigerate both mixtures at least 2 hours until firm.

Just before serving, loosen edge of Nesselrode layer from waxed paper with spatula; invert onto chocolate layer and remove waxed paper. Beat remaining 1 cup whipping cream in chilled small bowl until stiff. Spread over pie, covering surface completely. Sprinkle with reserved chocolate. Serve immediately. Refrigerate any remaining pie.

Pear Tart Tatin

8 servings

2 tablespoons margarine or butter
1/2 cup packed brown sugar
6 medium pears or tart apples (about 3 pounds), peeled, cored and cut into eighths
1/2 package (17 1/4-ounce size) frozen puff pastry, thawed
Pear Chantilly Cream (below)

Heat margarine and brown sugar in 10-inch ovenproof skillet over medium heat, stirring constantly, until melted. Stir in pears. Cook 20 to 25 minutes, stirring frequently, until syrup thickens; remove from heat. If desired, use two forks and arrange pear slices overlapping in a pinwheel pattern.

Heat oven to 400°. Roll pastry into 10 1/2-inch square on lightly floured surface. Cut into 10 1/2-inch circle. Fold pastry into fourths; cut slits so steam can escape. Place over pears in skillet and unfold; carefully tuck edge down around pears.

Bake 15 to 20 minutes or until brown. Let stand 5 minutes; invert onto heatproof serving plate. Serve with Pear Chantilly Cream.

PEAR CHANTILLY CREAM

1 cup whipping (heavy) cream
1 tablespoon pear liqueur, pear brandy, apple brandy or apple juice

Beat ingredients in chilled medium bowl until soft peaks form.

Pear Tart Tartin

Cranberry-Apple Pie

8 servings

A nice blend of flavors for those who find cranberries alone a bit too intense.

**Favorite Pastry for 9-inch Two-Crust Pie
    (page 259)**
1 3/4 to 2 cups sugar
1/4 cup all-purpose flour
**3 cups sliced peeled tart apples (about
    3 medium)**
2 cups fresh or frozen (thawed) cranberries
2 tablespoons margarine or butter

Heat oven to 425°. Prepare pastry. Mix sugar and flour. Arrange half of the apples in pastry-lined pie plate. Top with cranberries. Sprinkle sugar mixture over cranberries. Top with remaining apples. Dot with margarine. Cover with top crust that has slits cut in it; seal and flute. Cover edge with 2- to 3-inch strip of aluminum foil to prevent excessive browning; remove foil during last 15 minutes of baking.

Bake 40 to 50 minutes or until crust is brown and juice beings to bubble through slits in crust. Serve warm with ice cream if desired.

Partridge-in-a Pear-Tree Pie

8 servings

You can fashion other pastry cutouts for your Christmas pies: Use a cookie cutter (bell, star, tree) or cut around your own patterns.

3 cups (12 ounces) cranberries
1 1/2 cups sugar
**1 can (8 3/4 ounces) crushed pineapple,
    drained (reserve syrup)**
**Favorite Pastry for 9-inch Two-Crust Pie
    (page 000)**
3 tablespoons flour
1/4 teaspoon salt
1/4 teaspoon ground cinnamon
**1 can (8 ounces) pear halves, drained and
    cut into halves**
Sugar

Cook cranberries, 1 1/2 cups sugar, the pineapple and 1/4 cup of the reserved syrup, stirring constantly, until cranberries are tender, about 5 minutes. Cool.

Prepare pastry as directed—except flute bottom crust. Mix flour, salt and cinnamon; stir into cranberry mixture. Pour into pastry-lined pie plate. Gently press pear slices spoke-fashion onto cranberry mixture.

Heat oven to 400°. After rolling pastry for top crust, cut partridge, leaf and pear shapes (see photograph). Sprinkle with sugar, if desired; place on ungreased cookie sheet.

Bake pastry cutouts and pie until cutouts and pie are golden brown, 7 to 10 minutes for cutouts and about 40 minutes for pie. Arrange cutouts on pie.

Partridge-in-a-Pear-Tree Pie

Holiday Nut Bread

1 loaf (about 20 slices)

2 1/2 cups all-purpose flour
1/2 cup granulated sugar
1/2 cup packed brown sugar
1/4 cup shortening
1 1/4 cups buttermilk*
3 teaspoons baking powder
1 teaspoon salt
1/2 teaspoon baking soda
2 eggs
1 cup chopped nuts

Heat oven to 350°. Grease bottom only of loaf pan, 9×5×3 inches. Beat all ingredients except nuts in large bowl on low speed 15 seconds. Beat on medium speed 30 seconds, scraping bowl constantly. Stir in nuts. Pour into pan.

Bake 60 to 65 minutes or until toothpick inserted in center comes out clean. Immediately remove from pan. Cool completely on wire rack before slicing. Garnish top of nut bread with maraschino cherries and sliced green candied pineapple if desired. For best results, wrap and refrigerate at least 8 hours before slicing.

1 1/4 cups milk and 1 tablespoon white vinegar can be substituted for the buttermilk; mix and let stand 5 minutes.

Cherry-Nut Bread: *Decrease buttermilk to 1 cup and add 1/4 cup maraschino cherry juice. After beating, stir in 1/2 cup chopped drained maraschino cherries. Bake 1 hour 10 minutes to 1 hour 15 minutes.*

Date-Nut Bread: *Omit buttermilk. Pour 1 1/2 cups boiling water over 1 1/2 cups chopped dates; stir and let cool. Beat date mixture with remaining ingredients. Bake 1 hour 5 minutes to 1 hour 10 minutes.*

Cranberry-Orange Bread

1 loaf (24 slices)

2 cups all-purpose flour
3/4 cup sugar
1 1/2 teaspoons baking powder
1/2 teaspoon salt
1/2 teaspoon baking soda
1/4 cup butter or margarine, softened
1 tablespoon grated orange peel
3/4 cup orange juice
1 egg
1 cup fresh or frozen (thawed and drained) cranberries, chopped
1/2 cup chopped nuts

Heat oven to 350°. Grease bottom only of loaf pan, 8 1/2×4 1/2×2 1/2 inches or 9×5×3 inches. Mix flour, sugar, baking powder, salt and baking soda; stir in butter until mixture is crumbly. Stir in orange peel, orange juice and egg just until moistened; stir in cranberries and nuts. Spread in pan.

Bake 8-inch loaf 1 hour 15 minutes, 9-inch loaf 55 to 65 minutes or until toothpick inserted in center comes out clean; cool 5 minutes. Loosen side of loaf from pan; remove from pan. Cool completely before slicing.

TIP

Purchase chopped nuts for this quick bread or use your food processor to chop a large quantity of nuts. Freeze in 1-cup amounts to have ready for use any time.

Cranberry-Orange Bread

Pumpkin Bread

1 loaf (24 slices)

1 cup sugar
1 cup canned pumpkin
1/3 cup vegetable oil
1 teaspoon vanilla
2 eggs
1 1/2 cups all-purpose flour
1/2 cup coarsely chopped walnuts or pecans
2 teaspoons baking powder
1/2 teaspoon ground cinnamon
1/4 teaspoon salt
1/4 teaspoon ground cloves

Heat oven to 350°. Grease bottom only of loaf pan, 8 1/2×4 1/2×2 1/2 inches or 9×5×3 inches. Mix sugar, pumpkin, oil, vanilla and eggs in large bowl. Stir in remaining ingredients. Pour into pan.

Bake 50 to 60 minutes or until toothpick inserted in center comes out clean. Cool 10 minutes. Loosen sides of loaf from pan; remove from pan. Cool completely on wire rack before slicing. Store tightly wrapped in refrigerator up to 1 week.

Gingered Pear Bread

2 loaves (24 slices each)

3 cups chopped unpeeled pears (about 3 medium)
1 1/4 cups sugar
1/2 cup vegetable oil
1 tablespoon finely chopped gingerroot
3 eggs
3 cups all-purpose flour
3 1/2 teaspoons baking powder
1 teaspoon salt

Heat oven to 350°. Grease bottoms only of 2 loaf pans, 8 1/2×4 1/2×2 1/2 inches or 9×5×3 inches. Mix pears, sugar, oil, gingerroot and eggs in large bowl. Stir in remaining ingredients. Pour into pans.

Bake 8-inch loaves about 65 minutes, 9-inch loaves about 50 minutes or until toothpick inserted in center comes out clean. Cool 10 minutes. Loosen sides of loaves from pans; remove from pans. Cool completely on wire rack before slicing. Store tightly wrapped in refrigerator up to 1 week.

Cranberry Bread

2 loaves (24 slices each)

2 cups fresh or frozen cranberries, chopped
1 2/3 cups sugar
2/3 cup vegetable oil
1/2 cup milk
2 teaspoons grated lemon or orange peel
2 teaspoons vanilla
4 eggs
3 cups all-purpose flour
1/2 cup coarsely chopped walnuts or pecans
4 teaspoons baking powder
1 teaspoon salt

Heat oven to 350°. Grease bottoms only of 2 loaf pans, 8 1/2×4 1/2×2 1/2 inches or 9×5×3 inches. Mix cranberries, sugar, oil, milk, lemon peel, vanilla and eggs in large bowl. Stir in remaining ingredients. Pour into pans.

Bake 50 to 60 minutes or until toothpick inserted in center comes out clean. Cool 10 minutes. Loosen sides of loaves from pans; remove from pans. Cool completely on wire rack before slicing. Store tightly wrapped in refrigerator up to 1 week.

Fruited Christmas Wreath

1 large coffee cake (32 slices)

2 packages active dry yeast
1/2 cup warm water (105° to 115°)
1 1/4 cups buttermilk
1/2 cup granulated sugar
1/2 cup margarine or butter, softened
2 eggs
2 teaspoons baking powder
2 teaspoons salt
5 1/2 cups all-purpose flour
1 cup cut-up mixed candied fruit
1/2 cup chopped pecans
1 tablespoon grated lemon peel
1/2 cup powdered sugar
1 tablespoon milk

Dissolve yeast in warm water in large mixer bowl. Add buttermilk, granulated sugar, margarine, eggs, baking powder, salt and 2 1/2 cups of the flour. Beat on low speed, scraping bowl constantly, 30 seconds. Beat on medium speed, scraping bowl occasionally, 2 minutes. Stir in remaining flour, the candied fruit, pecans and lemon peel. (Dough will be soft and slightly sticky.)

Turn dough onto well-floured surface; knead until smooth and elastic, about 5 minutes. Roll into strip, 24×6 inches. Cut into 3 strips, 24×2 inches. Place close together on greased cookie sheet. Braid strips; shape into circle and pinch ends to seal. Cover; let rise in warm place until double, about 1 hour. (Dough is ready if indentation remains when touched.)

Heat oven to 375°. Bake until golden brown, about 30 minutes. Mix powdered sugar and milk; drizzle over wreath while warm. Decorate with green and red candied cherries, if desired.

Note: *For two small wreaths, divide dough after kneading into halves. Roll each half into rectangle, 18×3 inches. Cut into 3 strips, each 18×1 inch. Continue as directed—except bake 20 to 30 minutes. Omit powdered sugar and milk and brush with softened margarine or butter if desired.*

Sour Cream Coffee Cake

14 to 16 servings

This coffee cake is perfect to serve a crowd! When baked in loaf pans, you can serve one, and give the other as a gift.

1 1/2 cups sugar
3/4 cup (1 1/2 sticks) margarine or butter, softened
1 1/2 teaspoons vanilla
3 eggs
3 cups all-purpose or whole wheat flour
1 1/2 teaspoons baking powder
1 1/2 teaspoons baking soda
3/4 teaspoon salt
1 1/2 cups sour cream
Filling (right)
Light Brown Glaze (right)

Heat oven to 350°. Grease tube pan, 10×4 inches, 12-cup bundt cake pan or 2 loaf pans, 9×5×3 inches. Beat sugar, margarine, vanilla and eggs in large bowl on medium speed 2 minutes, scraping bowl occasionally. Beat in flour, baking powder, baking soda and salt alternately with sour cream on low speed. Prepare Filling.

For tube or bundt cake pan, spread one-third of the batter (about 2 cups) in pan and sprinkle with one-third of the filling (about 6 tablespoons); repeat twice. For loaf pans, spread one-fourth of the batter (about 1 1/2 cups) in each pan and sprinkle each with one-fourth of the filling (about 5 tablespoons); repeat once.

Bake tube pan or bundt cake pan about 1 hour, loaf pans about 45 minutes or until toothpick inserted near center comes out clean. Cool slightly; remove from pan to wire rack. Cool 10 minutes. Drizzle Light Brown Glaze over warm coffee cake. Serve warm or cool.

FILLING

1/2 cup packed brown sugar
1/2 cup finely chopped nuts
1 1/2 teaspoons ground cinnamon

Mix all ingredients.

LIGHT BROWN GLAZE

1/4 cup (1/2 stick) margarine or butter
2 cups powdered sugar
1 teaspoon vanilla
1 to 2 tablespoons milk

Heat margarine in 1 1/2 quart saucepan over medium heat until light brown; remove from heat. Stir in powdered sugar and vanilla. Stir in milk, 1 tablespoon at a time, until smooth and of drizzling consistency.

Fruit Swirl Coffee Cake

18 servings

For a smaller coffee cake, substitute 1 jar (10 ounces) any flavor fruit preserves for the pie filling and cut the remaining ingredients in half. Grease a 9×9×2-inch pan instead of the jelly roll pan, and prepare as directed.

1 1/2 cups sugar
1/2 cup (1 stick) margarine or butter, softened
1/2 cup shortening
1 1/2 teaspoons baking powder
1 teaspoon vanilla
1 teaspoon almond extract
4 eggs
3 cups all-purpose flour
1 can (21 ounces) cherry, apricot or blueberry pie filling
Glaze (right)

Heat oven to 350°. Generously grease jelly roll pan, 15 1/2×10 1/2×1 inch. Beat sugar, margarine, shortening, baking powder, vanilla, almond extract and eggs in large bowl on low speed, scraping bowl constantly. Beat on high speed 3 minutes, scraping bowl occasionally. Stir in flour. Spread 2/3 of the batter in pan. Spread pie filling over batter. Drop remaining batter by tablespoonfuls onto pie filling.

Bake about 45 minutes. Drizzle Glaze over warm coffee cake. Serve warm or let stand until cool.

GLAZE

1 cup powdered sugar
1 to 2 tablespoons milk

Mix ingredients until smooth and of drizzling consistency.

Apple-Filled Coffee Cake

6 servings

1/4 cup shortening
2 cups all-purpose flour
2 tablespoons sugar
3 teaspoons baking powder
1/2 teaspoon salt
3/4 cup milk
1/2 cup finely chopped peeled or unpeeled
    apple (about 1 small)
1 tablespoon sugar
1/2 teaspoon ground cinnamon
1 tablespoon margarine, melted
Glaze (right), if desired

Heat oven to 425°. Grease round pan, 8×1 1/2 inches, or square pan, 8×8×2 inches. Cut shortening into flour, 2 tablespoons sugar, the baking powder and salt with pastry blender in large bowl until mixture resembles fine crumbs. Stir in milk until dough leaves side of bowl and forms a ball.

Turn dough onto lightly floured surface; gently roll in flour to coat. Knead lightly 20 to 25 times. Divide dough into 12 equal parts; cover.

Mix apple, 1 tablespoon sugar and the cinnamon. Pat each part dough into 3-inch circle on floured surface. Place 1 rounded teaspoonful apple mixture in center of each circle. Bring edges of dough up over apple mixture; pinch and seal well to from a ball. Arrange balls, seam sides down, in pan. Brush with margarine.

Bake 17 to 19 minutes or until golden brown. Drizzle Glaze over warm coffee cake. Serve warm or let stand until cool.

GLAZE
1/3 cup powdered sugar
1 1/2 teaspoons milk
1/8 teaspoon vanilla

Mix all ingredients until smooth.

Cherry-Almond Coffee Cake

16 servings

1/3 cup finely chopped almonds
1 cup sugar
1/2 cup (1 stick) margarine or butter, softened
1/2 cup milk
1/2 teaspoon almond extract
1 container (15 ounces) ricotta cheese
2 eggs
2 1/2 cups all-purpose flour
1 cup dried cherries or prunes, chopped
1 cup chopped almonds, toasted if desired
3 teaspoons baking powder
1/2 teaspoon salt

Heat oven to 350°. Grease 12-cup bundt cake pan or tube pan, 10×4 inches. Coat pan with 1/3 cup finely chopped almonds. Beat sugar, margarine, milk, almond extract, ricotta cheese and eggs in large bowl on low speed until blended. Beat on medium speed 2 minutes, scraping bowl occasionally. Beat in remaining ingredients (batter will be very thick). Spread in pan.

Bake 55 to 65 minutes or until toothpick inserted near center comes out clean. Cool 20 minutes. Remove from pan; place on wire rack. Sprinkle with powdered sugar if desired. Serve warm or let stand until cool.

Cherry-Almond Coffee Cake

Christmas Brioche

2 loaves (12 slices each)

1 package regular or quick-acting active
   dry yeast
1/2 cup warm water (105° to 115°)
2 tablespoons sugar
1/2 teaspoon salt
5 eggs
1 egg white
3/4 cup (1 1/2 sticks) margarine or butter,
   softened
3 1/2 cups all-purpose flour
1/2 cup chopped nuts
1 cup mixed chopped candied fruit
1 egg yolk
1 tablespoon water
2 tablespoons apricot jam
2 teaspoons water

Dissolve yeast in warm water in large bowl. Add sugar, salt, 5 eggs, the egg white, margarine and 2 cups of the flour. Beat on low speed 30 seconds, scraping bowl constantly. Beat on medium speed 10 minutes, scraping bowl occasionally. Stir in remaining flour, the nuts and candied fruit until batter is smooth. Scrape dough from side of bowl. Cover with plastic wrap and let rise in warm place about 1 hour or until double. (Dough is ready if indentation remains when touched.)

Stir down dough by beating about 25 strokes. Cover bowl tightly with plastic wrap and refrigerate at least 8 hours.

Grease two 4-cup brioche pans or two 1 1/2-quart ovenproof bowls. Stir down dough. (Dough will be very soft and slightly sticky.) Divide dough in half; refrigerate one half. Shape one-fourth of the remaining dough into a cone shape, using lightly floured hands. Shape remaining three-fourths dough into flattened round, about 3 1/2 inches in diameter. Place flattened round in 1 pan, patting to fit. Make indentation, about 2 inches in diameter and 1 1/2 inches deep, in center of dough. Place cone-shaped dough, pointed side down, in indentation. Repeat with refrigerated dough. Cover and let rise in warm place about 1 1/2 hours or until double.

Heat oven to 375°. Beat egg yolk and 1 tablespoon water slightly; brush over top of dough. (Do not allow egg yolk mixture to accumulate around edges of pans.)

Bake 35 to 40 minutes or until golden brown. Immediately remove from pans. Mix apricot jam and 2 teaspoons water; brush over hot loaves.

Classic Brioche: *Omit nuts, candied fruit, apricot jam and 2 teaspoons water.*

Individual Brioches: *Grease 24 brioche pans or medium muffin cups, 2 1/2×1 1/4 inches. After stirring down chilled dough, divide in half; refrigerate one half. Shape remaining half dough into roll, about 7 1/2 inches long. Cut into 15 slices, each about 1/2 inch thick.*

Working quickly with floured hands (dough will be very soft and slightly sticky), shape 12 of the slices into balls; place in pans or muffin cups. Flatten and make a deep indentation in center of each ball with thumb. Cut each of the remaining 3 slices into 4 equal parts; shape each part into ball. Place 1 ball in each indentation. Repeat with refrigerated dough. Cover and let rise in warm place about 40 minutes or until double.

Heat oven to 375°. Beat egg yolk and 1 tablespoon water slightly; brush over top of dough. (Do not allow egg yolk mixture to accumulate around edges of pans.)

Bake 15 to 20 minutes or until golden brown. Immediately remove from pans. 2 dozen individual brioches.

Stollen

2 coffee cakes (12 slices each)

This rich, classic Christmas bread originated in Germany, where it is called Weihnachts-stollen. *Each province in the country has its own recipe and shape for the bread.*

3 1/2 cups all-purpose flour
1/2 cup sugar
1/2 teaspoon salt
**1 package regular or quick-acting active
    dry yeast**
3/4 cup warm water (105° to 115°)
**1/2 cup (1 stick) margarine or butter,
    softened**
3 eggs
1 egg, separated
1/2 cup chopped blanched almonds
1/4 cup chopped citron
**1/4 cup chopped candied cherries,
    if desired**
1/4 cup raisins
1 tablespoon grated lemon peel
Margarine or butter, softened
1 tablespoon water
Creamy Frosting (right)

Mix 1 3/4 cups of the flour, the sugar, salt and yeast in large bowl. Add water, 1/2 cup margarine, the eggs and egg yolk. Beat on low speed 1 minute, scraping bowl frequently. Beat on medium speed 10 minutes, scraping bowl frequently. Stir in remaining flour, the almonds, citron, candied cherries, raisins and lemon peel. Scrape batter from side of bowl. Cover and let rise in warm place 1 1/2 to 2 hours or until double. (Dough is ready if indentation remains when touched.)

Stir down batter by beating about 25 strokes. Cover tightly and refrigerate at least 8 hours.

Grease cookie sheet. Turn dough onto well-floured surface; gently roll in flour to coat. Divide in half. Press each half into oval, 10×7 inches. Spread with margarine. Fold lengthwise in half; press only folded edge firmly. Place on cookie sheet. Beat egg white and 1 tablespoon water; brush over dough. Cover and let rise 45 to 60 minutes or until double.

Heat oven to 375°. Bake 20 to 25 minutes or until golden brown. Cool 15 minutes. Drizzle Creamy Frosting over warm coffee cakes. If desired, decorate with almond halves, pieces of citron and candied cherry halves to resemble poinsettias, or dust frosting with powdered sugar. Serve warm or cool.

CREAMY FROSTING

1 1/2 cups powdered sugar
2 to 3 tablespoons water
1/2 teaspoon vanilla

Mix all ingredients until of drizzling consistency.

Holiday Almond Braid

1 loaf (32 slices)

5 to 5 1/2 cups all-purpose flour
1/2 cup sugar
1 teaspoon salt
2 packages regular or quick-acting active
    dry yeast
1/3 cup margarine or butter
3/4 cup milk
1/2 cup water
2 eggs
1 cup slivered almonds, toasted
2 1/2 teaspoons grated lemon peel
1/4 to 1/2 teaspoon ground mace or nutmeg
Glaze (right)

Mix 1 1/2 cups of the flour, the sugar, salt and undissolved yeast in large bowl. Cut margarine into small pieces. Heat margarine, milk and water until warm (105 to 115°); stir into yeast mixture. Stir in eggs, almonds, lemon peel, mace and enough remaining flour to make a soft dough. Grease top of dough. Cover tightly with plastic wrap and refrigerate at least 2 hours but no longer than 24 hours.

Lightly grease cookie sheet. Punch down dough. Divide into 4 equal parts. Roll 3 parts into 14-inch ropes. Place ropes close together on cookie sheet. Braid ropes loosely. Pinch ends together to seal. Divide remaining dough into 3 pieces. Roll each piece into 12-inch rope. Place ropes close together. Braid ropes; place on top large braid. Cover and let rise in warm place 30 to 50 minutes or until double. (Dough is ready if indentation remains when touched.)

Heat oven to 350°. Bake 40 to 50 minutes or until deep golden brown. Remove from cookie sheet to wire rack. Brush Glaze over warm braid.

GLAZE

1/2 cup powdered sugar
Dash of ground mace or nutmeg
3 to 4 teaspoons lemon juice

Mix all ingredients until smooth.

Panettone

2 loaves (16 slices each)

**2 packages regular or quick-acting active
     dry yeast**
1 cup warm water (105° to 115°)
1/2 cup sugar
**1/2 cup (1 stick) margarine or butter,
     softened**
3 eggs
1 teaspoon salt
1 teaspoon grated lemon peel
1 teaspoon vanilla
5 to 5 1/2 cups all-purpose flour
1/2 cup golden raisins
1/2 cup chopped citron
2 tablespoons pine nuts or walnuts
Margarine or butter, softened

Dissolve yeast in warm water in large bowl. Stir in sugar, 1/2 cup margarine, the eggs, salt, lemon peel, vanilla and 2 1/2 cups of the flour. Beat until smooth. Stir in raisins, citron, pine nuts and enough flour to make dough easy to handle.

Turn dough onto lightly floured surface; gently roll in flour to coat. Knead about 5 minutes or until smooth and elastic. Place in greased bowl; turn greased side up. Cover and let rise in warm place 1 1/2 to 2 hours or until double. (Dough is ready if indentation remains when touched.)

Punch down dough; divide in half. Shape each half into round loaf, about 6 inches in diameter. Place each loaf in ungreased round pan, 8×1 1/2 inches. Cut an X shape 1/2 inch deep on top of each loaf.

Generously grease one side of a strip of heavy brown paper, about 25×4 inches. Fit and coil paper around inside of pan, greased side toward center, forming a collar; fasten

with paper clip. Repeat for second loaf. Cover and let rise about 1 hour or until double.

Heat oven to 350°. Bake 35 to 45 minutes or until golden brown. Remove loaves from pans to wire rack; remove paper. Brush margarine on tops of loaves; cool.

Wine-and-Cheese Muffins

1 dozen muffins

2 cups Bisquick Original baking mix
2/3 cup white wine or apple juice
2 tablespoons vegetable oil
1 egg
**1 cup shredded Swiss, Gruyère or Cheddar
     cheese (4 ounces)**
**2 teaspoons chopped fresh or freeze-dried
     chives**

Heat oven to 400°. Line 12 medium muffin cups 2 1/2×1 1/4 inches, with paper baking cups or grease entire cup generously. Mix baking mix, wine, oil and egg with fork in medium bowl; beat vigorously 30 strokes. Stir in cheese and chives. Divide batter evenly among cups.

Bake about 20 minutes or until golden brown. Immediately remove from pan. Serve warm.

TIP

Buy shredded cheese, or cut a 4-ounce chunk of cheese. You can then shread without having to stop and measure.

416 BETTY CROCKER'S BEST OF BAKING

Parmesan-Pepper Rolls

1 dozen rolls

2 1/4 cups all-purpose flour
2 tablespoons sugar
2 tablespoons grated Parmesan cheese
1 teaspoon salt
1/4 teaspoon coarsely ground pepper
1 package regular or quick-acting active
   dry yeast
1 cup very warm water (120° to 130°)
1 egg
2 tablespoons vegetable oil

Mix 1 1/4 cups of the flour, the sugar, cheese, salt, pepper and yeast in large bowl. Beat in warm water, egg and oil until smooth. Stir in remaining flour until smooth. Scrape batter from side of bowl. Cover and let rise in warm place about 30 minutes or until double.

Grease 12 medium muffin cups, 2 1/2× 1 1/4 inches. Stir down batter, beating about 25 strokes. Divide among muffin cups. Let rise uncovered 20 to 30 minutes or until batter rounds over tops of cups.

Heat oven to 400°. Bake 15 to 20 minutes or until golden brown.

Cheese Straw Twists

About 4 dozen twists

These easy bread sticks are welcome additions to your bread basket—the crisp-tender morsels will melt in your mouth! For a peppery twist, mix 2 teaspoons cracked black pepper with the Parmesan cheese mixture. To serve as appetizers, cut the twists in half before baking.

2/3 cup grated Parmesan cheese
1 tablespoon paprika
1 package (17 1/4 ounces) frozen puff
   pastry, thawed
1 egg, slightly beaten

Heat oven to 425°. Line 2 cookie sheets with cooking parchment paper or heavy brown paper. Mix cheese and paprika. Roll 1 sheet of pastry into rectangle, 12×10 inches, on lightly floured surface with floured cloth-covered rolling pin.

Brush pastry with egg. Sprinkle with 3 tablespoons of the cheese mixture. Press cheese mixture gently into pastry. Turn pastry over. Repeat with egg and cheese mixture. Fold pastry lengthwise in half.

Cut pastry crosswise into 1/2-inch strips. Unfold strips and roll each end in opposite directions to twist. Place twists on cookie sheet.

Bake 7 to 8 minutes or until puffed and golden brown. Repeat with remaining sheet of pastry, egg and cheese mixture. Remove from cookie sheet to wire rack. Serve warm or cool.

Savory Cheese Swirl

1 loaf (16 slices)

You can substitute chopped, well-drained pimiento if red peppers are not available, and you'll have the same cheerful effect.

1/2 recipe Refrigerator Roll Dough (right)
1 cup shredded Swiss or mozzarella cheese (4 ounces)
1/4 cup finely chopped red or green bell pepper
2 tablespoons finely chopped onion
2 tablespoons mayonnaise or salad dressing
1 tablespoon chopped fresh or 1 teaspoon dried cilantro leaves
1/2 teaspoon ground cumin

Grease large cookie sheet. Roll dough into rectangle, 15×10 inches, on lightly floured surface. Mix 1/2 cup of the cheese and the remaining ingredients. Spread cheese mixture over dough to within 1/2 inch of edges. Roll up tightly, beginning at 15-inch side. Pinch edge of dough into roll to seal. Stretch and shape until even.

Cut roll lengthwise in half, using kitchen scissors. Place end of one strip, cut side up, in center of cookie sheet; loosely coil strip. Place second strip, cut side up, end-to-end with first strip; pinch end together. Continue coiling second strip loosely around first strip; tuck end under coil. Cover and let rise in warm place about 25 minutes or until double. (Dough is ready if indentation remains when touched.)

Heat oven to 375°. Bake 20 to 25 minutes or until golden brown. Immediately sprinkle with remaining cheese. Serve warm.

REFRIGERATOR ROLL DOUGH

1 package regular or quick-acting active dry yeast
1 1/2 cups warm water (105° to 115°)
1 cup unseasoned lukewarm mashed potatoes
2/3 cup sugar
2/3 cup shortening
1 1/2 teaspoons salt
2 eggs
6 to 7 cups all-purpose flour

Dissolve yeast in warm water in large bowl. Stir in potatoes, sugar, shortening, salt, eggs and 3 cups of the flour. Beat until smooth. Mix in enough remaining flour to make dough easy to handle.

Turn dough onto lightly floured surface; gently roll in flour to coat. Knead about 5 minutes or until smooth and elastic. Place in greased bowl; turn greased side up. Cover bowl tightly; refrigerate at least 8 hours but no longer than 5 days.

Punch down dough; divide into 4 equal parts.

Skillet Chile-Cheese Cornbread

12 servings

A down-home favorite, perfect served right from the skillet. For festive flair, just before baking arrange thin slices of red or green bell peppers in the shape of Christmas trees on top of the batter.

1 1/2 cups cornmeal
1/2 cup all-purpose flour
1/2 cup shredded Cheddar cheese
   (2 ounces)
1/4 cup shortening
1 1/2 cups buttermilk
2 teaspoons baking powder
1 teaspoon sugar
1 teaspoon salt
1/2 teaspoon baking soda
1/2 teaspoon chile powder
2 eggs
1 can (4 ounces) chopped green chiles,
   well drained

Heat oven to 450°. Grease 10-inch ovenproof skillet, round pan, 9×1 1/2 inches, or square pan, 8×8×2 inches. Mix all ingredients; beat vigorously 30 seconds. Pour into skillet or pan.

Bake skillet about 20 minutes, round or square pan 25 to 30 minutes or until golden brown. Serve warm.

Burgundy Meatballs

12 meatballs

2 pounds ground beef
1 cup dry bread crumbs
1/2 cup water chestnuts, finely chopped
1/2 cup milk
1 teaspoon salt
1 teaspoon Worcestershire sauce
1/8 teaspoon pepper
2 eggs
1 medium onion, chopped (about 1/2 cup)
Burgundy Sauce (below)
Chopped fresh parsley

Heat oven to 400°. Mix all ingredients except Burgundy Sauce and parsley. Shape mixture into 1-inch balls. Place in ungreased jelly roll pan, 15 1/2×10 1/2×1 inch.

Bake uncovered about 10 minutes or until done.

Prepare Burgundy Sauce. Stir meatballs into Burgundy Sauce. Meatball mixture can be covered and refrigerated up to 24 hours at this point. Heat meatball mixture to boiling; reduce heat. Cover and simmer about 10 minutes or just until meatballs are hot. Garnish with parsley.

BURGUNDY SAUCE

1/3 cup cornstarch
1/2 cup cold water
1 cup burgundy, dry red wine or beef broth
1 clove garlic, crushed
2 cans (10 1/2 ounces each) condensed
   beef broth

Mix cornstarch and cold water in 3-quart saucepan. Gradually stir in remaining ingredients. Heat to boiling, stirring constantly. Boil and stir 1 minute.

Curried Meatballs with Chutney Sauce

4 dozen appetizers

Chutney Sauce (below)
1 pound ground turkey
1/2 cup crushed buttery cracker crumbs
1/3 cup evaporated skimmed milk
2 tablespoons finely chopped green onions
1 1/2 to 2 teaspoons curry powder
1/4 teaspoon salt

Prepare Chutney Sauce. Heat oven to 400°. Mix remaining ingredients; shape into forty-eight 1-inch balls. Place in ungreased rectangular pan, 13×9×2 inches.

Bake uncovered 10 to 15 minutes or until no longer pink in center. Serve hot with Chutney Sauce.

CHUTNEY SAUCE

2/3 cup plain yogurt
1 tablespoon finely chopped chutney
1/4 teaspoon curry powder

Mix all ingredients. Cover and refrigerate 1 hour.

Southwest Riblets

About 28 appetizers

1 medium onion, chopped (about 1/2 cup)
2 tablespoons vegetable oil
1 tablespoon ground red chiles
6 dried juniper berries, crushed, if desired
3 cloves garlic, finely chopped
1/2 teaspoon salt
1/2 ounce unsweetened chocolate, grated
1 cup water
2 tablespoons cider vinegar
1 can (6 ounces) tomato paste
2 tablespoons sugar
3-pound rack fresh pork back ribs, cut
    lengthwise across bone in half

Cook onion in oil in 2-quart saucepan 2 minutes, stirring frequently. Stir in ground red chiles, juniper berries, garlic and salt. Cover and cook 5 minutes, stirring occasionally. Stir in chocolate until melted.

Pour water, vinegar and tomato paste into food processor or blender. Add onion mixture and sugar. Cover and process, or blend, until well blended.

Heat oven to 375°. Cut between pork back ribs to separate. Place in single layer in roasting pan. Pour sauce evenly over pork.

Bake uncovered 30 minutes; turn pork. Bake about 30 minutes longer or until done.

Mexican Cheese Puffs

24 puffs

1 cup Bisquick Original baking mix
3 tablespoons margarine or butter, softened
3 tablespoons chopped green chiles
1 egg
1 cup shredded Cheddar cheese (4 ounces)

Heat oven to 400°. Grease cookie sheet. Mix baking mix, margarine, chiles and egg in medium bowl. Stir in cheese. Drop dough by rounded teaspoonfuls about 1 inch apart onto cookie sheet.

Bake 10 to 12 minutes or until golden brown.

Pesto Pinwheels

40 appetizers

1 package (17 1/4 ounces) frozen puff
    pastry, thawed
1 cup Spinach Pesto (page 429) or other
    prepared pesto
1 egg, beaten

Heat oven to 400°. Roll each sheet of puff pastry on a very lightly floured surface into rectangle, 14×10 inches. Spread 1/2 cup of the Spinach Pesto evenly over each rectangle to within 1/2 inch of long sides. Loosely roll pastry from narrow end; brush edge of roll with egg and pinch into roll to seal. Cut into 1/2-inch slices, using sharp knife. Place on ungreased cookie sheet.

Bake 8 to 10 minutes or until golden brown.

Savory Stuffed Mushrooms

36 appetizers

36 medium mushrooms (about 1 pound)
1 small onion, chopped (about 1/4 cup)
1/4 cup chopped green bell pepper
2 tablespoons margarine or butter
1 1/2 cups soft bread crumbs (about
    2 1/2 slices bread)
1 1/2 teaspoons chopped fresh or
    1/2 teaspoon dried thyme leaves
1/2 teaspoon salt
1/4 teaspoon ground turmeric
1/4 teaspoon pepper

Remove stems from mushrooms; reserve caps. Finely chop enough stems to measure 1/3 cup. Cook mushroom stems, onion and bell pepper in margarine in 10-inch skillet about 5 minutes, stirring occasionally, until tender; remove from heat. Stir in remaining ingredients.

Heat oven to 350°. Lightly grease shallow baking dish, 12×7×1 1/2 inches, with nonstick cooking spray. Fill mushroom caps with bread crumb mixture. Place mushrooms, filled sides up in baking dish.

Bake uncovered 15 minutes. Set oven control to broil. Broil with tops 3 to 4 inches from heat about 2 minutes or until light brown.

Shrimp with Prosciutto

18 appetizers

2 tablespoons margarine or butter
2 tablespoons olive or vegetable oil
2 anchovy fillets in oil, finely chopped
1 tablespoon chopped fresh parsley
2 cloves garlic, finely chopped
18 raw jumbo shrimp (in shells)
9 thin slices prosciutto or fully cooked
    Virginia ham, cut in half
1/2 cup dry white wine
1 to 2 tablespoons lemon juice

Heat oven to 375°. Heat margarine and oil in baking dish, 9×9×2 inches, in oven until margarine melts. Mix anchovies, parsley and garlic; spread over margarine mixture in baking dish. Peel shrimp, leaving tails intact. Make a shallow cut lengthwise down back of each shrimp; wash out vein. Wrap 1 half-slice prosciutto around each shrimp. Place shrimp on anchovy mixture.

Bake uncovered 10 minutes. Pour wine and lemon juice over shrimp. Bake about 10 minutes longer or until shrimp are pink.

Cheese Triangles

35 appetizers

1 pound feta cheese*
2 eggs, slightly beaten
1/4 cup finely chopped chives
1/4 teaspoon white pepper
1 package (6 ounces) frozen phyllo sheets,
    thawed
1/4 cup (1/2 stick) margarine or butter,
    melted

Heat oven to 350°. Grease cookie sheet. Crumble cheese in small bowl; mash with fork. Stir in eggs, chives and white pepper until well mixed. Cut stack of phyllo sheets lengthwise into thirds. Cover with waxed paper, then with damp towel to prevent them from drying out. Use 2 sheets of phyllo for each strip. Place 1 heaping teaspoon cheese mixture on end of strip; fold phyllo strip end over end, in triangular shape, to opposite end. Place on cookie sheet. Repeat with remaining phyllo and cheese mixture. (Triangles can be covered and refrigerated up to 24 hours at this point.) Brush margarine over triangles.

Bake about 20 minutes or until puffed and golden.

Finely shredded Monterey Jack cheese can be substituted for the mashed feta cheese.

Peachy Cornish Game Hens

Peachy Cornish Game Hens

2 servings

2 Rock Cornish hens (3/4 to 1 pound each)
Salt
Margarine or butter, melted
Orange Rice (right)
1/4 cup peach jam or orange marmalade
1 teaspoon soy sauce
1 clove garlic, finely chopped

Heat oven to 350°. Sprinkle cavities of hens with salt. Place breast sides up, on oven rack in shallow pan. Brush with margarine.

Roast uncovered 45 minutes, brushing with margarine 3 or 4 times.

While hens are roasting prepare Orange Rice. Add to oven with hens 35 minutes before hens are done. Mix jam, soy sauce and garlic. Brush hens with jam mixture.

Roast uncovered about 15 minutes longer, brushing once with jam mixture, until juices run clear. Serve with Orange Rice.

ORANGE RICE

When grating orange peel, be sure not to grate in the white section—it has a bitter flavor.

1/2 cup uncooked regular long grain rice
1 teaspoon grated orange peel
1/4 teaspoon ground nutmeg
2 medium carrots, sliced (about 1 cup)*
1 cup hot chicken broth
2 tablespoons orange juice
1 tablespoon chopped fresh parsley

Heat oven to 350°. Mix rice, orange peel and nutmeg in ungreased 1-quart casserole. Stir in carrots and broth. Cover and bake 30 to 35 minutes or until liquid is absorbed. Sprinkle with orange juice. Add parsley; toss until well mixed. Let stand 5 minutes before serving.

*Use 1 cup frozen sliced carrots instead of preparing fresh carrots.

Roast Goose

6 servings

This is nice served with Apple-Raisin Dressing.

1 goose (9 to 11 pounds)
Salt
4 to 6 large potatoes, peeled and cut in half
Freshly ground pepper
Paprika

Heat oven to 350°. Trim excess fat from goose. Rub cavity of goose lightly with salt. Fasten neck skin of goose to back with skewer. Fold wings across back with tips touching. Tie drumsticks to tail. Prick skin all over with fork. Place goose, breast side up, on rack in shallow roasting pan. Insert meat thermometer so tip is in thigh muscle and does not touch bone.

Roast uncovered 3 to 3 1/2 hours, removing excess fat from pan occasionally, until thermometer registers 180° or drumstick moves easily and juices run clear. If necessary, place a tent of aluminum foil loosely over goose to prevent excessive browning.

One hour and 15 minutes before goose is done, place potatoes in roasting pan around goose. Brush potatoes with goose fat; sprinkle with salt, pepper and paprika. When done, place goose and potatoes on heated platter. Cover and let stand 15 minutes for easier carving. Garnish with kumquats and parsley, if desired.

Apple-Raisin Dressing

6 servings

3 medium stalks celery (with leaves), chopped (about 1 1/2 cups)
1 medium onion, chopped (about 1/2 cup)
1 cup (2 sticks) margarine or butter
8 cups soft bread cubes (about 13 slices)
1/2 cup raisins
1 1/2 teaspoons salt
1 1/2 teaspoons dried sage leaves
1/4 teaspoon pepper
3 medium tart apples, chopped (about 3 cups)

Heat oven to 350°. Grease rectangular pan, 13×9×2 inches, or 3-quart casserole. Cook celery and onion in margarine in 10-inch skillet, stirring frequently, until onion is tender. Stir in about one-third of the bread cubes. Place in deep bowl. Add remaining bread cubes and ingredients; toss. Place in pan.

Cover and bake 15 minutes. Uncover and bake about 15 minutes longer or until hot and slightly crisp.

Asparagus with Gruyère

6 servings

1 1/2 pounds asparagus*
1/2 teaspoon salt
1/4 cup (1/2 stick) margarine or butter
1/2 cup grated Gruyère or Parmesan cheese

Heat oven to 350°. Break off tough ends of asparagus as far down as stalks snap easily. Arrange in single layer in ungreased rectangular baking dish, 11×7×1 1/2 inches. Sprinkle with salt. Cover with aluminum foil.

Bake about 25 minutes or until tender.

Heat margarine over low heat until light brown; drizzle over asparagus. Sprinkle with cheese.

Bake uncovered 5 to 8 minutes or just until cheese softens.

2 packages (10 ounces each) frozen asparagus spears can be substituted for the fresh asparagus. Rinse asparagus with cold water to separate; drain. Increase first bake time to about 35 minutes.

Standing Beef Rib Roast with Yorkshire Pudding

6 servings

Yorkshire Pudding is an English classic, similar to a popover. However, instead of baking in individual cups, Yorkshire Pudding is baked in a pan, with the roast beef drippings. When puffed and golden, it is cut into squares and served with the roast beef.

4- to 6-pound beef rib roast
Salt and pepper
Yorkshire Pudding Batter (right)

Heat oven to 325°. Place beef roast, fat side up, on rack in shallow roasting pan. Sprinkle with salt and pepper. Insert meat thermometer so tip is in center of thickest part of beef and does not touch bone or rest in fat. Do not add water.

Roast uncovered to desired degree on doneness: 135° for rare, 23 to 25 minutes per pound; 155° for medium, 27 to 30 minutes per pound.

About 30 minutes before roast reaches desired temperature, prepare Yorkshire Pudding Batter. Heat square pan, 9×9×2 inches, or rectangular baking dish, 11×7×1 1/2 inches, in oven.

When roast reaches desired temperature, remove from oven. Increase oven temperature to 425°. Transfer roast to warm platter; cover with aluminum foil. Pour 1/4 cup drippings from roasting pan; place drippings in heated square pan. Pour in pudding batter.

Bake about 25 minutes or until puffed and golden brown. Cut into squares; serve with beef.

YORKSHIRE PUDDING BATTER

1 cup all-purpose flour
1 cup milk
1/2 teaspoon salt
2 eggs

Mix all ingredients with hand beater just until smooth.

Mushroom Pita Bites

8 servings

2 pita breads (6 inches in diameter)
2 cups sliced mushrooms (about 5 ounces)*
1 small red onion, thinly sliced
1/4 cup chopped green bell pepper
2 tablespoons chopped fresh or 2 teaspoons
    dried basil leaves
1 cup finely shredded mozzarella cheese
    (4 ounces)
1 tablespoon grated Parmesan cheese

Heat oven to 425°. Split each pita bread around edge in half, using knife. Place pita rounds, cut sides up, on ungreased cookie sheet. Arrange mushrooms on pita rounds. Top with onion and bell pepper. Sprinkle with basil and cheeses. Bake 8 to 10 minutes or until cheese is melted. Cut each pita round into 8 pieces.

* 1 can (4 ounces) mushroom stems and pieces, drained, can be substituted for fresh mushrooms.

Basil Brie in Pastry

6 servings

2 tablespoons grated Parmesan cheese
2 tablespoons finely chopped fresh or
    2 teaspoons dried basil leaves
1 round Brie cheese (14 ounces)
1/2 package (17 1/4-ounce size) frozen puff
    pastry, thawed

Heat oven to 400°. Grease cookie sheet. Mix Parmesan cheese and basil. Cut cheese round horizontally into 2 layers. Sprinkle basil mixture evenly over cut surface. Reassemble cheese round.

Roll pastry into rectangle, 12×10 inches, on lightly floured surface. Cut out one 10-inch circle. Place cheese in center. Bring pastry up and over cheese. Press to make smooth and even. Brush pastry lightly with water and press gently to seal. Place pastry-wrapped cheese, seam side down, on cookie sheet. Cut decorations for remaining pastry if desired; moisten pastry with water to attach.

Bake about 25 minutes or until golden brown. Cool on cookie sheet on wire rack 30 minutes before serving. Serve with assorted crackers or fruit, if desired.

Apricot-Pistachio Rolled Pork

12 servings

4-pound pork boneless top loin roast
   (single uncut roast)
1/2 cup chopped dried apricots
1/2 cup chopped pistachio nuts
2 cloves garlic, finely chopped
1/4 teaspoon salt
1/4 teaspoon pepper
1/4 cup apricot brandy or apricot nectar
1/4 cup apricot preserves
Crunchy Topping (right)

To cut pork roast into a large rectangle that can be filled and rolled, cut lengthwise about 1/2 inch from top of pork to within 1/2 inch of opposite edge; open flat. Repeat with other side of pork, cutting from the inside edge to the outer edge; open flat to form rectangle (see diagram).

Sprinkle apricots, nuts, garlic, salt and pepper over pork to within 1 inch of edge. Tightly roll up pork, beginning with short side. Secure with toothpicks or tie with string. Pierce pork all over with metal skewer. Brush entire surface with brandy. Let stand 15 minutes. Brush again with brandy. Cover and refrigerate at least 2 hours.

Heat oven to 325°. Place pork, fat side up, on rack in shallow roasting pan. Insert meat thermometer so tip is in thickest part of pork.

Roast uncovered 1 1/2 hours. Brush preserves over pork. Sprinkle with Crunchy Topping. Roast uncovered 30 to 60 minutes longer or until meat thermometer registers 160°. Cover and let stand 15 minutes before serving for easier carving.

Cut lengthwise about 1/2 inch from top of pork to within 1/2 inch of opposite edge; open flat. Repeat with other side of pork, cutting loose from inside edge; open flat to form rectangle.

CRUNCHY TOPPING

1 tablespoon margarine or butter
1/4 cup coarsely crushed cracker crumbs
2 tablespoons chopped pistachio nuts
1/4 teaspoon garlic salt

Heat margarine in 2-quart saucepan over medium heat until melted. stir in remaining ingredients. Cook and stir 1 minute; cool.

Duchess Potatoes

12 servings

For a different twist, use sweet potatoes or yams, and sprinkle with nutmeg or cinnamon.

4 pounds potatoes (about 12 medium),
   peeled and cut into pieces
2/3 to 1 cup milk
1/2 cup margarine or butter, softened
1/2 teaspoon salt
Dash of pepper
4 eggs, beaten
Margarine or butter, melted

Heat 1 inch water (salted if desired) in 3-quart saucepan to boiling. Add potatoes. Cover and heat to boiling. Cook whole potatoes 30 to

35 minutes, pieces 20 to 25 minutes or until tender; drain. Shake pan with potatoes over low heat to dry.

Heat oven to 425°. Grease cookie sheet. Mash potatoes until no lumps remain. Beat in milk in small amounts (amount of milk needed to make potatoes smooth and fluffy depends on kind of potatoes used). Add 1/2 cup margarine, the salt and pepper. Beat vigorously until potatoes are light and fluffy. Add eggs; beat until blended.

Drop potato mixture by spoonfuls into mounds onto cookie sheet. Or place in decorating bag with star tip and form rosettes or pipe in a border around meat. Brush with melted margarine.

Bake about 15 minutes or until light brown.

Crown Roast of Pork with Mushroom Stuffing

12 servings

7 1/2- to 8-pound pork crown roast
    (about 20 ribs)
2 teaspoons salt
1 teaspoon pepper
Mushroom Stuffing (right)

Heat oven to 325°. Sprinkle pork roast with salt and pepper. Place pork, bone end up, on rack in shallow roasting pan. Wrap bone ends in aluminum foil to prevent excessive browning. Insert meat thermometer so tip is in thickest part of meat and does not touch bone. Place a small heatproof bowl or crumpled aluminum foil in crown to hold shape of roast evenly.

Roast uncovered until thermometer registers 160° (medium), 20 to 25 minutes per pound; or 170° (well), 26 to 31 minutes per pound. Prepare Mushroom Stuffing.

One hour before pork is done, remove bowl and fill center of crown with Mushroom Stuffing. Cover only stuffing with aluminum foil during first 30 minutes.

When pork is done, place on large warm platter and allow to stand about 20 minutes for easiest carving. Remove foil wrapping; place paper frills on bone ends if desired. Remove stuffing to another bowl. To carve, cut roast between ribs.

MUSHROOM STUFFING

1 medium onion, finely chopped (about
    1/2 cup)
2/3 cup margarine or butter
8 cups unseasoned croutons
1 tablespoon chopped fresh or 1 teaspoon
    dried sage, thyme or marjoram leaves
1 teaspoon poultry seasoning
1 teaspoon salt
1/2 teaspoon pepper
1 pound fresh mushrooms, sliced, or 1 can
    (6 ounces) sliced mushrooms, drained
2 medium stalks celery, chopped (about
    1 cup)

Cook onion in margarine in Dutch oven over medium heat about 3 minutes, stirring frequently, until tender. Stir in half of the croutons. Cook, stirring frequently, until evenly mixed and croutons are softened. Mix in remaining croutons and ingredients.

TIP

Buy fresh mushrooms already sliced in the produce or deli section of your supermarket.

428 BETTY CROCKER'S BEST OF BAKING

Fruit-Stuffed Trout

4 servings

4 pan-dressed rainbow trout (6 to
    8 ounces each) or drawn trout
    (about 12 ounces each)
Fruit Stuffing (below)
2 tablespoons margarine or butter, melted
1 tablespoon lemon juice

Heat oven to 425°. Grease jelly roll pan,
15 1/2×10 1/2×1 inch. Stuff fish with Fruit
Stuffing. Close openings with skewers or
toothpicks if necessary. Place fish in pan. Mix
margarine and lemon juice; drizzle over fish.

Bake uncovered 15 to 18 minutes or until
fish flakes easily with fork.

FRUIT STUFFING

1 cup unseasoned croutons
1/3 cup diced dried fruit and raisin mixture
2 tablespoons margarine or butter, melted
2 tablespoons dry white wine or chicken
    broth
1/4 teaspoon salt
1/8 teaspoon ground allspice
1 green onion, chopped

Mix all ingredients until liquid is absorbed.

Almond Pilaf

8 servings

1 1/2 cups uncooked regular long grain rice
1 medium onion, chopped (about 1/2 cup)
1/4 cup (1/2 stick) margarine or butter
1/2 teaspoon ground allspice
1/2 teaspoon ground turmeric
1/4 teaspoon salt
1/4 teaspoon curry powder
1/8 teaspoon pepper
3 cups hot chicken broth
1/4 cup slivered blanched almonds

Heat oven to 350°. Cook rice and onion in
margarine in 10-inch skillet, stirring frequently, until onion is tender. Stir in allspice,
turmeric, salt, curry powder and pepper.
Place in ungreased 2-quart casserole. Stir in
broth.

Cover and bake about 40 minutes or until
liquid is absorbed and rice is tender. Stir in
almonds.

Brown Rice-Almond Pilaf: *Substitute brown rice for
the regular rice. Bake 60 to 70 minutes.*

Holiday Stuffed Pasta

8 servings

24 uncooked jumbo pasta shells
2 cups spaghetti sauce
2 cups ricotta cheese
1 cup shredded mozzarella cheese
    (4 ounces)
1/2 cup grated Parmesan cheese
2 tablespoons chopped fresh parsley
1/2 teaspoon pepper
2 eggs
1 cup Spinach Pesto (right) or prepared
    pesto

Heat oven to 350°. Cook pasta shells as directed on package; drain. Spread spaghetti sauce in rectangular pan, 13×9×2 inches. Mix remaining ingredients except pasta shells and Spinach Pesto. Fill each pasta shell with about 2 tablespoons cheese mixture. Arrange filled shells on spaghetti sauce. Cover pan with aluminum foil.

Bake about 45 minutes or until hot. Serve with pesto.

SPINACH PESTO

4 cups firmly packed spinach (10 to
    12 ounces)
1 cup firmly packed fresh or 1/2 cup dried
    basil leaves
1 cup grated Parmesan cheese
1 cup olive oil
1/2 cup chopped pine nuts or walnuts
1/2 teaspoon salt
1/4 teaspoon pepper
8 cloves garlic

Place 2 cups of spinach and remaining ingredients in food processor. Cover and process 1 minute. Add remaining spinach and process about 2 minutes, stopping processor occasionally to scrape sides, until finely chopped and smooth. (Or place all ingredients except spinach in blender. Cover and blend on high speed about 1 minute, stopping blender occasionally to scrape sides. Add spinach, 1 cup at a time, blending until smooth after each addition.) Store covered in refrigerator up to 3 days or in freezer up to 3 months.

Metric Conversion Guide

Volume

U.S. Units	Canadian Metric	Australian Metric
1/4 teaspoon	1 mL	1 ml
1/2 teaspoon	2 mL	2 ml
1 teaspoon	5 mL	5 ml
1 tablespoon	15 mL	20 ml
1/4 cup	50 mL	60 ml
1/3 cup	75 mL	80 ml
1/2 cup	125 mL	125 ml
2/3 cup	150 mL	170 ml
3/4 cup	175 mL	190 ml
1 cup	250 mL	250 ml
1 quart	1 liter	1 liter
1 1/2 quarts	1.5 liters	1.5 liters
2 quarts	2 liters	2 liters
2 1/2 quarts	2.5 liters	2.5 liters
3 quarts	3 liters	3 liters
4 quarts	4 liters	4 liters

Measurements

Inches	Centimeters
1	2.5
2	5.0
3	7.5
4	10.0
5	12.5
6	15.0
7	17.5
8	20.5
9	23.0
10	25.5
11	28.0
12	30.5
13	33.0
14	35.5
15	38.0

Weight

U.S. Units	Canadian Metric	Australian Metric
1 ounce	30 grams	30 grams
2 ounces	55 grams	60 grams
3 ounces	85 grams	90 grams
4 ounces (1/4 pound)	115 grams	125 grams
8 ounces (1/2 pound)	225 grams	225 grams
16 ounces (1 pound)	455 grams	500 grams
1 pound	455 grams	1/2 kilogram

Temperatures

Fahrenheit	Celsius
32°	0°
212°	100°
250°	120°
275°	140°
300°	150°
325°	160°
350°	180°
375°	190°
400°	200°
425°	220°
450°	230°
475°	240°
500°	260°

Note: The recipes in this cookbook have not been developed or tested using metric measures. When converting recipes to metric, some variations in quality may be noted.

Index

Numbers in *italics* refer to photos.